THE GENERALSHIP OF
ULYSSES S. GRANT

GENERAL ULYSSES S. GRANT, 1863

THE GENERALSHIP OF ULYSSES S. GRANT

BY J. F. C. FULLER

" Each epoch creates its own agents, and General
Grant more nearly than any other man imper-
sonated the American character of 1861-5. He
will stand, therefore, as the typical hero of the
Great Civil War."

WILLIAM T. SHERMAN.

A DA CAPO PAPERBACK

Library of Congress Cataloging in Publication Data

Fuller, J. F. C. (John Frederick Charles), 1878-1966.
The generalship of Ulysses S. Grant / by J.F.C. Fuller.
    p.   cm. – (A Da Capo paperback)
    reprint, with new pref. and introd. Originally published: London: J.
Murray, 1929.
    Includes index.
    ISBN 0-306-80450-6
    1. Grant, Ulysses S. (Ulysses Simpson), 1822-1885 – Military leadership. 2.
United States – History – Civil War, 1861–1865 – Campaigns. I. Title.
E672.F962   1991   91-19762
973.7′092 – dc20   CIP

This Da Capo Press paperback edition of *The Generalship of Ulysses A. Grant* is an unabridged reprint of the edition published in London in 1929, with the addition of a Preface and a Foreword written for the American editions. It is reprinted by arrangement with The Royal Society for the Prevention of Cruelty to Animals, sole beneficiary of the Estate of J.F.C. Fuller.

Published by Da Capo Press, Inc.
A Subsidiary of Plenum Publishing Corporation
233 Spring Street, New York, N.Y. 10013

Manufactured in the United States of America

THE CIVIL WAR

" For the whole country it was to be the bitterest of all ordeals—an agony of struggle and a decision by blood; but for one party it was to be a war of hope. Should the South win, she must also lose—must lose her place in the great Union which she had loved and fostered, and must in gaining independence destroy a nation. Should the North win, she would confirm a great hope and expectation, establish the Union, unify it in institutions, free it from interior contradictions of life and principle, set it in the way of consistent growth and unembarrassed greatness. The South fought for a principle, as the North did : it was this that was to give the war dignity and supply the tragedy with a double motive. But the principle for which the South fought meant standstill in the midst of change ; it was conservative, not creative ; it was against drift and destiny ; it protected an impossible institution and a belated order of society ; it withstood a creative and imperial idea, the idea of a united people and a single law of freedom. Overwhelming material superiority, it turned out, was with the North ; but she had also another and greater advantage : she was to fight for the Union and for the abiding peace, concord, and strength of a great nation."

WOODROW WILSON.

PREFACE TO THE BRITISH EDITION

In the United States of America, where chance and opportunity have played so large a part in fashioning history, to me it seems wonderfully appropriate that in the greatest and most vital war its people were ever engaged upon, the blindfolded goddess Fortuna should have placed her finger on a man so humble and obscure as Ulysses S. Grant, and have raised him to such a pinnacle of fame. Also does it seem to me curiously inappropriate that this pacific and somewhat puritanical nation should have benefited so amazingly from every war it has waged. The War of Independence sowed the seeds of a great people; the War of 1812–15 gave these people sure and certain economic foundations: the Mexican War vastly expanded their territories; the Civil War welded them into a nation; the Spanish War brought them into close contact with the outer world; and finally, the World War of eleven years ago, so it seems to me, has placed them on the economic road towards world dominion. And all this in a hundred and fifty years. Rome shudders; certainly the age of the great empires is still with us.

To-day we have learnt to abhor war, and, when we cannot avoid it, to entrust its loathly work to professional hands. To suggest that war has had its value, and may still have its value, that it has hitherto been an essential ingredient in civilisation, and that many of the greatest generals have been unprofessional men, is to proclaim oneself a heretic. Yet this is the dictum of history, which cares little about the fashions of the day or the emotions of a fleeting period.

It is because popular opinion on any serious subject, such as war and generalship, is nearly always wrong, that I have written this book, for in my opinion the Civil War in America is not only typically a war which proves this contention, but a war which is still so wonderfully modern, so close to us and of our day, that I believe much can be learnt from its history, its generalship, and its results. So much, in fact, that probably of all wars it is the most instructive in teaching us how to avoid the next war ; and if we fail to do so, how to win it, and what is equally important, how to win the peace which must, in its turn, follow it.

To-day there can be no question of doubt in my own mind that the Civil War in America was the first of the great modern wars, wars begotten of the Industrial Revolution and all this revolution includes. It was a war born of steam-power, which changed not only the historical structure of nations, but the traditional structure of armies. To-day we are faced by many similar changes ; for it may be said without fear of contradiction that we are now living in the throes of the second industrial revolution, a most powerful sequel which is daily adding to the might of coal and steam the might of oil and electricity.

In 1861 the Civil War, which had lain smouldering for two generations, burst into flame, and its causes, long and vehemently debated, were in fact little examined and understood.

The same sequence of events is to be witnessed before 1914, the same sequence follows 1919 as followed 1865, because the World War was but a thinly veiled European Civil War. The causes of these two wars were very similar, the natures of these two wars were very much alike, and the peace which followed the one and the other were equally chaotic. In brief, the statesmanship of 1900–29 learnt nothing from the statesmanship of 1850–79. In 1914 Europe drifted into war, and in 1919 she drifted into a so-called peace—nothing having been learnt from similar driftings in 1861 and 1865.

To-day what is the use of anathematising war, of outlawry and such-like hocus-pocus, if statesmen remain armoured by their ignorance against the reality of war—its origins, causes, and nature ? Similarly, what is the use of a military professionalism, which in this rapidly changing industrial age expects to win the next war with the tactics, organisation, and weapons of the last one ? With few exceptions, the age of the greatest generals in history antedates the age of the military academies. Since the advent of the war schools native genius has been crippled by pedantry, not because sound military education is in itself detrimental (such a contention would be absurd), but because the easiest thing to do in a school is to copy the past, and the past is something dead and gone, and frequently a thing which was misbegotten. In the days of the great captains, soldiers were free to blunder and learn from their blunders, their horsesense for war was not destroyed. To-day, as often as not, they school themselves into copying other people's blunders, or other people's successes, which change of circumstances has converted into tactical arsenic or strategical strychnine. Should they survive, then they find justification in a book, a doctrine, or a dogma. This is why professionalism has so often proved itself to be the dry rot of armies ; it does not probe into the viscera of living war, it merely rattles the skeletons of our military ancestors. And, be it remembered, the Civil War was a very unprofessional one.

Here, then, is the gist of this book—to write living history as well as truthful history—a difficult task ; for in my opinion all history has been diluted with about seventy-five per cent. of falsehood ; and more especially official history, which is normally meticulously accurate in fact and utterly false in spirit.

Having selected Grant as my hero, my task has been doubly a difficult one, because this great general was a silent and inarticulate man ; a man who normally did not confide his thoughts to others, yet a man who seldom if ever hurried towards a conclusion. To me he seems to have been typically non-academic ; thinking in facts and not in theories ; totally oblivious of his own genius ; always willing to listen to others, to trust in others when he believed in them, but seldom if ever to be led by them.

In order to decipher his generalship I have relied on three sources : the official records—the bones of my subject ;

personal memoirs and various historical works—the muscles ; and my own intuitions and deductions which I may liken to the nerves. This latter source may be very defective ; yet I feel not more so than the other two.

If I have belittled or exalted Grant below or above his true value—and I do not pretend to have studied the first two of my sources *au fond* (which would take a lifetime),— I am open to change my views. I have tried, however, to keep within historical facts and to relate the war and Grant's generalship to the years in which the war took place, and to Grant himself, that unimaginative, stolid, common-sense visionary I believe him to have been ; and I have done so with an eye on how this book can help us to-day in peace and in war, in statesmanship and in generalship.

I have not merely attempted to dig up political and military bones, but to endow these dead things with a little life, so that they may speak to us as if they were living things, and speak to us of their day in terms of our day. It is for this reason that in Part IV of my book I have dealt with the " Generalship of Peace " ; which, if it explains nothing else, will explain why it was that when Maurice de Saxe completed his memorable work—*Reveries upon the Art of War*, which he said treats " of a science which furnishes us with means for the destruction of the human race," he added an epilogue entitled—" Reflections upon the Propagation of the Human Species."

J. F. C. F.

ALDERSHOT.
May 5, 1929.

PREFACE TO THE AMERICAN EDITION

"I would like to see truthful history written. Such history will do full credit to the courage, endurance, and ability of the American citizen, no matter what section he hailed from, or in what rank he fought."—*Ulysses S. Grant.*

THE greatest event in European history was the discovery of the New World: to-day it could only be rivalled by landing on a habitable planet. The greatest event in American history was the Civil War; greater than the Rebellion, because separation from England was sooner or later inevitable. The man who most greatly influenced this war was Ulysses S. Grant; not because he was so clear-sighted a statesman as Lincoln, or so clever a tactician as Lee, but because he was the greatest strategist of his age, of the war, and, consequently, its greatest general.

The greatness of great men is an heirloom which is ever young; for it is the source of that historic spirit which gives character to a people, and which, when a people cease to follow it, leaves them bankrupt of moral strength. Thus, it seems to me that no earnest book on a great man, no matter how many may have been written, is altogether redundant; for greatness is not a thing which can be weighed and measured, but a force which flashing down the corridors of time reflects new possibilities from the ever-changing facets of human doings. What Grant was to the men and women of 1865 is not necessarily what he is to the men and women of to-day; not because Grant has changed, but because civilization has changed and is changing.

Because nothing human stands still, it has been the fate of most great men to lose their reality, to become separated from their mortal work, and to assume mythical or enigmatic forms. In this respect, I think that Grant has suffered his full share, and in this present age, in which elderly gentlemen are so deeply concerned in discovering peaceful platitudes whereon to found a Sunday-school universe, though Grant will never

be forgotten, his courage as a soldier and honesty as a citizen
are apt to become fallow land in American history as it is
cultivated to-day. Without courage and without honesty, a
nation is no more than a swarm of cowardly thieves; even
courageous vice is noble when compared to virtuous lethargy.

Grant was not of the type of Alexander, Cæsar, Frederick
and Napoleon: he was a simple-minded man of vision, and
one who for nearly forty years remained an obscure citizen of
the Great Republic. It is for this reason that I have dedi-
cated my book on his generalship to the Youth of America;
for I believe that the second greatest event in American
history was the recent World War, which, cracking the Old
World to its foundations, left the United States standing like
a granite rock.

The future of America rests with her youth; with the spirit
of freedom and not with the spirit of tradition which is en-
crusted on the bones of her mother Europe. To-day, in the
United States there are, so I feel, many potential Grants;
many simple-minded boys and girls of vision, humble and
hard-working, filled with a determination to conquer whatever
is their lot, and so gain that freedom which is the recompense
of victory. To these there is no greater example than Grant
their fellow countryman; not that they will attain to his fame,
but, however obscurely they may live, by emulating what was
great in him they may attain to some share of his greatness.
If they can face failure as he faced it; if they can meet success
as he met it, and remain human and unspoilt by defeat or
victory as he did, then their noblest goal—the greatness of
their civilization—is assured.

Life after all is a conflict—in peace as in war. Grant was
not only a great general, but an honest man, a somewhat rare
combination in the history of war, which should teach us not
only how to conquer our enemies, but how to master ourselves.
It is in this respect, I feel, that military history has been sadly
squandered; it has led us into realms of romance, or has
pointed the way to future slaughter; yet seldom has it shown
us how the greatness of war can be built into the goodness of
peace. It is here that men like Alexander and Napoleon fail

us, and others like Lee and Grant help us. The genius of the former is too distant from us; the greatness of the latter sufficiently far and yet sufficiently near to make it at once attractive and graspable.

Among the great soldiers of this second category, surely Grant is an example. From a humble worker, through perseverance he rose to be a general-in-chief in the greatest war of his age, and was twice chosen by his countrymen as their President. Such a romance as his staggers the Arabian Nights. It staggers them because it was not accomplished through any magic. Alexander was the son of a king, and Napoleon was hurled onto the summit of European affairs by a volcanic revolution. The Civil War in America was not a revolution, and Grant lived and died a simple citizen. He was no despot who grasped "the skirts of happy chance"; he was no slave become Calif, no Clovis shattering pots and proclaiming kingship by his sword. He was a great soldier, but above all he was a great American—the epitome of his age. On his deathbed he wrote: "The war begot a spirit of independence and enterprise. The feeling now is, that a youth must cut loose from his old surroundings to enable him to get up in the world." And again: "The war has made us a nation of great power and intelligence."

In writing this book my object has been to examine what Grant accomplished as a soldier; to show that as such he has not been fully appreciated, and that as he looked upon war as a necessary evil so long as peace remains imperfect, we also, after the greatest war in modern times, may find in his honesty and in his vision our direction towards creating a happier and less turbulent world. "Let us have peace," he said: well then—let us examine war.

J. F. C. F.

Aldershot,
May 5, 1929.

FOREWORD TO SECOND EDITION

SINCE this book was first published in 1929, a number of other books on the Civil War have appeared, but because this study is so largely based on the official records, I doubt whether any of them would cause me drastically to modify my estimate of General Grant. Those that I have read, and in particular Douglas Southall Freeman's monumental biography of R. E. Lee, if anything have reinforced it. To me, at least, Grant remains the greatest of the many remarkable Civil War generals, and a general who, better than most others, can teach soldiers of to-day their art.

Because warfare is now so different from what it was 100 years ago, this may seem an unwarranted assumption. The differences seem so enormous that the question may be asked: Has not the scientist replaced the general as the decisive factor in future warfare? The answer depends on what is meant by war. Should it be the obliteration of ourselves and our opponents in an exchange of nuclear ballistic missiles, then my answer is that the paean of victory must be raised for the scientist, although it will be indistinguishable from the dirge of defeat. But is warfare of mutual obliteration probable? I think not, and my reasons are not my personal predilections but historical facts.

The first is, that the atomic bomb has never again been used since first dropped in 1945. The second is, that although since 1945 a number of wars—in Greece, China, Korea, Indonesia, Indochina, Malaya, Egypt, and Algeria—have been fought, all have been limited in nature and restricted to the employment of conventional weapons. And the third that, though during this period more war-provoking incidents of a violent nature have occurred than in any comparable period in history, because of the universal terror that a nuclear catastrophe instills, the majority of them have not led to war.

What probabilities can be deduced from these facts? Firstly, that the wars of the future—it would be folly to imagine that there will be none—will remain limited; and secondly, because of this, generalship will take precedence over scientism. This is not to belittle the scientist, because in this age of science his task is to render unlimited war so total in effect that the only wars which can be fought with profit will be those of a limited nature in which—thanks to him—generalship will still dominate. Therefore it stands to reason that the generals of to-day and to-morrow can learn lessons of inestimable value from the generals of yesterday. As this is so, and I do not see how it can be disputed, I hope that this study of a great general may be not only of interest but of value to my readers.

March 12, 1958   J. F. C. F.

CONTENTS

CONTENTS

PART IV.—THE GENERALSHIP OF PEACE

CHAPTER XVII

THE FOUNDATIONS OF WAR

CHAPTER XVIII

THE FOUNDATIONS OF PEACE

CHAPTER XIX

GRANT AS CITIZEN AND MAN

APPENDICES

LIST OF ILLUSTRATIONS

GENERAL ULYSSES S. GRANT, 1863 . . *Frontispiece*

MAPS

PLANS

xxi

ABBREVIATED TITLES OF WORKS REFERRED TO IN THE FOOTNOTES

(*All other Titles are given in full*)

Abbreviation.	Author.	Full Title of Work.
Alexander .	. Alexander, E. P.	The American Civil War (1908).
Atkinson .	. Atkinson, C. F.	Grant's Campaigns of 1864 and 1865 (1908).
Atlanta .	. Cox, J. D.	Atlanta (1909).
Badeau .	. Badeau, A.	Military History of Ulysses S. Grant (1881).
Battine .	. Battine, C.	The Crisis of the Confederacy (1905).
B. & L. . .		Battles and Leaders of the Civil War (1884–8).
Beauregard .	. Roman, A.	Military Operations of General Beauregard (1883).
Bigelow .	. Bigelow, J.	The Campaign of Chancellorsville (1910).
Boynton .	. Boynton, H. V.	Sherman's Historical Raid. The Memoirs in Light of the Records (1875).
C.M.H. . .		Cambridge Modern History, VII (1903).
Church .	. Church, W. C.	Ulysses S. Grant (1906).
Cist . .	. Cist, H. M.	The Army of the Cumberland (1909).
Conger .	. Conger, A. L.	The Military Education of Grant as General (1921).
Corresp. . .		Correspondance de Napoléon Iᵉʳ (1858–69).
Cox . .	. Cox, J. D.	The March to the Sea, Franklin and Nashville (1906).

xxiii

Abbreviation.	Author.	Full Title of Work.
Davis . . .	Davis, Jefferson	The Rise and Fall of the Confederate Government (1881).
Ency. Brit. . .		Encyclopædia Britannica, 11th Edition.
Fiske . . .	Fiske, J.	The Mississippi Valley in the Civil War (1901).
Fitzhugh Lee	Lee, F.	General Lee (1894).
Force . .	Force, M. F.	From Fort Henry to Corinth (1908).
Ford . . .	Ford, H.	My Life and Work (1924).
Formby	Formby, J.	The American Civil War (1910).
Fry . . .	Fry, J. B.	Military Miscellanies (1889).
Grant	Grant, U. S.	Personal Memoirs (1885).
Greene	Greene, F. V.	The Mississippi (1909).
Henderson .	Henderson, G. F. R.	Stonewall Jackson and the American Civil War (1898).
Hosmer	Hosmer, J. K.	The American Civil War (1913).
Humphreys .	Humphreys, A. A.	The Virginia Campaign of '64 and '65 (1907).
Jones . . .	Jones, J. B.	A Rebel War Clerk's Diary (1866).
Livermore .	Livermore, W. R.	The Story of the Civil War (1913).
Longstreet .	Longstreet, J.	From Manassas to Appomattox (1896).
M.H.S.M. . .		Papers of the Military Historical Society of Massachusetts (1895–1918).
Nicolay	Nicolay, J. G.	The Outbreak of Rebellion (1882).
Nicolay & Hay	Nicolay, J. G., and Hay, J.	Abraham Lincoln : A History (1890).
N. & L. . .	Livermore, W. R.	Numbers and Losses in the Civil War in America (1900).

Abbreviation.	Author.	Full Title of Work.
Phisterer	Phisterer, F.	Statistical Record of the Armies of the United States (1901).
Pond	Pond, G. E.	The Shenandoah Valley in 1864 (1884).
Ropes	Ropes, J. C.	The Story of the Civil War (1894–8).
Schouler	Schouler, J.	History of the United States under the Constitution (1880–9).
The Science of War	Henderson, G. F. R.	The Science of War (1905).
Sheridan	Sheridan, P. H.	Personal Memoirs of P. H. Sheridan (1888).
Sherman	Sherman, W. T.	Memoirs of General W. T. Sherman (1875).
Sidney Johnston	Johnston, W. P.	The Life of General Albert Sidney Johnston (1879).
S.H.S.		Southern Historical Society Papers (1876–1909).
Swinton	Swinton, W.	Campaigns of the Army of the Potomac (1882).
Taylor, F. W.	Taylor, F. W.	The Principles of Scientific Management (1916).
Taylor	Taylor, R.	Destruction and Reconstruction, Personal Experiences of the Late War (1870).
W.R.		The War of the Rebellion (Official Records) (1880–1900).
Wood & Edmonds	Wood, W. B., and Edmonds, J. E.	A History of the Civil War in the United States (1905).
Woodward	Woodward, W. E.	Meet General Grant (1928).

INTRODUCTION

INTRODUCTION

THE GENERAL

"C'est la volonté, le caractère, l'application et l'audace qui m'ont fait ce que je suis."—NAPOLEON.

On April 9, 1865, two of the most remarkable men in the history of the United States of America met near Appomattox Court House. *Lee*, the aristocrat, was in full uniform, wearing embroidered gauntlets and carrying a burnished sword ; Grant, but a few years before an assistant in a leather store, without sword, appeared in the dress of a private soldier on which were stitched the straps of a lieutenant-general. Outwardly these two men were as unlike as could be, inwardly there was a link between them —their generalship.

In order to understand this word we must at once dismiss from our minds the popular illusion that generalship can be measured by victory or defeat ; for there is something more subtle than this in the drama of war, namely, the art of those who wage it. There, on the battlefield, is no carefully prepared stage, yet the audience is immense, for on a few square miles of ground are the eyes of the nations fixed. Everywhere is there turmoil, or vacant spaces riddled with death. A gathering of things growing, moving, struggling, eluding the grasp, dissolving and then sprouting up again. Behind it all, the unceasing rumble of wheels, and the whisperings of intriguing officials ; and in the centre of this tumult of fears, of hopes, and of things seen, suspected and unknown, stands a solitary figure—the general-in-chief.

" I consult no one but myself," said Napoleon, because in war there is no one else to whom a general can turn. The responsibility of every action lies heavily upon him. He may seek the advice of others, but others cannot share his

3

load. Their opinions may be good, bad, or indifferent, but the conditions in which they are fashioned can bear but a distant relationship to those in which he is labouring. His first quality is, therefore, fortitude.

To this supreme virtue must he add many others ; perseverance which is akin to it, and determination which is but perseverance ensouled. He must be physically strong, mentally alert, and morally unshakeable. He must understand men, weapons, and war, and above all—this is his philosopher's stone—he must understand himself, and see himself as his enemy sees him. Here I will quote from two men—Henderson, the soldier, who possessed a natural wisdom for war, and Faraday, the chemist, who possessed an inborn instinct for essentials. I will quote from these two, because it is my wish to show that in generalship but a hair divides the great soldier from the great civilian.

Henderson says, and he is considering the actions of General *Lee* before the battle of Gettysburg :

" War is more of a struggle between two human intelligences than between two masses of armed men ; and the great general does not give his first attention to numbers, to armament, or to position. He looks beyond these, beyond his own troops, and across the enemy's lines without stopping to estimate their strength or to examine the ground, until he comes to the quarters occupied by the enemy's leader ; and then he puts himself in that leader's place, and with that officer's eyes and mind he looks at the situation. . . ." [1]

Faraday, contemplating philosophy and not war, which is largely barbarity, gives so complete a picture of true generalship that it would be difficult to better it. He says :

" The philosopher " (the general) " should be a man willing to listen to every suggestion, but determined to judge for himself. He should not be biased by appearances ; have no favourite hypotheses ; be of no school ; and in doctrine, have no master. He should not be a respecter of persons,

---

[1] *The Science of War*, p. 283.

but of things. Truth should be his primary object. If to these qualities be added industry, he may indeed hope to walk within the vail of the temple of nature " (war).[1]

When applied to the soldier, it may seem to some a curiously inappropriate definition, because it runs counter to the jargon of the schools, their discipline, rules, maxims, unlimited offensives, pivots of manœuvre, *ad nauseam*; most if not all of which are completely out of date and inapplicable fifty years before they ruin themselves and their adherents on the battlefield. Professionalism has been and is still the curse of armies, because it rapidly petrifies, it is a thing of tradition, but not of fact. Of professional soldiership, as it was in his day, Marshal Saxe sarcastically remarks:

" War is a science so obscure and imperfect, that, in general, no rules of conduct can be given in it which are reducible to absolute cĕrtainties; custom and prejudice, confirmed by ignorance, are its sole foundation and support." [2]

It was because the Civil War in America was so un-professional a conflict that it is so vastly interesting, and its generalship so brilliant and instructive. In 1861 there were no generals in the United States Army who, from the European standard, could be classed as professional soldiers. A few were true students of war, a very different thing, and many had behind them the rough-and-tumble experiences of warfare in Mexico and of skirmishes with Red Indians and Mormons—these made them men and masters of men. When, a generation after this war, so eminent a soldier as Field-Marshal Lord Wolseley could say, " that had the United States been able, early in 1861, to put into the field, in addition to their volunteers, one Army Corps of regular troops, the war would have ended in a few months," [3] we are no longer left in doubt of the value of military professionalism in the World War of 1914–18, in

[1] *Scientific Method*, F. W. Westaway, p. 49.
[2] *Reveries upon the Art of War* (English edition, 1757), p. iii.
[3] *Henderson* (Introduction), p. x.

which generalship all but vanished. One European army corps in the continent of America, confronted by the riflemen of the South, would in a few weeks have met the fate of Braddock and his regulars on the Monongahela, or of Lord Percy and his Red-Coats at Lexington.

The greatest generals in history have always been more than mere professionals. Men who not only understood men as soldiers, but who understood their age. Men who ran counter to the professionalism of their day, and who, succeeding, unfortunately created schools of war which rapidly solidified and turned out pedants and pundits. The greatest were autocrats, men like Alexander, Cæsar, Frederick, and Napoleon, who combined statesmanship with soldiership—the knowledge of their day with the knowledge of war. To these few elect, the true Great Captains of history, in one direction was generalship simplified; for being autocrats they could concentrate their minds on one objective—the enemy—and were not compelled to squander their thoughts on a hydra-headed host of misbegotten operations, the offspring of political interference. Such men are their own government, and their own law.

Such men can show us the greatness of war. They can raise us to the sublimity of their art, but they can only vaguely teach us the common difficulties of generalship, because they are uncommon men in uncommon circumstances. To understand these difficulties we must descend lower in the military hierarchy, selecting as examples more ordinary beings, as great perhaps in genius, but less free to give it play.

When we turn to this second category, the general under political control, we find in almost all great wars, and certainly in the American Civil War, two major series of actions —the defeat of the enemy, and the establishment of unity of command. " Men are nothing," said Napoleon, " it is one man who matters." Again, " Let only one command in war," wrote Machiavelli, because " several minds weaken an army." When the truth of these sayings is realised, then are the surest foundations of generalship established ; and, as we shall see, it was not until Lincoln grasped this truth that the Great Rebellion passed from substance to shadow.

Setting aside the autocrat, we see that the general is the true military instrument of government. He has the will to act, and, possessing the power, he must understand how to act. This he can never do unless the political nature of the war is known to him. In their turn, must the Government understand its military nature. This common understanding is what is called grand strategy,[1] the national fabric upon which the war picture—grand tactics—is woven. Grand strategy secures the political object by directing all warlike resources towards the winning of the war, whilst grand tactics accomplishes action by converging all means of waging war against the forces of the enemy. In spite of their military ignorance at the outbreak of the war, Lincoln learnt the meaning of the first, and Grant of the second. Yet, it was not until the spring of 1864, when the great statesman met the great soldier, that these two saw eye to eye, and the meaning of Napoleon's words, " An army is nothing without a head," became manifest.

Looking back on this war, the vastest civil conflict in modern history, and considering how inadequately Federals and Confederates were prepared to meet it, it is a remarkable proof of the power of such turmoils, when compared to professional selection, to release military genius. No other war in modern times, not excepting the Revolutionary and Napoleonic wars, produced such a galaxy of generals; and with few exceptions, the most notable being *Lee*, those of more marked ability were under forty-five years of age.[2]

---

[1] Strategy, in all its forms, is a most perplexing word. Grand strategy, in my opinion, would be more comprehensible if called " political strategy," whilst strategy, as ordinarily understood, might be called " field strategy."

[2] In 1861 the average age of the following officers—(Federals) Grant, Sherman, Meade, Thomas, Rosecrans, Sheridan, Hancock, McClellan, McPherson, Burnside; (Confederates) *Lee*, " *Stonewall* " *Jackson, Joseph Johnston, Longstreet, Hood, Early, Morgan, Beauregard, Stuart,* and *Mosby* was 38·55 years. In the Napoleonic Wars the average age was much the same. Napoleon was of opinion that few generals of over forty-five were fit for active command. At the date of the Battle of Waterloo he was forty-six, and so was Wellington.

Youth is a tremendous asset to generalship. When in war old men command armies, republics rock and kingdoms totter, for war demands the audacity and energy of youth. In the Civil War the ablest generals were men who had been educated at West Point, and who had breathed the atmosphere of war in Mexico. Men of no formal school, no fixed doctrine, and of no set ideas. Men who in many cases, notably Grant and Sherman, had left the army years before the war, and in place of being asphyxiated by mess life had gained independence in the struggle for existence. The cramping military discipline of European armies, fettered by worn-out traditions, was unknown to them. The war found these men ignorant and unprepared, but seldom lacking in courage. They plunged into errors in place of avoiding them, and were sufficiently young in mind to learn, and profit by their mistakes. Grant is a wonderful example of this : of how a man of forty could begin with a Belmont and end with an Appomattox campaign. He was for ever learning, and though not endowed with outstanding genius, through sheer industry, perseverance, and self-education he accomplished his end far more thoroughly than many a more brilliant but less determined general would have done.

In so strange a war as this one, a new war begotten of a new weapon—the rifle—old ideas, and rigidity of system were out of place. Youth is flexible and adaptable, boldness is a characteristic of manhood, prudence of old age. Courage begets prestige—the magnetism of generalship. Of Major-General McDowell, a major in the old army, an historian writes " that he remembered the Major, but forgot the General, and went into the thick of the fight." [1] In this instance (the first battle of Bull Run) it may have been wrong to do so, but it was because so many of the generals of this period could forget that they were generals, and at times could transform themselves into majors, that the courage of their men was so astonishing. When things went awry, Grant went to the front, and so did

[1] *Formby*, p. 86.

Lee. " Back, General *Lee* ! . . . to the rear, General *Lee* ! "
was frequently heard in the thickets of the Wilderness.
This boldness was not only brave soldiership, but good
generalship, and had a few of the generals of the World
War gone forward when their men were going back, many
a reverse would have been avoided. What action could
have been more pregnant of victory than C. F. Smith's
at Fort Donelson ?

" General Smith, on his horse, took position in the front
and centre of the line. Occasionally he turned in his saddle
to see how the alignment was kept. For the most part,
however, he held his face steadily toward the enemy. He
was, of course, a conspicuous object for the sharpshooters
in the riflepits. The air around him twittered with minié
bullets. Erect, as if on review, he rode on, timing the gait
of his horse with the movement of his colors. A soldier
said : ' I was nearly scared to death, but I saw the old
man's white mustache over his shoulder, and went on.' " [1]

Smith was Grant's instructor at West Point, and he was
fifty-five years old at this time.

It was the personality of the American generals, more
so than their knowledge, which stood them in such good
stead, and in the end it is this undefinable quality, always
prolific in a forming nation, and generally deficient in a
formed one, which is one of the greatest assets of generalship. Discipline makes soldiers, but it is personality which
makes, and sad to say sometimes unmakes, generals.
Napoleon, one of the most astonishing personalities of any
age, saw this clearly, for he says :

" The personality of the general is indispensable, he is
the head, he is the all of an army. The Gauls were not
conquered by the Roman legions, but by Cæsar. It was
not before the Carthaginian soldiers that Rome was made
to tremble, but before Hannibal. It was not the Macedonian
phalanx which penetrated to India, but Alexander. It
was not the French Army which reached the Weser and
the Inn, it was Turenne. Prussia was not defended for

---

[1] *B. & L.*, I, p. 423.

seven years against the three most formidable European powers by Prussian soldiers, but by Frederick the Great." [1]

To this list, as we shall see, may be added : It was not the valiant soldiers of the South who in 1864 stood like a wall between Grant and Richmond, but *Lee*. And it was not the gallant men of the North who drove *Lee* from the Rapidan to the Appomattox, but Grant. Thus we see, that to appreciate the history of great battles, above all we must appreciate the personality of the generals who waged them, those men who wielded armies as their men wield weapons, and who imbued these living instruments with their determination to conquer. Yet when an army is so lacking in organisation, equipment, or training, that it cannot respond to the will of its general, all genius is in vain.

PRINCIPLES

"L'art de la guerre n'est que l'art d'augmenter les chances pour soi."
NAPOLEON.

Thus far I have dealt mainly with the moral forces of generalship, and it will be seen from what I have said how capricious they are, and how largely chance enters into them. Whatever type of man we examine, it is obvious that we cannot change to any considerable extent his native intelligence, his sense of humour, his courage, prudence, etc., etc. ; but we can increase his knowledge through education, and improve his talents by practice. We cannot endow him with genius, but we can teach him to think logically. Whilst his natural abilities enable him to accomplish his aim with some degree of art, method of work will greatly assist him to attain artistic results with the least loss of energy ; in other words, the method of science will be of immense value to him.

All arts are based on science, that is on co-ordinated knowledge, though this does not mean that a scientist must consequently be an artist. But when a man does

[1] *Mémoires écrits à Sainte-Hélène*, Montholon, II, p. 90.

possess artistic ability, whether his art be war, music, electric lighting, gardening, etc., then, if he can simultaneously think scientifically, he will be in a position to economise his faculties, his forces, his time, and the material he is making use of.

A battle may be a work of art, like a picture ; but from one battle it is not possible to deduce a science of war, because, though actions can be compared with actions, with the battle itself there is no comparison. Instead, let us take ten battles, a hundred battles, or a thousand battles, and analyse the generalship manifested in them ; then by degrees we shall establish several thousands of comparisons. Many we shall trace to the native genius of the generals ; but some we shall find cropping up in each battle fought when circumstances are fairly similar ; also that a few are patent to all forms of fighting—duels, skirmishes, combats, and battles between groups of armies. From these facts we can deduce certain generalisations known as the principles of war.

Taking all these facts, irrespective of their origin, we can assemble them under three major headings, namely, the instruments of war, the methods of war, and the conditions of war. The first includes armies, navies, and, to-day, air forces ; the second the rules, maxims, and principles of war ; and the third a multitude of circumstances—political, financial, economic, ethical, geographical, etc. In all the instruments of war will be found three elements, namely, protection, offensive power, and movement. Protected mobility is strategy, and protected offensive power is tactics. The object of the former is battle, not at any price, but at the lowest cost ; and of the latter the accomplishment of strategy, that is complete freedom of movement, and this is only possible when the enemy's strength is paralysed, dissipated, or destroyed.

The third category of facts, namely, conditions, in so far as they influenced the Civil War I will deal with in Part I of this book. Meanwhile I will examine the second category, and I should like to ask the student, or reader, to bear with me a little if this subject appears a dull one, because it is the key which I intend to use in unlocking the door of Grant's generalship. Rules and maxims I will not discuss, for they come and go as weapons, means of protection, and of movement change ; but principles are fundamental, and these I will now attempt to explain.

Expenditure of military force is an art, and like all other arts it is based on science. The science of war is the knowledge of human conflict in all its forms, whether the battle is a fight between two men, or between two or more nations. Without this science warfare must largely remain in an alchemical state, and be governed by chance and not by law. As force has to be expended, then the side which can best economise its force is the side which is more likely to win, or to sustain unnecessary loss. Economy of force is, therefore, the governing law of war. Granted this law, the next question is to decide on the nature of force ; and as an army is but a number of men, the forces of war must be sought in man himself. Human force is threefold ; it is mental, moral, and physical, and no one of these forms of force can be expended without influencing the remaining two. Economy in the expenditure of these constitutes the central problem of strategy and tactics.

The expenditure of force presupposes pressure and resistance which govern the direction force eventually takes. In war each side must have an object which provisionally fixes the direction of military operations. In order to maintain this direction, pressure and resistance must be exerted. These two factors if correctly employed lead to an economical distribution of force, and they should control the formulation of all plans of war. These three principles are, consequently, closely related to the mental sphere of force—to the thoughts in the head of the general-in-chief out of which he evolves his plan.

Before this plan can be transformed into physical action, that is executed by the men themselves, the troops must not only be willing but determined to carry it out. To do so their *moral* must balance their fear, consequently their determination to act must be supported by moral endurance. Further, to economise this endurance, they should aim at surprising the enemy, that is demoralising him. In the moral sphere of war we thus obtain three principles closely related to the former ones. They may be called the principles of the determination, endurance, and demoralisation of force (or surprise). It is in this moral sphere of war that the decisive battle is waged.

To attack the enemy's determination to win, physical action must be brought into play. Men must move, and movement depends on how far offensive action can be protected. Thus are obtained three physical principles of war, namely, those of mobility, security, and the disorganisation of force (or offensive action).

We thus obtain nine principles of war which govern the expenditure of force. Three are related to pressure, three to resistance, and three to the control of their resultants —the direction of the operation, the determination of all ranks to attain the object in view, and movement towards the objective itself.

These nine principles, which are expressions of the law of economy of force, form the foundations of the science of war, without which the art of war is solely determined by individual predilection, or chance. This science is expressed as an art through the instrument of war, the military organisation at the command of the general-in-chief, who, to act rightly, expends its force by applying the principles of war according to the everchanging conditions which surround him. These conditions can either assist or resist him, and by a correct, that is an economical, application of principles to conditions, he abstracts the highest assistance from all the forces which surround his army. For him to do so with true economy, it is necessary that the organisation of his army should be suitable to the nature of the operation in hand. This suitability consists in power to develop protected offensive action in the least possible time and at the greatest possible speed. From these considerations we see that not only are strategy and tactics complementary halves of the art of war, but that the geometric strategical ideas so favoured in former days, such as interior and exterior lines, lines of operation, concentric and excentric attacks, etc., etc., are but details of the art which should be as " fluid " as any other art, and is so when it is based on a full understanding of the science of war in place of haphazard improvisation.

This system of analysing war, condensed from my book *The Foundations of the Science of War*, I believe to be a useful one. It may not explain military genius, yet it does, so I think, explain the framework of this intuitive knowledge. General Lloyd, so it seems to me, gives the clearest definition of men of genius. He writes :

" They see at once the cause, and its effect, with the different combinations which unite them : they do not proceed by common rules, successively from one idea to another, by slow and languid steps, no : the *whole*, with all its circumstances and various combinations, is like a picture, all together present to their mind ; these want no geometry : but an age produces few of this kind of men : and in the common run of generals, geometry and experience will help them to avoid gross errors." [1]

I hope that my system will do likewise, when I apply it to the generalship of Grant. I do not intend to do so in a pedantic way, but I shall have the system in mind when I criticise his campaigns. When applied as a means of analysing plans of operation, that is the decisions arrived at by the general, I shall make use of the principles as follows. Those of concentration, distribution, and direction, as influenced by the determination of the general, I shall consider as appertaining more closely to strategy ; and those of offensive action, security, and mobility, as influenced by the endurance of the troops, as appertaining to tactics. Surprise, that is originality in the generals and unexpected

[1] *History of the Late War in Germany* (1766), General Lloyd, I, p. 19. By " geometry " Lloyd means " method."

action as it influences their men, I shall consider as being common to these two branches of the art of war.

If the reader will carefully examine these principles, he will find that they are of universal application—that is to say, they govern, so it seems to me, all forms of human activity. They are as applicable to work as to fighting, and, conversely, the methods of work, and particularly scientific management, are as important to fighting as to work. I know of no two books more useful in understanding the art of generalship than F. W. Taylor's *The Principles of Scientific Management,* and Henry Ford's *My Life and Work.* And because I feel that this is so, I hope that this book of mine, in which is examined the activities of one of the greatest generals of the last century, may assist those who would become masters of work to distil from the turmoil of war the more excellent generalship of peace. This is a use of military history which I believe to be original.

PART I
THE CIVIL WAR

CHAPTER I

NATURAL HISTORY OF THE WAR

IMMENSITY OF THE CONFLICT

" AT half-past four o'clock, on the morning of April 12th, 1861, while yet the lingering night lay upon the waters of the bay, leaving even the outline of Fort Sumter scarcely discernible, the assembled spectators saw a flash from the mortar battery near old Fort Johnson, on the south side of the harbor, and an instant after a bombshell rose in a slow, high curve through the air, and fell upon the fort." [1]

The Rubicon was crossed, sixty years and more of argument, of political facts and fictions, of expedients and unworkable panaceas, were, like a cobweb, swept aside by Captain *George S. James's* ten-inch shell. On April 14 the flag of the United States was hauled down, and Major Anderson surrendered the fort. Exactly four years later this same officer raised the Stars and Stripes to float once again over its then peaceful ruins.

During these four years what do we see ? A drama, the like of which had never been witnessed before ; a drama the United States is unlikely ever to look upon again : in fact, a unique event in the history of this turbulent world. During these four years the theatre of war was half the size of India ; the North enlisted nearly 3,000,000 men ; 2,200 combats were fought, 149 being important engagements ; 1,504 blockade runners were captured or destroyed ; approximately half a million men were killed or died, and to the North alone the war cost some $4,750,000,000. These figures rightly make us pause and wonder ; yet, in Europe, to so great a general as Moltke this colossal conflict was but a matter of " two armed mobs chasing each other around the country, from which nothing could

[1] *Nicolay*, p. 62.

be learned." Such is the military eye of the doctrinaire, the man who has soaked his brain in rules, and to whom all things warlike are to be measured on the bed of Procrustean regulations.

This war was far otherwise. It was one of the most extraordinary of wars ever fought—an epoch-making war in military and civil history. A war which foretold the coming of the World War of 1914–18, the tactics of which would have been vastly modified had Moltke studied those of this Civil War. For forty years his school of thought obsessed European armies, rendering them all but impervious to the changing conditions introduced by science and industry. It was a war within a nation in which the North was fighting, not a hostile army, but a hostile people; and in which both sides were equally imbued with the justice of their cause. A war on the one side undertaken to establish national independence, and on the other to maintain national unity. A war which moved in the highest moral spheres; an epic to the South, stern duty to the North, for both, according to their ideals, were fighting for the ashes of the dead, and the inheritance of those unborn. For the North it could be no other than a war of conquest, it could end in no treaty, no argument, no terms, except unconditional surrender, or separation. In its toils were gripped not only the future of America but the future of Western Civilisation; for the disruption of the United States would have resulted, rapidly or slowly, in changing the entire political and economic structure of Europe. Looking back on this war, and remembering that the North was beset by many internal foes, that, as Ropes aptly remarks, " the poetry of war hardly entered into the mind of the Northern volunteer," [1] and that offensive warfare had to be carried over half a continent, the outstanding marvel is that the North ever won. Thus, it seems to me, to talk of armed mobs is puerile. Is this all that can be learnt from such conflicts as the Peloponnesian War, the Thirty Years' War, and this Civil War? We shall see.

[1] *Ropes*, Pt. I, p. 106.

ETHICAL AND ECONOMIC ORIGINS OF THE WAR

The origin of all modern wars may be traced to economic causes, and in the last hundred years these causes find their source in the Industrial Revolution which, between 1760 and 1860, refashioned the world. In the sixteenth century the feudal barons of the Plantagenets were steadily replaced by the economically minded nobility of the Tudors, and in the following century we see numbers of the more truculent members of the old military aristocracy emigrating to the then infant American Colonies. In 1775 the descendants of these settlers led the Rebellion, and no sooner had liberty been won than internal discord arose. As early as 1799 we find William Cobbett writing in his *Porcupine* :

" The reader will do well to observe the point on which the Virginia politics turn. Virginia will either have majority in Congress or a separation of the States. . . . They [the States] can be held together by nothing but the Federal influences of the middle States, and more particularly that of Pennsylvania. If, therefore, this influence should decline in any considerable degree, a separation must inevitably take place, and happy will it be if it should come unaccompanied by a civil war, long, desolating, and bloody." [1]

The fact was, that as early as the end of the eighteenth century the Industrial Revolution had begun to sift the Americans into traders and planters. The first were a rising plutocracy, the second an all but stationary aristocracy. The first rapidly devoted themselves to manufacturing, the second remained an agricultural community. Then, when, to nurse their new-born industries, the North demanded protective tariffs, political swords were drawn, for the cotton monopoly of the South demanded free trade. In 1819 there were twenty-two States in the Union, and of these eleven were slave-holding and eleven free. Politically the two factions were equally divided, but should other States be created, as they must be, what then ?

---

[1] *Porcupine*, X, p. 183.

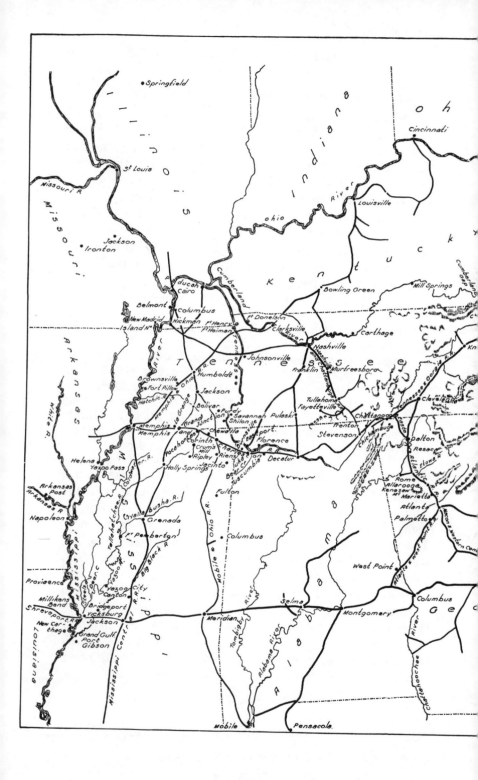

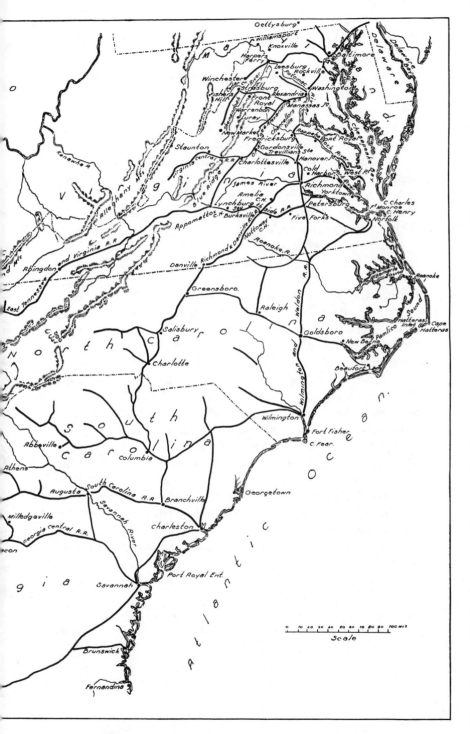

MAP No. 1.—THE THEATRE OF WAR, 1861-5.

We now come to the real cause of the war, the necessity of slavery to the existence of the patriarchal and agricultural society of the South. The squabble over the meaning of the Union, the interpretation of the Constitution, and the liberty of each State to decide upon its own government, were but the weapons whereby slavery could be maintained or abolished. Slavery was not a secondary issue as many suppose, but the main issue, confronted by a new world order, namely, the culture of the Industrial Revolution. Here we are faced by two tangled sets of problems—the ethical and the economic.

Ethically, slavery cut the Southern States adrift from not only the rest of America but from the whole of Europe. Slavery was repugnant to the nineteenth century, and though the war was not fought to abolish slavery, but to put down resistance to the National Government, without slavery the war could not have taken place. Jefferson Davis, in his book *The Rise and Fall of the Confederate Government*, maintains that the South was fighting for equality and not slavery. The whole mass of Secessionist literature contradicts this statement, and Alexander H. Stephens, the Confederate Vice-President, himself declared that slavery was the corner-stone of his Government.[1]

Slavery in one way or another touched almost every measure of legislation. Though it gave leisure to the ruling class of the South, namely, the slave-holders, it kept them conservative and stagnant, for as Woodrow Wilson writes in *The Cambridge Modern History* : " Wherever slavery was established, society took and kept a single and in-variable form ; industry had its fixed variety and pattern ; life held to unalterable standards." [2] All immigrants went to the North, in the South there was no place for them.

---

[1] He said: " Our new Government is founded upon exactly the opposite idea [viz. to that of all men being free and equal] ; its foundations are laid, its corner-stone rests, upon the great truth that the negro is not equal to the white man : that slavery, subordination to the superior race, is his natural and normal condition. Thus our new Government is the first in the history of the world based upon this great physical, philosophical, and moral truth."

[2] *C.M.H.*, VII, p. 413.

In the South the population remained practically stationary, no new markets being established, because the negro population supplied its own wants, and the poor whites were excessively poor.

Though the economic influence of slavery must ultimately have led to an Assyrian indolence which would have rotted the South, its worse feature at this time was its brutalising effect on human nature. Many Southerners realised this: *Robert E. Lee* was against it, *Thomas J. Jackson* (Stonewall) did not like it, yet supported it on Biblical authority. Colonel Henderson, when discussing this subject, mitigates it. He points out that the lot of the slave was frequently a happy one, and preferable to that of thousands of the denizens of European city slums.[1] He overlooks, however, the fact that personal liberty is the highest human happiness in a free society in which imprisonment for life is the severest punishment except death.

The slavery of poverty is an exceeding evil, but legalised slavery is diabolical, because no hope of redemption can exist. In my opinion, the *Journal of a Residence on a Georgian Plantation in 1838–9*, written by that noble woman Fanny Kemble, is one of the saddest books in history. To read of a transaction like the following, described by Harriet Martineau,[2] makes one wonder how it was that the whole Christian world was not ranged against the South. Three beautiful girls of the ages of fifteen, seventeen, and eighteen, were left as orphans. An ancestress of their mother had been a slave, but they showed no perceptible mulatto tinge. Their uncle was about to take them back to his home in New Hampshire, when their father's debtors claimed that they should be entered on the inventory of his effects. The uncle remonstrated. He was a poor man, nevertheless he offered to redeem them for more than they would fetch in the market for house or field labour. This offer was refused with scorn, and in the slave-market of New Orleans " they were sold,

---

[1] *Henderson*, I, p. 90.
[2] Quoted from *American Social History*, Allan Nevins, pp. 211, 212.

separately, at high prices, for the vilest of purposes." Such acts as this, disgracing North and South alike, fostered the Abolitionist Movement, which endowed the North with a crusading spirit. This precipitated the conflict.

Political Origins of the War

The shifting of the causes of a war from an economic to the political level is inevitable, for governments and not systems declare war. In the present instance this shifting began to take place in 1819, when the question of Missouri came before Congress. Should this Territory become a free or a slave State, this was the question? A compromise was arranged: Missouri was to enter the Union as a slave-holding State, and to compensate the balance Maine was to be a free State. Further still, slavery was to be prohibited from the extensive Louisiana Territory purchased from France in 1803.

No sooner was this compromise agreed upon, than the revolution in Spain and the European interference which followed it brought into the political arena the question of the future of the Spanish South American colonies. These had already been recognised by the United States as independent republics. Fearful that some European Power might occupy them before the United States could set its house in order, the Monroe Doctrine was promulgated. This declaration politically separated the New World from the Old.

Once safeguarded theoretically from outside pressure, Congress could devote the whole of its time to internal politics, and these took the form of the Tariff Act, known in the South as the " Tariff of Abominations." When, in 1828, this Act became law, the ships in Charleston harbour flew their flags at half mast, and though, in 1832, the Act was amended, the following year it was declared null and void by the Government of South Carolina, and no longer " binding on the State, its officers or citizens." Thus was the spirit of secession born.

Whilst these political quarrels were monopolising attention, Mexico abolished slavery, and in 1836 Texas revolted, was annexed by the United States, and in 1845 was admitted into the Union as a slave State. This led to the Mexican war of 1845–8, which many Americans, including Ulysses S. Grant, considered an unrighteous undertaking. In his *Personal Memoirs* he writes : " The Southern rebellion was largely the outgrowth of the Mexican war. Nations, like individuals, are punished for their transgressions. We got our punishment in the most sanguinary and expensive war of modern times." [1]

The result of this war was that the United States came into possession of an immense area including, in addition to Texas, the present States of California, New Mexico, Nevada, Arizona, Utah, with parts of Wyoming and Colorado. The question at once arose : should they remain free ? Whilst this problem was being debated, gold was discovered in California, and a rush to the goldfields followed. " The whole social condition of California was instantly changed. Labourers left their fields, tradesmen their shops. Seamen deserted their ships in every harbour . . . to send troops out here would be useless, for they would immediately desert." [2] As the circumstances were such that Congress could not establish a Government for California, the people themselves drew up and ratified a Free State constitution, and made formal application to be admitted into the Union. The South resisted this application. This resistance brought the question of slavery to the top in politics. The balance between free and slave-holding States could no longer be maintained, for in the great West and North-West, slavery was in fact, if not in law, excluded, because these territories were mainly inhabited by Northerners and free immigrants.

The disintegration of the Union had begun, for the South, having segregated itself through slavery, was now faced by the alternatives of either submitting to the eventual abolition of slavery, or to the setting aside of the Union. The ideal

[1] *Grant*, I, p. 56. [2] *C.M.H.*, VII, pp. 400, 401.

of those who originally drew up the Constitution was to establish a Union based on brotherhood. This ethical foundation was by now completely undermined, in place of brotherly affection between the States there were dissensions and hatred.

" A Union which could only be maintained by force was a strange and obnoxious idea to the majority. . . . According to his [the American citizen's] political creed his country was his native State, and such was the creed of the whole South . . . in taking up arms ' they were not, in their opinion, rebels at all,' they were defending their States. . . ." [1]

Slavery had in fact transformed them into a separate nation, ready to repel invasion, and to resist conquest.

Nature and Results of the War

The war was in every respect a desperate one, a war between advancing civilisation, the culture begotten by the French and Industrial Revolutions, and the older agrarian civilisation which preceded these events. It was in fact a war between coal and muscle, a war between two tremendous ideals, on the one side a great free Republic stretching from the Atlantic to the Pacific, developing the wealth of a continent, on the other—an Empire of Babylonian proportions, an immense feudal Arcadia " before which the intellect, the power, the splendor, and the government of all preceding ages and nations should fade and wane." [2] Whilst the North was magnetised by the future, the South was hypnotised by the past. It was a contest between what had been and what should be. To attain either end a sacrifice was demanded—the blood of half a million men to decide the course of destiny.

This war was the first great conflict begotten of the Industrial Revolution, the second was the World War of 1914–18 ; consequently, in the natural history of war these two stand in close relationship. Each sprang from economic

---

[1] *Henderson*, I, pp. 98, 99.   [2] *Nicolay*, p. 11.

causes ; each was preceded by a period of intensive inventiveness ; each was fought with comparatively new weapons, and was largely a war of entrenchments. In each, sea-power strangled the industrially weaker side, which sought to make up for numerical inferiority by novelty in means of attack. Each was faced by a neutral world which influenced its grand strategy, and both were brought to a conclusion through financial chaos, and economic exhaustion as much as by force of arms.

In the half-century preceding the outbreak of the war, what do we see ? Eli Whitney's cotton gin [1] transforming the South ; Fulton's steamships plying the waters of the Hudson, Delaware, Ohio, and Mississippi ; railways developing apace between 1840 and 1850 ; the electric telegraph established in 1844, and McCormick's reaper conquering the prairies of the west.

During the war these inventions were followed by others. The rifle, a comparatively new weapon, is used by both sides, its power is known, but its tactics are not understood ; hence entrenched battlefields and colossal slaughter. Late in the war a breech-loading rifle is adopted, even a magazine-loading rifle, and a machine gun is invented. Torpedoes, land mines, submarine mines, the telegraph, lamp and flag signalling, wire entanglements, are all used and developed ; and newspaper boys, as in the World War, are frequently seen not only behind but on the battlefields themselves. In sea warfare a complete revolution is established : the *Merrimac* and the *Monitor* in one day render obsolete the wooden navies of the entire world ; ramming replaces boarding, and in England Sir John Hay says : " The man who goes into action in a wooden ship is a fool, and the man who sends him there is a villain." The South, unable to rival the naval power of the North, turns to cunning, and seeks to fashion a submarine on the lines of Fulton's *Nautilus*. Though one Federal steamer, the *Housatonic*, is sunk by this strange vessel, hand-driven

[1] " Without the cotton gin, there can be hardly a doubt that the Civil War would not have happened."—*Woodward*, p. 65.

by eight men, she proved a dangerous ally—yet the idea is there, an idea which in 1917 nearly changed the course of European history.

Many other inventions might be listed, but sufficient have been mentioned to show, not only the peculiar nature of this war, but its close resemblance to the World War. Whilst the one was based on steam-power, and all this power includes, the other was based on oil-power and electrical power, the two new sources of power largely developed during the fifty years which preceded 1914. Not only do these inventions link together these two wars in structure, but their influence on the means of waging war is similar ; for, both in 1865 and 1918, war is brought to an end by the collapse of the industrially and financially weaker side.

The onslaughts of *Lee* in 1862–3, and of Grant in 1864–5, resulted in an attrition of man-power, but it was the moral attack of Sherman in Georgia and the Carolinas, and the economic attack of the Federal Navy and of Sheridan in Virginia, which brought the Confederacy to its knees. The South lost heart, prices soared ; already in November 1863 bread riots became frequent, for flour was selling at over $100 the barrel.[1] G. C. Eggleston writes that : " The householder must take his money to market in his basket, and bring his purchases home in his pocket-book." [2] After the World War, in Germany conditions were similar. A man entering a restaurant with a large leather bag was requested to leave it in the cloak-room. " In the cloak-room ? " he exclaimed. " Never ! Why, it is my purse."

From these few incidents it will be seen how much the statesmen and soldiers of Europe might have learnt from this war, had they dismissed from their minds the idea that its main lesson was that of two armed mobs of men chasing each other round a continent. Had they learnt these lessons, then would they have discovered what this war meant to America, and, understanding this, should have been able to apply this knowledge when, in 1919, the reconstruction of Europe confronted them. They would

[1] *Jones*, II, pp. 90, 284. [2] *A Rebel's Recollections*, Chap. IV.

have learnt that no war is worth winning which leaves nations in turmoil, for they would then have understood the spirit of the words engraved on the plinth of General Sherman's statue at Washington—" The legitimate object of war is a more perfect peace."

The Rebellion of 1775 founded the American nation, but it was the Civil War which fashioned this nation into one people. If the South had won, the Confederacy would in time have disintegrated, and North America to-day might be a European satrapy.

The supreme value of this war, and it seems to me no other event could have accomplished it, was to manifest to the South that liberty is the foundation of fraternity and unity, and that her Empire was but a dream. To squeeze out the spirit of the first rebellion ; to absorb the individual selfishness of North and South ; to establish a united spirit of self-reliance, and self-control ; to test the endurance of the people, and to discover whether they were worthy of future greatness.

Finally, not only did this war lead to the opening up of the vast unoccupied territories of the West, and so reveal to a united people the immensity of future prosperity, but it advertised to Europe and to the world, as nothing else could have done, the power of the United States. What this war was to America, so I believe, in spite of petty statesmanship and the lack of great men, the World War will one day be to Europe. Both were creative impulses shattering what was obsolete and releasing things new.

Such are the two great stepping-stones of our age, and unless we set our feet firmly on the one we may slip on the other as we step forward to the conquest of destiny—the unity of the world.

CHAPTER II

GRAND STRATEGY OF THE WAR

ABRAHAM LINCOLN AND THE WAR

" HE was beloved by his countrymen because he was the full embodiment of American life, American genius, American aspiration. No American statesman has equalled him in comprehending and interpreting the thought and will of the common people. He had realised the republican ideal that every American boy is a possible American President ; and he gave the national birthright a new lustre when, from the steps of the White House, he said to a regiment of volunteers : ' I am a living witness that any one of your children may look to come here as my father's child has. . . . " He lifted the Declaration of Independence from a political theory to a national fact. He enforced the Constitution as the supreme law. It was under him that for the first time the American Government attained full perfection in its twin ideals of union and liberty. . . . Commanding a million armed men, his sole ambition was to vindicate the doctrine that the majority must rule, that there can be no appeal from the ballot to the bullet. . . . Above all, it was his great Act of Emancipation that raised his administration to the plane of a grand historical landmark, and crowned his title of President with that of Liberator." [1]

This man was Abraham Lincoln, the noblest democrat of modern times. A man of humble origin, self-educated, human, alert, tolerant, and inflexibly honest. " Let us have faith," he once said, " that right makes might, and in that faith let us to the end dare to do our duty as we understand it." He saw clearly that " a house divided against itself cannot stand," and that the Government of the United States could not endure permanently " half slave and half free." Slavery he detested, but he did not

[1] *C.M.H.*, VII, pp. 547, 548.

allow this personal feeling to obscure his policy, which was to save the Union no matter what it cost.

In 1860 Lincoln was elected President, and was inaugurated as such on March 4 the following year. The difficulties which then confronted him were enormous ; not only had South Carolina, Georgia, Alabama, Florida, Mississippi, Louisiana, and Texas withdrawn from the Union, but he had been placed in power by only 1,866,452 votes, his three opponents scoring 2,813,741. This meant a divided political house, which if it fell must inevitably bring the Union to earth with it.

To accomplish his work, first he must keep in power ; secondly, he must win the war, for not otherwise could the Union be re-established. He had no military experience beyond a few weeks' campaigning against Red Indians in 1832 ; when, strangely enough, it is said that the oath of allegiance was administered to him by Jefferson Davis. He had at his disposal a microscopic navy, and a tiny army deprived of many of its best officers. Yet, though he knew nothing about war, he was possessed of a true military instinct, of which the following is an example. In 1863, a little before the Fredericksburg campaign opened, he said to General Hooker : " I would not take any risk of being entangled upon the river like an ox jumped half over a fence, and liable to be torn by dogs, front and rear, without a fair chance to gore one way or kick the other"; and about Richmond : " If left to me, I would not go south of the Rappahannock, upon *Lee's* moving north of it. If you had Richmond invested to-day, you would not be able to take it in twenty days. . . . I think *Lee's* army, and not Richmond, is your true objective point."

Lincoln had to form his policy in the following circumstances : the North was in no measure united ; the South was, and knowing the conditions which prevailed in the North, and knowing that the North must attack and continue to attack, these realisations, added to the inherent bravery of her armies, endowed the Confederacy with an invincible spirit.

European intervention (mainly French) was a standing menace until the spring of 1865. The British press (with the exception of the *Spectator*), voicing the opinions of the governing classes of Great Britain, was unanimously against the North, and Mr. Gladstone went so far as to congratulate Jefferson Davis on having "made a nation." Napoleon III was antagonistic to the United States as a whole. A man of uncommon vision, but of little balance, he considered that the progress of the United States was a menace to the Old World, and particularly so to French trade. His object apparently was to create a buffer State between Mexico and either or both parties in the Civil War.[1] No sooner had the war begun, than he began to interfere in Mexico. On June 10, 1863, Marshal Bazaine entered the city of Mexico, and, on April 10, the following year, Maximilian, Napoleon's protégé, was crowned Emperor.[2] Though, to-day, this may seem a petty affair, it must be remembered that Metz and Sedan had yet to be fought, and that behind Napoleon III stood the shadow of his mighty uncle.

Within the Government of the North there was division if not sedition. No part of American liberty had been more jealously guarded than freedom of speech and freedom of the press. Men like Vallandigham openly anathematised the war, the North, and Lincoln, and nothing could be kept secret from the newspapers, many of which were hostile.

We see, therefore, that Lincoln's difficulties were legion. He had to work within a conservative Government, influenced by a semi-hostile people and press, and an openly hostile Europe. He had to maintain his grip on the loyal slave States, and simultaneously build up a navy and an army, and carry war into the Confederacy. Fortunately for him, Jefferson Davis, though a man of considerable military knowledge, never had any policy outside the hope of foreign intervention, " he drifted from the beginning to the end of

---

[1] *Formby*, p. 245.

[2] *Schouler*, VI, pp. 428, 429. For French designs upon Texas, *see* Mahan's *The Gulf and the Inland Waters*, pp. 185, 186.

the war." [1]   Under him strategy was overridden by political expedients ; not only did he hope that cotton would pay for the war, but, should the blockade become effective, that European powers would intervene. " Cotton is king. . . . Europe cannot exist without it," was the dread obsession which smote the South with a palsy, and ruined the strategy of her generals.

GRAND STRATEGY OF THE SOUTH

On both sides the political object of the war was clear. The South aimed at gaining recognition as an independent nation ; the North at preventing this by compelling the South to re-enter the Union, and either abandon slavery, or accept compensation instead.

There were three courses of action open to the South, namely :

(1) To defeat the North, and win independence by force of arms.

(2) To induce Europe to intervene, stop the war, and compel the North to recognise the independence of the Confederacy.

(3) To tire the North out, and so compel the Union Government to abandon the contest.

The first was possible until Gettysburg and the fall of Vicksburg ; the second until the issue of Lincoln's Proclamation of Emancipation, and the third until September, 1864, when Sherman entered Atlanta and Sheridan defeated Early in the valley.

President Davis, having no policy beyond hoped-for intervention, had no grand strategy beyond a rigid defensive, interrupted from time to time by attempts on the part of his generals to take advantage of the central position occupied by the Confederacy. As Grant sarcastically said : " On several occasions he came to the relief of the Union Army by means of his *superior military genius*." [2]

---

[1] *B. & L.*, I, p. 110.   *Grant*, II, p. 87.

As President he was commander-in-chief *de jure*, but for him this was not sufficient ; for, though he never commanded an army in the field, he assumed the position of commander *de facto*. General *Beauregard* writing of him says :

" We needed for President either a military man of high order, or a politician of the first class without military pretensions. . . . The South did not fall crushed by the mere weight of the North ; but it was nibbled away on all sides and ends, because its executive had never gathered and wielded its great strength under the ready advantages that greatly reduced or neutralised its adversary's naked physical superiority. It is but another of the many proofs that . . . the passive defensive policy may make a long agony, but can never win a war." [1]

Nevertheless, it should not be forgotten that, in spite of his dictatorial will, it is difficult to see who could have replaced him. A people who rebel nearly always demand a dictator. *Lee* could not have taken his place, and towards the close of the war he refused to do so. Among the politicians of the seceded States, probably there was not one who would have done better than Davis, certainly none who would have maintained the war to its bitter end. Further, it should not be forgotten that in an amazingly short time he organised and put into the field a magnificent army ; that, in spite of the blockade and the lack of factories, he supplied this army with arms and the munitions of war. Not until the very end did he abandon hope in victory, and even when *Lee* surrendered to Grant, with a few gallant followers he headed off westwards to continue the war.

His indomitable will, his obstinacy, and lack of political sense both sustained and ruined his cause. After Fredericksburg, foreign intervention was possible ; and after Cold Harbor, a surrender on terms might have been acceptable to the North ; but like a Viking he preferred to go down fighting his ship without a thought of the crew. So mighty was his will to win, that in the last lap of the war, in order

---

[1] *B. & L.*, I, p. 226.

to continue the conflict, he agreed to abandon slavery, that corner-stone of the Confederacy. Man-power failing, he proposed to enlist negroes and to grant them emancipation for military service, thereby admitting the fallacy of slavery as an institution of government, and the right of any single State to maintain it. " Under that admission the vital spirit of the Southern cause—the preservation and perpetuation of slavery—expired. . . . Secession had been illogical from the first ; its own consequences had now rendered it ridiculous." [1] Indeed, an extraordinary man, by instinct a tyrant, by fate a politician ; and through combining these two without taking the field, the most magnificent failure in the history of his country.

Grand Strategy of the North

Except for slavery which cast its shadow over every event, the grand strategical problems which faced President Lincoln and the Union Government at the outbreak of the war were very similar to those which confronted the Allied Governments in 1914. The grand tactical idea of the North was to lay the entire Confederacy under siege, and slowly strangle it to death. Though this idea took form immediately after the capitulation of Fort Sumter, its full meaning was not understood until Grant became general-in-chief. Looking back on the war, we find that the following grand strategical problems faced Lincoln :

(1) The blockade of the Confederacy.
(2) The emancipation of the slaves.
(3) The control of the army.
(4) The recruiting of the army.

The first of these four problems was strategically the most important, for unless the South was cut off from the outer world, the length of the war might become intolerable to the North. Sea-power, consequently, formed the foundations of Northern grand strategy, and Lincoln was not slow to see this, for on April 19, 1861, he proclaimed a blockade

[1] *C.M.H.*, VII, p. 535.

of the Southern ports. Command of the sea was, however, purely theoretical, for there were only forty steam-vessels in the navy, and none armoured ; twenty-four of these were in commission and scattered over the seas, eight were useless, and eight were in dockyards without crews. All other ships were sailing-vessels. The total number of officers and men was 7,600. From this small beginning the Federal Navy expanded in a way which can be described only as magical. In 1865 it had in commission 671 ships, mostly steamers and many armour-plated, manned by 51,000 officers and men.

The coast to be blockaded ran from Chesapeake Bay to the Mexican frontier, a distance of 3,500 miles,[1] and to this enormous stretch of water must be added the Mississippi from New Orleans to Cairo. This river was, in fact, an inland western coast-line.

Besides blockade by sea and river, two further problems engaged the Federal Navy, namely, fortress attack and commerce destroying ; the latter being the most difficult problem of all.

The only offensive naval measure of importance adopted by the Confederacy was commerce raiding by a few auxiliary cruisers such as the *Alabama* and the *Sumter*. Blockade running was not an offensive measure, but an economic manifestation based on the calculation of profit and loss. " Thus the cotton exported by the blockade runners paid for all the imports of raw materials etc. . . . This is the secret of effectual blockade running. It must pay." [2]

---

[1] It must, however, be remembered that, excluding Norfolk, there were only nine harbours between Cape Charles and the Mississippi connected to the interior by railroads ; these were Newbern, Beaufort, Savannah, Brunswick, Pensacola, New Orleans, Charleston, Wilmington, and Mobile. The first six were closed before May 1, 1862 ; Charleston in September, 1863 ; Mobile in August, 1864 ; and Wilmington in January, 1865. According-ing to Lieut.-Colonel George A. Bruce, all should have been captured, or closed, in 1862. (*See M.H.S.M.*, XIII, pp. 400, 401.) Had this been done, the war would almost certainly have ended in the following year.

[2] Vice-Admiral Meurer in *Marine Rundschau*, April, 1927. Blockade running and its prevention have been inadequately dealt with by British and American naval historians. The best works to consult are : Soley's *The Blockade and the Cruisers*, Taylor's *Running the Blockade*, and Captain

In England the blockade rekindled the spirit of the merchant adventurers of Tudor times,[1] for blockade running appealed as a sport to English daring and greed for gain. Special blockade runners, "low, flat, slim, grey-painted boats" of about 600 tons burden, were built. These vessels mainly operated from the Bermudas, Nassau in the Bahamas, and Havana, where they shipped their cargoes and contrabands, and returned with bales of cotton which by ordinary merchantmen were shipped to Liverpool and elsewhere. Three successful voyages generally paid for one total loss. The profits made were enormous, sufficient for the captains to receive £1,000 a voyage, and the seamen £50 a head. The magnitude of these operations is obvious when it is realised that

"between October 26, 1864, and January [1], 1865, 8,632,000 lbs. of meat, 1,507,000 lbs. of lead, 1,933,000 lbs. of saltpetre, 546,000 pairs of shoes, 316,000 pairs of blankets, half a million pounds of coffee, 69,000 rifles, and 43 cannon" were obtained by the Confederates through the port of Wilmington alone, "while cotton sufficient to pay for these purchases was exported."[2]

When Wilmington fell, the Confederacy was strangled. Nor must it be overlooked that the economic-strategical effect of the blockade was really negligible until, as Admiral Meurer writes, "General Grant had succeeded in blockading the Mississippi, thereby cutting off the Western States of Texas and Arkansas, with their supplies of cattle and grain, from the Eastern cotton-producing area." Then, as he remarks, "the collapse of the Confederates was a matter of certainty."[3]

Once the blockade was established, anyhow in theory,

Robert's *Never Caught*. In a recent American work, *History of Sea Power*, by Stevens and Westcott, it is astonishing to find that the blockade during the Civil War is dismissed in a few sentences.

[1] See *Running the Blockade*, Taylor, p. 10.

[2] *C.M.H.*, VII, p. 557. See also the *Richmond Dispatch* of January 3, 1865, which quotes these figures for Charleston and Wilmington; but little could have entered the former of these ports.

[3] *Marine Rundschau*, April, 1927, and March, 1924.

the next problem was the reduction of the will of the South so as to compel the abandonment of the struggle, with its collateral—to prevent the South imposing its will by armed force on the North before the blockade attained its full effect. This problem may be examined under two headings —the moral and the physical attacks. The first aimed at justifying the political morality of the North, and simultaneously undermining that of the South; it centred on the question of emancipation.

Had it been possible for Lincoln to issue his Proclamation of Emancipation the day after Fort Sumter surrendered, a moral foundation to the whole of his grand strategy would have been laid. But it was not possible. First, the North was not ready for it, and, secondly, as he said himself : " I do not want to issue a document that the whole world will see must necessarily be inoperative like the Pope's bull against the comet." Nevertheless Lincoln had this problem in mind from the middle of 1861 to the middle of 1862 ; it was his trump card, and all he was waiting for was the right moment to play it. He realised its enormous strategical power : by liberating the negro, he placed him on the footing of a free-born citizen ; consequently, he could enlist him, and if he did so, sooner or later the South would be compelled to do likewise ; and immediately this happened, the Confederacy would be forced to throw down its cards and abandon the policy for which it was fighting. On July 13, 1862, he introduced this subject to Secretaries Seward and Welles, and " dwelt earnestly on the gravity, importance, and delicacy of the movement ; said he had given it much thought, and had about come to the conclusion that it was a military necessity, absolutely essential for the salvation of the nation, that we must free the slaves, or be ourselves subdued." [1]   Seward considered that emancipation must be supported by military success ; accordingly Lincoln drafted his Proclamation, and awaited victory.

It was not until *Lee* was repulsed at the battle of Antietam (or Sharpsburg) on September 17–19, 1862, that Lincoln

[1] *C.M.H.*, VII, p. 589.

warned his country that an emancipation decree would be published unless the rebellion ceased. And, in spite of Burnside's defeat at Fredericksburg, on December 13, this Proclamation was published on the first of the new year. As Colonel Livermore says : " The 1st of January, 1863, marks an era in the history of the United States of America, second only to the 4th of July, 1776." [1]

The effects of this Proclamation were immediate and stupendous : " The war now took a totally different turn. All hope of compromise was at an end. There was now no possible outcome but the ruin of the nation or the conquest of the South." [2] Negro regiments were at once enrolled, and by the end of the war 150,000 blacks had been enlisted in the Federal armies. In Great Britain the Proclamation was received with so much joy that fear of England recognising the Confederacy began to vanish. In the North, emancipation was generally welcomed ; nevertheless large numbers of officers and men openly declared that they would never have enlisted in a war for the abolition of slavery. In the South the Proclamation was received with a feeling akin to terror. General *Lee* declared " that Major-General Hunter had armed slaves for the murder of their masters," and Jefferson Davis issued a general order " that officers organising negro soldiers should be subject, if captured, to execution as felons."

The moral victory was thus won by the North, and in strategical effect it compensated for all the Confederate victories of 1861-2. Except for France, world opinion was now behind the North. In the World War of 1914–18 a somewhat similar turning-point was reached when the Germans most foolishly torpedoed the *Lusitania*. I will now examine the political relationships of the physical attack.

THE SOLDIER AND THE POLITICIANS

It is not my intention to discuss the evolution of the opposing armies, but only the influence of politics upon them.

---

[1] *Livermore*, Pt. III, Bk. I, p. 98.   [2] *Livermore*, Pt. III, Bk. I, p. 100.

The military forces of the United States were organised in three categories of troops, namely, Regulars, Volunteers, and Militiamen, of which, on the outbreak of the war, the first numbered some 16,000 officers and men for the most part scattered on police duty in the West. Under the Constitution, the President was *ipso facto* commander-in-chief; and, after the Confederacy was established, Jefferson Davis assumed this responsibility in opposition to Lincoln. In the South an entirely new army had to be created; in the North the minute regular establishment had to be expanded. The Federal problem was the more difficult, for as General Grant stated: the South " had a great advantage in having no army, but only a number of excellent officers, to create one." [1]   On both sides the first task was not so much the enrolment of the men as the selection of suitable officers. Regardless of seniority, Davis chose as officers men he considered capable and energetic, and on the whole he made few mistakes. Lincoln, surrounded by interested politicians, and having no one but that fine old soldier Lieut.-General Winfield Scott (then seventy-five years of age and quite out of his depth in this tremendous turmoil) to advise him, allowed some 600 junior regular officers to remain with their regiments, and filled many of the senior appointments with volunteers. Not only was this a grand-strategical mistake of the first order,[2] for it split the army into two camps, the quarrels of which influenced the entire war, but it was aggravated by Lincoln failing to establish a full hierarchy of general officers—generals, lieutenant-generals, etc. Until March, 1864, the highest grade was that of major-general, consequently subordination between officers of this rank was often in question, with the result that a lack of discipline is most noticeable among the higher commanders.

In criticising Lincoln, it must be remembered, however,

---

[1] *Formby*, p. 66.

[2] Lord Kitchener, the creator of the British New Armies in 1914, has frequently been criticised for not building on the existing Territorial (Volunteer) Army. Had he done so he would have committed the identical error Lincoln committed in 1861.

that his position was a difficult one. The South, from first to last, was a military camp ; the North, until the end of the war, was a house politically divided. When Grant took command of the 21st Illinois Regiment, as he tells us himself, not only was this regiment quite undisciplined, but Springfield, its station, and the State of Illinois were teeming with secessionists. Two democratic members of Congress from this State, McClernand and Logan, addressed his men. Grant was a little nervous, but as he says : " Logan followed in a speech he has hardly equalled since for force and eloquence. It breathed a loyalty and devotion to the Union which inspired my men to such a point that they would have volunteered to remain in the army as long as an enemy to the country continued to bear arms against it." [1] Such men naturally were eager to serve their country, and were of the greatest service to the Union. Can it be wondered, therefore, that Lincoln rewarded such men with high military appointments ; for it would have been an insult to their class had he commissioned them as subalterns or captains.[2]

Until the date of the first battle of Bull Run, or Manassas (July 21, 1861), the inherent faults in the Federal military system were hidden from view. This battle, in which the Confederates were as disorganised by success as the Federals by defeat, revealed the total lack of ballast among the politicians at Washington. Tactically an insignificant affair, politically Bull Run was a decisive victory for President Davis. Like the jinn from out its bottle, the defence of Washington loomed out of the dust of McDowell's retreating army, to cast its shadow over every campaign in the eastern theatre of the war until the battle of Cedar Creek (October 19, 1864). Henceforth the slightest threat to Washington shook to its foundations the whole of the Federal strategy ; and surely the most extraordinary instance of this was when, in March, 1862, the *Merrimac* appeared off Hampton Roads.

----

[1] *Grant*, I, p. 246.

[2] Similar appointments took place in the British Army in the World War. Sir Eric Geddes, a civilian, not only attained the rank of major-general but also that of rear-admiral, a somewhat unique honour.

Stanton, the Secretary of War,[1] at a Cabinet meeting presided over by President Lincoln, said :

" ' The *Merrimac* will change the whole character of the war ; she will destroy, *seriatim*, every naval vessel ; she will lay all the cities on the seaboard under contribution. I shall immediately recall Burnside ; Port Royal must be abandoned. I will notify the governors and municipal authorities in the North to take instant measures to protect their harbors.' He had no doubt, he said, that the monster was at this moment on her way to Washington ; and, looking out of the window, which commanded a view of the Potomac for many miles, ' Not unlikely, we shall have a shell or cannon-ball from one of her guns in the White House before we leave this room.' Mr. Seward, usually buoyant and self-reliant, overwhelmed with the intelligence, listened in responsive sympathy to Stanton, and was greatly depressed, as, indeed, were all members." [2]

This unseemly panic is an excellent example not only of the effect of a tactical novelty on the political mind, but of the liability to hysteria in the Union Government from the first battle of Bull Run onwards. At this time, McClellan had filled the capital with generals ; [3] but, as a general-in-chief, in place of endowing the Government with confidence, he depressed it. He held all politicians in the utmost contempt, and, apparently in retaliation, when, in March, 1862, he moved out to reoccupy Manassas, Lincoln seized the opportunity to relieve him of the supreme command of all the Federal armies, the first intimation of this important change reached McClellan through the newspapers.

The origins of much of this friction may be traced to Mr. Stanton.[4] He had his good points, for he instilled a sense of discipline into the army, and under his masterful

---

[1] Stanton was appointed Secretary of War in January, 1862.

[2] *B. & L.*, I, p. 705.

[3] A newspaper gravely announced that " a boy throwing a stone at a dog in Pennsylvania Avenue had hit three brigadier-generals."

[4] He was so rude, that Lincoln, who knew him at the Bar before the war, would not act in the same cases with him. *See* also General Grant's opinion : *Grant*, II, pp. 536, 537.

hand negligence and corruption disappeared.   Nevertheless, as Ropes says, he was

" utterly ignorant of military matters;   despising from the bottom of his soul what is known as military science; making no secret of his general distrust of educated officers; rarely, if ever, lending an intelligent support to any general in the service;   treating them all in the way in which the Committee of Public Safety treated the generals of the First French Republic;   arrogant, impatient, irascible, Stanton was a terror and a marplot in the conduct of the war." [1]

What between Lincoln's ignorance and at times high-handedness,[2] Stanton's infernal temper, and McClellan's secrecy and exaggeration, the first great Federal campaign was utterly ruined.   *Jackson's* dash down the valley causing a panic in Washington, Lincoln abandoned the idea of sending McDowell and his 40,000 men to McClellan, who was in sight of the spires of Richmond; in place he ordered him to move on Front Royal.   Thus was the Peninsula Campaign wrecked [3] by the sirens begotten of the battle of Bull Run, those unbalanced terrors of the political mind of the North.   Similarly, when, in 1864, Grant stood on the identical ground occupied by McClellan in 1862, another Confederate raid down the valley nearly wrecked his plans.   In my opinion, the first battle of Bull Run was of far greater value to the South than Fredericksburg and Chancellorsville together; it was a paralysing victory.

From the difficulties which arose between the Government and the Higher Command, difficulties which in the North were not overcome until, in March, 1864, Grant was appointed general-in-chief, and in the South until, in January, 1865, when the ship of State was sinking, the Confederate

---

[1] *Ropes*, Pt. I, p. 225.

[2] In March, 1862, without consulting McClellan, Lincoln appointed McDowell, Sumner, Heintzelman, and Keyes to command the Army Corps of the Army of the Potomac.

[3] McDowell, a good strategist, considered it a " crushing blow."   Further, he said : " It throws us all back, and from Richmond north we shall have all our large masses paralysed, and shall have to repeat what we have just accomplished " (18 *W.R.*, p. 220).

Congress conferred upon *Lee* [1] practically supreme power, I will now turn to the political relationship between the Union Government and its army.

On both sides the regimental organisation was much the same. Battalions were of ten companies, on establishment 600 to 800 strong, but normally averaging from 400 to 500 men, and sometimes much less. A varying number made up a brigade, and in the Federal service divisions consisted of two or three brigades, and in the Confederate usually of four brigades.

On April 29, 1861, President Davis set about to raise a volunteer army of 100,000 men ; but, by the close of the year, volunteering was found insufficient, and was superseded by the Conscription Act which became law early in 1862. The passing of this Act by the centralised Government at Richmond, though it proved beneficial to the army, struck a blow at the doctrine of State rights, and so was the first political step taken by Jefferson Davis in the undermining of his policy. In the summer of 1863 conscription led to a general disaffection, especially in North Carolina, this unrest crystallising into what became known as the Peace Party. The following year threats to secede from the Confederacy took form, and had not the war ended in the spring of 1865, it is very doubtful whether the South would not have revolted against conscription and so have abandoned the war.

The idea of compulsory service was even more repugnant to the North. Volunteering was resorted to, and within one year of the outbreak of the war 500,000 three-year volunteers were enrolled. At about the same time as the South adopted conscription, the Union Government, with a fatuity unrivalled in the history of war, stopped recruiting, and in place raised new units. Old salted regiments were allowed to waste away, and levies of nine-months' recruiting were accepted in their stead. These men on several

[1] Compare Alcibiades in the Peloponnesian War, and General Foch in the World War. In democratic countries Misfortune is dam of Unity of Command.

occasions were more dangerous to their own side than to the enemy.[1]

A resumption of enlistments was ordered in June, but all recruiting offices had been closed, and public enthusiasm, so necessary to recruiting, had vanished. Not being able to revive this excellent system which the Government had literally assassinated, on March 3, 1863, Congress passed a Conscription Law, which allowed, however, a commutation of $300 for personal service. The result was a three-days' riot in the city of New York, in which atrocities equalling the worst committed during the French Revolution were perpetrated ; $2,000,000 worth of property was destroyed, and some 1,000 persons killed and wounded. These excesses at an end, the law was enforced.

Though the men raised by this law fought well, generally speaking, they cannot be compared to the old volunteers, or to the Confederate soldier of the same period, of whom General *Alexander* writes :

" He was lean, sun-burned, and bearded ; often barefoot and ragged. He had neither training nor discipline, except what he acquired in the field. He had only antiquated and inferior arms until he captured better ones in battle. He had not even military ambition, but he had an incentive which was lacking to his opponents—brave and loyal as they were—he was fighting for his home." [2]

CONCLUSIONS AND A COMPARISON

Such, in brief, was the grand strategy of the war, that frame in which Grant eventually was called upon to shape

[1] During the Port Hudson operations General Banks complaining to General Halleck about his nine-months' men received the following reply : " The defection of your nine-months' men on the field of battle was a most criminal military offence which should have been promptly and severely punished in order to prevent a repetition of it by other troops. When a column of attack is formed of doubtful troops the proper mode of curing the defection is to place artillery in their rear loaded with grape and canister, in the hands of reliable men, with orders to fire at the first movement of disaffection." General Palfrey remarks : " This was excellent doctrine, but it came from a great distance " (*M.H.S.M.*, VIII, p. 50).

[2] *The Confederate Soldier*, E. P. Alexander.

his actions, and without a slight knowledge of this question it is not possible justly to appreciate his work.

In the war there were three great turning-points, namely, the first battle of Bull Run, the effects of which ultimately culminated in the establishment of unity of command; the capture of Fort Donelson, which led to the surrender of Vicksburg, and which evolved into Sherman's Atlanta campaign; lastly, the capture of Wilmington, which led direct to *Lee's* surrender at Appomattox Court House. All three of these, in one way or another, were closely connected with Grant.

Ultimately, the South was defeated by combined economic, moral, and physical pressure, which bears close comparison to a similar combined attack made on the Central European Powers by the Allied Governments during the World War. The grand-strategical methods of these two wars were identical, but their results were very different; for, whilst in the American Civil War the Confederacy was crushed physically, economically, and morally, the Central Powers were never morally defeated. The moral cause of the World War remained therefore alive in a wounded body when the Armistice of November 11, 1918, was agreed upon. The Treaty of Versailles in no way succeeded in binding up these wounds and so establishing the foundations of a healthy peace. Only such a peace could have justified four years of slaughter and destruction. It was an inglorious war, opening with a breach of faith to Belgium, and closing with a breach of faith to the world. Not so the Civil War, which though it began as a rebellion ended in establishing not only a united nation, but the most powerful and prosperous nation the world has as yet seen. Its end justified it. Thus it seems to me, that in spite of his many errors Lincoln must for ever find a permanent place in the temple of human history. If not to be reckoned amongst the greatest of the grand strategists, there can be no doubt that he is numbered amongst the most successful, because his goodness as a man eclipsed his errors as a strategist.

CHAPTER III

STRATEGY AND TACTICS OF THE WAR

Theatre of War

In 1861 the political theatre of the war—that is, the whole of the United States, in extent some 3,000,000 square miles—was populated by 31,000,000 people, of whom 9,000,000 were in the seceded States, and of these 3,500,000 were slaves. The tactical theatre—that is, the zone in which battles were fought—covered about a third of this area. It was bounded on the north by the rivers Missouri, Ohio, and Potomac; on the east by the Atlantic; on the south by the Gulf of Mexico, and on the west by the western boundaries of Louisiana, Arkansas, and Missouri.

The political theatre was by nature divided into three geographical areas:

(1) From the Atlantic to the Alleghany (or Appalachian) Mountains.

(2) From the Alleghany Mountains to the Mississippi.

(3) From the Mississippi to the Mexican frontier and the Pacific Ocean.

Until 1864 the first was the stage of the great political operations, such as the Peninsula campaign, and those of Antietam, Fredericksburg, Chancellorsville, and Gettysburg; in each of which the chief object was to win world support by seizing either Richmond [1] or Washington, or by striking at Pennsylvania—the key State of the North. The second was the great strategical arena, possessing a twofold value: first, the Mississippi endowed it with vast political and commercial importance; secondly, by moving up the Tennessee River, the Alleghany range could be turned

[1] The first capital of the Confederacy was Montgomery, Alabama. The Government moved to Richmond, 115 miles south of Washington, in June 1861.

from the South, and the Atlantic area attacked in rear. The third, a vast stretch of country, was strategically a weakness to the North (e.g. the Arkansas operations and the Red River campaign), but of great value to the South as a reservoir of man-power, a source of supply, and a link with Mexico, which, being neutral, could not be blockaded by the Federal Navy.

Throughout the war the military objectives were three in number, namely, the protection of the respective capitals, their capture, and the destruction of the opposing army. All operations centred round these objects, and were influenced not only by the nature of the theatre of war, but particularly by its communications.

In 1861 the United States was largely an undeveloped country, badly roaded, and east of the Mississippi extensively wooded. No European area of this date bears a close resemblance to it. It was a country well suited for guerrilla warfare, as the War of Independence had proved, and a most difficult one for organised armies with large baggage trains to operate in. Railways, being few, assumed the highest importance in the eastern area, and an importance second only to the rivers in the central one. From the Atlantic shore three main railways ran westwards to the Mississippi, namely, from Baltimore to St. Louis; from Washington, via Chattanooga to Memphis, and from Charleston and Savannah, via Atlanta, to Memphis and Vicksburg. From the Gulf another three railways ran northwards : from Pensacola, via Atlanta, Chattanooga and Nashville, to Louisville; from Mobile, via Meridian, Corinth, and Cairo, to St. Louis, and from New Orleans, via Jackson and Grenada, to Memphis. From the map of the theatre of war it will be seen that south of the Baltimore—Ohio railroad the East is connected by rail to the West at only two points, namely, Chattanooga and Atlanta, consequently these two towns were centres of the highest strategical value. Second to them, in the eastern area were Harpers Ferry, Lynchburg, Burksville Junction, and Petersburg ; and in the central area, Nashville, Corinth, Jackson (Mississippi), and Meridian.

As we shall see, most of the great strategical operations of the war pivoted on these places.

Turning to the Alleghany mountains, we find that their strategical influence was prodigious. Not only does this range, which is 100 miles broad and 1,000 miles long (extending from New York to Alabama), separate the eastern from the central area, but it forms the watershed of two systems of rivers : those flowing into the Atlantic, and those flowing into the Mississippi. The former, namely, the Potomac, Rapidan, Rappahannock, James, and smaller rivers in between, form tactical obstacles for an army advancing from Washington on Richmond, or *vice versa* ; the exception being the Shenandoah River, which rises near Staunton and joins the Potomac at Harpers Ferry. The latter, the Ohio, Cumberland, and Tennessee rivers are mainly of strategical importance, as waterways running from the Alleghany area into the Mississippi, the main means of communication from the north to south, with its western waterways—the Red and the Arkansas rivers.

The importance of the river systems in this war is clearly shown by the fact that six Federal armies were named after them—those of the Potomac, James, Ohio, Cumberland, Tennessee, and Mississippi.

The value of the Mississippi to the North was threefold :

(1) It cut the Confederacy in two, severing the eastern States from the western.
(2) It formed the main waterway from north to south, and, including the Ohio River, to as far as Pittsburg.
(3) It protected the right flank and rear of any army operating from Nashville round the southern extremity of the Alleghany Mountains.

The great strategical centres on the Mississippi were : New Orleans near its mouth, the largest town in the Confederacy ; then those cities at which the railways strike the river, namely, Vicksburg, Memphis, and St. Louis, with Cairo, between the last two, where the Ohio River flows into it.

Strategy of the War

Such was the geographical warp upon which the strategy of the war was woven. At first the design is not only obscure, but actually formless in the minds of the weavers. Objects exist, but how to transmute them into objectives—that is, how to work out methodically the progress from the one to the other—is so tangled with ignorance and enthusiasm, so confused by political considerations and social longings, so perplexed by the immensity of the work and the poverty of the means, that it is only after a full year of warfare the strategical woof begins to take form, and to present itself as a picture to the struggling masses, to their Governments, and to their generals : and still how vaguely.

From the first, the blockade is appreciated, but how to combine the war on land so as to take advantage of, or to resist, the war at sea is not ; because both sides, irrespective of their art, have no conception of a science of war whereon to found it. They press and they resist, they move this way and that, but pressure, and resistance, and movement beget no reasoned direction. Yet, at length, trial and error, those gropings in the dark, were by geography forced into line, and compelled to march forward according to a fixed strategical plan. This plan, as we shall see, was initiated by Grant, and, whatever may be his failings as a general, from the capture of Fort Donelson onwards, to him more than to any other man are due the strategical and tactical successes which followed its surrender.

From the outset of the war the strategical difficulties of the North pivot on the following factors : though the South initiated the war, unlike most such cases, the strategy of the South was defensive ; consequently the North was compelled to advance into its enemy's country in order to reduce it piecemeal, so that the very spirit of resistance might be pulverised. Logically this meant a war of offensive movement on the one side, and of defended positions combined with occasional sallies on the other. The deeper the North advanced into the South, the longer became its lines of communication, absorbing thousands of men in their protection who were faced not only by a hostile army but by a hostile nation in arms. Whilst the South fought the soldiers of the North, the North fought the people of the South, of which part was organised as regular formations, and part as guerrilla bands ever ready to swarm round the flanks and rear of their enemy, perpetually stinging and blinding him like a cloud of hornets. Nothing is more terrible than partisan warfare, and every partisan war has been a long war in spite of the superiority in regular formations of the invading side. La Vendée is an example of this, and a more recent one is the British war in South Africa (1899–1902), in which, towards its close, over a quarter of a million of regular soldiers were employed to hunt down some twenty-five thousand mounted riflemen—and it was the same in the German South-West African war against the Hereros. In short, the problem of partisan warfare is very similar to the maintenance of law and order during peace time—it normally takes ten or more policemen to catch an armed criminal, but seldom more than one armed criminal to do down a policeman.[1]

Whilst the Federal armies, as they advanced, dissolved in strength,[2] continually dropping detachments to protect their lines of supply,[3] for the first half of the war the Confederate forces presented no rear to attack : " No rear had to be protected," writes Grant. " All the troops in service could be brought to the front to contest every inch of ground threatened with invasion." [4] The one great strategical problem of the North was to manœuvre in such a way as to

---

[1] In the famous Sidney Street " siege " in London—some twenty years ago—a regiment of infantry and a battery of artillery, besides a large number of police, were called out to capture three armed desperadoes.

[2] This is the great difficulty which hitherto has confronted British operations against the partisan hillmen of the North-West Frontiers of India.

[3] " It is safe to say that more than half the National Army was engaged in guarding lines of supplies, or were on leave, sick in hospital, or on detail which prevented their bearing arms " (*Grant*, II, p. 505).

[4] *Grant*, II, p. 502.

create an enemy rear. This was accomplished from the West, the Western Federal forces moving southwards down the Mississippi, eastwards through Chattanooga, Atlanta, to Savannah, and then northwards towards Richmond. A right flank wheel of more than a 1,000 miles extending in time over three years; a strategical movement compared to which the German right flank wheel in 1914, however powerful, was child's play. Surely this wheel is one of the most amazing manœuvres in military history. It was not until Sherman was holding *Johnston* in North Carolina that the Confederates felt the full effect of this rear attack; which, by preventing *Lee* from being reinforced, enabled Grant to pound him to pieces, and prevent *Johnston* being succoured. Grant's pressure and Sherman's rear attack annulled the advantage hitherto possessed by the Confederates of operating on interior lines—that is, from a central position towards any point of the hostile circumference.

TACTICAL CHANGES, 1760–1860

If geography is considered as the warp of strategy, then strategy may be considered as the weft of tactics, which completes the web of war. To appreciate the tactical art of the Civil War, it is necessary to know a little about the tactical theories accepted by armies before its outbreak, for otherwise the employment of the weapons used in this war cannot be criticised, and without criticism no true lessons are learnt.

Throughout the history of the art of war, the tactics of the infantry attack have depended entirely upon whether cavalry action could or could not be developed from infantry action. In the days of Sparta, when practically no cavalry were used, infantry tactics were extremely simple : actions were in parallel order, one line of men advancing upon the other. If both lines were of equal length, victory was determined by endurance and skill at arms, the assault was the be-all and end-all of the attack. If one line were longer than the other, overlapping took place; the flanks of the

longer line, being unopposed, washed round the flanks of
the shorter, and pushed the shorter line inwards, when it
became a mob which either broke and fled, or was slaughtered.
Once cavalry are introduced we find that this arm is not
only employed to protect the infantry flanks, but to manœuvre
round the enemy's in order to strike him in rear—that is,
at his tactically weakest point. When this is possible,
the infantry attack assumes quite another form. It is
launched not to destroy the enemy's resistance by an assault,
but to hold him to his position ; to compel him to reinforce
his front, and so to deny to him the power of meeting the
outflanking manœuvres of the opposing cavalry, whose
activity is developed from the holding power of the infantry
with whom they are co-operating.

Shortly before the days of Frederick the Great, tactics
had reverted to the parallel order. He turned from
mass attacks to battles of manœuvre, his idea being to
outflank his enemy's line. He made full use of his artillery
to prepare the infantry attack, and of his infantry to hold
the enemy's line, and to assault one of its flanks, whilst
his cavalry, taking advantage of these operations, moved
round towards the enemy's rear.

During the Seven Years War, 1756–63, an old type of
infantry soldier was reintroduced in America and Austria,[1]
namely, light infantry, who were able to prepare the way
for the attacking lines and columns. Though, during this
war, they proved their value, after it their use was forgotten ;
for the leading soldiers of this day were blinded by Frederick's
superb manœuvres, and sought for the secret of his successes
in his drill. Few efforts were made by the military hierarchies
to combine light infantry and infantry of the line, until
the Wars of American Independence and of the French
Revolution once again accentuated the importance of the
skirmisher, or natural fighter.

During the Napoleonic wars we see the increasing value
of bullet-power in contradistinction to bayonet-power.
Skirmishers were freely used, and in the British Army trained

[1] See my *British Light Infantry in the Eighteenth Century*.

by Sir John Moore they attained to the highest state of tactical perfection.[1]

Napoleon was not a great tactician, he invented no new system of attack, depending more on strategy than upon tactics for his victories. Nevertheless he understood clearly the advantages of the holding attack. He himself said : " I attack so that the enemy will attack me," by which he meant : I make use of a comparatively small force to attack in order to compel the enemy to defend himself— that is, " to attack me." By pressing him I shall force him to draw on his reserves, and when all are drawn in his power to manœuvre will be reduced to zero ; then my reserves and cavalry will possess full liberty of movement to operate against his flanks and rear. This was the famous defensive order of Napoleon which he mentions in the wisest tactical maxim ever laid down, namely : " The whole art of war consists in a well-reasoned and extremely circumspect defensive, followed by rapid and audacious attack." Further still, the growing value of fire power was fully recognised by him. As he advanced in his career, more and more did he realise the power of artillery and its use to demoralise an enemy before the infantry assault was launched. He says :

" It is by fire and not by shock that battles are decided to-day. . . . The power of infantry lies in fire. . . . In siege warfare, as in the open field, it is the gun which plays the chief part, it has effected a complete revolution. It is with artillery that war is made." [2]

Though Wellington's tactics were different, they were based on a similar idea, but his defensive order was static in place of mobile. Instead of attacking, he took up a covered position, so to speak a natural trench line, and awaited attack. When the enemy was within fifty paces of him, his men rose, fired a volley or two, and, under cover of the smoke of their muskets, charged home with the bayonet. They attacked to destroy, and not to hold.

[1] See my *Sir John Moore's System of Training.*   [2] *Corresp.*, XIV, 11896.

Their attack was a true assault. These tactics succeeded again and again. Had Napoleon understood the use of the howitzer as Frederick understood it, they would never have succeeded, for Wellington's men would have been blown out of their covered positions long before the infantry attack developed. Succeeding as they did, they gave a totally false value to the assault. A retrogression in tactics set in, the idea of the attack pivoting on the bayonet in place of the bullet, and, as the war was left behind, and its personal experiences forgotten, infantry tactics once again crystallised round the idea of the assault. Lines of men closely supported by artillery advance in order to assault ; they may or may not be preceded by skirmishers, but normally they are followed by other lines, not to support the first by fire, but to replace its casualties so that the assault may be carried out by a wall of men with bayonets lowered. Such was the tactical theory, Macedonian in form, of the year 1860.

INFLUENCE OF THE RIFLE

The fifty years which followed the Battle of Waterloo are tactically most instructive. From the military point of view Napoleon might as well have never been born ; for not only were his methods not understood by soldiers in general, but by Clausewitz in particular. No sooner had the Emperor been incarcerated in St. Helena than the rigid school of war, the men of the hoplite mind, returned to power. Nevertheless, in spite of their ponderous notions, the Industrial Revolution swept on. Invention followed invention, and amongst these were two of extreme tactical importance, namely, the percussion cap, invented in 1814, and the cylindro-conoidal bullet, invented ten years later.

The rifle had long been known, but hitherto all rifles and muskets were fired by means of a flint and steel, and in rainy weather frequently misfired. The percussion cap signed the death warrant of the cavalry charge, and the conoidal bullet not only reduced the power of the infantry assault, but also revolutionised artillery tactics. In 1839 a percussion musket was issued to British infantry, and in 1851, they were equipped with the Minié rifle, a weapon with a killing range of 1,000 yards. In 1815 cavalry, artillery, and infantry were in close contact, and were operated by the general-in-chief as easily as a platoon is to-day. The guns were frequently placed in front of the infantry, and the cavalry close behind the foot-soldiers. All this was changed by the rifle. The cavalry can no longer attack infantry unless completely broken. The guns have to retire in rear of the infantry, and as the range of the rifle is increased, so is the distance between them and the infantry they are supporting. Thus the old battle order, which in idea had changed but little since the days of Gustavus Adolphus, was completely thrown out of joint ; yet few of these changes were even noticed, let alone understood, by the tacticians of Europe. In the Crimean War, British, French, Russians, and Turks fought as if everything was as it had been in the days of their fathers. Is it to be wondered at, then, that the soldiers of the United States, who, except for the Mexican War, had experienced no organised warfare since 1812–15, failed to appreciate the tactics of the rifle and of the rifled gun ?

In 1861 both sides were armed with a variety of muskets and rifles, and as late as the battle of Gettysburg we find smooth-bore muskets in the Confederate army. So little at first did the Confederate Government realise the value of the percussion rifle, that it was not until May, 1861, that Major *Huse* was sent over to England to purchase 10,000 Enfield rifles. So small a number appears extraordinary, even 100,000 would have been few enough. There seems to have been a fixed prejudice against this weapon, anyhow during the first year of the war. It is true that the South lacked copper and the means of making fulminate of mercury, but percussion caps are not a bulky cargo, and many hundreds of millions of them could easily be run into Wilmington, or some other port, by a single ship. In the North we find a similar prejudice against repeating rifles, for the older generals preferred muzzle-loaders ; they could not see that the difficulty of ammunition supply, upon which their opposition was mainly based, was completely outbalanced by the enormous advantage of being able to load when in a prone position.

The flint-lock musket had an effective range of about 100 yards, the Minié rifle of between 300 and 400 yards, consequently in the defence this weapon could beat back an attack at these ranges. This was the secret of most of the failures in assaults attempted during this war.

The original Confederate musket was ·69 of an inch in calibre ; after Gettysburg these cumbersome weapons were replaced by rifles of calibre ·58 and ·54. In the second year of the war the Federal cavalry began to receive breech-loading carbines and, later on, magazine rifles.[1] Of the last-mentioned weapon there were several kinds, such as the Spencer rifle [2] with a tube magazine holding seven rounds besides one in the breech ; the Henry rifle, improved by Winchester, holding seventeen rounds, and the Colt rifle, a revolver fitted with a stock. In 1864 the Spencer rifle was issued to the Federal cavalry, and before the end of the year to some of the Federal infantry as well. It was with reference to this weapon that the Confederates used to say : " Those confounded Yankees loaded up their guns in the morning, and shot all day." The effect of these weapons on the attacker was terrible, but in no way did it dislodge the idea of the assault. On October 7, 1864, on the Darbytown Road, *Field's* division was easily repulsed by two Federal brigades armed with Spencer rifles. Again, on November 30, this same year, at Franklin, Tennessee, Casement's brigade with these rifles decided the battle with terrific slaughter. It was said that " never before in the history of war did a command, of the approximate strength

---

[1] The magazine principle was not adopted by European armies until it was adapted to take cartridges of the size and shape considered suitable for military rifles. In 1863, the first mention of a machine gun—Requa's (see *Ency. Brit.*, eleventh edition, XVII, p. 239)—was made. This weapon was used in the trenches by General Gilmore before Fort Wagner. Gatling guns are said to have been invented during this war.

[2] Invented in 1861.

of Casement's, in so short a period of time kill and wound as many men." Of the breech-loading rifle General Alexander writes : " There is reason to believe that had the Federal infantry been armed from the first with even the breech-loaders available in 1861 the war would have been terminated within a year." [1]

As regards artillery, Major John Bigelow informs us that

" The artillery had practically no regimental organisation in either army. The pieces were muzzle-loading, and made of wrought or cast iron or brass. There was not a steel or a breech-loading piece in either army.

" The principal varieties used are given in the following table :

DESCRIPTION OF PIECE.	RANGE IN YARDS.	USED IN
Rifles.		
20-pounder Parrott gun.	4,500	Both armies.
10-pounder Parrott gun.	6,200	Both armies.
3-inch ordnance gun .	4,180	Both armies.
Smooth-bores.		
12-pounder gun . .	1,660	Army of the Potomac.
Light 12-pounder gun (Napoleon) . .	1,300	Both armies.
6-pounder gun . .	1,525	Army of Northern Virginia.
12-pounder howitzer .	1,075	Army of Northern Virginia.

" In addition to the guns above-mentioned there were in the Army of the Potomac a few 4½-inch ' ordnance ' guns, and in the Army of Northern Virginia a few Whitworth guns. . . ." [2]

The principal projectiles used were solid shot, percussion shell, shrapnel, grape, and canister. A piece could be loaded and fired from two to three times a minute.

The arms of the Federal cavalry were sword, revolver, and the breech-loading carbine, or the Spencer magazine carbine. The Confederate cavalry were virtually mounted infantry.

TACTICS OF THE WAR

The men of the North and South were of the same stock ; many coming from the same States, the same cities, and

---

[1] *Alexander,* p. 53.   [2] *Bigelow,* p. 22.

even the same homes. In the North there were more foreigners, consequently the Federal armies were less homogeneous ; artisans and mechanics abounded, these men making abler gunners than the men of the South, who, being accustomed to a free and out-of-doors life, excelled as infantry and cavalry. Though working under disadvantageous circumstances, the Northern soldier steadily improved. " What we have got to do," said *Albert Sidney Johnston*, " must be done quickly. The longer we leave them to fight the more difficult will they be to defeat." [1] Of the Southern soldiers General Winfield Scott said : They

" have *élan*, courage, woodcraft, consummate horsemanship, endurance of pain equal to the Indians, but they will not submit to discipline. They will not take care of things or husband their resources. Where they are there is waste and destruction. If it could be done by one wild desperate dash they would do it, but they cannot stand the waiting. . . . Men of the North on the other hand can wait ; they can bear discipline ; they can endure for ever. Losses in battle are nothing to them. They will fight to the bitter end." [2]

These words were spoken in February 1862.

At the beginning of the war discipline was not only indifferent, but almost non-existent on both sides. There were many reasons for this : Henderson attributes it to the " dogma of absolute equality," and because " the soldier was wont to regulate his action rather by the opinion of his comrades or by his own judgment than by the voice of his superior." [3] The Comte de Paris says much the same : The troops are brave, " but the bonds of subordination are weak in the extreme. . . . The will of the individual, capricious as popular majorities, plays far too large a part." [4] With the result—" In default of the mechanism which, in armies well organised, communicates to every man controlling influences as rapidly as do the nerves in the human

---

[1] *Confederate Veteran*, III, p. 83.
[2] *A Diary from Dixie*, Mrs. H. B. Chesnut, p. 182.
[3] *The Campaign of Fredericksburg*, G. F. R. Henderson, p. 18.
[4] *Campagne du Potomac*, pp. 144, 145.

frame, there were constant failures to transform a first advantage into a decisive success." [1] As the war advanced discipline improved, and frequently passed into heroism. In the winter of 1863, when the little Army of the Ohio under General Burnside was shut up in Knoxville, the country was swept by a blizzard.

" The half-naked soldiers," writes General Cox, " hovered around their camp fires, some without coats, some without pantaloons, some with tattered blankets tied like petticoats about their waists. An officer passing among them . . . was greeted with the cheery response, ' It's pretty rough, General, but we'll see it through ! ' " [2]

March discipline remained, however, indifferent throughout the war, and especially in the Confederate army. At the battle of Antietam, it is said that 20,000 Confederates were absent from the ranks. [3] Straggling was due to two main causes : the first, as General *Taylor* says, " when brought into the field the men were as ignorant of the art of marching as babes ; " [4] for they had never been trained to march. The second, more particularly so in the Confederate army, was lack of shoes, also falling out to plunder the Federal dead, who were nearly always better equipped. In May, 1862, *Johnston* wrote to *Lee* :

" Stragglers cover the country, and Richmond is no doubt filled with the ' absent without leave.' . . . The men are full of spirit when near the enemy, but at other times, to avoid restraint, leave their regiments in crowds. To enable us to gather the whole army for battle would require a notice of several days." [5]

When Sherman marched through Georgia, in 1864, he experienced the same difficulties :

" In some brigades every regiment was made to keep its own rear guard to prevent straggling, and the brigade provost guard marched in rear of all, arresting any who

---

[1] *Histoire de la Guerre Civile en Amérique*, I, pp. 343, 344.
[2] *Atlanta*, p. 16.   [4] *Taylor*, pp. 36, 37.
[3] *The Science of War*, p. 203.   [5] 14 *W.R.*, p. 503.

sought to leave the ranks, and reporting the regimental commander who allowed his men to scatter." [1]

Fraternising, as may be expected, was common between the two armies, and by no means confined to the men. An amusing case of this is to be found in the correspondence between Averell and *Fitzhugh Lee*. Averell left with a surgeon attending two wounded officers a sack of coffee and a note : " Dear Fitz : Here's your coffee. How is your horse ? " A few weeks after, Averell received a reply : " Your two officers are well enough to go home, where they ought to be. Send an ambulance to Kelly's, and you can have them." Sometime afterwards, President Lincoln visited the army, and seeing these notes he asked Averell, " Were you and General *Lee* friends ? " " Certainly, and always have been." " What would happen should you meet on the battlefield ? " " One or both of us would be badly hurt or killed." After a pause Lincoln said with emotion : " Oh, my God, what a dreadful thing is a war like this, in which personal friends must slay each other, and die like fiends ! " [2]

From discipline I will turn to drill. The drill book in use in the United States Army was *Hardee's Tactics*.[3] Movements were few and simple, column formations were seldom used, except on the line of march, and for attack and defence eight companies were drawn up in line of battle in two ranks, and were covered by the remaining two companies extended in skirmishing order. When the line approached the enemy, the skirmishers joined in on its flanks, and took part in the assault. The Federal formations were generally deeper than those of their opponents, who frequently made the mistake of attacking with lines of too little depth and insufficiently supported. " *Jackson* and Hancock were probably the best infantry leaders in the two armies, but neither succeeded in originating any clever innovation in infantry tactics." [4]

[1] *Cox*, p. 41.　　　　　　[2] *Bigelow*, pp. 73, 101, 131.
[3] For drill and drill books, see *The History of the United States Army*, W. A. Ganoe.　　　　　[4] *Battine*, p. 415.

Generally speaking, the tactics of this war hinged on the bullet and the trench. From the very beginning the power of the first made itself felt in a manner so unmistakable that there appeared to be no solution to it except by entrenching a front, or by delivering an attack with such a mass of men that some at least would live to reach the enemy's parapet. Assault after assault failed; in fact, it has been calculated that less than one out of every eight assaults succeeded. " One rifle in the trench was worth five in front of it. The attacking columns saw little more before them than a thin and continuous sheet of flame issuing beneath the head-log of the parapet, whilst they themselves marched uncovered against the unseen foe." [1] The attacker was under the enormous disadvantage of having to fire standing, and of having to halt in order to reload after each volley. The defender had the advantage of resting his rifle on the parapet, and was frequently assisted by one or more men to load for him, handing him loaded rifles. Even on the defence there was little accuracy of fire at ranges over 400 yards, which is proved by the fact that two opposing forces, separated by not more than 500 yards, could wait for hours before engaging.[2] Nevertheless, the era of short-range weapons closed with this war. This was never fully realised, and though " it was generally impossible for the assailants from a distance to bring a converging enfilade fire to bear upon the point of a position selected for assault either with guns or rifles," [3] and overhead fire was difficult, fire was never expected to drive an enemy out of his position unless it could be followed by a bayonet charge. The defender realising this often reserved his fire until the attacking line emerged at close range from its own smoke, when one volley was normally sufficient to throw it back in confusion. " A fire fight between attacking and defending infantry almost always ended in the success of the latter." [4] Colonel Henderson once asked a veteran of the war " whether men could be got to advance shoulder

[1] *Atlanta*, p. 129.   [3] *Battine*, pp. 409, 410.
[2] *Cist*, p. 99.   [4] *Battine*, p. 410.

to shoulder," and the answer he received was : " No ;
God don't make men who could stand that." [1] A Confederate
general said : " Whoever saw a Confederate line advancing
that was not as crooked as a ram's horn ? Each ragged
rebel yelling on his own hook, and aligning on himself." [2]

The solid shoulder-to-shoulder line had outgrown its useful-
ness, and, as is often the case in war, the weaker side discovered this first. In 1864, though the Federals still relied
on attacking in swarms of men, as happened again and
again in the Wilderness campaign, the Confederates adopted
small attack columns well protected by skirmishers. Successive lines of skirmishers were introduced, which moved forward
by successive rushes, and towards the end of the war many
of the attacks carried out by both sides were tactically far
in advance of anything witnessed either in the Sadowa
campaign of 1866, or in the Franco-Prussian war of 1870–71.

As regards artillery tactics, though at the outset of the
war each side possessed some technical knowledge of gunnery,
tactical training was deficient. Besides, much of the theatre
of war was unsuited to artillery. At the battle of Malvern
Hill (July 1, 1862) the Federal guns played a decisive part ;
they might equally well have done so at Gettysburg (July 1–3,
1863), for Meade deployed a large number of pieces, but he
made the common mistake of failing to concentrate their
fire on the point of attack. The main difficulty was,
however, not the selection of the target, but the maintenance
of the bombardment during the crisis of the battle. Ricochet
fire was impossible once the attackers began to close, and
indirect laying was never, as far as I know, attempted in a
land battle.[3]

Generally speaking, battlefields unsuited to artillery fire

---

[1] *The Science of War*, p. 263.   [2] *The Science of War*, pp. 263, 264.

[3] On April 18, 1862, indirect laying was used in the bombardment of
Fort Jackson. " The schooners took position about 3,000 yards below
the fort under cover of a wood on the right bank, and their mastheads were
dressed with bushes, that they might not be distinguished from the trees.
Though Fort Jackson was invisible from their decks, yet its exact position
had been ascertained by triangulation, and the fire of the mortar-boats
was extremely accurate " (*Wood and Edmonds*, p. 475).

were equally unsuited to cavalry attack. In the mounted arm the Confederates excelled. Not only were they a nation of horsemen, but their independent spirit suited them well to cavalry operations, and especially to mounted guerrilla fighting. For the first two years of the war the Federal cavalry were indifferent, but, after Grant became commander-in-chief, under Sheridan's skilful leadership they became more than a match for their opponents. Both sides, however, failed again and again to combine cavalry action with infantry operations, because they did not fully recognise that the main duty of this arm was to reconnoitre and not to fight. Scarcely knowing how to employ them when battle was imminent, cavalry were dispatched on raiding operations. *Lee* committed this mistake at Gettysburg, and Grant, more excusably so, shortly after he plunged into the Wilderness. If these raids had been directed against the immediate rear of the enemy's army, their tactical value might well have been incalculable. Instead, they were generally made against distant points on the enemy's line of communications, that is for strategical effect, and so lost much of their power ; for though terrifying, they were too distant to influence the main operations.

There was no important instance in this war, in which thousands of mounted men were used, of a cavalry charge succeeding against unbroken infantry. Cavalry frequently fought cavalry, for example at Kelly's Ford, on April 17, 1863, but sabres were seldom crossed, for such mounted attacks as took place were normally carried out with the pistol under cover of dismounted carbine or rifle fire.

Such were the tactics of the three arms, which in the earlier period of the war were seldom correctly combined, not so much because the men lacked skill or their generals tactical knowledge, but because one of the greatest difficulties of the war was the creation of an efficient staff. This took a long time to effect, and it was not until 1864 that experience produced one, certainly on the Federal side, which left little to be desired. This staff not only learnt how to handle with skill intricate combined operations, but to deal rapidly with the evacuation of enormous numbers of wounded and the replacement of ammunition.[1] This staff was assisted by an admirable corps of signallers using telegraphic as well as flag and lamp signalling. " Lines of flag and torch communication," writes Major Bigelow, " were often gotten up from one part of an army to another twenty or thirty miles long, and maintained day and night for months." [2]

Tactical Novelty and Generalship

Such were the main strategical and tactical conditions in which Grant was called upon to work and direct, whether as a subordinate general, or as general-in-chief. In April 1861 it may be said, without seeking for effect, that tactics were mainly conspicuous through their absence. Four years later the art of war had evolved at such a pace, that in military history we find no war which bears any comparison to this one until the Russo-Japanese war of forty years later. The rifle bullet ruled the field, and in each battle its power created some new and unexpected situation. Because of the bullet, nearly every battlefield, after Shiloh, saw part or all of one side or the other entrenched, the trenches being protected by abattis and slashings. We find wire entanglements creeping in, and used with terrible effect by General Butler at Drury's Bluff in May, 1864. " The enemy in falling over the telegraph wire were slaughtered like partridges [3] ; " or as General Weitzel, on whose front these entanglements were constructed, says : After his men " had twice repulsed the enemy with terrible slaughter,—he being piled in heaps over the telegraph wire,—they were ordered to fall back." On the other hand, the Confederates spoke of " the wire as a devilish contrivance which none but a Yankee could devise." [4] Besides wire entanglements we find trench warfare begetting stationary observation balloons, wooden wire-bound mortars, hand

---

[1] At the battle of Gettysburg the Federal artillery fired some 30,000 rounds, and at Chickamauga, the Federal infantry fired 2,650,000 rounds— as much as the Prussians fired in the whole of the Sadowa campaign.

[2] *Bigelow*, p. 20.   [3] *B. & L.*, IV, p. 212.   [4] *B. & L.*, IV, p. 212.

grenades, winged grenades, and many forms of booby-traps ; so many strange and new devices that with a little imagination we can easily transport ourselves from 1864–65 to 1914–15.

Now I come to an important point as regards generalship. Tactical and mechanical evolution moved so fast that every battle was in fact a new experiment. Because of the rifle bullet, and all that this projectile created, no general could base his operations on really known, that is fully tested out, quantities. Throughout the war he was surrounded by a tactical doubt, not the normal fog of war, but an uncertainty generated by the tactics he had been taught and the tactics the rifle bullet was compelling him to adopt. This tactical doubt we must always bear in mind when we criticise the generalship of this war. In the Napoleonic wars the tactics of the musket were known ; in this Civil War the tactics of the rifle had to be discovered. If, as we now know, it was by no means fully understood by generals in 1914–18, it seems to me then that many of the tactical errors committed by their forerunners in 1861–65 will, when we bear this fact in mind, become less glaring.

PART II
GRANT AS SUBORDINATE GENERAL

CHAPTER IV

FROM GALENA TO FORT DONELSON

EARLY YEARS

In the year 1858, in the streets of the city of St. Louis might sometimes be seen a man leading a horse and cart—a seller of faggots. The man was no longer young, about five feet eight inches in height, though he looked shorter, for he stooped slightly, and when he drew up to off-load his wood his limbs trembled, for he suffered from ague. He was a thick-set, muscular man whose dark-brown hair and beard showed no trace of grey.

To the passer-by he was one of many thousands who had failed to make good—that is, he was a poor, honest, hard-working fellow whose end seemed preordained—to do odd jobs until his days were numbered ; to die, and to be forgotten. Yet in the United States of America, then, as now, it would have taken a bold man to predict the end of a fellow citizen. *The Thousand and One Nights* is a romance founded on slender facts, on Eastern dreams which seldom come true without a knife, a bow-string, or a cup of poisoned coffee. But here in this vast tumultuous continent facts find room wherein to wind and unwind themselves into tremendous romances. No man can tell the destiny of another ; for there is magic in this land of vast possibilities, vast as its spaces, in which talent more so than birth sorts through the sieve of opportunity the human grist from the human chaff. This man, humble, work-worn, and disappointed, as he off-loaded his faggots, stood on the brink of his destiny as surely as the prince in the fairy tale when he lifted up the old peasant woman and her bundle of wood, and wading the river found on the far bank that in his arms rested a smiling princess.

69

The name of this humble seller of wood was Ulysses S. Grant, who, within a few years, was destined to command vast armies, to win great battles, and to be twice chosen by his countrymen as their President. If this is not romance —what is ?

In 1630, it is said that one Matthew Grant of Dorchester sailed from England with Winthrop, and settled in Massachusetts. From him was begotten in the eighth generation Ulysses S. Grant,[1] born in a two-room house at Point Pleasant, Clermont County, Ohio, on April 27, 1822. His father kept a tannery, and with him young Grant remained until he went to West Point Academy in 1839. Not liking the tanner's trade, he worked on the adjoining farm, grew to love horses, and became an expert horseman, winning a prize in a circus for riding a trick mule which had thrown every other boy.

Church, one of his biographers, tells us, that " he was a self-reliant, honest lad, energetic and industrious, but gave no sign of future greatness. He was gentle and kindly, and popular, especially with young girls, who were secure from rudeness of speech or action when in his company." [2] He was extremely trustful of others, and here I cannot forbear quoting an instance of this, because it is a key which unlocks the door of his character, and explains many of his eventual successes and failures. He was eight years old, and wanted to buy a horse from a Mr. Ralston who valued the animal at twenty-five dollars. His father informed him it was not worth more than twenty, and told him to offer that price, and if he would not accept it to offer twenty-two and a half, and if that would not obtain him, then to give the twenty-five. Little Ulysses went to Mr. Ralston's house and looking up said to him : " Papa says I may offer you twenty dollars for the colt, but if you won't take that, I am to offer twenty-two and a half, and if you won't take that to give you twenty-five." [3]

---

[1] He was christened Hiram Ulysses Grant, but was wrongly entered upon the West Point records as Ulysses Simpson Grant. As War Department records cannot lie this error stands to prove their veracity.

[2] *Church*, p. 13.   [3] *Grant*, I, p. 30.

When seventeen years of age he went to West Point, surpassed all the cadets in horsemanship, leapt an obstacle five feet six and a half inches high ; graduated in July 1843, and was promoted brevet second lieutenant to the 4th Infantry, first raised in 1796.

In the summer of the following year this regiment was moved to Texas, and in March, 1846, under General Taylor, it marched into Mexico and occupied Matamoras. During the Mexican War, which now took place, Grant was engaged in every battle except that of Buena Vista ; and it is interesting to note that his men were armed with flint-lock muskets, and that " the artillery was advanced a rod or two in front of the line " in order to fire. Such were his first experiences in battle tactics. At Monterey, he galloped through the bullet-swept streets in search of ammunition. He writes :

" Before starting I adjusted myself on the side of my horse furthest from the enemy, and with only one foot holding to the cantle of the saddle, and an arm over the neck of the horse exposed, I started at full run. It was only at street crossings that my horse was under fire, but these I crossed at such a flying rate that generally I was past and under cover of the next block of houses before the enemy fired." [1]

In this war he obtained his first insight into political military control. After the fall of Monterey, General Taylor, a Whig, having won his third battle, could not very well be relieved from duty, yet something had to be done to neutralise his growing popularity, so General Scott was sent out to Mexico to order him to march on the capital. " It was no doubt supposed that Scott's ambition would lead him to slaughter Taylor or destroy his chances for the Presidency, and yet it was hoped that he would not make sufficient capital himself to secure the prize." [2]

In February, 1848, the war ended, and in the summer of this year Grant married Miss Dent. After service in Panama,

[1] *Grant*, I, p. 116.   [2] *Grant*, I, p. 120.

and elsewhere, he resigned from the army in July, 1854, started a small farm and failed ; entered a real-estate business but with no success ; sold faggots in St. Louis, and in May, 1860, moved to Galena, Illinois, where he accepted a clerkship on a salary of $600 a year in a leather store managed by his younger brothers. There he was sitting on an empty crate when his destiny closed upon him.

GRANT'S FIRST COMMAND

In the winter of 1861, a young merchant of Galena, roused by the conditions of the day to a sense of patriotism, began drilling his company of militiamen, and one morning, as it happened, he found himself in front of the leather store of Grant Brothers. A wrong word of command caused a confused opening in the ranks, when hidden away behind the soldiers was seen a little man seated on a packing-box. Then it occurred to the young merchant that this was Captain Grant, late of the Regular Army. He asked him to take charge of his company, and handed him his sword. Grant buckled it on, and stepped out in front of the men. " As he drew his blade from its scabbard, and it flashed in the sunlight, his whole nature seemed transformed and to his fellow-townsmen was revealed the fact that here was a man who understood the business of war." [1]

Grant was a reader, and his readings led him to infer that Lincoln's election meant war, which, in common with others, he supposed would be a " ninety days' affair." Then came the bombardment of Fort Sumter, and Grant joined up as a clerk to assist in the Adjutant-General's office at Camp Yates ; because, as he said, " he thought it was his duty to offer his services." In May he obtained leave to visit his parents, and took the opportunity to go to Cincinnati to ask Major-General B. McClellan, who had his headquarters there, if he would accept him as a staff officer. He waited for two days in the great man's ante-room, watching " so many with quills behind their ears " until he was tired of seeing them. Then he returned to

[1] *Church*, p. 68.

his home, and wrote to the War Department at Washington
offering his services as a soldier, but no reply was vouched.
A little later, Governor Yates, who had formed a high opinion
of his force of character, sent for him, and offered him the
command of the 21st Illinois Infantry.[1] This regiment
was bordering on mutiny, it had been commanded by a
colonel " who wore two pistols in his belt and made speeches
on dress parade."

The day Grant took over command " the boys " had
been worked up to " a three-cheer-and-a-tiger state of
mind " by Mr. Logan, a member of Congress, and accustomed
to speeches from their old colonel they began to yell for—
" Grant ! Colonel Grant ! " Grant stepped forward, and
without exhausting the English language, made the following address : " Go to your quarters ! " On another occasion,
an Irish soldier, who was a terror to the camp, refused to
go to his. As a corporal and a file of men shrank from
arresting him, Grant went after him, knocked him down,
trussed him, and gagged him by tying a bayonet in his
mouth. The disciplining of the 21st had begun.

The regiment moved to Palmyra, and then to Salt River,
near which the Confederates under Colonel *Thomas Harris*
had established a camp. Grant moved out to attack it,
and in his *Memoirs* he writes :

" As we approached the brow of the hill from which it
was expected we could see *Harris'* camp, and possibly find
his men ready formed to meet us, my heart kept getting
higher and higher until it felt to me as though it was in my
throat. I would have given anything then to have been
back in Illinois, but I had not the moral courage to halt
and consider what to do ; I kept right on. When we
reached a point from which the valley below was in full
view I halted. The place where *Harris* had been encamped
a few days before was still there and the marks of a recent
encampment were plainly visible, but the troops were gone.
My heart resumed its place. It occurred to me at once that

[1] After Grant had become famous Yates prided himself on this act and
said : " God gave him to the country, and I signed his first commission."
(*General Grant*, James Grant Wilson, p. 85.)

Harris had been as much afraid of me as I had been of him. This was a view of the question I had never taken before ; but it was one I never forgot afterwards. From that event to the close of the war, I never experienced trepidation upon confronting the enemy, though I always felt more or less anxiety. I never forgot that he had as much reason to fear my forces as I had his." [1]

Thus Grant acquired the first virtue of generalship— fortitude.

Grant was not a coward, or even a highly strung man, his gallop at Monterey proves this ; but then he was under command and not in command, and here lurks a vast difference. At Salt River he began to experience that solitude of the general I have spoken of in the Introduction. It was not because he was without men, but because he was with men that he felt it. This is the difference between a brave scout and a determined leader : the one relies on himself, the other feels that each of his men is relying on him. His responsibility isolates him. That Grant learnt this supreme lesson during a morning's march, and in face of a vacant camp, shows that in this man there was something outside the common. He could learn ; he could analyse his fears, he could make them speak to him. Because he was a student of his own errors and weaknesses, much more so than an illumined genius, we see this man through toil and tribulation defeating his own ignorance, and " keeping right on " to the very end.

From Salt River the 21st moved to the town of Mexico, where Grant was assigned the command of a sub-district comprising three regiments of infantry and a section of artillery. Here he came under the command of General Pope, and soon after his arrival he was promoted to the rank of brigadier-general. In August he was moved to Ironton, and then to Jefferson City, where he came under the orders of Major-General Frémont, who was in command of the Western Department. Towards the end of August, 1861, he was ordered to take command of the district of

[1] *Grant*, I, pp. 249, 250.

South-Eastern Missouri; first he established his headquarters at Cape Girardeau, and then at Cairo, where he
arrived on September 4. Recognising the importance of
Cairo, and learning from a scout, the day after he arrived
there, that a Confederate force had moved out from Columbus
to seize Paducah at the mouth of the Tennessee, he telegraphed Department headquarters that he intended to start
for Paducah that night unless he received orders to the
contrary. Receiving no reply, to the consternation of its
citizens—he occupied Paducah; the struggle for the Mississippi had begun.

BATTLE OF BELMONT

The town of Columbus, eighteen miles south of Cairo,
stood on a high bluff commanding the Mississippi; it was
strongly fortified, and was described by General *Polk* as
" the Gibraltar of the West." On November 5, Frémont,
hearing that *Price's* army in Missouri had been reinforced
from Columbus, ordered Grant to make a demonstration
against this place, whilst Colonel Oglesby, one of Grant's
subordinates, was instructed to operate with a small column
towards New Madrid.

The following evening Grant left Cairo with 3,114 men in
transports escorted by two gunboats. At 2 a.m. on the 7th,
learning that troops had been sent over from Columbus
to Belmont to cut off Oglesby, he resolved to attack this
detachment. That evening he landed at Hunter's Point,
three miles above Belmont, which was a settlement of three
houses situated close to the right bank of the river, and
almost immediately west of Columbus. The Confederate
detachment consisted at first of a regiment and a battery.
It was encamped in a large field protected by felled timber.
Before Grant arrived, it was reinforced by four regiments
under General *Pillow*, bringing its total strength up to
about 2,500.

Leaving some five companies (about 250 men) at Hunter's
Ferry to protect the transports, at about 8 a.m. Grant
marched through a stretch of forest land and deployed his

small column into two lines facing Belmont—McClernand in front and Dougherty in rear. Advancing in this formation, the leading line struck a connected series of ponds and swamps, and, to circumvent them, apparently it moved to one flank and the rear line to the other ; with the result that, when on the far side of the ponds, one continuous line was formed. A hot engagement now took place, and *Pillow* was driven out of his camp towards the river, whereupon Grant's men broke ranks and pillaged the camp. " They behaved," says Badeau, " like so many schoolboys," [1] until Grant ordered the camp to be set on fire.

Pillow's men, much disorganised, were meanwhile hiding along the river bank, but finding that they were not pursued, and seeing some steamers putting out from Columbus to assist them, they began to work up the river, aiming to cut in between Grant and his transports. Some of these men appearing in rear of the disorganised Federals, the alarm " surrounded " was sounded, and a disorderly retirement on to the transports resulted. Once the men had embarked, Grant, supposing that the companies he had posted on landing were still out (as a matter of fact they were the first to re-embark), rode forward alone to call them in, and was nearly captured. Galloping back towards the river, as he writes, " my horse put his forefeet over the bank without hesitation or urging, and with his hind feet well under him, slid down the bank and trotted aboard the boat, twelve or fifteen feet away, over a single gang-plank." [2] Dismounting, Grant went to the pilot-house, threw himself down on a sofa, but, fortunately, at once got up, for as he did so " a musket ball entered the room, struck the head of the sofa, passed through it and lodged in the foot."

The losses in this battle were : Federals, 79 killed, 289 wounded, and 117 missing ; Confederates, 105 killed, 419 wounded, and 117 missing.

Such was Grant's first battle, and it cannot be said that his generalship was above that of an amateur, which is exactly what he then was. His determination to fight was

---

[1] *Badeau*, I, p. 17.   [2] *Grant*, I, p. 279.

right, for in all probability it saved Oglesby's column from capture. Further, the enemy, if defeated, were at his mercy, for the river was immediately in rear of them. The attack demanded extreme rapidity as it was made under the guns of Columbus, and not only could *Pillow* be easily reinforced, but Grant's rear could at any moment be threatened. To leave a detachment with the transports was right, but to advance without adequate ground reconnaissance was wrong, and what was still worse was not to hold reserves in hand; especially as his men had never as yet been under fire. That no pursuit was made was due to lack of reserves, quite as much as to lack of discipline on the part of his men. Further, having no reserve wherewith to form a rear-guard his withdrawal was chaotic.

It is easy to discover these errors now, but the extraordinary thing is that Grant himself discovered them at the time, and, as we shall see, through recognising how faulty had been his generalship, greatly improved upon it in his next battle.

Strategy taking Form

I must now retrace my steps, for in the autumn of 1861 the strategy which was to control the war began to shape itself; consequently, to understand it we must discover its origins, which are tangled in a host of cross-purposes.

Whilst in the East the capture of Richmond eclipsed all other problems, in the West chaos began to take form, and it centred round gaining control of Missouri, and driving the Confederates out of east Tennessee, which was loyal to the Union. The Western problem was complicated by the neutrality of Kentucky, the militia of which State, until October, 1861, was commanded by General Anderson of Fort Sumter fame, when General William T. Sherman relieved him. The occupation of Columbus by the Confederates, and of Paducah by Grant, violated this neutrality, with the result that in September Kentucky abandoned her impossible position and joined the North.

The occupation of Paducah by Grant led to General *Albert Sidney Johnston* being appointed to command the Department of the West, which embraced the States of Kentucky and Tennessee. Realising the importance of the Tennessee and Cumberland rivers, the main lines of communication in his command, he blocked them with two forts, Henry and Donelson, a little north of the points where the Memphis—Ohio railway crosses these rivers. Simultaneously, *Johnston* ordered General *Buckner* to occupy Bowling Green, and General *Zollicoffer* to move from Knoxville to Cumberland Gap.

Though these forces stretched from the Mississippi to the Cumberland mountains, the declaration of Kentucky was at once seized upon by President Lincoln to realise a wish he had for long desired, namely, the relief of east Tennessee. With unerring political sense he saw the advantage of carrying the war into this area. Not only would its occupation relieve a loyal population from oppression and add man-power to the Union, but a successful move in this direction would threaten the main lateral railways of the Confederacy, namely, those running through Chattanooga and Atlanta. How to found this scheme on sound strategy was quite beyond him.

On November 1, 1861, General McClellan was called to Washington to succeed General Scott as Commander-in-Chief. His plan of campaign was to strike at Richmond by sea and land, and pivoting the whole of his strategy on this idea he fell in with Lincoln's wishes, and supported the proposal of a campaign in east Tennessee ; for he saw that any army operating against Knoxville and Chattanooga must draw Confederate forces from Richmond towards these places. However desirable such a campaign might be, it was obviously unsound to inaugurate it as long as strong Confederate forces held Missouri and western Tennessee ; for these could fall on the rear of any Federal army advancing south and east of them.

To prepare for this campaign, McClellan's first step was to replace that erratic adventurer, Frémont, by Major-

General Henry W. Halleck, who, on November 9, assumed command of the Department of the Missouri, which included the States of Missouri, Arkansas, and that part of Kentucky which lay west of the River Cumberland. His next was to replace Sherman, whom he sent to St. Louis, by General Don Carlos Buell, appointing him to the Department of the Ohio, which embraced the State of Tennessee and the remaining portion of Kentucky. His idea apparently was for Buell to advance into east Tennessee whilst Halleck protected his right flank and rear. He failed to see, however, that for such a combined operation to be securely founded it was essential for both these Departments to be placed under a single head.

Had Buell and Halleck been of similar mentality, co-operation might have been possible ; but this was not so. Buell was an educated soldier, a man of imagination, a strict disciplinarian, a skilful trainer of troops, and, though apt to be slow, one who could be relied upon for sound judgments. Halleck—and I will deal somewhat more fully with him, because throughout the war he was a thorn in Grant's side— was a cautious, witless pedant who had studied war, and imagined that adherence to certain strategical and tactical maxims constituted the height of generalship. He was one of a type to be met with in every war, a type which seems to attract politicians ; for men of Halleck's stamp are nearly always promoted. In his case, not only was he given an important command in the West, but later on was selected as Commander-in-Chief, and, even after he had been superseded by Grant, he remained on at Washington as Chief of the Staff—that is, as military adviser to Lincoln. It may be said, without fear of contradiction, that throughout the war Halleck was worth much more than the proverbial army corps to the Confederate forces.

Buell, who was a far abler soldier than McClellan, at once saw the folly of attempting an invasion of east Tennessee without the support of carefully co-ordinated operations in western Kentucky and western Tennessee. On November 27 he recommended " the movement of two flotilla columns up the

Tennessee and Cumberland,"[1] also a movement on Nashville, all three to take place in conjunction with the advance into east Tennessee. McClellan, failing to see the connection between these operations and the one he had in mind, urged him to secure east Tennessee first, and only after this had been done to move on Nashville.[2] On December 3 he wrote to Buell again, and his letter is so extraordinary, and shows so clearly the chaotic strategical outlook at Washington, that I will quote a paragraph of it. He says :

" I still feel sure that the best strategical move in this case will be that dictated by the simple feelings of humanity. We must preserve these noble fellows from harm ; everything urges us to do that—faith, interests, and loyalty. For the sake of the eastern Tennesseans who have taken part with us I would gladly sacrifice mere military advantages ; they deserve our protection, and at all hazards they must have it."[3]

After such an appreciation from the Commander-in-Chief, can we blame Lincoln for the grand-strategical errors he so often made ?

On December 10 Buell very rightly objected to this proposal, considering that the movement must be merged " into the general line of operations."[4] Meanwhile, on December 6, McClellan suggested to Halleck that he should make a diversion up the rivers to distract the enemy's attention away from Buell. Halleck replied that he had no troops to spare. At length, on December 29, Buell wrote to McClellan saying :

" It is my conviction that all the force that can possibly be collected should be brought to bear on that front of which Columbus and Bowling Green may be said to be the flanks. The center, that is, the Cumberland and Tennessee where the railroad crosses them, is now the most vulnerable point. I regard it as the most important strategical point in the whole field of operations." He also added : " It is quite essential, too, that success should be speedy. . . ."[5]

[1] 7 *W.R.*, pp. 450, 451.   [3] 7 *W.R.*, p. 468.
[2] 7 *W.R.*, p. 457.   [4] 7 *W.R.*, p. 487.
[5] 7 *W.R.*, pp. 520, 521.

Though Buell had no intention of moving forward at this time, McClellan, not being prepared to move on Richmond for months, and apparently wishing to allay the complaints which his delays were giving rise to, as well as to induce Buell to initiate his campaign, ordered Halleck to make a demonstration ; then he went sick, and Lincoln requested Halleck and Buell to enter into direct communication. Accordingly, on January 3, 1862, Buell suggested to Halleck that he should dispatch two gunboat [1] expeditions accompanied by 20,000 men up the Tennessee and Cumberland rivers.[2] Halleck, disapproving of this, replied in his usual pedantic way : " It strikes me that to operate from Louisville and Paducah or Cairo against an enemy at Bowling Green is a plain case of exterior lines, like that of McDowell and Patterson, which, unless each of the exterior columns is superior to the enemy, leads to disaster ninety-nine times in a hundred." [3]

McClellan, now recovered, agreed with these views, and instructed Buell to advance into east Tennessee without waiting for Halleck. Thereupon Buell ordered Brigadier-General George H. Thomas to attack *Zollicoffer*, who had advanced to near Somerset on the Cumberland river. This he did, and, on January 19, decisively defeated him at Mill Springs.

To return to Grant. After the battle of Belmont, Halleck confirmed Grant in the appointment assigned to him by Frémont, but changed his designation from District of South-East Missouri to that of the District of Cairo. On January 6, obeying McClellan's instructions, he ordered Grant to carry out a demonstration.

Grant, soon after he was appointed to the District of Cairo, had formed the opinion that to break the line of the Tennessee river would be a disaster to the enemy,[4] and the day upon which Halleck wrote to him he had asked sanction [5] to see Halleck at St. Louis, his object being to obtain from

---

[1] The river gunboat programme was put in hand by the Federal Government in the spring of 1861. This fleet was ready in January, 1862.

[2] 7 *W.R.*, p. 529.   [3] 7 *W.R.*, p. 533.

[4] See *M.H.S.M.*, VII, p. 8, and also Buell's letter to Halleck on January 3, 1862, 7 *W.R.*, pp. 528, 529.   [5] 7 *W.R.*, p. 534.

him permission to move on Forts Henry and Donelson. Leave to do so was refused, and, receiving his instructions concerning the demonstration, Grant ordered General Smith to threaten Forts Heiman and Henry, whilst he and McClernand threatened Columbus with one column and the Tennessee river with another. As a result of his expedition, Smith reported to Grant that he considered it practicable to capture Fort Heiman. " This report of Smith's," says Grant, " confirmed views I had previously held, that the true line of operation for us was up the Tennessee and Cumberland rivers. With us there, the enemy would be compelled to fall back on the east and west entirely out of the State of Kentucky." [1] On January 22 Grant once again asked to see Halleck. This request was sanctioned ; so he went to St. Louis on the 23rd, but scarcely had he begun to explain his ideas, than, as he says : " I was cut short as if my plan was preposterous. I returned to Cairo very much crestfallen." Nothing daunted, on the 24th he forwarded to Halleck a report on Smith's reconnaissance. Then, talking the whole question over with Commodore Foote, who was in command of the gunboat flotilla, both he and Foote telegraphed Halleck on the 28th that Fort Henry could be captured.[2]

We come now to a question of personality. Halleck was by nature not only stupid, but jealous and ambitious. As long as he was asked to play second fiddle to Buell he refused to play at all. But directly Thomas won the battle of Mill Springs, which reflected glory upon Buell, he began to bestir himself, and turned over Grant's suggestion of January 6. Though, on the 23rd, he told Grant that his idea of capturing the forts was preposterous, he had already on the 20th (the day after Mill Springs) written to McClellan advocating a move up the Cumberland and Tennessee rivers, the object of which was to capture Nashville. He said : " This would turn Columbus, and force the abandonment of Bowling Green." [3]

He added, however, that he could not accomplish this with less than 60,000 men, suggesting to McClellan that part if

---

[1] *Grant*, I, p. 286.   [2] 7 *W.R.*, pp. 120–121.   [3] 8 *W.R.*, p. 509.

not all of Buell's forces should be transferred to his command. Receiving no definite answer to this letter [1] (and being urged on by Grant, who on the 29th followed up his telegram of the 28th with an explanatory letter),[2] not waiting for further instructions from Washington, he telegraphed to Grant to prepare to take and hold Fort Henry.[3] Grant received this order on February 1, written instructions following the next day.

CAPTURE OF FORT HENRY

" There was one general always ready to move on receipt of orders "[4]—this was Grant. For the battle of Belmont he started within twenty-four hours of receiving orders ; on his recent demonstration he had done likewise, in spite of the rain ; for as he himself says : it " will operate worse upon the enemy, if he should come out to meet us, than upon us." Now he did so again, and within twenty-four hours the embarkation of his troops began.

Johnston's position was a precarious one, *Zollicoffer* had been defeated and driven back ; at Columbus he had General *Polk* with 18,000 men, and under himself at Bowling Green was an active army 25,000 strong. Bowling Green was connected to Columbus by the railway which passed over the Cumberland and Tennessee rivers at bridges a little south of Forts Donelson and Henry, which were garrisoned by 2,000 and 3,000 men respectively ; both being under the command of General *Tilghman*. As long as these forts were held, *Johnston* could make use of his interior position with effect, but should they fall his line would be cut in two, and not only would he be compelled to evacuate Bowling Green, but *Polk*, in all probability, would be forced to withdraw from Columbus. . *Johnston* did not expect an attack by land, as the weather was bad, but ever since General Smith's reconnaissance he feared a gunboat offensive.

Grant not having sufficient transports to carry the whole of his force, some 17,000 strong, in one trip, on the 4th moved

---

[1] 7 *W.R.*, p. 930. [3] 7 *W.R.*, p. 121.
[2] 7 *W.R.*, p. 121. [4] *M.H.S.M.*, VII, p. 7.

forward McClernand's division under protection of seven
gunboats, four of which were armoured, and landed the
troops eight to nine miles below Fort Henry. From these he
reconnoitred the river, and returned with the transports to
Paducah to bring up Smith's division on the 5th. Before all
his troops had assembled Grant was ready with his plan of
attack.

Fort Henry was situated on the eastern bank of the Tennessee about twelve miles west of Fort Donelson, which was
constructed on the western bank of the Cumberland. Both
forts were too large, Fort Henry covering ten acres, and Fort
Donelson no less than one hundred. Fort Henry was badly
sighted, for not only was the ground low and swampy, but
from the western bank of the river it was commanded by
Fort Heiman, a small, half-finished work, as well as by the
high ground on its own bank to the north and east of it. It
was armed with seventeen guns.

Grant instructed General Smith to land a brigade on the
western bank during the night of the 5th/6th, and get in
rear of Fort Heiman—this he did and found it evacuated.
The rest of his command was ordered to move at 11 a.m. on
the 6th, and out-flank Fort Henry whilst the gunboats
steamed up the river and bombarded it frontally. By this
manœuvre Grant hoped to capture the entire garrison, and
so prevent it reinforcing Fort Donelson.

At about 12.30 p.m. the gunboats, mounting some fifty
guns, opened fire at about 2,000 yards' range. Then closing
to 350 yards—unnecessarily close—they rapidly silenced the
guns of the fort. *Tilghman*, seeing that the situation was
hopeless, wisely ordered the garrison to retire to Fort Donelson ; this it succeeded in doing at insignificant loss. At
2 p.m. he surrendered the fort, whereupon two gunboats
were at once sent up the river to destroy the Memphis and
Ohio railway bridge : *Johnston* was now cut off from *Polk*.

" The effect of the capture of Fort Henry," writes Ropes,
" on the people of the whole country, North and South, was
electrical. . . . It was accomplished, too, so suddenly and
so unexpectedly that the spirits of the Northern people

were elated beyond measure, while those of the people of the South were correspondingly depressed." [1]

That this fort had been compelled to surrender by the action of the fleet alone seemed to show that the North possessed an irresistible weapon. *Johnston* was of opinion that the strongest works could be reduced by iron-clad gunboats. This was not true, as the next operation will show.

CAPTURE OF FORT DONELSON

Fort Donelson was a bastioned earthwork standing on a bluff a hundred feet above the water. On the east of it flowed the River Tennessee ; on the north and south it was protected by two streams, namely, Hickman Creek and Indian Creek, and on its western flank, following the crest of a ridge between the two creeks, a line of rifle pits, protected by abattis, had been dug. On its northern face it was protected by two water batteries of twelve guns and a ten-inch columbiad sited some thirty to forty feet above the water ; a number of guns were in the fort itself.

In spite of the strength of Fort Donelson, the rapid reduction of Fort Henry had so shaken General *Johnston's* confidence that he decided forthwith to evacuate Bowling Green. General *Beauregard*, who happened at this time to be on a visit to *Johnston's* headquarters, wisely urged *Johnston* to march on Donelson, and attack Grant before he could be reinforced. In place, *Johnston* sent 12,000 men to Donelson, raising its garrison to rather over 18,000 ; and on February 11 and 12 retiring on Nashville with the remainder of his force, some 14,000 strong, he entered this town on the 16th. If this were not bad enough, he placed General *Floyd*, an inexperienced and incompetent officer, in command of the fort. What *Johnston's* plan really was it is difficult to discover. The truth of the matter appears to be, that though he was a typical fighting soldier with a high reputation, like many another of this kind, a disaster upset his balance. The fall of Fort Henry was so unexpected that it completely

---

[1] *Ropes*, Pt. II, p. 18.

bewildered him, and imagining that the gunboats bereft him of power to attack, he was paralysed ; in short, he had not the mental training to see things in correct tactical perspective.   The result was that he adopted a half-measure : he aimed at holding Fort Donelson as long as he could, and of saving half his army ; trusting that the other half would be able to cut its way out.   In my opinion, General *Johnston* was a very common type of brave and stupid soldier, and his action at the battle of Shiloh in no way disproves this.

Fort Henry having fallen, Grant was naturally elated, and though he also was for a time spellbound by the unexpected ease with which the gunboats had reduced the fort, he was in no way thrown off his balance.   It is true that in the midst of exultation he had written to Halleck that he would " take and destroy " Fort Donelson on February 8, but he soon realised that this was impossible ; for the fleet had to refit, and steam back down the Tennessee and then up the Cumberland.   He felt, however, " that 15,000 men on the 8th would be more effective than 50,000 a month later," [1] which shows that his judgment was perfectly sound.

Remembering his mistake at Belmont, the day after the fall of Fort Henry Grant reconnoitred Donelson.   As he says :

" I took my staff and cavalry . . . and made a reconnaissance to within about a mile of the outer line of works at Donelson.   I had known General *Pillow* in Mexico, and judged that with any force, no matter how small, I could march up within gunshot of any intrenchments he was given to hold. I said this to the officers of my staff at the time.   I knew that *Floyd* was in command, but he was no soldier, and I judged that he would yield to *Pillow's* pretensions.   I met, as I expected, no opposition in making the reconnoissance and, besides learning the topography of the country on the way round Fort Donelson, found that there were two roads available for marching ; one leading to the village of Dover, the other to Donelson." [2]

Whilst Grant impatiently waited for the fleet to refit, Halleck rushed up six regiments of reinforcements, but as

---

[1] *Grant*, I, p. 298.   [2] *Grant*, I, pp. 294, 295.

Colonel Bruce says : " he rendered the greatest service to the country that can be credited to him during the war by remaining in his office at St. Louis." [1] Grant's plan was to surround Fort Donelson on the land side and to attack it from the river with the gunboats, an operation similar to that undertaken against Fort Henry. Halleck did not approve or disapprove of this attack, as Grant says : " He said nothing whatever to me on the subject." [2] On the night of the 11th Grant moved McClernand's division out a few miles to clear the roads ; ordered Smith to leave General Lewis Wallace and 2,500 men to guard Forts Henry and Heiman ; and instructed Colonel Thayer, commanding the six reinforcing regiments, to turn his transports about, and move under escort of the fleet. Then with the remainder of Smith's division he moved out of Fort Henry on the 12th. On approaching Fort Donelson, Smith took up position with his left on Hickman Creek, and McClernand with his right on the Cumberland, and his front facing Indian Creek. Both divisions, though not entrenched, held strong positions along the crest of the ridges, their guns being sunk in the ground, and the men not required to serve them being ordered to seek cover from fire behind the crest line.

To save time, for the roads were in a terrible condition, the column marched without transport, shelter-tents had not yet come into use, and, as camp fires could not be lit in such close proximity to the enemy, the men suffered severely from the wet and bitterly cold weather, their discomfort being increased by ill discipline, many having thrown away their blankets and overcoats whilst on the line of march. Grant had but two educated officers with him, namely, General Smith and Lieut.-Colonel McPherson.

On the 12th and 13th there was some slight skirmishing, and McClernand, without orders, attempted to assault a battery, and was repulsed. All was going well at Fort Henry, and its landward side having been strengthened, Lewis

---

[1] *M.H.S.M.*, VII, p. 15.

[2] *Grant*, I, p. 296. This statement is questioned by Ropes ; see *Ropes*, Pt. II, footnote p. 37.

Wallace was ordered up, and, when Thayer arrived, on the 14th, Wallace took command of his brigade and such other reinforcements as had been sent forward, his own men rejoining Smith's division. Wallace was assigned to the centre between Smith and McClernand, his command being called the 3rd Division.

On the evening of the 13th the fleet arrived. Grant's plan was to hold the enemy within his lines whilst the gunboats attacked him. " Some of the gunboats were to run the batteries, get above the fort and above the village of Dover."[1] By 3 p.m. on the 14th, Foote steamed up-stream opening fire at a mile and a half from the fort, and then closed to within two to four hundred yards of the water batteries. Foote's flagship was hit fifty-nine times, and he himself was wounded. So heavy was the fire from the batteries, and so ineffective was the gunboat bombardment, that the fleet was compelled to withdraw, most of the ships being seriously damaged.[2]

Both Grant and Foote have been criticised for closing to within point-blank range. It is true that at Fort Henry this action had proved effectual, as the batteries were on the water level ; but at Fort Donelson they were well above the gunboats, which could not bring their full armament to bear on them, and in their turn were hit by a plunging fire. It must be remembered, however, that Grant's plan was to pass above the fort towards Dover, and according to Colonel Bruce he had asked Foote to send a single gunboat up-stream past the batteries to attack them in rear. This Foote did not do. Nevertheless, the possibility of this happening terrified *Floyd*, who now determined to evacuate the fort. That

---

[1] *Grant*, I, p. 302.

[2] H. W. Wilson, the well-known naval writer, says : " In the attack on Fort Donelson, which commanded the upper Cumberland, the gunboats were directed by Grant to run past the fort and take it in reverse, at the same time cutting it off from the Confederate forces. This work they accomplished, though they suffered severely from the guns of the fort ; and their presence on the river above the fort was the strategical cause of the sally of the garrison, which resulted in Grant's first complete victory." (*C.M.H.*, VII, p. 558.) I have been unable to trace Wilson's authority for his assertion that the gunboats passed the batteries.

evening a council of war was held, consisting of Generals
Floyd, *Pillow*, and *Buckner*, and it was decided at dawn the
following day to attack the Federals and so open a road by
which the army could retire to Nashville.[1] Whereupon
Floyd, making no arrangements, tactical or administrative,
ordered the attack to be made, with the result that early on
the 15th McClernand's division was driven back in confusion,
as was also Wallace's. Thus far the operation was crowned
with success, and all that remained was to effect a rapid
withdrawal. No arrangements had, however, been made for
this, no rations had been issued, no wagons loaded, and no
rear-guard detailed. Not knowing what to do, *Pillow*, who
had directed the main attack, lost his head and ordered the
troops back to their entrenchments, *Floyd* agreeing with
this extraordinary action.[2]

On the Federal side there was much confusion. Before
daylight on the 15th, Foote, not being able to leave his flagship on account of his wound, asked Grant to visit him. This
he did, but failed to appoint a commander during his absence.
On his return he was met by a staff officer " white with fear,"
who informed him that his troops had been scattered. Galloping forward, he found that McClernand, who had attacked
with all three of his brigades in line, had lost control ; but
that Smith, a trained soldier, having distributed his men in
depth—skirmishers, firing-line, supports, brigade reserves,
and a whole brigade in divisional reserve—had his troops
well in hand.[3] Grant, as Lewis Wallace says, now showed
his metal :

" His face flushed slightly. With a sudden grip he crushed
the papers in his hand. But in an instant these signs of
disappointment or hesitation—as the reader pleases—cleared
away. In his ordinary quiet voice he said : ' . . . Gentlemen, the position on the right must be retaken.' With that
he turned and galloped off." [4]

[1] 7 *W.R.*, p. 268.
[2] 7 *W.R.*, pp. 283, 314, 318, and *Buckner's* report 7 *W.R.*, pp. 332, 333.
[3] *Conger*, p. 11.
[4] *B. & L.*, I, p. 422.

Grant's actions were as follows :

(1) He ordered McClernand and Wallace to withdraw out of cannon range and entrench.

(2) He sent a message to Foote urgently asking him to make a demonstration : " If," he wrote, " all the gunboats that can will immediately make their appearance to the enemy it may secure us a victory."[1]

(3) He ordered Smith to prepare to assault the works in front of him.

(4) Then he returned to Wallace and McClernand, and ordered them to advance and reoccupy their former lines.[2]

Turning to Colonel J. D. Webster of his staff, he said : " Some of our men are pretty badly demoralised, but the enemy must be more so, for he has attempted to force his way out, but has fallen back ; the one who attacks first now will be victorious and the enemy will have to be in a hurry if he gets ahead of me."[3] Grant's presence roused officers and men to high enthusiasm. Galloping down the regiments, he shouted : " Fill your cartridge-boxes quick, and get into line ; the enemy is trying to escape, and he must not be permitted to do so."

" This," as he says, " acted like a charm. The men only wanted someone to give them a command."[4]

Smith, the good soldier that he was, had already reconnoitred his front before receiving Grant's order to assault, and within an hour of receiving this order he advanced :

" Birge's sharpshooters, deployed on each flank, opened skirmishing fire. The column advanced silently, without firing, crushed down the abattis, covered the hill-side with battalions, heedless of the fire from the garrison, pressed on to the works, leaped over, formed in line, and drove the defending regiment to further shelter."[5]

The key point of the fort was thus carried.

[1] 7 *W.R.*, p. 618.

[2] 7 *W.R.*, pp. 179, 180. (McClernand's report.)

[3] *Grant*, I, p. 307.

[4] *Grant*, I, p. 308.

[5] *Force*, p. 55.

That night, whilst Grant slept in a negro hut, and Smith with his troops on the frozen ground they had won, " inside the fort occurred one of the most remarkable scenes of the war."[1] *Floyd* summoned a second council of generals. *Pillow* suggested another attempt to cut their way out. *Floyd* and *Buckner* considered this impracticable, consequently a surrender was decided upon. Thereupon *Floyd* turned his command over to *Pillow*, and *Pillow* turned it over to *Buckner*.

Thus, whilst the junior general was left to open negotiations with Grant, the two senior ones,[2] accompanied by some 3,000 men, escaped from the fort under cover of night. *Forrest* with his cavalry and some other troops, about 1,000 in all, also made their way out, passing between Grant's right and the river.

Floyd and *Pillow* having abandoned their army, *Buckner* sent a letter to Grant proposing an armistice so that terms of capitulation might be agreed upon. To which he received the famous answer :[3]

> " HEADQUARTERS ARMY IN THE FIELD,
> CAMP NEAR FORT DONELSON,
> *February* 16, 1862.

General S. B. Buckner,

    Confederate Army.

Sir : Yours of this date, proposing armistice and appointment of commissioners to settle terms of capitulation, is just received. No terms except unconditional and immediate surrender can be accepted. I propose to move immediately upon your works.

> I am, sir, very respectfully,

> Your obedient servant,

> U. S. GRANT,
> *Brigadier-General Commanding.*"

[1] *Badeau*, I, p. 47.
[2] For the amazing conversation between these three generals, see *Force*, p. 58.
[3] 7 *W.R.*, p. 161.

Though *Buckner* considered these terms unchivalrous, he had no choice but to accept them. Thereupon he surrendered with 11,500 men and 40 guns.[1] Grant's losses were approximately 3,000 killed, wounded, and missing.[2]

Such was Grant's first great battle, in which it will be seen that his generalship was a vast improvement on that shown at Belmont. His success in no way turned his head. He generously acknowledged that by his bravery and coolness Smith had saved the situation, and in his report his praise is for others and not of himself.

On the other hand Grant's superior, Halleck, on the following day telegraphed to McClellan : " I must have command of the armies in the west. Hesitation and delay are losing us the golden opportunities. Lay this before the President and Secretary of War. May I assume the command ? Answer quickly." [3] Such was the moral difference between these two men.

As regards the origins of this battle, Colonel William P. Johnston, son of General *Albert Sidney Johnston*, writes : " There has been much discussion as to who originated the movement up the Tennessee River. Grant *made* it, and it made Grant." [4]

Donelson, says Colonel Bruce, was Grant's battle.

" Many soldiers were engaged in it, but his genius brought the victory. His quick comprehension of the whole situation on his return to the field ; his divination of the enemy's plan and object ; his clear sight of the empty lines on the left ; his speedy ride to Smith's division and infusion into its commander of that energy and promptness which the emergency demanded, make up a rounded whole of the

[1] 7 *W.R.*, pp. 944 and 159. Badeau, however, says : " Sixty-five guns, seventeen thousand six hundred small arms, and nearly fifteen thousand troops fell into the hands of the victor." (*Badeau*, I, p. 50.)

[2] 7 *W.R.*, p. 169.

[3] 7 *W.R.*, p. 641.

[4] *B. & L.*, I, p. 547.

comprehensive vision of a battlefield and perfect conduct of a battle that has never been surpassed."[1]

In another place this same officer writes : " The most damaging blows inflicted upon the South, up to the time *Lee* surrendered, . . . were received in the Donelson campaign, and, what naturally followed from it, the capture of New Orleans . . . and . . . the Vicksburg campaign."[2] Is there justification for such praise ? I think there is. First, the moral effects of this victory were enormous. Colonel Henry Stone, no great admirer of Grant, says :

" The exultation throughout the North-West—especially in Illinois and Indiana, which States furnished more than half the soldiers in the Union Army at Fort Donelson—and the consternation in the insurgent regions in the South-West, were not surpassed, if they were equalled, by those of three years later, when Petersburg was captured and Richmond abandoned. The hilarity at Chicago, and the panic at Nashville, cannot be described."[3]

Secondly, the material results were immense : Nashville was evacuated and so was Columbus, and the loss of this last-mentioned place enabled General Curtis, on March 7, totally to defeat the Confederates under *Van Dorn* at Pea Ridge in Arkansas, securing beyond further question the State of Missouri—a most important Federal gain. It won Kentucky, and laid Tennessee open to invasion. At a single blow not only did this victory sweep back the whole line of the Confederate defences in the West, but it deprived the South of an invaluable recruiting ground. At Donelson Grant not only captured *Buckner's* 11,500 men, but large numbers of prospective Southern recruits. As Colonel Bruce says : " If General Grant had captured at Donelson 75,000 men his campaign there would have passed unchallenged as the greatest event of the war."[4] And, as it happens, Colonel Livermore has calculated[5] that Tennessee, a populous State,

[1] *M.H.S.M.*, VII, p. 14. [3] *M.H.S.M.*, VII, p. 35.
[2] *M.H.S.M.*, VIII, p. 142. [4] *M.H.S.M.*, VII, pp. 25, 26.
[5] *M.H.S.M.*, VII, p. 26.

could furnish 175,000 men of between the ages of eighteen and forty-five, and as at this time there were between fifty and seventy-five thousand Tennesseans in the Confederate army, Grant's victory at Donelson not only opened the way to Vicksburg, Chattanooga, Atlanta, and *Johnston's* surrender at Durham Station, but it deprived the South of at least 100,000 soldiers.

CHAPTER V

BATTLE OF SHILOH

Origins of the Battle

The fall of Fort Donelson found Halleck completely bewildered ; not only did he fail to realise the importance of this victory, but he was quite unprepared to take advantage of it. Grant had persistently advocated the operation, and Halleck had as persistently opposed it. Then, without obtaining McClellan's approval, he suddenly agreed to it with the result that Buell's operations, following Thomas's victory at Mill Springs, were unhinged ; McClellan had to abandon the invasion of east Tennessee ; Buell, being too scattered, could not take advantage of the Confederate defeat, and Halleck, himself imagining that he was unable to spare troops from Missouri, did nothing. Thus it came about that Grant remained isolated, and had *Johnston*, at Nashville, been a really able general he was in an excellent position to concentrate a superior force against him, and had he done so he might well have retrieved his misfortunes. Such was the muddle resulting from Halleck's generalship.

On the day before the surrender of Donelson, Halleck had written to McClellan saying : " I have no definite plan beyond the taking of Fort Donelson and Clarksville."[1] Well might McClellan exclaim : " Of all the men whom I have encountered in high position, Halleck was the most hopelessly stupid. It was more difficult to get an idea through his head than can be conceived by anyone who never made the attempt. I do not think he ever had a correct military idea from beginning to end."[2] Grant saw quite clearly what should be done, but Halleck did not trouble to seek his advice. He saw that " the way was open to the National forces all over the

[1] 7 *W.R.*, p. 616.   [2] *Church*, p. 118.

South-west,"[1] and had they vigorously pursued *Johnston*, Chattanooga, Corinth, Memphis, and Vicksburg would have been theirs. Halleck had, however, no .plan, and when, in reply to his letter of February 15, McClellan directed him to move on Nashville by the quickest route,[2] fearing *Beauregard*, who at Columbus was in a precarious position, instead he kept Grant at Fort Donelson, and when Clarksville was occupied he sent Foote's gunboats back to Cairo. For ten days after the fall of Donelson he remained without a plan. He argued that Buell should go to Nashville, and writing to the Assistant Secretary of War he said : he could only " go ahead," if he (the Secretary) would " divide the responsibility with [him] me."[3] As Ropes remarks : " A most singular proposition for a general to make."[4] On February 24, three days after this amazing suggestion, *Johnston* abandoned Nashville.

What was the reason for this delay ? Stupidity in the first instance, and jealousy in the second—the result of no unity of command in the West. For long Halleck had striven to gain this command for himself, and had he sent Grant forward, this general would have come under Buell's orders. Buell, in his turn, did not want to be absorbed by a self-seeking and incompetent pedant. In place of pushing on to Nashville, Halleck sent letter after letter to the War Department urging that he should be given the command of all the troops west of the Alleghanies.[5] Eventually, after McClellan had been relieved of his appointment of general-in-chief, and General Curtis's victory at Pea Ridge (March 7 and 8) had reflected further glory upon Halleck, on March 11[6] President Lincoln wisely decided to put an end to dual command in the West, and created the Department of the Mississippi. He made, however, the egregious mistake of appointing Halleck to command it.

---

[1] *Grant*, I, p. 317. *See* also 7 *W.R.*, p. 648.
[2] 7 *W.R.*, p. 625.
[3] 7 *W.R.*, p. 648.
[4] *Ropes*, II, p. 48.
[5] 7 *W.R.*, pp. 636, 641, 655.
[6] The date of War Order No. 3, by which McClellan was relieved from the supreme command of the armies.

Whilst this unsoldierlike wrangle was in progress, on February 24 Buell occupied Nashville, from where no pursuit of *Johnston* was attempted, as it was considered that the roads were in too bad a condition for such a task. Meanwhile *Johnston*, in spite of the roads, moved the bulk of his forces from Nashville on February 18, and marching to Murfreesboro, and then through Shelbyville and Decatur, he arrived with 20,000 men at Corinth a month later. Here he was met by *Bragg* with 10,000 well-drilled troops, and shortly afterwards was joined by *Cheatham's* division from Columbus,[1] troops from Island No. 10, and various other detachments.

The pursuit being deemed impossible, Buell suggested that a blow should be directed against the Memphis—Charleston railroad, which, at Corinth, was intersected by the railway running from the State of Mississippi through Jackson, in Tennessee, to near New Madrid and Island No. 10, where Confederate works closed the Mississippi to the Federal fleet ; at this time, these works were being besieged by General Pope. Buell's aim was to strike at a point which *Johnston* would be compelled to defend, and so forced to accept battle. On the contrary, Halleck proposed to move his army up the Tennessee, not to bring the Confederates to battle, but with the sole object of making a series of raids against their communications. His instructions were emphatic, namely, on no account was a general engagement to be brought on.[2]

On March 1, Halleck decided[2] to carry out these raids, which were to destroy the railway bridges over Bear Creek, and the connections at Corinth, Jackson, and Humboldt. The following day he telegraphed to McClellan accusing Grant of insubordination, of refusing to answer his letters, and of sitting down and enjoying his recent victory " without any regard to the future."[3] On the 4th he telegraphed Grant : " You will place Maj.-Gen. C. F. Smith in command of expedition and remain yourself at Fort Henry.[1] Why do

---

[1] Evacuated on March 2.   [2] 7 *W.R.*, p. 674.

[3] For this amazing accusation, see *Grant*, I, p. 326 ; *Badeau*, I, pp. 60–5 ; *M.H.S.M.*, VII, p. 37 and p. 108 ; and 7 *W.R.*, pp. 679, 680, 682, and 683.

you not obey my orders to report strength and positions of your command ? " [2] Consequently Smith was ordered[3] to lead the raiding forces up the Tennessee ; which operation was fated to result in the battle of Shiloh.

PITTSBURG LANDING

In the vicinity of Fort Henry five divisions were assembled, namely, those of Generals Smith, McClernand, Lewis Wallace, Hurlbut, and Sherman. On March 5 the advanced party arrived at Savannah, the main body following on the 11th. Three days later General Smith sent Sherman's division to destroy the railway near Eastport. It moved up the Tennessee thirty-two miles above Savannah, and, on the 15th, attempted to march to Iuka and destroy the railroad at that place. On account of torrents of rain this attempt failed, and, as the transports on their return passed Pittsburg Landing, nine miles above Savannah and on the western bank, Lieutenant-Commander Gwin, of the gunboat *Tyler*, pointed this place out to Sherman, and told him that on March 1 he had had a small fight there. Thereupon Sherman suggested to Smith to send a division to this landing so that another attempt on the Memphis—Charleston railroad might be made. Smith agreed to this, and sent Hurlbut's.[4] Thus, through a pure accident Pittsburg Landing was occupied.

The eventual assembly of the army at this place has been much criticised, criticism being influenced far more by the battle which was fought than by the object of the expedition. As General Force says: " The divisions were not camped with a view to defence against an apprehended attack; but they did fulfil General Halleck's instructions to General C. F.

---

[1] Then under water six feet deep.

[2] *Grant*, I, p. 326 ; 11 *W.R.*, p. 3. Why did General Halleck pick this quarrel with Grant ? The reason is obvious : because he was jealous of him. He was afraid that Grant might gain fresh laurels, and possibly supersede him. Directly he was appointed Commander-in-Chief of the Federal forces in the West (March 11), he reinstated Grant (March 13) and lied to him in order to excuse his behaviour (*Grant*, I, p. 327). As Lieut.-Colonel Ephraim C. Dawes says : " Perhaps he no longer feared him as a possible rival." (*M.H.S.M.*, VII, p. 108.)

[3] 7 *W.R.*, p. 638.　　　　[4] *M.H.S.M.*, VII, pp. 109, 110.

Smith, to select a depot with a view to the march on to Corinth."[1] Not only was the camping ground extensive,[2] but the locality itself was extremely strong defensively,[3] as it was flanked on the east by the Tennessee and Lick Creek, and on the west by Snake and Owl Creeks. It is true that the river lay behind the encampments; but this disadvantage, should a withdrawal become necessary, was largely mitigated by the Federal command of the river, as well as the eventual support of Buell.

When Grant arrived at Savannah, as he did on March 17,[4] he found Sherman's and Hurlbut's divisions encamped at Pittsburg Landing on the two roads leading to Corinth. Lewis Wallace's division was at Crump's Landing, and the remainder of the troops, including the newly formed division of Prentiss, at Savannah. Realising the faulty tactical distribution of the army, for the river divided it, within an hour of landing Grant ordered McClernand's, Prentiss's,[5] and Smith's[6] divisions to move to Pittsburg Landing, the first to encamp in rear of Sherman, the second in front of Hurlbut, and the third in rear of these two.

On the day Grant arrived at Savannah Sherman wrote to him as follows :

" I have just returned from a reconnaissance towards Corinth and Purdy, and am strongly impressed with the importance of this position, both from its land advantages and its strategic position. The ground itself admits of easy defense by a small command, and yet affords admirable camping-ground for a hundred-thousand men."[7]

---

[1] *Force*, p. 103.   [2] 10 *W.R.*, p. 27.

[3] Colonel *William P. Johnston* says : " A formidable, natural fortification. With few and difficult approaches guarded on either flank by impassable streams and morasses, protected by a succession of ravines and acclivities, each commanded by eminences to the rear, this quadrilateral seemed a safe fastness against attack ; hard to assail, easy to defend. Its selection was the dying gift of the soldierly C. F. Smith to his cause."

[4] 11 *W.R.*, p. 43.

[5] 11 *W.R.*, p. 52. Prentiss's division was formed from various regiments sent to Savannah to reinforce Grant.

[6] While C. F. Smith was in command of the expedition, W. H. L. Wallace commanded his division, and succeeded Smith when shortly afterwards he went sick and died.   [1] 10 *W.R.*, p. 27.

Halleck had instructed Grant to act on the defensive, and not to bring about a general engagement until Buell should arrive[1]—Buell having been ordered by Halleck to march on Savannah. Though Grant considered that an immediate advance would find the enemy unprepared, he had no choice but to obey. On the 18th Halleck telegraphed him : It was reported that the enemy had moved from Corinth in order to cut off the transports below Savannah ; then he added : " If so General Smith should immediately destroy the railroad communication at Corinth."[2] Grant, chafing under enforced inaction, determined to carry out this work himself, and so wrote to Halleck informing him that he intended to start on the 23rd or 24th.[3] Halleck, surprised by this promptness, replied on the 21st : " Corinth cannot be taken without a general engagement, which from your instructions is to be avoided."[4] Thereupon Grant, on the 23rd, wrote to Smith :

" Carry out your idea of occupying, and particularly, fortifying Pea Ridge. . . . I am clearly of the opinion that the enemy are gathering strength at Corinth, quite as rapidly as we are here, and the sooner we attack, the easier will be the task of taking the place."[5]

There is much to be said for both these courses. From one point of view Halleck was right in considering that the whole of his forces should be concentrated before an advance was made on Corinth ; from another, Grant was right in suggesting an immediate advance before the enemy could concentrate his forces. Halleck was suffering from over-caution, his chronic complaint ; Grant, so I think, from over-confidence begotten of his comparatively easy victories at Forts Henry and Donelson, which led him to underrate *Johnston's* pugnacity. Halleck's plan was still based on the idea of a raid ; yet he was now engaged in massing an over-whelming force in the neighbourhood of Savannah. It would appear that his strategical outlook was, as usual,

[1] 11 *W.R.*, p. 51.   [4] 7 *W.R.*, p. 674.
[2] 11 *W.R.*, p. 46.   [5] 11 *W.R.*, p. 62.
[3] 11 *W.R.*, p. 51.

completely out of focus, and that Grant, fully occupied in organising and drilling his army (numbers of his men had never fired a shot), was daily expecting the order to advance —to carry out the raid and not to fight a decisive battle. Though Grant's lack of caution and his eventual surprise can in no way be exonerated, it is frequently overlooked that Halleck was in command ; that his controlling idea was a raid ; that he had authorised the concentration of Grant's 68,000 [1] men at Pittsburg Landing, and that he had ordered Buell to proceed to Savannah with 37,000 more.   Further, he must have realised that the Confederate forces at Corinth were demoralised,[2] and, consequently, a rapid raid might well prove successful ; but if it could not be carried out, then the whole project ought to have been abandoned.

On March 18 three of Buell's divisions were at Columbia, ninety miles from Savannah ; Grant might expect therefore their arrival by the 24th or 25th.   Unfortunately the bridges over the Duck river (Columbia) had been burnt by the Confederates and this delayed Buell's advance by ten days.   On March 27 McClernand, having recently been promoted to the rank of Major-General, claimed by seniority the command of the troops at Pittsburg Landing ; whereupon Grant informed Halleck that when Buell arrived he would move his headquarters to the Landing, and command in person, as he did not trust McClernand.   On April 4 Buell telegraphed Grant that he would arrive at Savannah the following day.[3]

On March 23, as we have seen, Grant had instructed Smith to fortify Pea Ridge—this was never done.   Further, in his *Memoirs* he says that he ordered McPherson, his only military engineer, to lay out a line to entrench, but, on

---

[1] 12,000 were absent, and 12,000 unfit for duty (10 *W.R.*, p. 112).

[2] On March 18 General *Bragg* says : " The disorganised and demoralised condition of our forces . . . gives me great concern " (11 *W.R.*, p. 340). When Buell was sent forward, Halleck appears to have changed his mind, for according to Buell he was not intended to succour Grant's army, but to form a junction with it " for an ulterior offensive campaign." Halleck does not, however, appear to have warned Grant of this change, or to have considered him in any danger.

[3] 11 *W.R.*, p. 91.

McPherson's advice, he cancelled this order because this line would have had to be dug in rear of the encampments, and because, as he writes : " I regarded the campaign we were engaged in as an offensive one and had no idea that the enemy would leave strong entrenchments to take the initiative when he knew he would be attacked where he was if he remained."[1] This, in my opinion, is the true reason why the encampments were not entrenched—Grant did not believe that the enemy would dare to attack. Ropes blames Halleck ; he says : " It was due to his negligence that this position was not entrenched, for only once did he allude in his letters to Grant to the necessity of taking this obvious precaution."[2] This I consider unfair criticism, for a subordinate should not require to be told so elementary a fact. Grant should have entrenched, not to fight a defensive battle but an offensive one, in the event of his being attacked, in other words : so that he would be able to develop his offensive power from a secure base. The truth of the matter is, as he says himself—and Grant is nothing if he is not frank : " Up to that time the pick and spade had been but little resorted to at the West."[3]

Grant, who visited Pittsburg Landing daily, on April 4 met with an unfortunate accident. Whilst riding to the front, where some firing was heard, his horse stumbled, came down, and he was severely bruised. He says : " My ankle was very much injured, so much so that my boot had to be cut off. For two or three days after I was unable to walk except with crutches."[4] On the 5th General Nelson with a division of Buell's army arrived at Savannah, and was at once ordered by Grant to move up the east bank of the river where he could, as occasion required, be ferried to Crump's or Pittsburg Landing. Learning that Buell would be at Savannah the next day, and that he desired to meet him,[5]

---

[1] *Grant*, I, p. 333.   [2] *Ropes*, Pt. II, p. 59.
[3] *Grant*, I, p. 357. *Lee* made the same mistake at Antietam.
[4] *Grant*, I, p. 335; 11 *W.R.*, p. 93.
[5] Buell arrived at Savannah on the evening of the 5th, but he did not report to Grant that night.

Grant, returning to Savannah late on the 5th, breakfasted at an early hour on the 6th, and, in spite of his crushed leg, was about to mount his horse in order to ride over to Buell's headquarters, when he heard heavy firing from the direction of Pittsburg Landing. At once he sent an order to General Nelson to move to the river bank opposite Pittsburg, and wrote a hasty letter to Buell explaining the situation. Then, at 7 a.m., by transport he started for the front, called at Crump's Landing and instructed Lewis Wallace to hold himself in readiness to move at short notice. At 8 o'clock he was at Pittsburg Landing.

THE FEDERAL SURPRISE

On March 24[1] *Johnston* arrived at Corinth, completing his concentration on the next day. General *Bragg*, who had preceded him, wished to attack the Federal forces at Pittsburg and Crump's Landings, but *Beauregard* objected to this ; for, at the time, he considered it wiser to let the Federals advance on Corinth, and then attempt to cut them off from their base on the river. Later, he changed his mind ; for, according to General *Jordan*, it was *Polk* and *Beauregard* who initiated the final idea of an advance, though *Johnston* at first did not like it.[2] Late on April 2 *Johnston*, learning that Buell was advancing rapidly " from Columbia, by Clifton, on Savannah,"[3] at 1 a.m. on the 3rd ordered his troops to hold themselves in readiness to move at short notice, with five days' rations and one hundred rounds of ammunition.[4] In this *Johnston* was supported by *Lee*, who wrote to him on March 26 saying : " I need not urge you, when your army is united, to deal a blow at the enemy in your front, if

---

[1] *Force*, p. 108. *Ropes* (II, p. 61) says March 18 and quotes 7 *W.R.*, p. 259, which states that the head of his column under *Bragg* arrived there on this day.

[2] *B. & L.*, I, pp. 594, 595.

[3] 11 *W.R.*, p. 387. He was advancing, but not rapidly.

[4] According to Colonel Ephraim C. Dawes (*M.H.S.M.*, VII, p. 132), *Johnston*, after a full discussion with General *Bragg* and General *Jordan* (the Assistant Adjutant-General of the Army), decided to make the attack. (See *Beauregard*, I, p. 270, and *Sidney Johnston*, p. 551.)

possible, before his rear gets up from Nashville. You have him divided, and keep him so if you can."[1]

According to his son :

" General *Johnston's* plan of campaign may be summed up in a phrase : It was to concentrate at Corinth and interpose his whole force in front of the great bend of the Tennessee, the natural base of the Federal army : this effected, to crush Grant in battle before the arrival of Buell."[2]

This was to be accomplished by turning Grant's left, throw him back on Owl Creek, and so cut him off from the Tennessee.

In the afternoon the advance began, the intention being to attack Grant on the morning of the 5th. Shiloh Church, a small wooden building two and a half miles south-west of Pittsburg Landing and within Sherman's front line, was but twenty-three miles away. The roads were, however, in bad condition, and the march discipline of *Johnston's* men was so indifferent that they covered only a few miles on the 4th. Against a vigilant enemy all surprise would have been lost, but fortune was to favour the Confederates, and when the advance was resumed on the 5th, *Johnston* was so confident of success that he said : " I intend to hammer 'em. I think we will hammer them beyond doubt." That night *Hardee's* pickets were so close to the encampments of Sherman and Prentiss, that drums were heard beating retreat and tattoo, " and a band serenading some newly arrived general made music for the enemy as well as for the recipient of the compliment."[3] Meanwhile, numbers of rabbits and squirrels, disturbed by the Confederate advance, scudded in and out of the Federal lines.

Before I examine the causes of one of the most complete surprises recorded in the history of this war, I will briefly describe the nature of the battlefield, and detail the strength of the opposing armies.

Few positions could be found so favourable for defence, and so unfavourable for attack, as that of the battlefield of

---

[1] *Force*, p. 110.   [2] *B. & L.*, I., p. 550.   [3] *M.H.S.M.*, VII, p. 57.

Shiloh, or Pittsburg Landing. The ground was thickly wooded and broken, interspersed with patches of cultivation, and cut up by streams and ravines. The Federal flanks were secured by the Tennessee and Lick Creek on the left, and by Owl Creek and Snake Creek on the right. A series of ravines skirted the front, and another series, about a mile behind this front, formed an admirable second line of defence. Such a position, unless it could be surprised, was to all intents and purposes invulnerable to frontal attack—it was a natural fortress which a few trenches and a little abattis would have rendered impregnable to assault.[1]

The composition of the two armies was as follows : *Johnston's*—72 regiments and 7 battalions of infantry, 8 regiments of cavalry, and 19 batteries of artillery, in all 40,335 men. Grant's—63 regiments of infantry, portions of 4 regiments of cavalry, and 21 batteries, in all 44,895 men.[2] In Sherman's and Prentiss's divisions the majority of the men were raw recruits. In Sherman's Colonel Stone informs us that not a man had as yet been in action, and that only two of his regiments were commanded by officers who had received any military training.[3] Colonel Peter J. Sullivan of the 48th Ohio often addressed his men as " gentlemen," and would say, " please to present arms."[4] In spite of these raw men and untrained officers, Sherman, in place of taking the utmost precaution to guard himself against surprise, fell under the extraordinary obsession that a Confederate attack was a sheer impossibility. I will briefly examine this spell, for it constitutes an interesting psychological study.[5]

Whoever is in supreme command is ultimately responsible for failure. Halleck was in supreme command, but I consider that, as he was at St. Louis and had only recently taken

---

[1] For a full description of the ground, see *M.H.S.M.*, VII, pp. 44–5, and *Badeau*, I, pp. 73–4.

[2] *M.H.S.M.*, VII, p. 52. See also, 10 *W.R.*, p. 112 ; and *Force*, pp. 113–16. *Grant* (I, p. 366) gives his strength at 38,000.

[3] *M.H.S.M.*, VII, p. 46. [4] *M.H.S.M.*, VII, p. 124.

[5] Grant always denied that he was surprised. After the battle a visitor said to him : " General Grant, were you not surprised by the Confederates ? " To which Grant answered : " No, but I am now." See Appendix I.

over the Department of the Mississippi, it would be most
unfair to blame him. Grant was at Savannah. He should
most certainly have ordered his subordinate commanders to
entrench themselves, and though he must share the onus of
failure with Sherman, Sherman's reports entirely misled him.
Grant is to blame for not entrenching ; for not appointing a
second in command to act for him when he was away from
Pittsburg Landing, and for not issuing instructions as to the
action to be taken in the event of an attack. He was, however, not to blame for the surprise itself.

In his *Memoirs* General Sherman writes :

" I always acted on the supposition that we were an
invading army ; that our purpose was to move forward in
force, make a lodgment on the Memphis and Charleston road,
and thus repeat the grand tactics of Fort Donelson, by
separating the rebels in the interior from those at Memphis
and on the Mississippi River."

All this is excellent, but then he adds :

" We did not fortify our camps against an attack, because
we had no orders to do so, and because such a course would
have made our raw men timid."[1]

Such an excuse cannot be accepted, for the first order
Sherman issued after the battle was that :

" Each brigade commander will examine carefully his
immediate front, fell trees to afford his men a barricade, and
clear away all underbush for 200 yards in front, so as to
uncover an approaching enemy. With these precautions
we can hold our camp against any amount of force that can be
brought against us."[2]

Sherman, rightly, was in the habit of sending out daily
reconnaissances, and this fact makes his obsession all the
more extraordinary. On the 4th it was reported that the
enemy were in considerable strength at Pea Ridge. A
prisoner corroborated this information, but he would not

---

[1] *Sherman*, I, p. 229.
[2] 11 *W.R.*, p. 103. An officer on General *Beauregard's* staff wrote : " The
total absence of cavalry pickets from General Grant's army was a matter
of perfect amazement." (*Boynton*, p. 34.)

believe him. On this same day one of Colonel Appler's pickets was fired on, whereupon Appler ordered his regiment, the 53rd Ohio, into line, and sent his quartermaster to inform Sherman of the fact. Sherman said to him : "Tell Colonel Appler to take his d—d regiment to Ohio. There is no force of the enemy nearer than Corinth."[1] On the 5th, when *Johnston's* leading troops were but two miles from his camp, Sherman wrote to Grant :

"I have no doubt nothing will occur to-day more than the usual picket firing. The enemy is saucy, but got the worst of it yesterday, and will not press our pickets far. I will not be drawn out far unless with certainty of advantage, and I do not apprehend anything like an attack on our position."[2]

Grant was so misled by Sherman's confidence, that when General Nelson arrived at Savannah on the 5th, and suggested that his division should cross at once to Pittsburg Landing, Grant promised to send transports on "Monday or Tuesday, or some time early in the week," as "there will be no fight at Pittsburg Landing; we will have to go to Corinth, where the rebels are fortified. If they come to attack us we can whip them, as I have more than twice as many troops as I had at Fort Donelson."[3] And that evening he wrote to Halleck : "Our outposts had been attacked by the enemy apparently in considerable force. I immediately went up, but found all quiet. . . . I have scarcely the faintest idea of an attack [general one] being made upon us."[4]

Early on the 6th Colonel Peabody, of the 25th Missouri regiment, sent out a reconnaissance which was at once driven back. General Prentiss called out to him : "What do you mean by bringing on an engagement, when you know we are not ready ?" Colonel Peabody answered sharply : "I did not bring it on. It is coming without my assistance."[5] Then the Confederate skirmishers emerged from the bushes, and Sherman seeing them exclaimed : "My God ! we are attacked."[6] At last his eyes were opened.

[1] *M.H.S.M.*, VII, p. 117.
[2] 11 *W.R.*, pp. 93, 94. He suspected, however, the proximity of small bodies of the enemy.   [3] 10 *W.R.*, p. 331.
[4] 10 *W.R.*, p. 89.   [5] *M.H.S.M.*, VII, p. 59.   [6] *M.H.S.M.*, VII, p. 141.

As the Confederates fired into Sherman's and Prentiss's encampments, a severe but disjointed fight took place which ended in a general stampede : breakfasts were left on the mess tables, the baggage unpacked, and knapsacks, stores, colours, and ammunition were abandoned.[1] At the time there were hundreds of sick in the camp,[2] and such of these men who could walk, hospital attendants, teamsters, cooks, officers' servants, and sutlers rushed to the rear, throwing into confusion, and sometimes into panic, whole regiments as they turned out to form up. Such was the Federal surprise at about 6 a.m. on April 6.

GRANT'S MOVEMENTS ON APRIL 6

Johnston's attack formation was in three lines preceded by a strong swarm of skirmishers. Each line was approximately 10,000 strong, a distance of about 500 yards being maintained between them, with some 7,000 men in reserve. The first line consisted of *Hardee's* corps, to which was added a brigade from *Bragg's* ; the second, of the remainder of *Bragg's* corps ; and the third, of *Polk's* corps, and *Breckinridge's* division.[3] This formation was ill-suited to the wooded and broken ground, for, as the army advanced, an inextricable commingling of commands took place, such confusion resulting that the three corps commanders agreed to divide the tangled mass of men between them, *Hardee* taking charge of the left, *Polk* of the centre, and *Bragg* of the right.[4]

I do not intend to describe in detail the fighting on the 6th, for it was a struggle of brute force, and a battle of broken combats. Both sides were surprised : the Federals because they were unprepared for the attack; the Confederates because they ignored to adapt their tactics to the ground, and because *Johnston's* generalship was of the most ′meagre order. In fact, from the opening of the battle until his death, he

[1] *B. & L.*, I, p. 559.
[2] *M.H.S.M.*, VII, p. 141. In all there were about 11,000 non-combatants in the camps. (See 10 *W.R.*, p. 112.) Probably the unwounded stragglers numbered some 4,000 to 5,000.
[3] 10 *W.R.*, p. 386. (*Beauregard's* Report.)
[4] 10 *W.R.*, p. 408. (*Polk's* Report.)

¹ *M.H.S.M.*, VII, p. 14.   ³ *M.H.S.M.*, VII, p. 35.
² *M.H.S.M.*, VIII, p. 142.   ⁴ *M.H.S.M.*, VII, pp. 25, 26.
        ⁵ *M.H.S.M.*, VII, p. 26.

[1] 11 *W.R.*, p. 51.
[2] 11 *W.R.*, p. 46.
[3] 11 *W.R.*, p. 51.
[4] 7 *W.R.*, p. 674.
[5] 11 *W.R.*, p. 62.

plantation, from where on the 29th it was moved in transports to Hard Times.   Here it was landed and re-embarked
in readiness to move over to Grand Gulf.   Porter then
opened fire on the batteries ; but finding that his bombardment had little effect, because they were sited high up on
the bluff, Grant decided to re-land his troops and move the
transports past the batteries under cover of night.   At first
he intended to move as far south as Rodney, but learning
from a negro that above Rodney a landing could be effected
at Bruinsburg, from where a good road led to Port Gibson,
he decided to land here and so place his army in rear of the
Grand Gulf bluff.

Early on the morning of the 30th McClernand's corps
and one division of McPherson's corps re-embarked at De
Shroon's and landed on the eastern bank of the river at
Bruinsburg.   Meanwhile, Sherman with Blair's division and
eight gunboats made a vigorous demonstration against
Haines's Bluff in order to distract *Pemberton's* attention from
his left flank.

When this landing was effected, writes Grant :

" I felt a degree of relief scarcely ever equalled since.
Vicksburg was not yet taken it is true, nor were its defenders
demoralised by any of our previous moves.   I was now in
the enemy's country, with a vast river and the stronghold
of Vicksburg between me and my base of supplies.   But I
was on dry ground on the same side of the river with the
enemy.   All the campaigns, labours, hardships and exposures
from the month of December previous to this time that
had been made and endured, *were for the accomplishment of
this one object*." [1]

The Rear Attack

Four months of ruse and feints, of wrestling with swamps,
bayous and forests, of labours seldom equalled in war, were
the mist which covered this landing.   *Pemberton* had been
completely misled ; concentrating his forces between Grand
Gulf and Haines's Bluff, his left flank was but lightly guarded,
and was at once turned by the first flight of the invading

[1] *Grant*, I, pp. 480, 481. Italics are mine.

army. By 2 a.m., on May 1, McClernand's leading division
had advanced eight miles east of Bruinsburg ; there it came
into contact with the enemy, who attempted to hold up
Grant's advance on the Bayou Pierre until reinforcements
could arrive from Vicksburg. At dawn the battle of Port
Gibson opened ; and, at 10 a.m., Grant, with no escort
but his staff, arrived on the field, and at once assumed command. Seeing that McClernand could not dislodge the
enemy on his left, Grant ordered up two brigades of Logan's
division of McPherson's corps, and turned the enemy's
right flank. The Confederates then evacuated Port Gibson,
and retiring northwards over the Bayou Pierre destroyed
the bridges as they fell back. McPherson was at once sent
in pursuit, and, on the 3rd, drove the Confederate forces
over the Big Black river, with the result that Grand Gulf
threatened in rear was evacuated ; whereupon Grant having
secured his bridge-head, at once moved his depots from
Bruinsburg to this place.

Grant was now faced by a problem unique in the history
of war. He was operating in an enemy's country with his
enemy's main forces located between his base of supply at
Memphis and his base of operations at Grand Gulf. The
fleet commanded the Mississippi, but to depend on this line
of supply meant the eventual crippling or loss of many ships,
as well as daily uncertainty in the delivery of supplies ; for
every convoy had to be escorted past the Vicksburg batteries,
and casualties inevitably resulted. Vicksburg was not only
immensely strong, but was connected by railway to the
interior, with Jackson a most important junction but forty-
five miles east of it. Consequently, either the fortress could
be rapidly reinforced, or, should the Confederates concentrate an army at Jackson, Grant might easily be caught
between two fires. On April 30 Colonel Livermore [1]
estimates the opposing forces as follows : Grant—51,000
operating against Vicksburg and Grand Gulf; 5,000 at
Helena, 33,000 between Memphis and Corinth, and 8,000
in western Kentucky and Tennessee. *Pemberton*—17,000 at

[1] *Livermore*, Pt. III, Bk. II, p. 271.

Vicksburg and Haines's Bluff, 9,000 between Vicksburg and Port Gibson, 5,000 at Jackson and 10,000 scattered through the State of Mississippi. In the vicinity of Vicksburg *Pemberton* could concentrate, therefore, from thirty to forty thousand men to meet Grant's 51,000.[1] Though largely outnumbered, his position, according to all the rules of war, was by no means a hopeless one, for Grant was operating in an enemy's country, and presumably would have to make large detachments in order to protect his line of supply. Further still, the country was broken and wooded, and therefore admirably suited to defensive warfare. To hold Grant at Vicksburg whilst forces were concentrating at Jackson did not appear to him to be a difficult task.

Grant's problem was the reverse, in fact it would be almost impossible to devise a more desperate one. The whole of his strategy pivoted on the question of supply. At first, he proposed [2] to detach an army corps of some 15,000 men to move down the Mississippi, and co-operate with General Banks against Port Hudson. Should this place be captured, then he could change his base of supply from Memphis to New Orleans, and once this was done, his army corps would return and his operations could begin. Though this plan was in agreement with conventional strategy, he abandoned it,[3] because Banks informed him that he would not be ready to move on Port Hudson until May 10, and, then, only with 15,000 men. Fully appreciating the time factor, Grant says : " I therefore determined to move independently of Banks, cut loose from my base, destroy the rebel forces in rear of Vicksburg and invest or capture the city." [4] In brief—to attack the enemy in rear. As we shall see, not only in this campaign but at Chattanooga

---

[1] As is usual in this war, it is most difficult to arrive at correct strengths. Greene (p. 136) estimates *Pemberton's* force at over 50,000, and states that Grant began his campaign with about 41,000, and at no time prior to the siege had over 45,000. Grant (I, p. 481) says that on May 7 he had 33,000, and that the enemy had nearly 60,000. In *Battles and Leaders* (III, p. 549) it is stated that Grant's effective force ranged from 43,000 at the beginning to 75,000 at the close of the campaign.

[2] 38 *W.R.*, p. 192.   [3] 36 *W.R.*, p. 30.   [4] *Grant*, I, pp. 491, 492.

and in 1864–5, the central idea in Grant's strategy was to
aim at the rear attack ; that is, to strike the enemy at
the decisive (most profitable) point—his back. Simultaneously, by cutting loose from his base he protected himself against an attack in rear by leaving himself without a
rear to be attacked. This plan completely bewildered
Pemberton, who failing to grasp the audacity of Grant's
strategy, and not believing that he would dare to advance
without first securing his communications, based his operations on the assumption that such an action was impossible.

Besides the undoubted strategical soundness of Grant's
decision, as long as his army could be supplied and fed, the
political situation demanded that not a minute should be
lost.   On May 2 the disastrous battle of Chancellorsville
was begun, and if Grant did not act now, at once, not only
might he be recalled, but the terror begotten by *Lee's* bold
manœuvres might so paralyse the higher command at
Washington, that his army might be broken up.

On April 4, as we have seen, Grant informed Halleck of
his probable intentions ; but now that he was on the point
of putting them into force he kept silent.   As Badeau says :

" Believing that he would not be allowed to make the
campaign if he announced his plan beforehand, Grant did
not now inform the general-in-chief of what he contemplated.
It was fortunate that he took this precaution.   Not one
syllable of encouragement had reached him since starting
from Milliken's Bend, and the President wrote, after all was
over : ' When you got below and took Port Gibson, Grand
Gulf, and vicinity, I thought you should go down the river
and join General Banks ; and when you turned northward,
east of the Big Black, I feared it was a mistake.' " [1]

Directly Halleck (who, according to Grant, "was too learned
a soldier to consent to a campaign in violation of all the
principles of the art of war ") [2] learnt of Grant's movement,
he at once sent him orders to return and co-operate with
Banks.   Fortunately there was no telegraph line in operation
south of Cairo, and this order reaching Grant after his move-

---

[1] *Badeau*, I, p. 221 ; 109 *W.R.*, p. 406.   [2] *Church*, p. 163.

ment had begun could not be obeyed. "Had the general-in-chief, however, been able to reach his subordinate, the Vicksburg campaign would never have been fought." [1]

Grant's position at this moment was indeed one of the most extraordinary ever faced by a general. He was confronted, so he calculated at the time, by a force double his own. He knew that the Government, reeling under Hooker's defeat at Chancellorsville, must be aghast at the news that he was about to plunge into the region of the Mississippi, and cut loose from his communications in face of two hostile armies, one pivoted on a powerful fortress and the other on an important railroad junction. His army was without proper transport :

" . . . the ammunition train was a curious assemblage of fine carriages, farm wagons, long coupled wagons with racks for carrying cotton bales,—every vehicle, indeed, that could be found on the plantations which had been used either for work or pleasure. These vehicles were a nondescript outfit, drawn by oxen and mules wearing plough harness, or straw collars and rope lines." [2]

On April 29 Grant had ordered [3] Sherman to cease his demonstration against Haines's Bluff, and to march with all haste to Hard Times. On May 3 he directed [4] him to organise a supply train of 120 vehicles, and ferry them over to Grand Gulf where they were to be loaded with 100,000 rations from the transports. This would give five days' rations for Sherman's corps, and two days' for McClernand's and McPherson's, these two corps having already three days' rations with them. These were all the rations Grant intended to carry.

Sherman expostulated. It seemed to him quite impossible to supply the army over a single road. He urged Grant to "stop all troops till your army is partially supplied with wagons, and then act as quickly as possible, for this road will be jammed, as sure as life." [5] To this Grant replied :

[1] *Badeau*, I, p. 221.   [3] 38 *W.R.*, p. 246.
[2] *Church*, p. 164.   [4] 38 *W.R.*, p. 268.
[5] 38 *W.R.*, p. 285.

" I do not calculate upon the possibility of supplying the army with full rations from Grand Gulf. I know it will be impossible without constructing additional roads. What I do expect is to get up what rations of hard bread, coffee, and salt we can, and make the country furnish the balance." [1] Well may Badeau write :

" So Grant was alone ; his most trusted subordinates besought him to change his plans, while his superiors were astounded at his temerity and strove to interfere. Soldiers of reputation and civilians in high place condemned, in advance, a campaign that seemed to them as hopeless as it was unprecedented. If he failed, the country would concur with the Government and the generals. Grant knew all this, and appreciated his danger, but was as invulnerable to the apprehensions of ambition as to the entreaties of friendship, or the anxieties, even, of patriotism. That quiet confidence in himself which never forsook him, and which amounted indeed almost to a feeling of fate, was uninterrupted. Having once determined in a matter that required irreversible decision, he never reversed, nor even misgave, but was steadily loyal to himself and his plans. This absolute and implicit faith was, however, as far as possible from conceit or enthusiasm ; it was simply a consciousness, or conviction, rather, which brought the very strength it believed in ; which was itself strength, and which inspired others with a trust in him, because he was able thus to trust himself." [2]

Such was the simple honesty and amazing fortitude of this remarkable man.

Once standing on dry ground at Port Gibson, what was Grant's plan ? His most obvious course would have been to have marched direct upon Vicksburg. He was but twelve miles from Warrenton, and the only formidable obstacle which lay in his path was the Big Black river. A *bon général ordinaire* would undoubtedly have moved north ; not so Grant. He knew that a Confederate force under *Gregg*, of what strength he was uncertain, was collecting towards the east and north-east of Vicksburg. Were he

[1] 38 *W.R.*, p. 285.   [2] *Badeau*, I, p. 222.

to advance on Vicksburg, this force would certainly move there also, and he might be outnumbered. So, instead, he determined not to push in between the two armies before they could combine, but to move on to Jackson in order to draw the Confederate forces east of Vicksburg towards that all-important junction; defeat them in its vicinity, before *Pemberton* could sally out of his fortress, and then destroy the railroad at Jackson. By so doing he would not only protect his rear when the time came for him to advance westwards against Vicksburg, but he would simultaneously cut Vicksburg off from its base of supply. In short, his idea, rather than plan, was to manœuvre against the Vicksburg line of communications in order to isolate the fortress, and, simultaneously, destroy that force of the enemy which was so placed that it could operate against his rear.

The secret of success did not, however, depend so much on the boldness of this idea, as upon the rapidity of its execution, and no man since the great Napoleon exclaimed " It may be that I shall lose a battle, but I shall never lose a minute " understood so fully the value of time as Grant did. His dispatches teem with indications of this—here are a few examples which are certainly worth quoting : To Sherman, on May 3, he wrote : " It is unnecessary for me to remind you of the overwhelming importance of celerity in your movements." [1] To Hurlbut, on the 5th : " Send Lauman's division to Milliken's Bend. . . . Let them move by brigades, as fast as transportation can be gotten." [2] To the commissary at Grand Gulf : " There must be no delay on account of either lack of energy or formality," load up " regardless of requisitions or provision returns." To an officer of his staff : " See that the commissary at Grand Gulf loads all the wagons. . . . Issue any order in my name that may be necessary to secure the greatest promptness in this respect. . . . Every day's delay is worth two thousand men to the enemy." And again on the 6th : Rush " forward rations with all dispatch. . . . How many teams have been

[1] 38 *W.R.*, p. 268.   [2] 38 *W.R.*, p. 274.

loaded with rations and sent forward ? I want to know as near as possible how we stand in every particular for supplies. How many wagons have you ferried over the river ? How many are still to bring over ? What teams have gone back for rations ? " [1] These urgent instructions remind one of Napoleon's orders, such as : " If the enemy is not at Memmingen, descend on us like lightning," and, " You see at a glance that never did circumstances demand a more active and rapid movement than this . . . activity, activity, swiftness, I commend to you ! "

Grant's tremendous energy electrified his men, everywhere was there activity. McPherson was pushed up to Hankinson's Ferry to protect the left flank ; reconnaissances were sent out daily to examine the roads and country, and foraging parties swarmed over the cultivated areas collecting supplies. Nothing was left undone which would speed up the advance, and assist in maintaining it at maximum pressure once the move forward was ordered.

On May 7, according to Livermore,[2] Grant at the head of 39,500 men was faced by the following forces : 3,600 in Vicksburg ; 2,000 at Warrenton ; 2,000 near Haines's Bluff ; 1,000 at Jackson, and 23,400 under *Pemberton* ready to advance against him. On the 6th McPherson was ordered to draw in all troops north of the Big Black, and to picket the ferries until the troops were well advanced.

Grant's plan was to keep the Big Black on his left, or strategic, flank, using it as a shield ; to advance Sherman's and McClernand's corps under cover of it to the Vicksburg-Jackson railway between Edward's Station and Bolton, whilst McPherson's corps was to move by way of Utica to Raymond, and thence on to Jackson.

On the 7th the move forward began, and on the 12th Sherman and McClernand reached Fourteen Mile Creek, and McPherson encountering *Gregg's* brigade two miles west of Raymond drove it back, and bivouacked on the outskirts of the town. Grant had now gained the position he wanted, his left flank rested on the Big Black, and his right was secured

[1] *Badeau*, I, pp. 223, 224.　　　[2] *Livermore*, Pt. III, Bk. II, p. 280.

by *Gregg's* defeat, so I will turn to his adversary and see
what he was doing.

CHAMPION'S HILL AND THE BIG BLACK RIVER

The reason why *Pemberton* was so completely surprised
by Grant's move south of Vicksburg can only be explained
by the fact that he considered it to be another of the many
feints carried out by his opponent during the winter.
Realising, on May 1, that Grant had landed in force, he
telegraphed to the War Department and to *Johnston* for
reinforcements.[1] *Johnston* at once ordered him to unite
all his troops against Grant, whilst Jefferson Davis, believing
that Grant's movement was nothing more than a raid,[2]
instructed him to hold on to Vicksburg and Port Hudson.
These orders were contradictory, and *Pemberton* being under
the impression that Grant must within a few days fall back
for lack of supplies, inclined to the second order ; this led
to his being surprised yet again. He decided, therefore,
first to hold the line of the Big Black, so that when the
opportunity arose he could fall upon Grant's line of supply
(which did not exist), and secondly, to keep open the Vicksburg—Jackson railway, which was of vital importance
to him.

On the 3rd *Pemberton* assembled the bulk of his forces
between Vicksburg and the right bank of the Big Black,
and, on the 11th, he ordered *Gregg*, if attacked, to retire
towards Jackson ; but should Grant move on Edward's
Station he instructed him to fall on his flank and rear.
On the 12th, *Gregg*, as we have seen, was compelled by
McPherson to adopt the first course.   On the 13th *Pemberton* ordered three divisions, *Bowen's*, *Loring's*, and *Stevenson's*,
to advance on Edward's Station, and, on the following day,
a position a mile south of the Station was occupied.   This
day, *Johnston* having arrived at Jackson from Tullahoma,
and finding the railway occupied by Sherman, telegraphed to

---

[1] 38 *W.R.*, pp. 807, 810, 817 ; and 36 *W.R.*, pp. 214, 259.
[2] 36 *W.R.*, p. 327.

Richmond : " I am too late," [1] and immediately ordered *Pemberton* to attack Grant in rear. He says :

" I have arrived and learn that Major-General Sherman is between us. . . . It is important to re-establish communications, that you may be reinforced. If practicable, come up on his rear at once. To beat such a detachment would be of immense value. The troops here could co-operate. All the strength you can quickly assemble should be brought. Time is all-important." [2]

Pemberton, still of opinion that Grant must fall back were he to strike at his line of supply, set aside *Johnston's* order, and informed him that, early on the 15th, 17,000 men would be moved to Dillon's—" The object is to cut the enemy's communications and force him to attack me. . . ." [3]

Meanwhile, what was Grant doing ?

On the 12th McPherson's corps was ordered to move on Clinton and destroy the railway, whilst Sherman and McClernand converged on Raymond, these movements being preparatory to the occupation of Jackson ; for as Grant says : " As I hoped in the end to besiege Vicksburg I must first destroy all possibility of aid. I therefore determined to move swiftly towards Jackson." [4] During the night of the 13th, and on the morning of the 14th, it rained in torrents, nevertheless Grant pushed on at top speed, and it was as well he did so, seeing that *Johnston*, a man of far greater ability than *Pemberton*, had already arrived.

On the 14th McPherson moved from Clinton towards Jackson, and Sherman from Mississippi Springs advanced towards the same place ; whilst McClernand protected the rear of these two divisions by sending a brigade to Clinton, and by occupying Raymond with the bulk of his force. The attack on Jackson was at first delayed by the rain, as it was feared that ammunition might be spoilt if the men opened their cartridge-boxes.[5] At 11 a.m. the battle

[1] *Davis*, II, p. 404.   [3] 36 *W.R.*, p. 262.
[2] 38 *W.R.*, p. 870.   [4] *Grant*, I, p. 499.
[5] This was before the days of metallic cartridges.

opened, and at 4 p.m. the town was carried, and thirty-five guns and several hundreds of prisoners were captured.

Forced out of Jackson, *Johnston* withdrew up the Canton road, and, on the 15th, wrote to *Pemberton* as follows : " The only mode by which we can unite is by your moving directly to Clinton, informing me, that we may move to that point with about 6,000." [1]

At this time the situation of the Confederate forces was a ludicrous one : *Johnston* was moving north to unite with *Pemberton*, and *Pemberton* was moving east and south-east from Edward's Station to cut the imaginary communications of Grant's army. On the night of the 14th *Pemberton* had 9,000 men about Vicksburg, which was not threatened, and some 14,000 were moving south of Edward's Station, whilst *Johnston*, now about Calhoun, headed 12,000, with 10,000 reinforcements on their way to join him. Thus we see 45,000 men in three detachments faced by an equal force well concentrated, and ready to strike at any one in overwhelming strength. *Pemberton*, who, on the night of the 15th, had arrived in the neighbourhood of Raymond, there received *Johnston's* second order to unite with him, and fearing to disobey it, though it was very similar to the first,[2] he abandoned his attack on Grant's line of communications and determined to move north.

The dispatch sent by *Johnston* to *Pemberton* on the 13th (38 *W.R.*, p. 870), in which he ordered him to operate against Grant's rear, was sent out by three messengers, one of whom happened to be a Federal soldier enlisted in the Confederate army. This man took his copy to General McPherson, who at once forwarded it to Grant, who received it on the evening of the 14th. Supposing that *Pemberton* would obey the order contained in it, and was now moving from Edward's Station to unite with *Johnston*, he at once issued orders for the 15th : McPherson to move back to Bolton—" the nearest point where *Johnston* could reach the road " ; McClernand to turn his forces towards Bolton, " and make all dispatch in getting there " ; whilst Sherman's corps,

[1] 38 *W.R.*, p. 882.   [2] 38 *W.R.*, p. 870.

less Blair's division, was to remain at Jackson, and destroy
the railways.[1] By the evening, Grant had concentrated
in all seven divisions, about 32,000 men, between Bolton
and Raymond, and that night he opened his headquarters
at Clinton.

Early on the 16th, whilst his pickets were skirmishing on
the Raymond road, *Pemberton* informed *Johnston* that,
as he considered he could not move on Clinton, he would
return to Edward's Station, and take the Brownsville road.

Early on the morning of the 16th Grant learnt from two
men employed on the Vicksburg—Jackson railroad that the
night before *Pemberton* with some 25,000 men was marching
eastwards. Thereupon he ordered up Steele's division of
Sherman's corps, which was on the road within an hour of
receiving the order. McPherson's corps, on the right, he
directed to advance by the Clinton road on Champion's
Hill; and McClernand's corps, on the left, to move by
the Middle and Raymond roads on Edward's Station.
By 7.30 a.m., skirmishing having begun, Grant rode forward
and joined McPherson's corps; and later on he ordered
McClernand to push forward and attack. Grant's object
was that McClernand should pin the enemy down on his
front and right, whilst McPherson turned his left. This
order was repeated several times, but with little result.

Pemberton's position was a strong one; not only did
his front command the three roads along which Grant's
leading divisions were advancing, but his left was protected
by Champion's Hill and Baker's Creek, as well as by a number
of precipitous ravines, and by woodland and much undergrowth, "difficult," as Grant says, "to penetrate with
troops even when not defended." This difficulty soon
manifested itself, and a close examination of it is illuminating,
as it explains many of the lost opportunities and wasted
attacks which were experienced a year later in the Wilderness of Virginia.

Though Smith's division on the Raymond road was the
first to encounter the enemy, its advance was painfully

[1] 38 *W.R.*, pp. 310, 311, 312.

slow, as was also that of Osterhaus on the Middle road. These divisions were confronted by a weak but well-placed force, and had McClernand ordered a charge, he would have cleared his front in a few minutes. The ground was, however, thickly wooded, and not being able to ascertain the strength of the enemy, with extreme caution he groped his way forward, and throughout the day never made his strength felt. Meanwhile, on the right, Hovey's division had become closely engaged, and to protect its right flank Logan's division was pushed beyond it to attack Champion's Hill

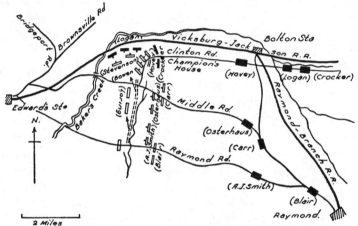

PLAN NO. 2. BATTLE OF CHAMPION'S HILL, MAY 16, 1863.

from the north. Still pressed in front, Hovey was reinforced by Crocker.

The situation was now as follows: Hovey, in spite of Crocker's assistance, could make little impression on Champion's Hill; on his left McClernand, failing to assault, in no way restricted the enemy's freedom of movement towards his left; Logan, unknown to himself, and to Grant, had worked his way behind the enemy on Champion's Hill, and was actually in line parallel to their rear, and in command of the only road by which *Pemberton* could retreat. Further still, a brigade of McArthur's division, which a few days before had crossed over to Grand Gulf, was coming up on McClernand's left flank. Unknown to Grant, *Pemberton's* army was to all intents and purposes surrounded, when Hovey once again calling for reinforcements, Grant, fearing that his front might be broken, ordered McPherson to disengage part of Logan's division and move it round to his support. An assault was then made, and the enemy driven back, not because of it, but because their line of retreat was now opened. Grant at once sent forward Osterhaus's and Carr's divisions in pursuit, ordering them to push on to the Big Black, and to cross that river if they could. That night McPherson's command bivouacked six miles west of the battlefield, and Carr and Osterhaus at Edward's Station. The losses in this battle were as follows : Grant's army, 2,438, and *Pemberton's* 4,082.[1]

Of the battle Grant writes : " Had McClernand come up with reasonable promptness, or had I known the ground as I did afterwards, I cannot see how Pemberton could have escaped with any organised force." [2] This is probably true, nevertheless it should not be inferred that McClernand was altogether an indifferent general ; he was not brilliant, but there were many less competent than he. He wasted several hours in slowly reconnoitring and working forward, and in no way assisted the attack on Champion's Hill (the losses in his division were only 158 men) ; but had he assaulted, and had he found the enemy strongly posted, he might well have been driven back with heavy losses and would have been blamed for his failure to reconnoitre. Again, Grant had no maps, and did not know the country ; further, it was so blind, that when Logan straddled *Pemberton's* line of retreat he did not realise that he had done so. These two facts, namely, the difficulties of reconnaissance,[3] and the dangers of assaulting in a wooded country, must always be borne in mind when examining the battles of this war ; for if they are overlooked, not only will tactical

---

[1] *Livermore*, Pt. III, Bk. II, p. 310.   [2] *Grant*, I, pp. 519, 520.

[3] Grant says (36 *W.R.*, p. 53): " The delay in the advance of the troops immediately with McClernand was caused, no doubt, by the enemy presenting a front of artillery and infantry where it was impossible, from the nature of the ground and the density of the forest, to discover his numbers."

lessons be missed, but many of the actions fought will appear ridiculous.

Defeated at Champion's Hill, *Pemberton* abandoned his intention to move north and unite his forces with those of *Johnston*. It is true he could no longer move by the Brownsville road, but he could have retired under cover of darkness across the Big Black, burnt the bridges, and abandoning Vicksburg have saved his army by moving north and then east towards Canton. Instead, he fell back on the Big Black, and reported to *Johnston* that he had about sixty days' rations at Vicksburg, but that, when Grant advanced, he would have to abandon Haines's Bluff. *Johnston* replied : " If it is not too late, evacuate Vicksburg and its dependencies, and march to the north-east." [1] This message was received by *Pemberton* at noon on the 18th, whereupon he assembled a council of war which decided that as Vicksburg was " the most important point in the Confederacy " it could not be abandoned.[2]

Early on the 17th Grant's pursuit was continued, and about midday, the Confederate line being broken, as *Pemberton* himself says : " It very soon became a matter of *sauve qui peut*." [3] In a state of high demoralisation he withdrew to Vicksburg ; [4] many stragglers had already made their way there, the bridges over the Big Black were burnt, and Haines's Bluff was abandoned.

On the morning of the 18th Sherman, making use of the only pontoon train in Grant's army, crossed the Big Black at Bridgeport, and that night, accompanied by Grant, reached Walnut Hills. The true goal of the campaign was won, namely, high dry ground free from enemy interference, and upon which could be established a base of supplies. Turning to Grant, Sherman exclaimed : " Until this moment, I never thought your expedition a success. I never could see the end clearly, until now. But this is a campaign ;

---

[1] 36 *W.R.*, p. 241 ; 38 *W.R.*, p. 888.
[2] 38 *W.R.*, p. 890.   [3] 36 *W.R.*, p. 267.
[4] General *Loring's* division, unable to cross the Big Black, retreated on Jackson, and joined up with *Johnston's* forces.

this is a success, if we never take the town."[1] Indeed, an amazing success, the greatest in Grant's life, and from a purely strategical point of view one of the greatest in military history.

SIEGE AND SURRENDER OF VICKSBURG

Handing Haines's Bluff over to the navy, Grant at once re-established his line of supplies, and issued orders to carry the fortress by storm at two o'clock on the 19th, " relying," as he says, " upon the demoralisation of the enemy, in consequence of repeated defeats outside of Vicksburg."[2] This assault failed, for though, during the last two days, the Confederates " had run like sheep . . . now they were in intrenchments which had been prepared long before . . . they felt at home. Their demoralisation was all gone. . . ."[3]

Though this assault failed, there was every excuse for it, but on the 21st Grant determined to make a second which was less excusable in spite of the fact that his reasons[4] for it were well considered, and are worth recording.

(1) *Johnston* was at Canton raising an army to attack Grant in rear.

(2) If Vicksburg could be taken by storm, Grant could turn upon *Johnston* and drive him out of Mississippi.

(3) Reinforcements required elsewhere would have to be diverted to Vicksburg as long as this fortress held out.

(4) The troops were impatient to carry Vicksburg, the weather was growing hot and water was scarce.

(5) The men (like all Anglo-Saxons) were in no mood for the drudgery of pick and spade work.

Grant says : " The attack was ordered to commence on all parts of the line at ten o'clock a.m. on the 22nd with

---

[1] *Badeau*, I, p. 281.   [2] 36 *W.R.*, p. 54.

[3] *Greene*, p. 170. Grant, throughout his career, never fully understood the " moralising " effect of entrenchments.

A similar case occurred in March, 1918. When the British were defeated by the Germans, they fell back and halted only when they reached their old front line some thirty to forty miles in rear ; then, quite " at home," nothing could move them.

[4] 36 *W.R.*, p. 54 ; *Greene*, p. 169 ; *Badeau*, p. 308.

a furious cannonade from every battery in position. All
the corps commanders set their time by mine so that all
might open the engagement at the same minute." [1] Every
possible preparation was made, and it might well have
succeeded, had not Grant committed the error, which he
repeated the following year in the Wilderness and at Cold
Harbor, of ordering a simultaneous assault *all along the line*,
in place of overwhelming the tactical points by artillery
and rifle fire, and assaulting in between and then turning
them by a flank.

"Suddenly . . . as if by magic, every gun and rifle
stopped firing. . . . The silence was almost appalling, at
the sudden cessation of the firing of so many field guns
(about 180), and the crackling of so many thousands of sharpshooters' rifles. But the silence was only for a short time.
Suddenly, there seemed to spring almost from the bowels
of the earth, dense masses of Federal troops, in numerous
columns of attack, and with loud cheers and huzzahs, they
rushed forward at a run with bayonets fixed, not firing a
shot, headed for every salient advanced position along the
Confederate lines. . . . As they came within easy range
(almost as soon as they started) the Confederate troops,
not exceeding 9,938 men, along the $3\frac{1}{2}$ miles of assault,
deliberately rose and stood in their trenches, pouring volley
after volley into the advancing enemy ; at the same time
the troops in reserve advanced to the rear of the trenches,
and fired over the heads of those in the trenches. Every field
gun and howitzer belched forth continuously and incessantly
double-shotted discharges of grape and canister. . . ." [2]

This description of the assault, written by General *S. D.
Lee*, speaks for itself. It failed, because, being delivered
in line over a wide front, no covering fire could support
it. Unfortunately, McClernand, believing that his troops
had gained a secure footing in the enemy's entrenchments
and not troubling to verify it, sent several urgent appeals
to Grant for aid, and a second assault was ordered which
failed as disastrously as the first. Though Grant was not

[1] *Grant*, I, p. 531.
[2] *Publications of the Mississippi Historical Society*, III, p. 60.

altogether to blame for this waste of life, in common with practically all the leading generals of this war (and what is still more astonishing, with most of the leading generals of the World War of fifty years later) he failed to grasp the utter folly of Badeau's special pleading, written to exonerate him, namely : " Neither can the generalship which directed this assault be fairly censured. The only possible chance of breaking through such defences and defenders was in massing the troops, so that the weight of the columns should be absolutely irresistible." ¹ No greater and more costly heresy has ever been propounded than this, for as Commandant Colin says : " It is well known that there never is any shock . . . an impulse never comes from the rear, because it is never due to material pressure but to the influence of superior will imposed by a chief who is seen in front. . . . Generally speaking, the frontal fight does not lead to a solution." ²

Assaults having failed, a regular siege was resorted to.

The fortress, or rather entrenched camp, of Vicksburg was some four miles long and two miles wide ; its outer line of works, which followed the ravines and ridges, extended over seven miles. Grant's lines were twice as long, and besides he had to prepare his rear to withstand attack, for *Johnston* was assembling a powerful army in the neighbourhood of Canton. On May 29 Grant informed Halleck that unless Banks could come to his assistance, large reinforcements would be required; these demands were promptly met by the general-in-chief, and a month later Grant's army numbered 71,141 men and 248 guns.³

The siege was carried out methodically, a line of circumvallation being dug from Haines's Bluff to Warrenton, and one of countervallation from the Yazoo to the Big Black river ; this latter line being held by Sherman and some 30,000 men. On July 3, at 10 a.m., white flags appeared on the Confederate works, and an aide-de-camp crossed over to the Federal lines bearing a letter from *Pemberton* proposing

---

¹ *Badeau*, I, p. 328. ² *The Transformations of War*, pp. 5, 6.
³ *Greene*, p. 188.

an armistice, to which Grant at first replied that no conditions could be considered except " unconditional surrender." *Pemberton* objecting to this, Grant modified his decision to a surrender on terms, in spite of the fact that a council of war of his generals, the only one he ever held, objected to this change. The reason why he did not insist on unconditional surrender was that, had he done so, the prisoners could not have been paroled, and at much inconvenience to the army they would have had to be transported to Cairo. " Besides this, Grant hoped to demoralise the whole interior country still in rebellion, by spreading this dispirited mass of men among the yet unconquered remainder." In my opinion, there was another reason : not only at this very moment was the battle of Gettysburg being fought, but the moral effect on the North of a surrender on July 4 [1] could not fail to be of enormous political importance. Grant never lost sight of the fact that battles are but means towards political ends, and not ends in themselves ; and in this case he was willing to forgo the personal applause which greeted him on the unconditional surrender of Fort Donelson, because he saw that it was to the national advantage that he should do so.

At 10 a.m. on Saturday, July 4, the garrison of Vicksburg, some 31,000 men in all, marched out of the fortress, stacked their arms in front of their conquerors, and laying their colours upon them returned to the town, whereupon both armies began to fraternise.

Johnston and 27,000 men were on July 1 encamped between Brownsville and the Big Black. On the 4th, immediately after *Pemberton's* surrender, Sherman, at the head of 40,000 men, moved out against him. On the 6th he crossed the Big Black, *Johnston* retiring to Jackson, where he hoped that scarcity of water would compel his antagonist to assault. On the 16th Jackson was evacuated, whereupon Sherman decided not to follow up his retreating enemy, as he would

---

[1] *Pemberton* also realised the moral importance of July 4. He says : " I believed that upon that day I should obtain better terms. Well aware of the vanity of our foes. . . ." (36 *W.R.*, p. 285).

have to cross ninety miles of country destitute of water, but instead to destroy the railroads at Jackson. On the 25th he returned to Vicksburg.

The losses in this campaign are instructive, for quite unjustly Grant has been handed down to history as a butcher of men. Since April 30 he had won five battles, had taken Vicksburg and occupied Jackson, at a cost to himself of 1,243 killed, 7,095 wounded, and 535 missing, a total of 8,873 casualties.[1] He had killed and wounded about 10,000 Confederates and had captured 37,000,[2] among these were 2,153 officers of whom fifteen were generals ; also 172 cannon fell into his hands.

The disparity between the losses of the contending forces was entirely due to Grant's strategy. Basing his plan of campaign on surprise, and accepting risks which nothing but surprise could justify, in the first eighteen days after he crossed the Mississippi he defeated the enemy at Port Gibson, established a temporary base at Grand Gulf, marched 200 miles, and won the battles of Raymond, Jackson, Champion's Hill, and the Big Black river—these four within the space of six days. During the whole of this period his men had but five days' rations, and for the rest lived on the country. Well may Greene say : " We must go back to the campaigns of Napoleon to find equally brilliant results accomplished in the same space of time with such small loss." [3]

At 7 a.m., on July 9, Port Hudson surrendered unconditionally to General Banks, and, on the 16th, " the steamboat *Imperial* quietly landed at the wharf in New Orleans, arriving direct from Saint Louis, laden with a commercial cargo, having passed over the whole course of that great thoroughfare of commerce undisturbed by a hostile shot or challenge from bluff or levee on either shore." [4] The South had been cleft in twain ; Vicksburg, and not Gettysburg, was the crisis of the Confederacy.

[1] *Badeau*, I, p. 399 ; 37 *W.R.*, p. 167, gives a total of 9,362.
[2] 36 *W.R.*, p. 58.
[3] His losses during the first eighteen days were about 3,500, *Pemberton's* 8,000, as well as 88 pieces of artillery. (*Greene*, pp. 170, 171.)
[4] *Nicolay and Hay*, VII, p. 327.

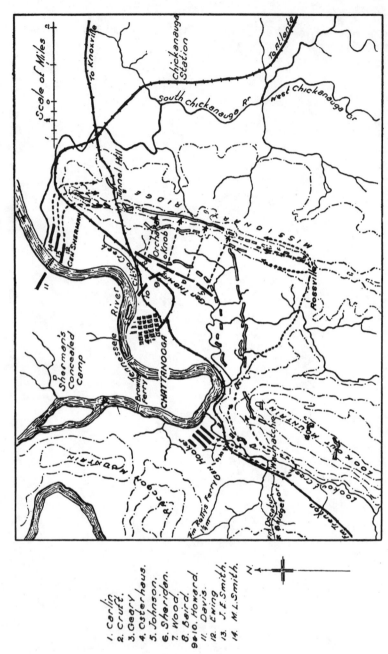

MAP No. 3.—BATTLE OF CHATTANOOGA, NOVEMBER 23-4, 1863.

1. Carlin.
2. Cruft.
3. Geary.
4. Osterhaus.
5. Johnson.
6. Sheridan.
7. Wood.
8. Baird.
9&10. Howard.
11. Davis.
12. Ewing.
13. J. E. Smith.
14. M. L. Smith.

CHAPTER VIII

BATTLE OF CHATTANOOGA

THE MOBILE PROJECT

ON July 18 Grant, now promoted to the rank of Major-General in the regular army, suggested to Halleck that an expedition should be sent from Lake Pontchartrain [1] with the object of taking Mobile, from where, by operating against the rear of *Bragg's* army, he might be compelled to detach troops from Chattanooga, and so facilitate a Federal advance on that town. Or, to move through Georgia, and devastate the country, for it was mainly from this State that *Lee* was drawing his supplies. This idea was not only tactically sound, but a brilliant strategical conception ; for now that the command of the Mississippi had cut the Confederacy in half, an advance from Mobile to Montgomery would practically limit the tactical theatre to Virginia, the Carolinas, and Georgia. In fact, as Badeau says : " It is not improbable that the capture of Mobile, at this time, would have shortened the war by a year."

Though this proposal was repeated by Grant during August and September, Halleck would not listen to it. He made every possible excuse, such as cleaning up the country, repairing the fortifications of Vicksburg and Port Hudson, assisting Banks to clear out Western Louisiana, and the necessity to operate in Texas. The truth would appear to be, that for purely political reasons Lincoln had set his mind on two projects : the first was the reopening of trade in the conquered Mississippi territories, and the second the occupation of Texas, which was threatened by the machinations of Napoleon III. On October 11 Halleck wrote to Grant saying : " I regret equally with yourself that you

---

[1] 38 *W.R.*, pp. 529, 530. Immediately north of New Orleans.

could not have forces to move on Mobile, but there were certain reasons which I cannot now explain, which precluded such an attempt." [1] Once again, through sheer ignorance of strategy, had Lincoln missed an opportunity of shortening the war.

The Mobile operation being forbidden, Grant's magnificent army, now a body of trained veterans, was broken up, just as it had been the year before. The Ninth Corps was sent to Kentucky; 4,000 men to Banks in Louisiana, 5,000 to Schofield in Missouri; a brigade to Natchez, and the remainder was employed in the thankless task of hunting down guerrilla bands.[2] On August 7 Grant was instructed further to deplete his army by sending the Thirteenth Corps under General Ord to Banks. To arrange this move he went in person to New Orleans, and met with a serious accident, his horse shying at a locomotive and throwing him. Then, on September 13, he received an urgent telegram from Halleck ordering him to send all " available forces to Memphis and thence to Corinth and Tuscumbia, to co-operate with Rosecrans " for the relief of Chattanooga.[3]

ADVANCE ON CHATTANOOGA

Buell's advance into east Tennessee, interrupted, as we have seen, by the campaign against Forts Henry and Donelson, was not begun until June 10, 1862, and then only under conditions imposed by Halleck which compelled Buell to repair the Memphis and Charleston railroad from Corinth to Decatur, and put it in running order as a line of supply.

---

[1] 53 *W.R.*, p. 274. These reasons were : events in Mexico, and re-establishing the national authority in Western Texas.

[2] It must never be forgotten that throughout the war the difficult problem of the guerrilla faced Grant and other Federal commanders. In the East this form of warfare was to a certain extent organised ; in the West it was murder, robbery, and terrorism. When caught guerrillas were usually shot. General Crook and some cavalry once fell in with a party of twenty guerrillas. He killed twelve and the rest were taken prisoners. " He regrets to report that on the march to camp the eight prisoners were so unfortunate as *to fall off a log* and break their necks." This was in Tennessee. (*M.H.S.M.*, XIV, p. 81.)   [3] 52 *W.R.*, p. 592.

This caused endless delay, and when, on June 27, *Bragg* succeeded *Beauregard* to the command of the Confederate forces opposing Buell, a series of cavalry raids by *Morgan* and *Forrest* [1] were carried out against his communications, and no sooner was the railway repaired than it was re-broken.

Early in August *Bragg* occupied Chattanooga, and thence marched into middle Tennessee, and later into Kentucky. Though Buell was then at the head of 50,000 men, this move persuaded him to abandon his advance on Chattanooga, and to fall back in order to cover Nashville. On September 14 he concentrated his forces in the neighbourhood of Bowling Green ; the drawn battle of Perryville followed, and the Confederate forces retired unmolested. On October 30 Buell, who had utterly failed in this campaign, and who should have reached Chattanooga long before *Bragg*, was superseded by General Rosecrans, who took command of what henceforth was to be known as the Army of the Cumberland.

In spite of Halleck's protests, Rosecrans refused to invade east Tennessee until he had collected 2,000,000 rations at Nashville, which for a time would render him independent of the railroads, and it was not until December 26 that he advanced from Nashville against *Bragg*, who had concentrated his army at Murfreesboro. Here, on the 31st, a desperate battle was fought between 43,400 Federals and 37,712 Confederates,[2] in which the losses of the former amounted to 13,249, and of the latter to 9,865.[3] Tactically, this battle was drawn ; nevertheless, on January 3, 1863, *Bragg* withdrew to Tullahoma, and Rosecrans, too exhausted to pursue, occupied Murfreesboro.

When Grant was operating against Vicksburg, he was anxious that Rosecrans should advance against *Bragg* and

---

[1] *Forrest* " was to become in the West . . . the counterpart of Jackson in the East, with this striking distinction between them, that while the latter was always invoking the aid of the Lord, the former never ceased to be in close alliance with the Devil." (*M.H.S.M.*, VIII, p. 121.)

[2] *B. & L.*, III, p. 613 ; 29 *W.R.*, p. 674.

[3] 29 *W.R.*, pp. 215, 681 ; *B. & L.*, III, pp. 611, 612.

so prevent him reinforcing *Johnston*.[1] On June 2 Burnside, with the Army of the Ohio, who was to advance from Lexington, Kentucky, and co-operate with Rosecrans, was ordered to send large reinforcements to Grant, and it was not until June 23 that Rosecrans resumed his long-interrupted move against *Bragg*, whilst Burnside advanced towards Knoxville on August 16. Thereupon *Bragg* evacuated Tullahoma on July 1, and crossed the Tennessee. Once Burnside was in a position to co-operate, Rosecrans's plan was to feint at *Bragg's* right, and cross the Tennessee below Chattanooga. *Bragg* was completely deceived by this manœuvre, and, on September 9, Rosecrans took possession of the town.

Thus far Rosecrans's strategy left nothing to be desired, but, thinking that *Bragg* was in full retreat, he pushed on in pursuit, and with his army in no order for battle he suddenly found himself confronted by a concentrated enemy. To extricate himself from this predicament, on September 19–20, he was compelled to fight the battle of Chickamauga,[2] in which he was severely beaten, and was saved only from complete destruction by the gallant defence of General Thomas—the Rock of Chickamauga. Retiring on Chattanooga, he abandoned Lookout Mountain which commanded the town. This battle was one of the most bloody of the war ; 55,000 to 60,000 Federals met from 60,000 to 70,000 Confederates, the former losing 16,336 and the latter 20,950 in killed, wounded, and missing.[3] At Chattanooga Rosecrans was besieged, whereupon Grant was called upon to relieve him.

GRANT TAKES COMMAND

The Confederate victory at Chickamauga, though a terrible blow to Federal prestige, led to the inestimable advantage of establishing unity of command west of the Alleghanies.

---

[1] About the same time, in order to prevent reinforcements being sent to Grant, *Lee* decided to invade the North. This decision led to the Gettysburg campaign. (*Longstreet*, p. 331.)

[2] Indian for—" The River of Blood."

[3] *B. & L.*, III, pp. 673–6 ; *Cist*, p. 228.

It struck terror into the heart of the Government, and abruptly awakened Lincoln from his dreams of campaigning in Texas, and of peaceful trading, to see the immensity of that strategical reality—the importance of Chattanooga. Hitherto the Departments of the Tennessee, Cumberland, and Ohio had respectively been commanded by Grant, Rosecrans, and Burnside, and Halleck at Washington was incapable of establishing co-operation between them. Now they were to be fused into one—the Military Division of the Mississippi.

On September 29 Halleck telegraphed Grant to send all possible reinforcements to Rosecrans ; and on October 3 he wrote : " It is the wish of the Secretary of War that, as soon as General Grant is able to take the field, he will come to Cairo and report by telegraph." [1]   To which Grant, still crippled, replied from Columbus : " Your dispatch of 3rd, directing me to report at Cairo, was received at 11.30 a.m. the 9th inst. I left same day with my staff and head-quarters, and have just reached here, *en route* for Cairo." [2] From Cairo he was ordered to Louisville, and on his way there, at Indianapolis, he met Stanton, " pacing the floor rapidly in his dressing-gown," who at once placed him in command of all the troops between the Alleghanies and the Mississippi, with the exception of those under Banks—a course suggested by Grant nearly a year before.

Grant at once assumed command, and having assigned the Department of the Cumberland to General Thomas, on the 19th, he set out by rail for Chattanooga. The last forty miles of this journey had to be done on horseback, and General Howard tells us that " at times it was necessary to take the General from his horse. The soldiers carried him in their arms across the roughest places. Yielding to no weakness or suffering, he pushed through to Chattanooga, reaching General Thomas the evening of October 23." [3]

Before Thomas took command, the condition of the Army of the Cumberland can be described only as deplorable. Rosecrans had quarrelled with Halleck, had been defeated, and now occupied an all but untenable position : his back

[1] 53 *W.R.*, p. 55.   [2] 53 *W.R.*, p. 375.   [3] *Church*, p. 199.

was against the Tennessee river, his left rested on, or near, Citico Creek, his front faced Missionary Ridge,[1] which rose to a height of from 300 to 400 feet above the plain, and which was separated from Lookout Mountain, on his right, by the Rossville Gap through which ran Chattanooga river. This mountain, 2,400 feet high, dominated the town of Chattanooga and the railway which ran thence up Lookout Valley to Decatur and Trenton. The Confederate entrenchments began on the north end of Missionary Ridge, ran along the ridge, spanned the Chattanooga Valley, and ended on Lookout Mountain. The importance of this mountain lay in the fact that it commanded the railway. It was abandoned by Rosecrans because he considered that his weakened army was not strong enough to hold it, and General William F. Smith is of opinion that he was right in not holding it, for had he done so he would have " diminished his force in the front by about 8,000." [2]   Personally I consider that either Lookout Mountain should have been held or Chattanooga abandoned ; for to remain there with the mountain in the hands of the enemy was to risk not only the loss of the town but the loss of the army.   Colonel Livermore supports this contention : he considers that it was because Rosecrans exaggerated *Bragg's* strength that the mountain was not held.   On October 1 *Bragg* had 41,972 [3] men on a line seven miles long, and Rosecrans 38,928,[4] " equal to 6,500 men per mile of a possible line of six miles from Citico Creek across the point of Lookout Mountain to Lookout Creek."   Further, he says : " The example of the Confederate defence for six weeks of seven miles of intrenchments at Vicksburg, five months before with 22,000 effectives against a force as large as, or greater than *Bragg's* . . . would have amply justified Rosecrans in the attempt to hold the line from Citico to Lookout Creek." [5]

Having lost his railroad communications, which on

---

[1] Called so by the Indians, who, in former times, allowed the missionaries to pass no farther west. Rossville was named after the famous Cherokee chief John Ross. Chattanooga is the Indian for " The Eagle's Nest."

[2] *M.H.S.M.*, VIII, p. 156.

[3] 53 *W.R.*, p. 721.

[4] 52 *W.R.*, pp. 914, 915.

[5] *M.H.S.M.*, VIII, pp. 285, 286.

September 30 were raided by *Wheeler* and his cavalry, who destroyed 400 wagons with their loads and teams,[1] a crippling blow to the transportation of the army, Rosecrans made no effort to run boats down the river. There were two at Chattanooga, and these could have brought up 200 tons of supplies daily from Bridgeport to a point near Williams Island, whence the wagon haul was but four or five miles to the town.[2] Instead, supplies were hauled over a circuitous and mountainous route north of the river, a distance of sixty to seventy miles. The result was that neither could the troops be properly rationed nor the animals fed. Boynton says :

" Thousands of horses and mules . . . died from want of food. There were Brigade headquarters where the officers lived chiefly on parched corn, there were regimental head-quarters where the daily food was mush or gruel ; there were officers of high rank who lived for days on sour pork and wormy mouldy bread." [3]

This statement is corroborated by General Smith [4] and by Grant, the latter saying that nearly 10,000 horses and mules died, and

" not enough were left to draw a single piece of artillery or even the ambulances to convey the sick . . . the beef was so poor that the soldiers were in the habit of saying . . . that they were living on ' half rations of hard bread and *beef dried on the hoof.' " [5]

---

[1] 53 *W.R.*, pp. 114, 231.

[2] 52 *W.R.*, p. 890 ; 53 *W.R.*, p. 102 ; 54 *W.R.*, pp. 67, 74.

[3] *Boynton*, p. 69. This was written in 1875, and it is strange to find this same officer writing in 1892 : " At no time did the men suffer, and at no time were the troops of the Cumberland either discouraged or demoralised." (*M.H.S.M.*, VII, p. 381.)   [4] *M.H.S.M.*, VIII, p. 167.

[5] *Grant*, II, p. 25 ; 56 *W.R.*, p. 216. General Fuller says : " Ten thousand dead mules walled the sides of the road from Bridgeport to Chattanooga. In Chattanooga the men were on less than half rations. Guards stood at the troughs of artillery horses to keep the soldiers from taking the scant supply of corn allowed these starving animals. Many horses died of starvation, and most of those that survived grew too weak for use in pulling the lightest guns. Men followed the wagons as they came over the river, picking up grains of corn and bits of crackers that fell to the ground. Yet there was no murmur of discontent." (*B. & L.*, III, p. 719.)

It would be difficult to find a more perfect example of an army paralysed by the inefficiency of its commander, who in this case had completely collapsed under the shock of defeat. Dana, writing to the War Department on October 16, said :

" Nothing can prevent the retreat of the army from this place within a fortnight. . . . General Rosecrans seems to be insensible to the impending danger, and dawdles with trifles in a manner which can scarcely be imagined . . . all this precious time is lost because our dazed and mazy commander cannot perceive the catastrophe that is close upon us, nor fix his mind upon means of preventing it. I never saw anything which seemed so lamentable and hopeless." [1]

Such was the state of affairs which faced Grant when he arrived at Chattanooga on the evening of October 23.

A New Line of Supply and a Plan

At Shiloh and at Vicksburg Grant had commanded an army ; now he was called upon to command three armies, the armies of the Cumberland, Ohio, and Tennessee, reinforced by Hooker's corps from the Army of the Potomac, in combination and in circumstances which could scarcely be worse.

Grant's immediate problem was to establish a workable line of supply. He at once realised that the key of this problem lay in securing command of Lookout Valley, and had *Bragg* realised that this valley was the key to Chattanooga he would have held it in force as well as the passes over Racoon Mountain, and Grant's problem would have been an impossible one to solve.

Hooker was then at Bridgeport, where, on October 1, he had been ordered by Rosecrans to bridge the river. It was useless bringing him forward unless a footing could be gained on the left bank of the Tennessee near Brown's Ferry, so that the enemy might be driven from the hills commanding this point. On the 19th General William F. Smith had

---

[1] 50 *W.R.*, pp. 218, 219 ; see also 50 *W.R.*, pp. 202, 215.

reconnoitred Brown's Ferry, and had come to the conclusion that this was the most suitable place at which to cross the river.   Immediately after his arrival, on the 23rd, Grant approved of Smith's scheme, and on examining the ferry the following morning he decided to force a crossing on the 27th.

At 3 a.m. on the 27th, 1,500 men under the command of Smith left Chattanooga in fifty-two boats which hugged the right bank until they reached a signal light indicating the point at which they were to cross the river and land.   The men then bent to their oars, landed, and rushing the weak Confederate pickets, occupied the hills on the left bank and entrenched them.   So thoroughly was this work done that at 3.30 p.m. Smith was able to telegraph General Thomas's chief-of-staff : " This place cannot be carried now." [1]   Thus was Chattanooga saved at a cost of four men killed and seventeen wounded.

That night Hooker's advanced guard entered Lookout Valley, and, at 3 p.m. on the 28th, the head of the main body reached Wauhatchie.   At 11 p.m. General Thomas telegraphed Halleck that

" the wagon-road is now open to Bridgeport.   We have, besides, two steam-boats, one at Bridgeport and one here, which will be started to-morrow. . . . By this operation we have gained two wagon-roads and the river to get supplies by, and I hope in a few days to be pretty well supplied. . . ." [2]

Thus, within five days of Grant's arrival in Chattanooga, the road to Bridgeport was opened, and within a week the troops were receiving full rations, were being reclothed and resupplied with ammunition, " and a cheerfulness prevailed not before enjoyed in many weeks.   Neither officers nor men looked upon themselves any longer as doomed." [3]

On the night of the 28th/29th *Longstreet* made a night attack on Hooker at Wauhatchie.   This was easily repulsed, the Federals being assisted by their mules, which taking fright stampeded towards the enemy, who in their turn

[1] 54 *W.R.*, p. 54.   [2] 54 *W.R.*, p. 41.   [3] *Grant*, II, p. 38.

broke and fled imagining that a cavalry charge was upon them. By 4 a.m. on the 29th the battle was over, and the " Cracker line " was never again disturbed.[1] Having secured a workable line of supply, Grant's next task was to consider the question of Burnside, and to bring up Sherman's corps from Corinth. On October 27 " a dirty, black-haired individual, with a mixed dress and strange demeanour " approached Sherman's house in Iuka. It was Corporal Pike, who had paddled down the Tennessee under the enemy's fire, and who brought a message to Sherman ordering him to move with all possible haste to Bridgeport, at which place he arrived on November 13. Meanwhile Burnside's position at Knoxville was causing the highest alarm at Washington, and Grant was plied with dispatch after dispatch urging that something must be done for his relief.

Longstreet had quarrelled with *Bragg*, and either to put an end to this bad feeling, or believing that it would be possible to move *Longstreet* to Knoxville, a hundred miles away, destroy Burnside, and withdraw him again to Chattanooga before Grant was ready to attack, President Davis instructed *Bragg* to send him to Knoxville. *Longstreet* started on November 4, and Grant, hearing of this on the 7th, ordered [2] Thomas to attack *Bragg*, and so draw *Longstreet* back. Thomas replied that he could not comply with this order as he was unable to move a single piece of artillery. Grant then directed him to take " mules, officers' horses, or animals wherever he could get them." [3] Thomas, as we shall see later on, though an excellent fighting officer, was, strategically, a man of parochial vision. He never could realise that in war situations constantly arise in which it is

---

[1] On the 29th Grant inspected the pickets, and as he was under fire he took only a bugler with him. On passing a post, he heard a soldier shout : " Turn out the guard for the commanding general." He replied : " Never mind the guard." Scarcely had he uttered these words, than a little way off a Confederate sentry called out : " Turn out the guard for the commanding general—General Grant ! " Grant saluted, and rode on—truly a strange and picturesque war.

[2] 56 *W.R.*, p. 634. [3] 56 *W.R.*, p. 73.

better to strike with an imperfect instrument than to wait until perfection is gained. He could never understand that actions depending on a combination of forces seldom permit of all being equally well prepared to strike. He was a staunch and efficient subordinate, but the interdependence of combined movements seems to have been beyond him.

Thomas, much perturbed by this order, rode out on the 7th with General Smith to examine the approaches leading from the mouth of the South Chickamauga towards Missionary Ridge. On this reconnaissance Smith pointed out to Thomas that the ground lent itself to a turning operation against *Bragg's* right flank, which, if successful, would not only threaten his rear, but separate him from *Longstreet* in east Tennessee. On their return they informed Grant of their conclusions, and he at once countermanded his order.[1]

Grant, having studied this new proposal, ordered Smith carefully to explore the country, and to prepare bridging material for a second bridge at Chattanooga, or Brown's Ferry, and for a bridge across the South Chickamauga. On the 14th Grant informed [2] Burnside that Sherman would cross South Chickamauga Creek in a few days' time, and that a general attack would then be launched on *Bragg*. On the 16th Grant took Thomas, Smith, and Sherman out to a position overlooking the mouth of the creek, and Sherman, after having carefully examined the ground, shut up his long glass with a snap, and said—" I can do it." [3]

In brief, Grant's plan was to effect a double envelopment with the forces under Sherman and Hooker pivoted on Thomas's army. Sherman was to attack *Bragg's* right, envelop it, and threaten or hold the railway in *Bragg's* rear. This would compel *Bragg* either to weaken his centre, or lose his base at Chickamauga Station. Hooker was to advance from Lookout Valley to Chattanooga Valley, move on to Rossville and threaten Missionary Ridge from the left.[4]

---

[1] 55 *W.R.*, p. 29 ; *B. & L.*, III, p. 716.
[2] 55 *W.R.*, p. 30.
[3] *M.H.S.M.*, VIII, p. 195 ; *Grant*, II, p. 58.   [4] *Grant*, II, p. 55.

Thomas was to hold the centre, and was to move forward in conjunction with Sherman, and oblique to the left so as to form a continuous battle front.[1]

The main difficulty which confronted Grant was, that from Lookout Mountain and Missionary Ridge *Bragg* could watch every move which took place in or around Chattanooga. In order to mislead *Bragg*, Sherman was ordered to cross the river at Bridgeport, move his leading division by the Trenton road and then throw some troops on Lookout Mountain in order to convey to *Bragg* the idea that Grant's intention was to attack his left ; on the 18th a brigade was encamped on the mountain.[2] Sherman's remaining divisions were to take the Brown's Ferry road, move towards South Chickamauga Creek as if their intention was to go to Knoxville, and then hide themselves in the hills opposite the mouth of the creek, where they could not be observed from Lookout Mountain. One brigade of this force was to move on to the North Chickamauga, where 116 pontoons were in readiness to be floated down the river in order to effect a landing on the left bank. " All things," said Sherman, were " prearranged with a foresight that elicited my admiration." [3]

These movements partially misled *Bragg*, and, had not the rain and the shocking condition of the roads delayed Sherman, they might well have completely succeeded. At 9.45 p.m. on the 20th *Hardee*, in command of *Bragg's* left, ordered the passes over Lookout Mountain to be blocked, and said to a subordinate commander : " Direct your advanced brigade to make obstinate defence, so as to give time to send reinforcements. Be constantly on the alert. General *Bragg* is under conviction that a serious movement is being made on our left." [4] Unfortunately for Grant, Sherman's command was not ready to cross on the night of the 22nd,[5] and on the afternoon of the 21st the march of his division from Trenton towards Wauhatchie was seen.

[1] 55 *W.R.*, pp. 130, 131 ; *B. & L.*, III, p. 716 ; 56 *W.R.*, pp. 154, 181.
[2] 55 *W.R.*, p. 583.   [3] 55 *W.R.*, p. 571.   [4] 55 *W.R.*, p. 668.
[5] Originally ordered for the 21st. See 55 *W.R.*, p. 31.

The result was, that on the afternoon of the next day *Bragg* began to move troops to his right.[1]

On the night of the 22nd a deserter came into the Federal lines, and reported that *Bragg* was falling back. His story was that two divisions had been sent towards Sherman, who was expected to attack Steven's Gap (over Lookout Mountain) and that most of *Bragg's* army was massed between his headquarters and the mountain. This information, assuming it to be correct, exactly fell in with Grant's plan of drawing *Bragg* away from the point decided on for Sherman's attack. Whether he realised this at the time I am unable to say, but he had received news [2] that Knoxville had been attacked (telegraphic communication with Burnside was cut); and being daily worried by the authorities in Washington to do something to assist Burnside, he apparently thought that *Bragg's* move was a ruse to cover the sending of more troops against Knoxville. Further still, on the 20th, he had received the following cryptic letter from *Bragg* : " As there may still be some non-combatants in Chattanooga, I deem it proper to notify you that prudence would dictate their early withdrawal." [3] Grant knew that this letter was meant to deceive him, but coupling it with the information furnished by the deserter, his anxiety about Knoxville,[4] as well as the fact that Sherman could not cross the Tennessee until the night of the 23rd/24th, and that the flooded river was threatening destruction to the bridges, he ordered [5] Thomas to make a reconnaissance in force on the morning of the 23rd, in order to verify *Bragg's* position. This was done, and that day Thomas moving forward established his lines parallel to *Bragg's*, and within a mile of the western flank of Missionary Ridge. This movement materially

---

[1] 55 *W.R.*, p. 671.   [2] 56 *W.R.*, p. 206.   [3] 55 *W.R.*, p. 32.

[4] Grant says : " Hearing nothing from Burnside, and hearing much of the distress in Washington on his account, I could no longer defer operations for his relief. I determined, therefore, to do on the 23rd, with the Army of the Cumberland, what had been intended to be done on the 24th." (*Grant*, II, p. 62.) This is not altogether correct, for on the 24th Thomas was to conform to Sherman's movement ; but it does accentuate the fact that anxiety to relieve the political situation was uppermost in Grant's mind.

[5] 55 *W.R.*, p. 32.

changed the task given to Thomas in Grant's order of the 18th,[1] also it awoke *Bragg* to the danger threatening his right flank, and on the night of the 23rd he ordered *Walker's* division to move from near Lookout Mountain to Missionary Ridge,[2] and a brigade to occupy a position near the mouth of the South Chickamauga.[3]

THE BATTLE

By the night of the 23rd Sherman's command, with the exception of Osterhaus's division, still west of Brown's Ferry, was ready to move. Osterhaus was ordered to report to Hooker, should he not be able to cross by 8 a.m. on the 24th, and at midnight Sherman's landing force, under General Smith, advanced upstream from the North Chickamauga. At two o'clock the following morning a landing was effected near the mouth of the South Chickamauga, when the work of ferrying over Sherman's infantry was at once begun. By daylight two divisions had crossed. A bridge 1,350 feet in length was then thrown over the Tennessee, being finished a little after noon, and another across the South Chickamauga, when a brigade of cavalry was moved over under orders to proceed to the neighbourhood of Charleston and destroy the railroad.

At 1 p.m. Sherman began his advance in three divisional columns with the left leading and covered by the South Chickamauga, whilst the right was echeloned back in order to refuse this flank. At 3.30 p.m. the heads of the columns reached the detached hill north of Missionary Ridge, and in place of pushing on to the tunnel, Sherman ordered his division to halt there and entrench for the night. " This," General Smith, amongst others, proclaims, " was the blunder of the battle." [4]

For a moment I will pause, and examine Sherman's problem, for though it has been debated by a score of historians, in my opinion it has as yet never been fully analysed. The date was November 24, consequently by half-past

[1] 55 *W.R.*, p. 31.   [3] 55 *W.R.*, pp. 745, 746.
[2] 55 *W.R.*, p. 718.   [4] *M.H.S.M.*, VIII, pp. 202, 228.

four it would be getting dark. Throughout the day drizzling rain fell, and the clouds were low.[1] Even before four o'clock it was so dark on Lookout Mountain, that Hooker had to suspend his operations.[2] Though we are told that the whole of Sherman's cavalry was over both bridges by 3.30 p.m.,[3] we are not told when his artillery began to cross, but it could not have done so much before 2 p.m., probably later, for during the night of the 23rd/24th, Thomas, having no artillery horses, had to borrow Sherman's in order to move forty guns of the Army of the Cumberland forward on the north side of the Tennessee " to aid in protecting the approach to the point where the south end of the bridge was to rest." [4]

In brief, Sherman's position seems to have been as follows : Tunnel Hill was one and a half miles away ; visibility was poor, night was approaching, and only part of his artillery was up. If he advanced to the tunnel, which might, as far as he knew, be strongly held, he could not have arrived there until dark, and once there his right flank would have been a mile and a half to two miles from Thomas's left flank, and well in advance of it. If attacked in flank, he risked being rolled up and thrown back on to the South Chickamauga. In any case, in the dark he would have found it extremely difficult to select a tactically sound position and entrench it. I do not say that he should not have risked an advance, but I do consider that these circumstances ought to be carefully weighed up before Sherman is condemned. In my opinion, Sherman's blunder was not that he halted where he did, but that apparently he did not make it clear to Grant that he was not actually on the northern end of Missionary Ridge, for that night Grant wrote to Thomas, saying : " General Sherman carried Missionary Ridge as far as the tunnel with only slight skirmishing. . . ." [5]

Whilst Sherman was advancing, Thomas stood fast, and Brown's Ferry bridge breaking before Osterhaus's division

---

[1] *Grant*, II, p. 68.
[2] *Grant*, II, p. 72.
[3] *Grant*, II, p. 69.
[4] *Grant*, II, p. 66.
[5] 55 *W.R.*, p. 44.

could cross over, at 12.30 a.m. on the 24th, Thomas, under instructions from Grant, ordered Hooker to " take the point of Lookout." [1]

Early on the 24th Hooker advanced, and working his way through the mist climbed the mountain as far as the base of the " upper palisade," that is to the foot of the precipitous wall of rock which tops the mountain. During the night he worked forward small parties of sharpshooters who drove the enemy off the summit.

" Just before sunrise a group of soldiers stepped out on a rock which forms the overhanging point of the mountain. They carried a flag, but held it furled, waiting for the sun. The instant the rays broke full upon them they loosened its folds, and the waiting thousands below beheld the stars and stripes." [2]

That evening Grant reported his position to Washington, and the following day received replies from both Lincoln and Halleck. The former bade him to " Remember Burnside," and the latter answered : " I fear that Burnside is hard pushed, and that any further delay may prove fatal," which was scarcely encouraging, and shows how persistently Grant had been pressed to move. A little after midnight, he ordered [3] Sherman to advance as soon as it was light in the morning, and to Thomas he wrote : " Your attack, which will be simultaneous, will be in co-operation. Your command will either carry the rifle-pits and ridge directly in front of them, or move to the left, as the presence of the enemy may require." [4] Further : " If Hooker's present position on the mountain can be maintained with a small force, and it is found impracticable to carry the top from where he is, it would be advisable for him to move up the valley with the force he can spare and ascend (i.e. to the top of Lookout Mountain) by the first practicable road." [4] Obviously " top of Lookout Mountain " was a slip for " top of Missionary Ridge," [5] and Thomas, recognising this, at

[1] 55 W.R., p. 106.   [3] 55 W.R., p. 43.
[2] M.H.S.M., VII, p. 391 ; see also, 55 W.R., p. 112.   [4] 55 W.R., p. 44.
[5] See footnote M.H.S.M., VIII, p. 232, and Grant, II, p. 75.

10 a.m. on the 25th ordered Hooker to march " on the Rossville road toward Missionary Ridge,"[1] that is towards the southern extremity of Missionary Ridge. A little later on, Grant, who was with Thomas at Orchard Knob, decided that Thomas should not move forward with Sherman, but wait until Hooker had reached Missionary Ridge ;[2] obviously in order to take advantage of Hooker's success of the 24th should it be followed by an equal success the next day.

As I have related, one of the results of Thomas's reconnaissance in force on the 23rd was that *Bragg* moved a division from Lookout Mountain to Missionary Ridge. Though this move facilitated Hooker's advance, it was destined to delay Sherman's. On the morning of the 23rd *Cleburne's* division and one brigade of *Buckner's* were at Chickamauga Station *en route* to join *Longstreet*.[3] Immediately after Thomas attacked, *Bragg* ordered this force to march to his headquarters, and from there *Cleburne* was instructed to place his division immediately behind Missionary Ridge. Early on the 24th, whilst Sherman was still crossing the Tennessee, *Bragg* ordered *Cleburne* to send a brigade to the east Tennessee and Georgia railroad bridge over the South Chickamauga, in order to protect his line of retreat, and at 2 p.m. he ordered him to move his remaining three brigades to the northern end of Missionary Ridge near the railway tunnel, and " preserve the brigade in " his " rear at all hazards." Actually, when Sherman arrived at the position he occupied on the night of the 24th/25th, *Cleburne* had only one brigade entrenched between him and the tunnel.[4] On the morning of the 25th *Cheatham's* division and a brigade from *Stevenson's* arrived from Lookout Mountain, the rest of *Stevenson's* division not coming up until later in the day.[5]

The morning of the 25th was clear and bright, and as the

[1] 55 *W.R.*, p. 115.
[2] *Grant*, II, p. 75, and 55 *W.R.*, pp. 34, 96, 112, 113.
[3] 55 *W.R.*, p. 745.   [4] *M.H.S.M.*, VIII, p. 205.
[5] 55 *W.R.*, pp. 701, 726.

day remained so, Grant from Orchard Knob had a full view of the left of the battlefield. Sherman advanced at daylight as ordered, and after a two-hour contest Grant, from his observation post, saw " column after column of *Bragg's* forces moving against him." Thereupon Grant ordered Thomas to send Baird's division to reinforce Sherman, but it was not required, whereupon " *Bragg* at once commenced massing in the same direction." [1] " This," says Grant, " was what I wanted. But it had now got to be late in the afternoon, and I had expected before this to see Hooker crossing the ridge in the neighbourhood of Rossville, and compelling *Bragg* to mass in that direction also." [2]

Meanwhile, Sherman could not understand what was delaying the advance of Thomas, and, at 12.45 p.m., he asked, " Where is Thomas ? " [3] To which Thomas replied : " I am here ; my right is closing in from Lookout Mountain towards Missionary Ridge." [3] Grant was still holding Thomas back, for the circumstances of battle had compelled him to modify his original plan. Sherman having been checked, there was now little hope of turning *Bragg's* right ; but, directly Hooker turned *Bragg's* left, *Bragg* would be compelled to denude his centre in order to reinforce his left. This was the movement Grant was waiting for, before launching Thomas against the enemy's weakened centre.

Though Hooker had advanced early on the 25th, the retiring enemy burnt the bridge over Chattanooga Creek. This delayed his crossing for some hours, and he did not reach Rossville gap until after 3 p.m. When he did, he immediately carried it and swept on to Missionary Ridge. He did not, however, report this success to Thomas. As Grant considered that Sherman's position was critical, at 3.30 p.m. he ordered Thomas to advance and carry the " rifle pits " at the foot of the ridge.[4] Which order, when

---

[1] 55 *W.R.*, p. 34.　　　[2] *Grant*, II, p. 78.　　　[3] 55 *W.R.*, p. 44.
[4] 55 *W.R.*, p. 34. Thomas, always slow, delayed to do so, and nearly an hour later Grant ordered the advance himself. (*Grant*, II, p. 79.)

referred to Grant's instructions, issued to Thomas a little after midnight on the 24th, was obviously the first step towards carrying the ridge itself. In spite of the quibbles raised over this order by a number of historians, and particularly by General Smith, the Official Records of the war leave its full meaning in no doubt. General Baird in his report says that an officer of Thomas's staff brought him an oral order to carry the rifle pits, and told him that " this was intended as preparatory to a general assault on the mountain, and that it was doubtless designed by the major-general commanding that I should take part in this movement, so that I would be following his wishes were I to push on to the summit." [1]

Dana says : " The storming of the ridge by our troops was one of the greatest miracles in military history." [2] It was nothing of the sort ; instead, it was an act of common sense. Missionary Ridge was protected by two entrenched lines, each held by men at one pace interval, and the artillery fire from the ridge was plunging, and consequently not fully effective. When the first line, that is the line of rifle pits mentioned by Grant, was taken, its defenders fell back, many of them rushing through the second line. General *Manigault*, who commanded a brigade in *Hindman's* division, says : " All order was lost, and each striving to save himself took the shortest direction for the summit. . . . The troops from below at last reached the works exhausted and breathless, the greater portion so demoralised that they rushed to the rear to place the ridge itself between them and the enemy." [3] Obviously Grant intended the ridge to be taken, and not foreseeing the eventual demoralisation of the garrison of the forward Confederate line, he ordered the line of rifle pits to be carried first. The attacking troops, seeing their enemy run, instinctively ran after him, and so it happened they carried the ridge in one bound in place of two. The impossibility of holding a line of men back when an enemy is flying from before it is well known to every soldier who

---

[1] 55 *W.R.*, p. 508. See Appendix II.   [2] 55 *W.R.*, p. 69.
[3] *Alexander*, pp. 477, 478.

has taken part in such an engagement. The continued advance was not due to a miracle, but to the instinct of the fighting spirit; this does not in any way detract from the gallantry of Thomas's superb assault, but it does explain it.

This charge succeeding, Hooker's advance, which had already made itself felt, proved the decisive blow of the battle, for, shattered in front, *Bragg* could not possibly meet this flank attack. In place of winning the battle with his left, as originally planned, Grant won it with his right. That he should have done so after his mistaken move of Thomas on the 23rd, does not reflect adversely on his generalship; instead, it shows that his plan and distribution were flexible, that is, that they could be adapted to circumstances as they arose. This, after all, is one of the greatest tests of generalship. The pursuit was abandoned on the 28th, for Grant's immediate problem was the relief of Burnside.

On the 27th Grant, having ascertained that *Bragg* was in full retreat, ordered Sherman to march on Knoxville.[1] He arrived there on December 6, to find that *Longstreet* had raised the siege on the 4th, and was in full retreat up the Holston Valley. On the 20th Grant moved his headquarters to Nashville, leaving Thomas in command at Chattanooga.

In this battle Grant's losses were 5,815 out of a total force of about 60,000.[2] *Bragg*, who after *Longstreet* had left him had only 33,000 troops in line, lost 6,175 stand of arms, 40 guns, 5,471 prisoners,[3] and about 3,000 in killed and wounded.

THE MOBILE PROJECT RENEWED

Grant's victory at Chattanooga opened the road to Atlanta, and Atlanta was the back door of *Lee's* army.

---

[1] On the 27th Grant instructed Thomas to send Granger's corps to Knoxville. On the 29th he found that he had not yet started, so he sent Sherman instead. (*Grant*, II, pp. 90–92.)

[2] *B. & L.*, III, p. 711. [3] *Cist*, p. 258.

Grant had seen this clearly ever since the fall of Vicksburg, and now that Chattanooga was his, he says :

" I expected to retain the command I then had, and prepared myself for the campaign against Atlanta. I had great hopes of having a campaign made against Mobile from the Gulf. I expected after Atlanta fell to occupy that place permanently, and cut off *Lee's* army from the west by way of the road running through Augusta to Atlanta and thence south-west. I was preparing to hold Atlanta with a small garrison, and it was my expectation to push through to Mobile if that city was in our possession ; if not, to Savannah ; and in this manner to get possession of the only east and west railroad that would then be left to the enemy." [1]

On December 7, from Chattanooga, suggesting this plan to Halleck, he wrote as follows :

" . . . I take the liberty of suggesting a plan of campaign that I think will go far towards breaking down the rebellion before spring. . . .
" I propose, with the concurrence of higher authority, to move by way of New Orleans and Pascagoula on Mobile. I would hope to secure that place, or its investment, by the last of January. Should the enemy make an obstinate resistance at Mobile, I would fortify outside and leave a garrison sufficient to hold the garrison of the town, and with the balance of the army make a campaign into the interior of Alabama and possibly Georgia. The campaign, of course, would be suggested by the movements of the enemy. It seems to me that the move would secure the entire States of Alabama and Mississippi and a part of Georgia, or force *Lee* to abandon Virginia and North Carolina. Without his force the enemy have not got army enough to resist the army I can take. . . ." [2]

On the 21st Lincoln agreed [3] to this plan, but only should *Longstreet* be first ejected from east Tennessee. Grant, realising that on account of the severity of the winter a direct advance against *Longstreet* was not practicable until the spring, determined to move Sherman on Meridian. On

[1] *Grant*, II, pp. 100, 101.   [2] 56 *W.R.*, pp. 349, 350.   [3] 56 *W.R.*, p. 457.

January 15 he informed Halleck that Sherman was then
concentrating at Vicksburg, that he would move on Meridian,
and thoroughly destroy the railways, after which he would
return, " unless opportunity of going into Mobile with the
force he has, appears perfectly plain." In this same letter
he wrote :

" I look upon the next line for me to secure to be that
from Chattanooga to Mobile ; Montgomery and Atlanta
being the important intermediate points. To do this,
large supplies must be secured on the Tennessee river, so
as to be independent of the railroads from here [Nashville]
to the Tennessee for a considerable length of time. Mobile
would be a second base. The destruction which Sherman
will do to the roads around Meridian will be of material
importance to us in preventing the enemy from drawing
supplies from Mississippi and in clearing that section of
all large bodies of rebel troops. I do not look upon any
points except Mobile in the south, and the Tennessee river
in the north, as presenting practicable starting-points from
which to operate against Atlanta and Montgomery." [1]

Thus was outlined the idea which in the main, as we shall
see, was carried out by Sherman in his grand wheel against
Lee's rear.

A copy of this letter was sent to Sherman, and, on
January 19, Grant informed Thomas that he was to co-
operate in this movement, and that he particularly wanted
him " to keep up the appearance of preparation for an advance
from Chattanooga." [2]

In brief, Grant was preparing to cast his net over an
area of a thousand miles in extent. Thomas, in the centre,
was confronted by *Joseph E. Johnston,* who had relieved
Hardee [3] ; Schofield, now in command of the Department
of Ohio, was holding *Longstreet* in east Tennessee, and
Sherman was about to move out from Vicksburg eastwards
through Mississippi and Alabama, and by threatening

---

58 *W.R.*, pp. 100, 101.   [2] 58 *W.R.*, p. 143.

[3] After the battle of Chattanooga, *Bragg* was made Commander-in-Chief
and replaced by *Hardee.* *Hardee,* not desiring the responsibility thrust
upon him, was shortly afterwards relieved by *Johnston.*

Johnston in rear, whilst Thomas operated against his front, compel the Confederate Government to call upon *Longstreet* to evacuate east Tennessee, and come to *Johnston's* assistance.

A prettier piece of strategy than this has seldom been devised, for not only would it compel the Confederates to evacuate east Tennessee, but it prepared the way for any eventual move against Mobile, Montgomery, and Atlanta from the West.

Sherman advanced from Vicksburg on February 3 ; General Sooy Smith and 7,000 cavalry [1] having been ordered, on the 1st, to advance from Memphis and join hands with him at Meridian. Smith, an indifferent soldier, however, delayed [2] his move until the 11th, and failing to accomplish his task, turned back on the 22nd. On the 14th [3] Sherman entered Meridian, and so completely destroyed the railroads at this place, that in the autumn of this year, when *Hood* cut loose from Atlanta, the time taken up in wagoning his supplies round the breaks detained him at Florence for nearly a month, and so enabled Thomas to collect his scattered forces and defeat him at Nashville.[4]

This raid caused the greatest excitement throughout the Confederacy, troops being sent from Mobile and from *Johnston's* army to bring Sherman to book. This general, not waiting, however, for their arrival, fell back, and reached Canton on the 28th.

On the 12th Thomas was ordered to make a reconnaissance in force towards Dalton, but the usual delays followed, and he did not leave Chattanooga until the 22nd. *Longstreet* having fallen back, Schofield followed him up, but the roads were so bad that he was prevented going far. Such was the situation which faced Grant in the West when, on March 3, he was called to Washington.

[1] 57 *W.R.*, pp. 174, 181.   [3] 57 *W.R.*, p. 175.
[2] 57 *W.R.*, p. 175 ; 56 *W.R.*, p. 316.   [4] *Badeau*, I, p. 558.

CHAPTER IX

GRANT'S GENERALSHIP, 1861-3

THE EXPERIMENTAL PERIOD

SINCE the coming of the Industrial Revolution, the tactics and strategy of each great war have been largely based on trial and error, and none more so than those of the American Civil War and the World War of 1914–18, which in nature are, however, separated by one great difference : though both opened as stupendous strategical and tactical experiments, the former was conducted by amateur statesmen and soldiers who had never studied the meaning of such a conflict, whilst the latter was controlled by professional men, deeply versed in diplomacy, international politics, and the theory of absolute warfare as expounded by Clausewitz and others. Curious to relate, the errors of the Prussian trained experts were even more flagrant than those of the amateurs, the reason being, that though these experts had studied war deeply they had failed to relate their work to the conditions of the civilisation in which they lived ; instead, they laboured in a world which existed long before their day, namely, that of pre-industrial civilisation—the age of agrarian culture. They could not see that war is as much a product of things living as of things dead ; that to relate it to history is for practical purposes valueless, unless simultaneously it is related to the active world-forces of the ever-changing present. And the result ? Whilst these professionals started their war on political and military theories, each and every one of which was founded on a fallacy, the amateurs, having no theories except of the vaguest to perplex them, through their native horse-sense, discovered their errors. Whilst to the statesmen and soldiers of 1861–3 failure was an illumination, to those of 1914–16 it was in most cases a mist, which, silting between theory and fact, obscured the reality of their mistakes. The one, like children, could learn fully, for knowledge was slight, and imagination still vivid ; the other, like pedants, attempted to make the end fit the means, and were dumbfounded when it would not do so. This does not prove that theory is useless, but that idols have feet of clay, and that theory must be based on the facts of the living present, and not on those of a dead past ; for the present all such facts are fictions. This is why I devoted a chapter to the natural history of the Civil War, for unless we use the living historic sense of things, like a candle, to light up the dark mansion of generalship, when we search through its dusty rooms for living men, in their place we shall merely uncover the mouldering skeletons and mildewed doctrines of dead warriors.

Compared to the year 1914, the year 1861 was little more than a kindergarten entertainment. In both these years it was obvious that the enemy had some day to be defeated : but how ? This was the question which was not understood. In both, the fundamental reason for this was the same : there was no unity of command. In Europe, this unity was grudgingly agreed upon only when a death-rattle began to choke the Allied cause. In America, we see it established in March 1864 ; but even before this date attempts were made to found it. For example, in the spring of 1862, when Halleck took command in the West ; again when Halleck went to Washington in July, 1862 ; and again when Rosecrans's defeat at Chickamauga resulted in Grant's appointment in the autumn of 1863, to the command of the Military Division of the Mississippi. This last unification was the stepping-stone to the establishment of complete unity of command the following year.

For nearly three years, Lincoln, who was an amateur war statesman, stood perplexed between how to win the war, and whom to trust with this task. Lincoln's supreme difficulty was : whom could he trust ? One general after another failed him ; they did so because they also were amateurs, for, with the solitary exception of Grant, they failed to understand that a general is an instrument of government. They had no comprehension of grand strategy, that is, of the relationship between policy and war. McClellan, probably the ablest of the failures, never grasped this essential. In 1862 he behaved like a wilful schoolboy, and the following year we find him intriguing against Grant. Grant never intrigued ; further still, he never overlooked the political situation, and the necessity of conforming to it. When McClernand, quite wrongly, was given command of the river expedition, Grant, in place of butting his head against Lincoln's, at once modified his plan. When in the late winter of 1862–3 political conditions in the North were desperate, he waged three months of toilsome warfare in the swamps of the Mississippi because these conditions demanded activity, and simultaneously he converted this waste of tactical energy into a strategic smoke cloud to cover his eventual advance. Finally he accepted the surrender of Vicksburg on terms, because he felt that the political situation demanded it.

In 1861 there existed a hazy grand strategy entirely divorced from grand tactics. The problem then was : Lincoln must learn the full meaning of the first, and discover a general who could appreciate the full meaning of the second. For nearly three years he searched in vain, the reason being that such a man did not exist ; circumstances had to create him, to educate him, and to point him out. At length he discovered a man he had never seen—Grant, the self-made soldier. Not a man from the East, which flamed before the doorsteps of the White House, but a man from out the twilight of the West, a somewhat silent man, who blew no trumpet and who had no axe to grind, a strange contrast to the McClellans and the Hookers. A man who once had been seated on a packing-box in a leather store at Galena ; who had passed through many ordeals, but who had never as yet been defeated. Who had met *Floyd, Pillow, Buckner, Van Dorn, Pemberton,* and *Bragg,* every one of whom was either captured or superseded after the meeting. Grant was Lincoln's last experiment, and his

choice, as we shall see, proved Lincoln's ability to solve
the war problem successfully.

GRANT'S COMMON SENSE

In examining the campaigns fought by Grant during the
first three years of the war, we must dismiss from our minds
all the jargon of the military schools, and particularly the
geometric strategy and tactics of Baron de Jomini, whose
histories and *Art of War* were the textbooks of European
armies.   Grant, in 1861, knew none of these things, and in
all probability he had never heard of Jomini.   Quite un-
educated in military matters, he relied entirely on his
personality and his common sense, intuitively understanding
that war is nothing more than an equation between pressure
and resistance ;   that all direction springs from these two,
and if the direction of an operation is to be profitable its
object must be a desirable one, and its objective, or goal,
an attainable one with the means at hand.   Grant's common
sense is so remarkable, that in itself it constitutes a military
lesson of no small importance, namely, that the art of war
—strategy and tactics—is nothing more than action adapted
to circumstances.   This goes to prove that all theoretical
systems of war must be so flexible in nature that they can
be easily moulded to whatever circumstances confront a
general.   In 1861 Grant possessed no theory of war, not
for five minutes could he have argued on strategy with
Halleck.   I doubt whether he could have ever done so,
even in 1865 ;   but when he was faced by a problem, he
could look at it in an eminently common-sense way, and in
so detached and unselfish a manner, that throughout his
life he seems to have been quite oblivious of his genius ;
for common sense is genius and of no common order.

Grant was not, as we have seen, a great artist of war ;
for his tactics were frequently crude and remained so
throughout his career, but as a natural scientist of war he
was of the type who, so I think, would have pleased Thomas
Huxley, for this philosopher defined science as " organised

common sense," common sense being, in his opinion, " the
rarest of all the senses." Had Grant possessed a love for
war, which he certainly did not ; that is, had he been so
fascinated by war as to examine it, study it, and live with
its idea as the one controlling influence of his life ; and had
he belonged to a military people in a warlike age, he might
well have risen to a place among the Great Captains of history.
But he disliked war, looking upon it in no romantic light ;
for to him it was the necessary retribution for evil done.
In spite of the fact that his wife kept slaves, slavery was
an evil institution, the war with Mexico was a dishonourable
act, consequently the Civil War was the exorcism Nature
rightly demanded to banish the evil and to re-establish the
good. It was a great national purification in which he had
to play his part ; yet the astonishing thing is that except
as a soldier Grant failed in every peaceful work he undertook. Throughout his life he never seems to have realised
that in his native common sense and in his personality
were the raw materials of great soldiership.

His common sense was such that he possessed the inestimable gift of being able to learn from his own mistakes,
as well as from the mistakes of others. He was in no way
bound by conventions or by traditions ; he had a horror
of precedents and formalities, and at times, such as during
his advance from Port Gibson, he would cast them aside
in order to speed up his work. He was a stubborn man,
yet always willing to listen to the suggestions of his subordinates, so much so that many have considered that such
men as Rawlins, his chief-of-staff, were his brains. I can
find no proof of this in his campaigns, for in them he appears
to have been his own law, his textbook being the war itself.
Though a slow thinker, he studied this book minutely, and
particularly the chapters concerning his own operations.
To illustrate this I cannot do better than quote what he
himself says as regards the value of military history :

" Some of our generals failed because they worked out
everything by rule. They knew what Frederick did at one
place, and Napoleon at another. They were always thinking

about what Napoleon would do. Unfortunately for their
plans, the rebels would be thinking about something else.
I don't underrate the value of military knowledge, but if
men make war in slavish observances to rules, they will
fail. No rules will apply to conditions of war as different
as those which exist in Europe and America. Consequently,
while our generals were working out problems of an ideal
character, problems that would have looked well on a black-
board, practical facts were neglected. To that extent I
consider remembrances of old campaigns a disadvantage.
Even Napoleon showed that, for my impression is that his
first success came because he made war in his own way,
and not in imitation of others. War is progressive, because
all the instruments and elements of war are progressive.
I do not believe in luck in war any more than luck in business.
Luck is a small matter, may affect a battle or movement,
but not a campaign or a career." [1]

Here we see Grant's common sense : conditions and not
rules governed his actions. He did not resist circumstances,
instead he analysed them.

At Belmont he had no real reserves, at Donelson he had,
but here his administrative arrangements were of the
meagrest, and not only did the men suffer but the battle
suffered. At Shiloh he was mentally as unprepared for
the battle as his men were physically so. Thus far he
had never been full-heartedly attacked, now he was, and
his first action was to push forward ammunition, a lesson
he learnt at Donelson ; next to form up the stragglers and
broken units into a reserve, another lesson he had learnt
at the same place. At Shiloh his main lesson was the value
of a general reserve, that is, of a formed body of fresh
troops which can renew the attack against an exhausted
enemy. Further, he learnt the value of establishing a
defensive base to an offensive operation. These lessons
may be considered extremely elementary, but this does
not detract from their value ; for, as Clausewitz says :
" It is the simple which is difficult in war."

Throughout the experimental period of the war the

[1] *Church*, pp. 188, 189.

value of a strong reserve had escaped the notice of McDowell, McClellan, Buell, and Burnside, as well as most of the other generals. *Lee* never mastered the use of reserves until his defeat at Gettysburg ; but Grant did so after Shiloh, as may be seen in his Corinth, Vicksburg, and Chattanooga campaigns. In the last of these, his centre, Thomas and the Army of the Cumberland, was kept in reserve throughout the first day of the battle ; and at Vicksburg Grant's columns were so distributed that any one of them could act as a mobile reserve to strike the enemy in flank or rear, a lesson he had tested out at Iuka and Corinth.

At Holly Springs, *Van Dorn's* raid taught him the enormous advantage of living on the country, a lesson applied in his campaign south of Vicksburg, and one upon which Sherman based his march through Georgia.

At Shiloh he was surprised, at Vicksburg he prepared one of the most elaborate and successful surprisals ever effected in war. At Chattanooga he again applied it, and had he made better use of his cavalry, had he, in place of sending them off to destroy the railway, ordered them forward to co-operate with Sherman in seizing Tunnel Hill, *Bragg's* army should have been annihilated. The true use of cavalry he had not yet mastered, though Shiloh might have taught him this lesson.

In brief, Grant's lessons may be grouped under three headings, namely, those which concern the instrument, the method, and the conditions of war ; such as ammunition-supply, the rear attack, and the political factors. From these he built up his art of war, in which he excelled in protected-mobility, that is in strategical action, rather than in protected-offensive power—tactics. In this respect he resembles Napoleon, whose tactics were frequently faulty. I will now turn to Grant's second quality—his personality.

Grant's Personality

" If you cannot earn—learn " is a common saying, and as I have just shown it is one automatically, rather than consciously, applied by Grant. Yet the discovery of errors, and the ability to avoid repeating mistakes, lose much of their practical value unless they are governed by a strong personality, a quality not easy to define, and one which lends itself better to illustration.

The first quality of soldiership is courage, without which all other virtues lose form, tone, and colour. Courage not only fortifies the will of the general, but it magnetises the will of his men. Whoever possesses courage, possesses prestige in its most powerful form, for throughout history heroism has stirred the hearts of men and women infinitely more so than reason has their minds. Of courage there are two forms—physical and moral, which are so closely related that it is quite impossible to separate them. Grant possessed these two in abundance ; for he was not only a man who scorned danger, when it was profitable to scorn it, but a man who scorned untruth, that is, if he considered his opinion was right, no physical danger or moral responsibility could shake him from his purpose. At Salt river he kept " right on," not because he did not fear, but because he did fear, and had sufficient command over himself to throttle his fears. At Belmont it is the same ; as yet he is no general, but in spite of danger he was the last to leave the field, as a trusty captain is the last to leave a sinking ship. In this instance it is not because he fought bravely that he commands our admiration, but because, single-handed, he braved imminent personal danger in order to make certain that not a man of his had been left behind. Such acts as this distinguish a leader from his men, they render him conspicuous, and ennoble him in their eyes. To them he becomes a hero, and it is heroism which magnetises the human soul, and impels the human will to challenge even the impossible.

His first speech to his regiment, the 21st Illinois, was not a jest, it was an act of moral courage. There was no humbug about this man, and a vast amount of common sense. How many others would have exclaimed : " Go to your quarters " ? How many another would not have been surprised by the sudden call for a speech, and being unbalanced would have said something pleasant and jocular. Grant saw before him a *canaille* and not a regiment, and when they shouted he saw a still greater *canaille*, and he treated his undisciplined rabble as such. When, in 1796, Bonaparte, " of poor aspect, and with the reputation of a mathematician and a dreamer," first met his generals in conference (and some, such as Augereau, were anything but friendly) he hitched up his sword, adjusted his hat, explained his orders to them, and dismissed them. They were dumbfounded : not a word of praise, not a request for an opinion, merely an order. Augereau afterwards admitted to Masséna ţhat " this little devil of a general inspired him with awe." He is overwhelmed by the stronger personality ; he makes no answer, for mentally he is paralysed.

In the Vicksburg campaign Grant's moral courage has seldom been equalled, certainly seldom surpassed. His plan met with no support, and was opposed by his subordinate commanders. Sherman, a fine soldier, strenuously objected to it ; but Grant, having thought it out, and having meditated upon it, knew that it was a good plan, and no better being suggested he refused to change it. Here his moral courage drew its strength from a firm knowledge of the situation. A man who knows has the courage to act, but in war chance and uncertainty play so large a part that the average man either follows his innate stupidity, or leans upon the advice of others, in order to share the responsibility of his decisions with his staff, or with his subordinates. Such men rely on councils of war, and in the World War these were re-christened " Conferences "— and they destroyed one operation after another.

Courage begets energy, but unless a general is bodily and mentally active, and unless he is endowed with a will to press on, the energy of courage is apt to effervesce. In war, energy may be, and frequently is, misdirected ; but even waste of energy is better than lethargy, that unforgivable sin of generalship. Grant's energy is quite extraordinary : fit, or sick, nothing can stop him. He is always ready to act, he is never obsessed by difficulties, he never exaggerates difficulties, or paints mental pictures of imaginary situations. At Belmont he is reputed to have said : " Don't be too anxious about what the other fellow is going to do to you, but make him anxious about what you are going to do to him." At Shiloh, though half-crippled, and all was in tumult, he moved everywhere. His ride to Chattanooga is an epic of energy, and men who can create such epics are those who may be called born leaders. In them is an enormous source of power which will out, and in spite of ignorance it often happens in war that the man of energy is the man of destiny. He is like a hurricane—he is the true thunderbolt of war.

Courage and energy will sometimes sweep a general off his feet. Men like Charles XII of Sweden cannot stand still, for battle intoxicates them like strong wine. This wild enthusiasm for glory is entirely foreign to Grant ; to him it would have appeared ridiculous, for of all the generals of the Civil War—with the possible exception of Thomas— he was the coolest and the most perfectly balanced. At Donelson and Shiloh, in spite of chaos, he has complete mastery over himself, his heart never runs away with his head ; wherever he appears, his presence, like ice, allays the fever. He is totally unlike General Rosecrans, an able strategist, one of the ablest of this war, but a man who collapsed under defeat. Grant is at his best when tumult surrounds him, because he is unaffected by it, and though he may issue no single order, his presence at once counteracts panic, it allays fear, it induces confidence. His imperturbable appearance and his inevitable cigar restore a broken line more firmly than a fresh division. In this respect, his imperturbability, he closely resembles the Duke of Wellington.

This confidence in himself, which instilled confidence in others, was based on his determination. No matter what might be the difficulties, he never failed to see a thing through. Nevertheless, he never adhered to a plan obstinately or in spite of conditions. This we clearly see at Chattanooga ;

but nothing would induce him to give up the idea behind his plan. Like Napoleon, he seldom had a fixed plan, and when he made a plan he frequently changed it : but the idea of his plan he never abandons. Once riding round the lines at Vicksburg he stopped at the house of a rebel woman for a drink of water. The woman taunted him, asking him if he ever expected to take the fortress. " Certainly," he replied. " But when ? " " I cannot tell exactly when I shall take the town, but I mean to stay here till I do, if it takes me thirty years." Such was Grant.

A man who is a " stayer " is not usually speedy. But I feel the reader will agree, that during the years 1861-3 there were few generals who realised the value of speed and time so fully as Grant. With him " activity " is a daily watchword, and though often he tried his troops to the utmost, no loss of *moral* resulted. It is sloth and not activity which rots discipline. From the day he set out from Holly Springs towards Vicksburg until the day he took over the appointment of general-in-chief, his armies were in constant movement. He was always pressing, seldom resisting, because he understood what may be called the " strategy of pressure " ; by which I mean, that an enemy who is continually attacked has no time to think, to plan, or to regain his tactical breath.

Such was Grant's vigorous personality, and it magnetised his men. This we see at Fort Donelson. It was his " fire baptism," and it was his personality rather than his generalship which won through. Here he turned a defeated line into a conquering line, a line which having fallen back in disorder was, a few hours later, to stand victorious on the enemy's parapets. His magnetism at Chattanooga is most remarkable. He moralised an army not by a display of heroics, but by silent common sense. The men who were without a head, for Rosecrans had lost his, he supplied not only with a head but with a heart, and a few weeks later Missionary Ridge was theirs.

Curiously enough, the secret of Grant's personality, the real secret of his success as a general, may be summed up in the words of an old magical formula, the secret of secrets, written by some long-forgotten hand in the twilight of the Middle Ages. It is: "To know, to will, to dare, and to remain silent."

GRANT AS STRATEGIST

Throughout the history of war few great generals, whether in supreme or subordinate command, have simultaneously proved themselves to be great at strategy and good at tactics. In ancient times, when battles consisted of hand-to-hand encounters, in the art of generalship tactics predominated; and this is clearly seen in the actions of such men as Alexander, Hannibal, Belisarius, and Edward III. In modern times it has been the reverse, the art of the general depending more on distribution, concentration, and direction, than upon the combined use of arms and weapons in battle. Frederick the Great never understood the value of light infantry, and Napoleon failed to grasp the power of the howitzer. The reason for this is obvious, namely, the more senior a commander becomes the more is he divorced from actual fighting; and the larger his command grows the more has he to concentrate on administration and organisation, and leave leadership and tactics to his subordinates. These facts must be kept in mind when we criticise Grant.

In its broadest sense, strategy is nothing more than protected movement with the object of developing offensive power against the most vulnerable point in the enemy's military distribution of forces. This point is always the rear of an army, or the enemy's base of operations. Protected movement is guaranteed by a correct appreciation of conditions, the position of the enemy's forces, their strength, his probable intentions, the ground, weather, communications, etc., followed by a distribution of force which will result in restricting the enemy's mobility and simultaneously concentrate strength unexpectedly against the most vulnerable, or decisive, point. From this definition it will be realised how complex the art of strategy is, and why it is that so few generals show a high strategical ability.

If Grant was unfortunate in possessing no knowledge of this art, it was more than fortunate for the Federal cause that his first small command should place him in the neighbourhood of Cairo, the great strategical centre of the West, the hub of a system of communications, water and rail, leading to St. Louis, Pittsburg, Knoxville, Chattanooga, Mobile, and New Orleans. He was by nature a man of situations ; by which I do not mean that he was a creative genius, a creator of situations which would assist his work, but an analyser of the situations in which he found himself, or was placed. At Cairo he at once realised the importance of Paducah, and though not authorised to do so he occupied this strategical centre. Once occupied, his ideas on strategy began to grow : he saw that a successful move against Forts Henry and Donelson would not only compel the Confederates to abandon Kentucky, but would open up the line of the Tennessee, whereby a move could be made on Corinth and Chattanooga, and the Confederate forces in Tennessee separated from those in Arkansas.

At first this may have been somewhat of an uncertain vision, but on the fall of Forts Henry and Donelson it became concrete, and had Grant been in command in place of Halleck there can be little doubt that he would have rapidly occupied Corinth and Memphis, and from these centres have moved upon Vicksburg, cutting the Confederacy in half in the summer of 1862, in place of in that of 1863 as he eventually did. When Vicksburg surrendered, his next idea was to move on Mobile, in order to establish a base of operations against Georgia and the eastern Confederate States. From Paducah to Appomattox, as we shall see, Grant's strategical plan, upon which all actions were to pivot, was maintained in spite of all difficulties ; this in itself constitutes one of the most remarkable cases of concentration of purpose and maintenance of direction to be found in the history of war.

What was the idea behind this plan ? Strategically, it

was the rear manœuvre leading whenever possible to the
rear attack. The move on Forts Henry and Donelson was
a manœuvre against the rear of Bowling Green, which would
have been followed, had Grant been in command, by a
move on Corinth, that is—a manœuvre against the rear of
Nashville and Memphis. The manœuvres at Corinth and
Iuka were tactical, aiming at a rear attack. At Vicksburg
we see rear manœuvres and attacks intimately combined.
First, Sherman was sent down the Mississippi to attack
Pemberton in rear, whilst Grant manœuvred against his
front ; and later, when a footing was gained south of the
fortress, Grant, so to say, abolished his own rear so that
he might protect himself from the very type of attack he
intended to launch against his enemy. He at once moved
on Jackson, not because it was occupied by the enemy's
main army, but because it was the most vulnerable point
in rear of Vicksburg. Jackson in his hands, the rear
manœuvre was developed into the rear attack at Champion's
Hill, which failed, and the result was the siege of Vicksburg.
At Chattanooga he found Rosecrans's army attacked in
rear, because *Bragg* commanded Lookout Valley, and his
first action was to re-establish its line of supply ; his next,
to plan a battle which would threaten *Bragg's* rear by turning
his right. Chattanooga won, the Mobile operation was
once again suggested, so that from Montgomery a rear
manœuvre might be made against Atlanta ; and in Sherman's
Meridian campaign we see the same idea.

Grant has gone down to history as a bludgeon general,
a general who eschewed manœuvre and who with head
down, seeing red, charged his enemy again and again like
a bull : indeed an extraordinary conclusion, for no general
in this war, not excepting *Lee*, and few generals in any other
war, made greater use of manœuvre in the winning of his
campaigns, if not of his battles. Without fear of contradiction, it may be said that Grant's object was consistent ;
strategically it was to threaten his enemy's base of operations, and tactically to strike at the rear, or, failing the rear,
at a flank of his enemy's army. This being so, the pivotal

idea in his generalship was absolutely sound, and firmly
based on economy of force.

Throughout the campaigns under review, the direction
of Grant's movements was governed by this idea ; nevertheless, in spite of his natural stubbornness, when circumstances demanded a change of direction, he did not hesitate
to modify his movements, and yet without abandoning this
idea. When *Van Dorn* destroyed his supply depot at Holly
Springs, there is little doubt that, learning he could live on
the country, he might with no great difficulty have continued his advance on Grenada, and quite possibly have
taken Vicksburg from the east. But it was because he was
threatened by a political rear attack—the appointment of
McClernand—an attack which he felt would lead to the
destruction of his idea, and consequently of his strategy,
that to maintain this idea he shifted his line of operation
from the railway to the river, increasing his tactical difficulties enormously. In spite of these difficulties, his final
plan is not far removed from his original one. According
to his first plan Sherman was to operate against Haines's
Bluff whilst he moved down from Grenada ; in his final
plan, Sherman feinted at Haines's Bluff, and he moved up
from Port Gibson.

From direction of movement I will turn to distribution
and concentration of force, and here again we shall see that,
between the battles of Belmont and Chattanooga, Grant
became a master of these principles, and in spite of the
fact that the word " principle " would have conveyed to
him little or no meaning. At Belmont distribution could
scarcely have been more faulty ; at Fort Henry and Fort
Donelson it was amateurish ; at Shiloh it was non-existent,
because security was altogether wanting ; then came a
remarkable change. At Iuka and Corinth one force held
while another was ready to hit ; neither battle led to a
complete success, nevertheless the idea of a correct distribution of force is to be seen in each. At Vicksburg the
columns of Sherman, McClernand, and McPherson were so
distributed that any one of them could resist whilst the

other two pressed—that is, concentrated against the enemy opposing the resistance. The first concentration, as I have already stated, was made against Jackson, because this railway junction was what may be called a centre of strategical mobility. In 1914 Paris occupied a similar position with reference to the advancing German right wing. In 1905 General von Schlieffen had planned that this right wing was to envelop Paris, and so destroy it as a centre of mobility before this wing moved east and struck the French armies in rear ; but in 1914 this plan was modified by General von Kluck moving forward east of Paris in a south-easterly direction. Immediately this centre of mobility became active, an army was assembled there, and the German right wing was threatened in rear ; this manœuvre led to the battle of the Marne.[1] Grant, as we have seen, was wiser than the younger Moltke ; from Port Gibson he did not move on Vicksburg—his goal, nor on *Pemberton's* army—his objective, but on Jackson, the centre of mobility ; and by concentrating his forces against it he protected his rear as I have already described.[2] Once Jackson was occupied, Grant concentrated his forces against *Pemberton*, and driving him across the Big Black, made use of this river as a wet moat to protect his rear whilst he lay siege to Vicksburg. Throughout this entire campaign, concentration and distribution of force march hand in hand, and the economy of force resulting is truly remarkable ; in all, Grant lost some 9,000 in killed and wounded and 400 prisoners to the Confederates' 10,000 killed and wounded and 37,000 prisoners. In other words, Grant's total loss was exactly one-fifth of his opponent's.

At the battle of Chattanooga Grant's distribution is in

[1] In November, 1917, during the battle of Cambrai, the city of Cambrai became a centre of mobility, with the result that directly the initial British attack was checked, the Germans rushed up reinforcements and, on the 30th, counter-attacked the British right, broke through, and all but succeeded in taking the British left in rear.

[2] Grant's operations against the Confederate forces at Jackson and Vicksburg bear a marked resemblance to those of Napoleon against Blücher at Ligny and Wellington at Quatre Bras in 1815.

form classical, for it closely resembles that established in the Macedonian army by Philip in the fourth century B.C., and made use of by his son Alexander the Great throughout his astonishing career. Philip's organisation, consciously or unconsciously, was modelled on that of the human body; it was a three-fold organisation, the central phalanx was the trunk and the two cavalry wings attached to it the arms which, hinged on the trunk and protected by it, could punch right or left. It is not the place here to enter into the detail of this organisation, but, in my opinion, it was the most perfect ever devised for war, and with certain modifications remains so.

At Chattanooga what do we see ? A three-fold order of battle : Thomas's army is the phalanx, or trunk ; Hooker's the right wing and Sherman's the left—the wings moving forward and threatening whilst the centre holds firm and protects their inner flanks.[1] Grant's plan was to knock out *Bragg* with his left, and because the blow failed several writers have stated that Grant's plan failed. In detail it did, because Sherman did not knock out *Bragg*, but in idea it did not. The left wing being hung up, the right wing swung forward, and threatening the left flank and left rear of *Bragg's* army, distracted his centre, which was assaulted and overthrown by Thomas. It was because Grant's distribution was flexible that he was able to modify his plan and yet maintain his idea ; had it been rigid, Sherman's failure would have ended the battle, and *Bragg* would either have remained in position or have retired. In actual fact, Sherman's failure did lessen the chances of annihilating *Bragg*, but it in no way prevented Grant severely defeating his enemy. Grant's distribution of force was masterful, because it permitted of a concentration of force against *Bragg's* centre or flanks, according to circumstances, and it permitted of the ultimate direction of Grant's will—the defeat of *Bragg*—being maintained. It is in this distribution that we see his generalship far more clearly than in the final results of this battle.

[1] As will be seen in Chapter XIV, Sherman made use of this formation during his Atlanta campaign.

In my definition of strategical action I stated that strength must be concentrated unexpectedly against the decisive point. Unexpected action is surprise, and though Grant as a man was anything but original, from 1861 onwards we see him eagerly striving in most of his battles to gain concentration of force through surprise.

The foundation of his originality is not so much imagination, for Grant was not imaginative, as a quick and rational grasp of conditions, his determination to see things through, and the rapidity with which, once he had made up his mind, he moved and acted. Fort Henry was surprised by a sudden attack, and so would Fort Donelson have been had not the weather delayed Grant's advance. Here he was severely checked, in fact surprised by the Confederate sortie ; but when he learnt that *Buckner's* men had three days' rations in their haversacks, he at once inferred that they were attempting to cut their way out, and that, consequently, they must be massed on the left of their position ; therefore, that on the right of their position the chances were that he would not be opposed in strength. Through this rapid process of reasoning which, considering the circumstances, shows how little Grant's imagination was affected by the tumult around him, he fathomed the situation and at once ordered Smith to assault.

Grant's behaviour at Donelson coincides to the letter with Napoleon's description of a general-in-chief, which is as follows :

" The first quality of a general-in-chief is to have a cool head which receives exact impressions of things, which never gets heated, which never allows itself to be dazzled, or intoxicated, by good or bad news. The successive or simultaneous sensations which he receives in the course of a day must be classified, and must occupy the correct places they merit to fill ; because common sense and reason are the results of the comparison of a number of sensations each equally well considered. There are certain men who, on account of their moral and physical constitution, paint mental pictures out of everything : however exalted be their reason, their will, their courage, and whatever other good qualities they may possess, nature has not fitted them to command armies, nor to direct great operations of war." [1]

At Shiloh Grant was surprised, and, whether he considered that he was so or not, the fact remains that he was never surprised again, and that afterwards he generally aimed at surprising his enemy. At Iuka *Price* escaped from a trap through a disregard of orders on the part of Rosecrans, and at Corinth *Van Dorn* just failed to be surrounded because of the lethargy of this same general. The series of surprisals at Vicksburg I have already entered into so fully that I will not examine them again. At Chattanooga surprise was aimed at from the moment Grant arrived at that place; Brown's Ferry was surprised, and Sherman was moved secretly from the right to the left of the Federal position, and had the weather not delayed the launching of the battle there can be little doubt that he would have completely surprised *Bragg*. This surprise failing, the next day Hooker, having carried Lookout Mountain, suddenly fell upon the Confederate left flank. Except for Shiloh, there was not a single battle fought by Grant between 1861 and 1863 in which he did not effect a surprise; it was for this reason that his casualties were comparatively low, and his expenditure of force economical.

GRANT AS TACTICIAN

Whilst strategy is largely influenced by communications, the limitations of which are generally well known in war, for during peace time they are daily tested, tactics depend mainly on the powers of the weapons used; powers which can only be fully proved out in war itself. Further than this, in modern times, the development of weapons has been so rapid and so great that tactics when compared to strategy have become the more uncertain branch of the art of war.

In brief, the aim of all tactical actions is to develop

[1] *Corresp.*, XXXII, pp. 182-3.

mobility, or to prevent it being developed, from protected offensive power ; in other words, tactical movement depends on hitting or threatening to hit the enemy, and simultaneously on preventing the hitter or threatener from being hit or threatened. We have seen how Grant accomplished this at Iuka, Corinth, and Chattanooga, in each of which battles one of his forces constituted the base of action of the other. At Champion's Hill he failed, because McClernand was over-cautious, this over-caution wrecking the opportunity created by McPherson's holding attack.

In battle, the first action of an attacker is to immobilise his enemy—that is, to hold or to fix him. He does so by pressure which compels his adversary to resist, to reinforce his resistance from his reserves, and so lose power to manœuvre. The second action is to demoralise his enemy and his enemy's command by a distracting attack—that is, an attack which draws him away from his intention by surprising him or threatening him in a quarter the security of which is vital to his plan. Of such operations, the rear attack, or its threat, is usually the most effective. Grant was thus distracted at Belmont, and directly he realised that his rear was threatened, not only was he compelled to change his plan, but his men took fright and became demoralised. At Fort Henry he planned to outflank the position ; at Donelson he wanted the gunboats to steam above the fort and above the village of Dover ; during his first move on Vicksburg, Curtis's advance from Helena towards *Pemberton's* rear was a distracting attack, and so was Sherman's, against *Johnston's* rear, in his advance on Meridian.

Once the enemy's plan is upset, the next action is that of disruption—the disorganisation, or breaking up of the organisation, of the enemy's army by actual attack. Thomas's attack at Chattanooga was such an act ; it decided the battle, but it did not complete it. To complete an attack demands a pursuit—the act of destruction—which is virtually a new attack, and when possible it should be carried out by fresh troops, because victorious troops are normally as disorganised as defeated ones, and when both victor and vanquished are equally exhausted, the latter, influenced by self-preservation, will retire more rapidly than the former will advance.

As I mentioned in the Introduction of this book, security, mobility, and offensive action, as influenced by the endurance of the troops, are principles of war intimately related to tactics : I will now consider these in turn.

In peace training, security is usually neglected, because no danger exists ; consequently fear is not experienced. The " valour of ignorance " replaces courage, with the result that a fallacious value is given to offensive action. Though Grant must have realised this during the war in Mexico, at Belmont he acted like a novice ; there were no reconnaissances, and no reserves, solely a linear fire attack. At Donelson he did reconnoitre, and when McClernand and Wallace's troops were driven back, he withdrew and entrenched them before ordering Smith forward. It was a wise precaution, and one which shows that Grant had learnt one of the most important applications of the principle of security, namely, never to attack without a reserve in hand. A reserve is always a tactical base of operations, a fulcrum to work from, and a reservoir of strength from which may be developed resistance to sudden, or unexpected, pressure.

At Shiloh we see an exceptionally strong defensive position bereft of all its protective value through what can only be described as gross negligence. Grant, apparently bewildered by the large force entrusted to him, and surrounded by untrained officers and men, overlooked the possibility of attack, and trusting to Sherman, who was obsessed by the idea that the enemy would not attack, experienced one of the most startling surprisals of the war. He made no use of entrenchments or of the small force of cavalry under his command, and the excuse that his men were untrained and that the country was not suited to cavalry action bear no weight whatsoever. As I have already stated when examining this battle, in my opinion he was flagrantly surprised.

Rapidity of movement was the physical mainspring of Grant's generalship; seldom has there been a general who so fully appreciated the meaning of Frederick the Great's words : " To advance is to conquer." I have already noted this characteristic so often that I will do no more than mention a few cases. An immediate advance was made on Paducah, Belmont, and Fort Henry ; at Donelson there was a delay on account of the weather, but even then Grant was so anxious to move forward that he eventually did so without his supply train. During the Vicksburg campaign, once at Port Gibson, his movements can only be described as electric ; compared to Halleck after the battle of Shiloh, and to McClellan in his Peninsula campaign, Grant moved like lightning. At Chattanooga it was the same, and it is for this reason that men like Thomas irritated him. Thomas was one of the most successful tacticians of the war, but he refused to seize time by the forelock. He was a man who was never ready to move unless he felt certain of success. As a general-in-chief he would have been as impossible as McClellan, because he would have missed opportunity after opportunity through ceaseless preparation. Grant, in this respect, was exactly the reverse, and his desire to move before the enemy could prepare to meet his blow led him in several of his attacks into serious difficulties. " Who risks nothing gains nothing " was a saying of Napoleon's, and one which can be well applied to Grant.

Badeau, comparing the generalship of Grant and Halleck, says : " Grant believed that, in war, what is won is only a fulcrum on which to rest the lever for another effort. One was essentially a defensive, the other an offensive general ; one always prepared for defeat, the other always expected to win." [1] This is very true, and exactly describes Grant's outlook on offensive action. He was always ready to move, and ready to move against his enemy ; he was never petrified by numbers or situations, and never through fear or caution did he exaggerate the strength of his enemy. At Donelson, when repulsed, he refused to abandon the offensive. At

[1] *Badeau*, I, p. 127.

Shiloh it was the same, and on the evening of the first day of the battle he ordered Sherman to continue the attack in the morning, because he realised that when both sides are in a state of disorder, the side which pushes the attack is the side which is more likely to win. This proved true at Donelson and Shiloh, but at Vicksburg it failed.

The reasons for this failure hinged on two factors which, throughout his career, Grant never fully appreciated, namely, the defensive power of the rifle, and the enhancement of this defensive power by field works—entrenchments, rifle-pits, slashings, and abattis. Grant understood as fully as any other general of this war the value of life, and the folly of unnecessary slaughter. He was not blind to the value of endurance, and this is proved by his paroling the garrison of Vicksburg; for, as it will be remembered, he was of opinion that these men when they returned to their homes would have a demoralising influence on those who were still fighting. He understood full well the value of *moral*, and the detrimental influence of casualties on *moral*; but what he did not understand was that the muzzle-loading rifle, when compared to the old musket, was a far more powerful weapon in the defence than in the attack. Most other generals in this war shared with him this failing.

In the Mexican War Grant's experiences were based on the flint-lock musket. In that war assaults had more often than not succeeded, and be it remembered that the range of the musket was so restricted that artillery could frequently continue to protect the assaulting troops until they were within charging distance. The increased range of the rifle drove the guns back, with the result that the assault could no longer be supported by them, and as the rifle became more efficient this support became more and more problematical.

In the West, during the years 1861-3, the Confederate forces for the most part were indifferently armed, and assaults were frequently successful; in 1864-5, in the East, except for the magazine carbines, they were generally as well armed as the Federals. The result was that the assault became more and more difficult, and it may be said that it proved only an economical form of attack when the defender was excessively weak, when he was unprepared, when he was surprised, or when the assault was most carefully prepared and supported.

In the first assault on Vicksburg Grant's theory (when an enemy is disorganised an assault will overwhelm him) broke down, because he failed to realise that a mob of men entering an entrenched line is automatically reorganised by the actual trench they occupy. They are no longer a mob, in place they are a line of men, nearly as well organised, and far more securely protected, than when they were in line in the open field. There is no possibility of manœuvre, their tactics are reduced to their very simplest form ; for all the men have to do is to turn about, and open fire on the advancing attacker. If they are not outflanked, and if they are sufficiently well armed, or numerous, to fire three to four rounds a minute to each yard of front, it is almost a mathematical certainty that the assault will be shattered. Further still, artillery can still closely co-operate with the defence.

The second assault at Vicksburg was a tactical error, and this Grant realised, for not only did he regret having ordered it, but as it will be remembered, in his next battle—Chattanooga—he was extremely cautious in handling Thomas's frontal attack. He planned the assault in two stages : first, the lower line of rifle-pits was to be carried, and only after it was captured was the line along the crest of Missionary Ridge to be assaulted. The men, however, decided matters for themselves, and, refusing to make two bites at the cherry, they carried the ridge in one rush.

I cannot help feeling that Grant learnt a lesson here which he never forgot, namely, the danger of hesitation, and the decisive effect of a successful frontal attack. He cannot have failed to have recognised that had McClernand assaulted the Confederates at Champion's Hill, *Pemberton* would have been annihilated. His own assaults at Vicksburg failed ; this caused him to hesitate ; then came the assault on

Missionary Ridge, which persuaded and convinced him of the feasibility of the frontal attack, and its devastating effect when successful. This lesson we must bear in mind when we examine his campaign in Virginia ; for I am convinced that it is the clue to the understanding of his assaults in the Wilderness and at Cold Harbor. Had it not been for his success at Missionary Ridge, I am of opinion that in 1864 his tactics would have been different ; for he was an extremely rational man, and though stubborn by nature, I do not believe that he would have sacrificed men's lives as he did, unless he was convinced that the success of any one of these assaults would have been so great as to prove decisive.

PART III

GRANT AS GENERAL-IN-CHIEF

CHAPTER X

THE PLAN OF CAMPAIGN

MILITARY AND POLITICAL SITUATION, 1864

THE victory of Chattanooga crowned Grant's work in the West, bringing to a close a series of strategical campaigns the ultimate aim of which was to establish a footing on the southern extremity of the Alleghany mountains, in order to be in a position to manœuvre against the rear of Confederate forces in the East. There, as I have pointed out in a former chapter, military operations had in nature been political, and strategical results negligible. Lincoln realising this turned to Grant.

On March 3 he was ordered to Washington; on the 9th he received his commission as lieutenant-general, a grade restored by Congress on February 26, and on March 10 he went to the front. From this date until May 4, when he crossed the Rapidan, he had approximately eight weeks wherein to grasp the political and military situation in the East; to concentrate large numbers of scattered troops; to organise them into a small number of powerful armies; to distribute them according to the demands of strategy, and to elaborate a plan of campaign for all the forces in the Union. Eight weeks was not long for this work, when it is considered that in the World War of 1914–18 many single battles took a longer time to mount, and in a microscopic area when compared to that which faced Grant. Curiously enough, this limitation of time has been often overlooked by those who have criticised Grant's Virginian campaign.

Besides this time factor, it is important to realise Grant's personal situation. In the East he was only known by name, and the East being the political sphere of the war, in the eyes of most of the eastern soldiers the western theatre was little more than a strategical backwater. It was as if in the World War a British general had been called from Mesopotamia to France to take over, not only command of the British armies in the west, but also to direct the strategy of the armies of the entire Empire. Not only was he personally unknown to the Army of the Potomac, to Lincoln and to most of the politicians at Washington, but he was to be faced not by a *Pemberton* or a *Bragg*, but by *Lee*, the most renowned general of the day, and to be confronted by a task which had broken McDowell, McClellan, Pope, Burnside, and Hooker, and which had halted Meade.

Grant, on assuming supreme command, found the Union forces divided into twenty-one corps distributed among nineteen military districts, exclusive of the Army of the Potomac under Meade, which faced *Lee* on the northern bank of the Rapidan. On its right was an army under Sigel, scattered in West Virginia and along the Shenandoah ; and on its left another under Butler, which occupied Norfolk and the mouth of the river James. In the West, Thomas and the Army of the Cumberland were at Chattanooga ; Sherman was moving from Vicksburg to rejoin him ; and Schofield at the head of the Army of the Ohio was still operating against *Longstreet* in east Tennessee ; whilst an army of some 30,000 men under the direction of Banks was advancing up the Red river towards Shreveport in Louisiana. All these forces, as Grant said, were acting independently and without concert, " like a balky team, no two ever pulling together." [1]

" So the struggle was protracted, the cost enhanced, and the expenditure of human life increased. A score of discordant armies ; half a score of contrary campaigns ; confusion and uncertainty in the field, doubt and dejection, and sometimes despondency at home ; battles whose object none could perceive ; a war whose issue none could foretell —it was chaos itself before light had appeared or order was evolved." [2]

[1] *Badeau*, II, p. 8.　　　　[2] *Badeau*, II, p. 9.

Though the armies of both sides had by now become veteran forces, the politicians had as yet learnt little from the struggle ; not only did cross-purposes replace unity of purpose, but the Councils at Washington, as Swinton writes, continued to rule alternately by " an uninstructed enthusiasm and a purblind pedantry." [1] Whilst the masses of the people were eager for strong measures, and were ready to undergo all privations, " the politicians feared that strong measures would lose votes, and therefore deemed it a political necessity to coax and bribe men to serve their country instead of compelling their service as a sacred duty." [2] Their fearfulness and lack of policy had so encouraged the peace party in the North, that Grant realised that the problems which confronted him were as much political as military, and, to save the North from a moral dry rot, his problem was not merely one of winning the war in the most economical way, but of crushing the rebellion in the shortest possible time. It was at this crisis he declared that he did not intend to manœuvre, and there is little doubt that his words fitted the political situation, for time prohibited delay and demanded fierce action. He realised that Washington must be protected ; but more clearly than any other general he saw that the policy of shielding the capital against *Lee's* thrusts should be replaced by one which would compel *Lee* to guard himself against his blows. His intentions are clearly set forth by Badeau, and I will quote what he says, for being on Grant's staff he was fully acquainted with his views. He writes :

" Accordingly, when placed in supreme command, he at once determined to use the greatest number of troops practicable against the armed force of the enemy. This was the primal idea, the cardinal principle with which he began his campaigns as general-in-chief—to employ all the force of all the armies continually and concurrently, so that there should be no recuperation on the part of the rebels, no rest from attack, no opportunity to reinforce first one and then another point with the same troops, at different seasons ;

[1] *Swinton*, p. 403.   [2] *M.H.S.M.*, IV, p. 183.

no possibility of profiting by the advantages of interior lines ; no chance of furlough troops, to reorganise armies, to re-create supplies ; no respite of any sort, anywhere, until absolute submission ended the war." [1]

In brief his central idea was concentration of force from which he intended to develop a ceaseless offensive against the enemy's armies, and the resources and *moral* of the Confederacy. This demanded unity of direction in its full meaning, consequently, having been appointed generalissimo, he intended to act as such. Further still, he saw that a pivot to his whole strategy could only be established by fixing *Lee* ; he determined, therefore, simultaneously to become *de facto* commander of the Army of the Potomac, leaving the detail of executive command to Meade. Frequently he has been criticised for this action ; yet had he remained as Halleck did at Washington, it is difficult to believe that Meade would have brought *Lee* to book ; and had he replaced Meade, it is equally difficult to see how he could possibly have simultaneously directed the strategy of the war. In the circumstances, not only do I consider that Grant was right to act as he did, but that he showed remarkable courage in shouldering the whole onus of the war, and in fixing the responsibility of defeating *Lee*, or being defeated by him, on his own shoulders. This arrangement was not a perfect one, and Grant realised it ; but he saw that he was confronted by a choice of evils, and what was so characteristic of him was, that in place of seeking for an ideal solution, he chose what he believed to be the lesser evil of the two, and at once set to work, leaving all detail to Meade—the man on the spot.

In this resolution he was nobly supported by Lincoln who, having learnt his lesson, said to him that " all he wanted, or had ever wanted, was some one who would take the responsibility and act." [2] He at once agreed to a rapid reshuffle of commanders : Halleck unfortunately was to become chief of the staff and remain at Washington ; Meade to continue in command of the Army of the Potomac ; Sherman

---

[1] *Badeau*, II, pp. 9, 10.   [2] *B. & L.*, IV, p. 100.

to take over the command of the Department of the Mississippi, and McPherson to command the Army of the Tennessee. This decided upon, Grant reduced the number of military departments to eighteen, and nominated their commanders.[1] The bulk of the troops, other than those required for protective purposes, he merged into three main armies, namely, the Army of the Potomac to confront *Lee* ; that of Sherman to operate against *Johnston*, and that of Butler, based on Fort Monroe, to hold on to this important position (for to abandon it would have enabled the Confederacy to gain unrestricted communication with Europe), until it could co-operate with the Army of the Potomac, and eventually unite with it.

On March 4, a few days before Grant was appointed to chief command, on Meade's recommendation, the five corps of the Army of the Potomac had been consolidated and reorganised in three ; the Second under Hancock, the Fifth under Warren, and the Sixth under Sedgwick, all officers of experience ; the Cavalry Corps was placed under Sheridan. It was a faulty organisation, as the three infantry corps were so large and cumbersome as to be quite unsuited to the forest warfare they were destined to be engaged in.   To this army was added the Ninth corps, under Burnside, to co-operate with Meade, but to remain under the direct orders of Grant.

STRATEGICAL FOUNDATIONS OF GRANT'S PLAN

When, in February, 1862, Fort Donelson surrendered, Grant, an all but unknown soldier, emerging from out the gloom of the West, opened a line of strategical action from which, two years later, he, as the first soldier in the Union, was to reap full advantage.   If Appomattox was the sunset of the Confederacy, then indeed was Donelson the dawn of Federal victory.

Strategically, his operations between the fall of Donelson and the defeat of *Bragg* at Chattanooga had led to two supremely important results : the first was the establish-

[1] For the full list, see *Badeau*, II, pp. 29-32.

ment of a base of operations at Chattanooga, from which
an army could operate against the rear of *Lee's* forces in
Virginia; the second, the holding of the line of the
Mississippi and the communications running east of it; consequently the establishment of yet another base of operations
from which any Confederate force moving against the right
flank or rear of a Federal army advancing from Chattanooga
towards Richmond might itself be taken in flank. Had he
been allowed to occupy Mobile—as we have seen him constantly urging—the strategical scaffolding of his forthcoming
campaign would have been as complete as could be desired.

His intention now was to make full use of this scaffolding;
to fix *Lee* with his eastern armies, and to manœuvre against
his rear with his western. In order to realise what this
gigantic concentration of force entailed, I will turn to the
Confederate distribution.

Lee's headquarters were at Orange Court House; the
Army of Northern Virginia, which he commanded, was
organised in three infantry corps and a cavalry corps,
namely, the First under *Longstreet*; the Second under *Ewell*;
the Third under *Hill*, and the cavalry under *Stuart*. There
were in all 66,351 present for duty, of which 61,025 were
effectives.[1] *Breckinridge* was in the Valley with about
11,500 men; *Pickett's* division of *Longstreet's* corps was in
North Carolina and southern Virginia, and numbered about
10,000; *Beauregard* and some 15,000 men were in North
Carolina, and the garrison of Richmond numbered about
6,000. On May 1, at Dalton, *Johnston's* army numbered
71,235.[2] Though there were many other detachments, such
as *Kirby Smith* and some 40,000 men between Arkansas
and Mexico, these were the main forces Grant had to reckon
with, and equate with three vital strategical factors—the
security of Washington, the fixing of *Lee*, and the grand
manœuvre against *Lee's* rear.

---

[1] *N. & L.*, p. 111; *Humphreys*, pp. 14–17.

[2] *Atlanta*, p. 243. The difficulty of computing strengths may be gauged
from the following returns : *Johnston*, July 10, 1864—total 135,092, present
73,849, effectives 50,932 ; *Hood*, July 31, 1864—total 136,684, present
65,601, effectives 44,495.

To protect Washington, the simplest operation was to place the Army of the Potomac between *Lee* and the capital. McClellan had neglected to do this, and his campaign had in consequence been wrecked. But again, Burnside and Hooker had both advanced overland, and had failed to penetrate the defensive area of the Wilderness, which was in fact a natural outwork protecting Richmond on its northern flank.

Grant considered the feasibility of a coastal movement south of the James, and at first seems to have favoured it. He argued that he could form two armies each in strength equal to *Lee's*, that he could move one by sea to the James and by leaving the other on the Rapidan eliminate the danger to Washington. By this means he hoped to combine the tactical defensive with the strategical offensive.[1] This was only a passing idea and he soon abandoned it ; for not only did it entail a division of force, but, in the circumstances, time was insufficient to mount such an operation ; further still, no move by sea could be made with secrecy.[2] Grant himself says : " If the Army of the Potomac had been moved bodily to the James river by water, *Lee* could have moved a part of his forces back to Richmond, called *Beauregard* from the south to reinforce it, and with the balance have moved on to Washington." [3] Ropes, who is hostile to Grant's plan of campaign, agrees that this appreciation is sound, and adds : Had Grant followed in the footsteps of McClellan, " I see no reason to suppose that the first battle of the campaign, though fought on the banks of the Chickahominy, would have been any less murderous or indecisive than the sanguinary struggles in the Wilderness, at Spottsylvania, or at Cold Harbor itself." [4]

Having decided on an overland advance, Grant's next

---

[1] *Swinton*, pp. 406–9.

[2] The following case shows how difficult it was to keep anything secret : On May 5, a little before midnight, Grant gave Colonel Rowley of his staff verbal instructions for the night, then he says : " Three days later I read in a Richmond paper a verbatim report of these instructions." (*Grant*, II, p. 144.)

[3] *Grant*, II, p. 141.   [4] *M.H.S.M.*, IV, p. 370.

problem was to determine the direction of his forward movement : should he move against *Lee's* left or right ? On April 9 he was still undecided ; this day he wrote to Meade as follows :

"*Lee's* army will be your objective point. Wherever *Lee's* army goes, you will go also. The only point upon which I am in doubt is whether it would be better to cross the Rapidan above, or below him. . . . By crossing above, *Lee* is cut off from all chance of ignoring Richmond and going north on a raid ; but if we take this route, all we do must be done whilst the rations we start with hold out ; we separate from Butler, so that he cannot be directed how to co-operate. By the other route, Brandy station can be used as a base of supplies, until another is secured on the York or James river." [1]

To move by the left, that is against, or around, *Lee's* right, was tactically disadvantageous but strategically sound. The Wilderness was the worst possible area to fight in ; but Grant soon realised that tactics must be subordinated to strategy. Butler's army could not be withdrawn, because Fort Monroe and the surrounding country constituted an area of vital importance. If Grant moved by his right, Butler would be entirely separated from him, and concentration of force would be impaired ; further still, Grant would be tied down to the Orange and Alexandria railway as his line of supply, and many thousands of men would be absorbed in its protection ; this alone cancelling out any advantage of fighting through more open country. Soon he saw that the Federal command of the sea was the backbone of his strategy, and that he could take advantage of it as he had of the Mississippi in the West. He realised that as tactics are based on strategy, in its turn strategy is based on administration ; that is, if action depends on movement, movement depends on supply. The sea could supply him and evacuate his wounded ; for by moving near to the coast he could constantly change his base of supply ; this obviously was a great advantage. Tactically there

[1] 60 *W.R.*, p. 827.

was a hope, but only a hope, that he would be able to get through the tangle of the Wilderness undisturbed. Meade and Humphreys were strongly of the opinion that *Lee* would be content to hold his lines on the Mine Run, as he had done in the Mine Run campaign in November, 1863. He decided, therefore, to advance by his left flank, and on April 29 wrote the following dispatch to Halleck :

" My own notions about our line of march are entirely made up, but as circumstances beyond my control may change them, I will only state that my effort will be to bring Butler's and Meade's forces together.

" The army will start with fifteen days' supplies ; all the country affords will be gathered as we go along. This will no doubt enable us to go twenty-five days without further supplies, unless we should be forced to keep in the country between Rapidan and the Chickahominy, in which case supplies might be required by way of the York or the Rappahannock rivers. . . . When we get once established on the James river, there will be no further necessity of occupying the road south of Bull Run." [1]

To Meade he wrote : " Should a siege of Richmond become necessary, siege guns, ammunition, and equipments can be got from the arsenals at Washington and Fort Monroe." [2]

It has often been asserted that in the forthcoming campaign Grant was outgeneralled, and was compelled by *Lee* to abandon the overland route and his entire plan. It is true that he hoped to destroy *Lee's* army before it could fall back on Richmond ; nevertheless, like Napoleon's ideal general, he painted no mental pictures and refused to found his campaign on a hope. Nothing is certain in war, and because Grant did not believe that Chance plays so important a part as most generals do, he determined to chance nothing, and in place he prepared for a change of base. He foresaw the possibility of having to establish himself on the river

---

[1] 60 *W.R.*, pp. 1017, 1018. Before the Wilderness campaign opened, Grant informed his two army commanders that it was his intention " to put both their armies south of the James river in case of failure to destroy *Lee* without it." (See 67 *W.R.*, pp. 15, 16 ; 60 *W.R.*, pp. 828, 885, 904.)

[2] 60 *W.R.*, pp. 880, 881, 889, and 107 *W.R.*, p. 1158.

James, and besides this he made ready to lay siege to Richmond. As events testify, few generals have been so clear-sighted as Grant.

Having decided on his main line of direction, the next problem was one combining security and concentration of force. On his right flank lay the well-roaded and fertile Shenandoah Valley—the strategical race-course of the war. Whenever hard pressed, as in 1862 and 1863, the Confederate armies had used it in order to threaten Washington, and so compel the North to assume the defensive. It was the direct line of political attack, and the frequent advances down it, more than any other factor in the Confederate strategy, had prolonged the war ; and be it remembered, the only hope left to the South of gaining their independence was to prolong it, and so weary out the North.

In the spring of 1864 General Sigel was in command of an army 32,061 strong [1] in the Department of West Virginia, which included the Shenandoah Valley. His troops, of which 11,000 were cavalry, were much split up on account of the activity of the Confederate guerrillas, but he had a strong column under Crook in the Kanawha region, and another under himself distributed near the Potomac line. Grant set him two problems : the first was to operate with Crook's column against the Virginia and Tennessee railway and New River bridge ; and the second, for his own column to protect the Baltimore and Ohio railroad, not by sitting on it but by menacing the Virginia Central railroad at Staunton, which operation would simultaneously distract attention from Crook. This defensive plan of campaign, attempted through offensive action, proved, as we shall see, too complex and bold a one for Sigel, and Grant has been blamed for having entrusted him with it. Still more has he been blamed for maintaining General Butler in command of the Department of Virginia and North Carolina ; to this general I will now turn.

Grant's main idea was, as I have already stated, to fix *Lee* and to manœuvre against his rear. Subordinate to

[1] *Pond*, p. 263.

this he determined that Butler's army should operate against *Lee's* base, Richmond, and its neighbourhood, whilst he himself moved upon him through the Wilderness. By so doing, Butler would prevent *Lee* from being reinforced, and would distract his army. Simultaneously, Butler's advance would cover the James, and eventually, should Grant's forward movement prove successful, his and Grant's armies were to unite.

Ropes has severely attacked this plan, stating that it was " an inexcusable mistake for Grant ever to have entertained it." [1] His first criticism is against Butler, and he states that Grant should have insisted on his removal. Like many historians he entirely overlooks the political situation, a factor Grant never overlooked. Grant did not know Butler or Sigel, and being new to the East was naturally averse to wholesale removals. He realised, however, that Butler, though an able organiser and administrator, was an indifferent general, and he had urged Lincoln to replace him by General William F. Smith; but the President had refused to do so, because Butler was a commanding personality in politics. He had been outlawed by Mr. Davis's cabinet,[2] was a political power in the North, and carried with him thousands of weavers to the Union cause. Grant realised that the political security of Lincoln was at this time of greater importance than the military efficiency of Butler; and Lincoln realised it also, for soon after his successful presidential campaign in the following winter he removed Butler from his command.

Ropes's second criticism is : That to allot nearly 40,000 men to Butler was an infringement of economy of force ; that 10,000 would have been sufficient, and that the rest should have been added to the Army of the Potomac. Ropes's objection is apparently based on Grant deciding

---

[1] *M.H.S.M.*, IV, p. 368.

[2] " Insults offered by the ladies of New Orleans to Union soldiers provoked the celebrated order in which he directed that women so doing were to be considered for police purposes as women of the town " (*Atkinson*, p. 364). Colonel George A. Bruce compares him to Fouché, Napoleon's minister of police. (*M.H.S.M.*, XIV, p. 87.)

to advance on two lines of operation, a movement so often decried in textbooks on strategy, and especially by Jomini, whose works Ropes appears to have studied; he entirely overlooks, however, that free sea communication existed between Grant and Butler, and that, as I shall refer to later on, difficulties of supply prohibited a vast increase in the strength of the Army of the Potomac.

Thirdly, Ropes attacks Grant for Butler's eventual landing at Bermuda Hundred, and considers that his correct action should have been to advance on Petersburg. But this is what Grant intended. On April 1 he visited Butler at Fort Monroe, and learnt from him that he preferred the route by the south side of the river. This exactly coincided with his own views, and he pointed out to Butler the importance of obtaining possession of Petersburg.[1] Richmond was to be his " objective point," that is the focal point in his campaign, but Petersburg, as a railway junction, was the key to Richmond—for when this junction was once gained Richmond must fall. On April 2 he confirmed this interview in writing, and said : " When you are notified to move, take City Point with as much force as possible " ;[2] and again on April 16, " What I ask is, that . . . you seize upon City Point, and act from there, looking upon Richmond as your objective point." [3] Grant did not—though knowing Butler to be an indifferent general, I think he might have—directly mention Petersburg ; but a glance at the map will show that had Butler landed, as he said he intended to, at City Point, from there he must take Petersburg before taking Richmond. To advance on Richmond without taking Petersburg was to expose the whole of his rear to attack, for Petersburg was an important centre of strategical mobility.

Having examined in some detail the foundations of Grant's strategy in the East, I will now turn to the grand manœuvre directed against *Lee's* rear. Grant writes : " There could have been no difference of opinion as to the first duty of the armies of the Military Division of the

---

[1] 95 *W.R.*, pp. 15, 16.　　[2] 60 *W.R.*, p. 795.　　[3] 60 *W.R.*, p. 885.

Mississippi. *Johnston's* army was the first objective, and that important railroad center, Atlanta, the second " [1]— Atlanta occupied, the range of the Alleghanies would be turned. On April 4 he wrote to Sherman saying :

" You I propose to move against *Johnston's* army, to break it up, and to get into the interior of the enemy's country as far as you can, inflicting all the damage you can against their war resources. I do not propose to lay down for you a plan of campaign ; but simply to lay down the work it is desirable to have done and leave you free to execute it in your own way. Submit to me, however, as early as you can, your plan of operations." [2]

Again on the 18th he wrote to Sherman explaining that if the two main attacks should promise great success, the enemy might abandon one part of his line of defence and seek to unite his forces at some central point, hoping that " the [Federal] army meeting with no resistance will rest perfectly satisfied with their laurels." Then he added :

" But you have had too much experience in travelling light and subsisting on the country to be caught by any such ruse. I hope my experience has not been thrown away. My directions, then, would be, if the enemy in your front shows signs of following *Lee*, follow him up to the full extent of your ability." [3]

To assist Sherman, Grant intended to move upon Mobile by land while the navy closed the harbour. From Mobile his plan was to advance northwards towards Montgomery, and distract *Johnston* by threatening his rear, whilst Sherman pressed him in front. The plan, like all others thought out by Grant, was admirably conceived, but it depended on Banks in Louisiana being able to co-operate. At this time Banks at the head of 40,000 men was engaged on the Red river campaign, a useless political operation which neither Grant nor Banks supported, but which had progressed too far to permit of it being stopped suddenly.

[1] *B. & L.*, IV, p. 99.   [2] 59 *W.R.*, p. 246.   [3] 59 *W.R.*, p. 409.

On March 15 (18 ?) he wrote to Banks as follows :

" It will, however, be my desire to have all parts of the
Army, or rather all the armies, act as much in concert as
possible. . . . I look upon the conquering of the organised
armies of the enemy as being of vastly more importance
than the mere acquisition of territory." [1]

He then instructed him to take Shreveport as rapidly as
possible, after which 10,000 men under General A. J. Smith
were to be sent to Sherman, and 25,000 to be held in readiness
to move against Mobile.   On the 31st he sent him orders [2]
to concentrate the 25,000 men against Mobile ; but Fate
decided otherwise, for, on April 8, Banks was attacked and
decisively defeated, losing nineteen pieces of artillery, many
wagons, and an immense quantity of supplies.   The result
of this disaster was that Sherman had to face *Johnston*
single-handed ; but the interesting point to note is, that
Banks was to play the same part to Sherman as Butler was
to play to Meade.   Whilst Meade fixed *Lee* to enable Sherman
to manœuvre, Butler was to distract *Lee*, and Banks *Johnston*,
by subsidiary rear manœuvres and attacks.   Not often has
so perfect a plan of developing mobility from a protected
offensive base been devised, for, as Grant said to Meade
on April 9 : " So far as practicable, all the armies are to
move together, and towards one common center," [3] the
whole being pivoted on the Army of the Potomac.

Besides these grand operations, Grant had to decide on
many minor ones, his essential dispersions being as follows :
guarding prisoners ; protecting railways ; hunting down
guerrillas ; holding the Sioux and other Indians in check,
and watching the frontier of Canada.   The following subsidiary commanders were appointed : Dix to command
the troops in New York and New England ; Couch in
Pennsylvania ; Lewis Wallace in Maryland ; Augur in
Washington ; Heintzelman in the central West ; Pope
in Minnesota ; Rosecrans in Missouri ; Wright on the
Pacific coast ; Carleton in New Mexico, and Steele in

[1] 62 *W.R.*, p. 610.   [2] 67 *W.R.*, p. 15.   [3] 60 *W.R.*, p. 827.

trans-Mississippi. I mention these duties and commanders as it·is frequently overlooked by those who criticise Grant's Virginian campaign that he had many other regions to consider. To me it is quite extraordinary how in this maze of operations he was able to maintain his object, namely, holding the Army of Northern Virginia in so tight a grip that his other armies could manœuvre towards the common centre—Richmond.

TACTICAL FOUNDATIONS OF GRANT'S PLAN

In the forthcoming attack *Lee's* distribution [1] was influenced by the topography and communications south of the Rapidan quite as much as by the position of his enemy and the crossings over this river. It was obvious that Grant would advance either by the Orange and Alexandria, or the Richmond—Fredericksburg railway. The second was of no great importance to *Lee*, but the first was vital; for should Charlottesville be captured, the probabilities were that Lynchburg would be attacked, and the East Tennessee and Virginia railroad would be lost to the Confederacy. Whilst the Orange—Alexandria line ran through fairly open country, protected on its western flank by the Blue Ridge, the railway from Richmond to Fredericksburg was crossed by a series of rivers flowing at right angles to it; also it was strongly protected by the Wilderness which stretched westwards and south-westwards from Fredericksburg.

Bearing these conditions in mind, *Lee* distributed his troops in such a manner that he could take in flank a Federal force advancing by either of these railways. Army headquarters and, *Hill's* corps were established at Orange Court House, *Ewell's* along the Mine Run, and *Longstreet's* at Gordonsville; all three covered by *Stuart's* cavalry corps, the main body of which was quartered on the lower Rappahannock in the neighbourhood of Fredericksburg. Should Grant advance by *Lee's* left, then *Hill* supported by *Ewell* would oppose him, when *Longstreet* could manœuvre against one or other of the Federal flanks. Should he advance by

[1] See Appendix III.

Lee's right, then *Ewell* supported by *Hill* would do likewise, and again *Longstreet* could manœuvre. As regards the second of these operations, the rivers which form the Mattapony and the Pamunkey would be of high tactical value to *Lee* ; because, whilst from his position he could move eastwards between them, Grant moving southwards would be compelled to cross them. To *Lee* they formed protected avenues of approach, to Grant—wet ditches which would have to be stormed.

Grant's object was to destroy *Lee's* army ; he knew that the Southern cause was waning ; he knew that in the Confederate armies desertions were growing apace, and that what *Lee* feared most of all was a heavy casualty list ; [1] for power to stay the war out was now the aim of the grand strategy of the South. Grant's grand tactics were based, therefore, on the attrition of *Lee*, an attrition which was to lead to such an attenuation of his strength that he would be compelled to use his entire force on the defensive ; this would deny him freedom of movement, and would consequently fix him.

Grant had to fight *Lee*, and as he himself says : " It was better to fight him outside of his stronghold [Richmond] than in it," [2] consequently he had no alternative to attacking hastily constructed entrenchments and inflicting casualties, except that of manœuvring *Lee* at small cost to him into the fortifications of Richmond. As Humphreys, Meade's chief-of-staff, says :

" But move as we might, long-continued, hard fighting under great difficulties was before us, and whatever might be the line of operations adopted, the successful execution of the task of the Army of the Potomac could only be accomplished by the vigorous and untiring efforts of all belonging to that army, and by suffering heavy losses in killed and wounded, and that the whole army well understood." [3]

[1] " It is pathetic to read in Lee's messages to his Government the ever-recurring phrase, ' By God's blessing our casualties are small.' " (*Atkinson*, p. 20.)

[2] *Grant*, II, p. 141.   [3] *Humphreys*, p. 9.

In brief, this was the essence of Grant's plan : All four armies were to attack simultaneously ; but all four attacks were not to develop an equal degree of force. This continued movement Grant hoped would prevent any one Confederate army reinforcing the other. Sigel's attack was, as we have seen, based on a defensive idea, and Butler's and Sherman's on that of manœuvre. Meade's attack, the pivot of this combined operation, was otherwise. It was to be an attack in such overwhelming force that *Lee* would suffer so heavily that the Confederate Government would be unable to reinforce any other army—this, it was expected, would have a demoralising influence on *Johnston*. It was also to be a continuous attack, in order to prevent *Lee's* army recuperating, and to impede his sending men on furlough or to work in the fields or the workshops, as had frequently been done during the intervals between battles in the past. Further than this, no exchange of prisoners was to take place.

Grant's army, that is the Army of the Potomac and Burnside's corps, numbered about 115,000 officers and men of all arms " equipped for duty," [1] distributed as follows : Sheridan's Cavalry Corps (13,287) covering the front from north-west of Culpeper Court House on the right to near Richardsville on the left ; Army headquarters and the Fifth Corps under Warren (25,663), at and around Culpeper Court House ; the Second Corps, under Hancock (28,333) south of Brandy Station, and the Sixth Corps, Sedgwick (24,213) north of this same place. The Ninth Corps, Burnside (22,762), stretched from a little north of Rappahannock Station to within a few miles of Manassas Junction : it was kept well back and in general reserve, so that should *Lee* fall upon the right flank of Meade's army after it had crossed the Rapidan, it could attack *Lee's* left flank ; or should *Lee* remain on the Mine Run, then it could operate against *Lee's* left flank and rear. The whole army was so placed that it could effect a direct advance along the Orange and Alexandria railroad, or, by swinging slightly

[1] " Present for duty "—127,095 (67 *W.R.*, pp. 198, 285, 915). See App. IV.

to its left front, cross the Rapidan at the fords west of Fredericksburg. This last-mentioned movement was the line of advance decided upon by Grant.

Most historians have severely criticised Grant for his Wilderness campaign, but amongst the few who have troubled to analyse his plan Ropes is the only one I know of who has definitely recommended a different one : he writes :

" There was but one way which was certain to give the Army of the Potomac the advantage of choosing its battle-ground, and that was the way adopted by General Sherman in his Atlanta campaign, which was conducted contemporaneously with this campaign of Grant's in Virginia. That way was to flank the enemy out of position after position, until by some fortunate combination of circumstances he could be brought to bay in a place where our great superiority of numbers would tell ; and had General Grant, before he crossed the Rapidan, reinforced his army with the garrison of Washington [1] and, I may add, with one of Butler's corps also, no one, in my judgment, would ever have had reason to complain of his choice of the overland route to Richmond. With such a force at his command he could have received General *Lee's* attack at the Wilderness with his main body and also have seized Spottsylvania with 30,000 or 40,000." [2]

A brief examination will show that this plan, which on the face of it may appear to be a sound one, is exactly the reverse.

Ropes's first error, and a fundamental one, is that like most of Grant's critics he has treated the campaign between the Rapidan and the Chickahominy as a single operation of war, and has overlooked the fact that it was part of a combined operation. Secondly, he has missed Grant's object, which was not to flank *Lee* out of one position after the other until he sought refuge behind the fortifications of Richmond, but to hammer him to such an extent that *Johnston* could not be reinforced. It was largely because

---

[1] Ropes says : 40,000 and 50,000 men.   [2] *M.H.S.M.*, IV, p. 371.

he hammered *Lee,* and after two days' fighting, as we shall see, compelled him to adopt a Fabian policy, that Sherman's manœuvre was so successful. Had *Lee* been able to fall back intact on Richmond, he could have held its fortifications and simultaneously have spared reinforcements for *Johnston.* The suggestion that Grant should have operated as Sherman did is, therefore, most inapt. Had Grant done so, he would have had either to assault Richmond, a more costly task than attacking field entrenchments, or have invested the fortress as he eventually had to do, but with this difference : that, as *Lee* would not have suffered severely, *Johnston* would have been reinforced and Sherman held back. There was no alternative to attacking *Lee* in the field except attacking him behind permanent fortifications, and what Ropes means by " until by some fortunate combination of circumstances he could be brought to bay in a place where our great superiority of numbers would tell," he does not even hint at. To trust on " fortunate circumstances " is about as helpful in war as was once the examination of the liver of a goose.

To turn from these two cardinal errors to the action suggested, which embraces an army of some 187,000 strong, Ropes overlooks the fact that Butler's 38,000 men contained 27,000 who otherwise could have reinforced *Lee* ; and to have stripped the Departments of Washington and the Susquehanna of their entire garrison, which, on April 30, numbered 39,394 " present for duty," [1] would have been a political blunder equal to McClellan's in 1862. Supposing, however, that Grant had been able to mass 187,000 men, then Ropes entirely overlooks two factors, namely, the nature of the country and supply : the first I will deal with in the next chapter, the second I will briefly examine here.

To have added 60,000 men to Grant's army would have enormously increased its train, which, for his 127,000 men, numbered over 4,000 vehicles. These, if assembled on one road, would have stretched from the Rapidan to Richmond, a distance of 65 miles. This train was already too cumber-

[1] 60 *W.R.*, pp. 1047, 1052 ; 81 *W.R.*, pp. 47, 48.

some, and it proved a constant source of delay and anxiety. If Grant could have solved the problem of supply, then I consider that the 60,000 additional troops would have been better employed in moving direct on Orange Court House with the object either of fixing *Lee's* left flank, or of falling on his rear, whilst the Army of the Potomac and Burnside's corps advanced on the lines laid down for them.

CHAPTER XI

FROM THE RAPIDAN TO SPOTTSYLVANIA

ORDERS FOR THE ADVANCE

ON May 2, General Meade issued his orders [1] for the advance on Wednesday, May 4 ; they are concise and clear, and show that the staff work of the army left little to be desired. In brief, the movements laid down were as follows :

Cavalry Corps.—The 2nd Cavalry Division (Gregg) to move to Richardsville on the 3rd, and, at 2 a.m. on the 4th, should the Rapidan be unfordable, to cross the river by a canvas pontoon bridge, and when the Second Corps arrived to move to Piney Branch Church, throwing out reconnaissances towards Spottsylvania Court House, Hamilton's Crossing, and Fredericksburg. In this position the division was to remain so as to cover the passage of the army trains, and, when they arrived, to move with them covering their left flank.

At midnight the 3rd, the 3rd Cavalry Division (Wilson) to move to Germanna Ford, cross the Rapidan by pontoon bridge and hold the crossing until the Fifth Corps arrived ; then move to Parker's Store, sending out reconnaissance to Robertson's Tavern, the New Hope Church, and Ormond's or Robertson's.

The 1st Cavalry Division (Torbert) to move on the 4th with the trains, and cover their advance. On the 5th to cross the Rapidan and protect the right flank of the trains while crossing the river.

Fifth Corps.—The Fifth Corps (Warren) to begin its advance at midnight the 3rd, bridge the river at Germanna Ford and move to the vicinity of the Wilderness Tavern ; thence, on the 4th to advance past the head of Catharpin

[1] 68 *W.R.*, pp. 331–4.

Run, crossing the Orange Court House Plank Road at Parker's Store.

Sixth Corps.—The Sixth Corps (Sedgwick) to move at 4 a.m. on the 4th following the Fifth Corps to Germanna Ford, and after crossing the Rapidan to bivouac on the heights beyond. The river to be bridged at Culpeper Mine Ford.

Second Corps.—The Second Corps (Hancock) to send forward at midnight on the 3rd two divisions and part of the bridging train to bridge the Rapidan at Ely's Ford ; the remainder of the corps to follow, moving by Stevensburg and Richardsville road. After crossing the Rapidan, the Second Corps to move to the vicinity of Chandler's and Chancellorsville.

Reserve Artillery.—The Reserve Artillery (274 heavy guns) to move at 3 a.m. on the 4th in rear of the Second Corps ; cross the river at Ely's Ford and halt for the night at Hunting Creek.

Trains.[1]—The subsistence and other trains to assemble in the vicinity of Richardsville, and cross the Rapidan at Ely's Ford and Culpeper Mine Ford.

Headquarters.—Headquarters to be on the road of the Fifth and Sixth Corps, and to be established at night between these corps on the Germanna Plank Road.

BATTLE OF THE WILDERNESS

In accordance with these orders, the Army of the Potomac moved towards the Rapidan. At what hour the movement actually took place remains in doubt. Captain Charles H. Porter says : " Promptly at the hours designated in the orders " ;[2] and Major-General James H. Wilson—that not " a single division did start at the time ordered except mine." [3] From *Lee's* right flank on Mine Run, Germanna Ford lay about nine miles, and Ely's Ford thirteen to the

---

[1] " The total number of vehicles and animals with the army was 4,300 wagons (in addition to the artillery and 835 ambulances), 33,991 public and private horses, and 22,528 mules." (*Atkinson*, p. 119.)

[2] *M.H.S.M.*, IV, p. 18.   [3] *M.H.S.M.*, XIII, p. 40.

east ; and be it remembered that Grant did not want to engage *Lee* in the Wilderness : he hoped to push through the greater part of it without fighting ; to compel *Lee* to abandon his entrenched position and to bring him to battle in the more open country beyond the forest. Whatever he may himself say, and whatever others have said about this operation, it was a manœuvre and not an advance to an attack. It is true that he did not overlook the possibility of a flank attack, but it is untrue that he intended to march on *Lee* and engage him.

To understand what the Wilderness was like is to realise the nature of the fighting which took place in it. It was not a forest in the ordinary meaning of the word, but

" a deserted mining region, the home of the whip-poor-will and the bat and the owl. Between the numerous creeks and rivulets are oak-covered ridges and knolls. The sweet-gum and the cedar and the low pine lift their tops just above the dense undergrowth. Ravines bar the way, and the tangled thickets can be traversed only along the winding cow-paths." [1]

It was a region which would have rejoiced the heart of Hannibal or Arminius ; nevertheless it did not terrify Grant, though he fully realised its hidden terrors. Humphreys says : " To handle large bodies of troops in battle in such a field was exceedingly difficult. Except along the main roads and in the open ground of the farms artillery would be of little use." [2] Of the fighting Badeau writes : It was

" a wrestle as blind as at midnight, a gloom that made manœuvres impracticable, a jungle where regiments stumbled on each other and on the enemy by turns, firing sometimes into their own ranks, and guided often only by the crackling of the bushes or the cheers and cries that rose from the depths around." [3]

Again, Swinton says :

" In that horrid thicket there lurked two hundred thousand men, and through it lurid fires played ; and, though no array

[1] *M.H.S.M.*, IV, p. 42.   [2] *Humphreys*, p. 11.   [3] *Badeau*, II, p. 113.

of battle could be seen, there came out of its depths the crackle and roll of musketry like the noisy boiling of some hell-cauldron that told the dread story of death." [1]

I quote from these various writers, all of whom witnessed the fighting in 1864, because, without realising these conditions, it is impossible to criticise Grant's tactics. It was not paucity of numbers which impeded Grant—Ropes's idea—but the over-heavy formations made use of by him ; the consequent loss of men, and the inevitable disorganisation which heavy losses lead to. To hold *Lee* off, and simultaneously move on Spottsylvania, as Ropes suggests, is a perfectly sound manœuvre ; but one demanding extremely flexible and intelligent tactics.

Grant was in fact faced by a form of fighting which neither he nor his men were prepared for, namely, Indian warfare. He was eventually to win through and at heavy cost ; but only after having experienced many of the difficulties which overcame Braddock at the Monongahela river in 1755, and Ferguson at King's Mountain in 1780.[2] Had he understood that in such a region fighting must consist in either hand-to-hand encounters or sharp-shooting ; that not only would every position be entrenched, but that every tree was an entrenchment and every bush an entanglement ; that each attack would take place in a defile, and that between attacks there could be little combination or co-operation, he would most certainly have acted differently.

Though the Confederates never understood these tactics so fully as the famous Bouquet, or the English Hessian mercenaries, or the American Backwoodsmen of 1775–81, they did understand them far better than Grant's men, and what was of equal importance to them was their knowledge of the country, and its many tracks and paths, whilst Grant knew little more than what his map showed him, and the maps of the Wilderness in 1864 were about as indifferent as maps could be. For instance : Todd's Tavern was shown

---

[1] *Swinton*, p. 429.

[2] For the fighting of this period, see my *British Light Infantry in the Eighteenth Century*.

one mile north, South Bend, on the river Po, two and three-quarter miles west, and Spottsylvania Court House two and a half miles west of their correct positions. Gayle House was variously printed as " Jet House " or " Myer's Farm " ; Durrett House, called after Mr. Durrett, a doctor, was immortalised on the map as " Dirt." [1] Unless we realise these difficulties and deficiencies, it is next to impossible to appreciate Grant's actions correctly.

To turn to Grant's antagonist—*Lee*—he was not surprised. He had foreseen that the Federal advance would be made by Germanna and Ely's Fords, and he deliberately chose the Wilderness as his battlefield. His plan as usual was a bold one ; he knew that with an army but a little more than half as strong as Grant's it was folly to meet his enemy in the open. He determined, therefore, to co-operate with the country, and make use of it to reinforce his weakness. He did not intend to defend the Rapidan, nor did he plan to attack Grant when half over the river ; for as a soldier he possessed much of the spirit of the gambler, so he decided to play for the highest possible stake, namely, the annihilation of the Army of the Potomac. His plan was to wait until the whole of Grant's forces had crossed to the south side of the Rapidan, and then, when they and their immense trains were entangled in its thickets, to fall upon their right flank ; to pen Grant up as he had penned up Hooker, and destroy his army or drive it back in rout over the river. He made one mistake, and a cardinal one : he left *Longstreet's* corps at Gordonsville, far too distant should he be required rapidly to support *Ewell* or *Hill*. The boldness of his plan astonished Grant, in fact it surprised him ; equally was *Lee* himself astonished and surprised by the determination of his adversary.

On the morning of the 4th, Grant's movements being observed from *Lee's* signal station on Clark's Mountain, the following Confederate movements were ordered [2] : *Ewell* to Locust Grove on the Orange Pike Road ; *Hill* to the neighbourhood of Verdierville on the Orange Plank Road, and

---

[1] *M.H.S.M.*, IV, pp. 80, 241, 293.   [2] 68 *W.R.*, pp. 950, 951.

Longstreet, who did not move until 4 p.m., to Brock's Bridge, and from there, on the 5th, to Richard's Shop (near Craig's Meeting House) on the Catharpin Road. *Stuart's* cavalry were ordered to operate against Grant's left flank.

On the morning of the 5th, before *Ewell* moved down the Pike Road, *Lee* instructed [1] him to regulate his march by that of *Hill* on the Plank Road, and, if possible, not to bring on a general engagement until *Longstreet* came up. At about 6 a.m. *Ewell* halted the head of his leading column two miles west of Wilderness Tavern, sending a division forward down the Spottswood Road to the Germanna Plank Road. At 7.15 a.m. Meade arrived at Warren's headquarters, and learning of the whereabouts of the enemy he said to him : " They [the enemy] have left a division to fool us here, while they concentrate and prepare a position towards the North Anna ; and what I want is to prevent those fellows getting back to Mine Run." [2] Thinking he was confronted by a rear-guard, he directed Warren to halt his column and to attack the enemy with his whole force. Grant now rode up, and joining Meade, these two generals established their headquarters on a knoll in the open ground near Wilderness Tavern and Lacy Farm, remaining there during the battle.

Meade's orders for the 5th,[3] issued at 6 p.m. on the 4th, had included the following moves : Hancock to Shady Grove Church with his right extended towards Parker's Store ; Warren to Parker's Store with his right extended towards Wilderness Tavern ; Sedgwick to Wilderness Tavern, and Burnside to move to Germanna Ford. Now that the enemy was met, though Grant had hoped to move through the thickets of the Wilderness without fighting, he at once abandoned his manœuvre, and turned on *Lee,* his " objective point." Sedgwick was ordered [4] to send Wright's division to support Warren's right, and Getty's division to support his left, and at 9 a.m. Hancock was ordered [5] to support

[1] 68 *W.R.,* p. 953.
[2] *Swinton,* p. 421.
[3] 68 *W.R.,* p. 371.
[4] 68 *W.R.,* pp. 403, 404.
[5] 68 *W.R.,* p. 407.

Getty. His corps did not, however, begin to arrive until 2 p.m., and at 4 p.m. Getty was ordered to attack whether Hancock was ready or not. Hancock, hearing the roar of battle, came to the support of Getty, the struggle continuing until nightfall.

I will now examine Grant's generalship on this first day of the battle.

On the 4th the Army of the Potomac, though it met with no resistance, was halted early in the day: the head of the Second Corps reaching Chancellorsville between 9 and 10 a.m. ; the head of the Fifth Corps arriving at Wilderness Tavern between noon and 1 p.m., and the Sixth Corps being well across the Rapidan by the afternoon. There can be little doubt that, had the march been continued, Warren could have reached Parker's Store, and Sedgwick Wilderness Tavern. The reasons for this early halt were, that Grant was afraid of uncovering his trains, and also, I think, that he did not expect *Lee* to cross the Mine Run. More than one writer has suggested that the Fifth and Sixth Corps should have pushed on, leaving the protection of the trains to Torbert's cavalry and the Ninth Corps. Humphreys says, however, that this " would have left the right too open during the forenoon of the 5th," [1] and in the circumstances this observation is sound. Nevertheless the question may be asked : were these circumstances inevitable ?

Failing the annihilation of *Lee's* army, Grant's grand tactical problem was to fix *Lee* so that Sherman's manœuvre might be facilitated ; similarly, his minor tactical problem should have been to fix *Lee* in order to cover his manœuvre towards the open country. He clearly saw the greater problem, but he failed to see the lesser, and not seeing it, and consequently not being prepared to meet it, he was compelled by *Lee* to change his plan.

To fix *Lee* demanded that a part of his force, for instance the Fifth and Sixth Corps, strongly supported by cavalry, should have advanced on the 4th to the line Wilderness Tavern—Parker's Store—Shady Grove Church, and have en-

[1] *Humphreys,* p. 20.

trenched themselves across the main road and tracks leading
from Mine Run eastwards.   Had this been done, Grant
could have crossed the whole of his trains over the Rapidan
on the 6th ; and under cover of this protective force have
manœuvred against *Lee's* right flank on the 6th or 7th.
Had *Lee* not attacked, as he did, no disadvantage would
have resulted, for the only change would have been that the
Second and Ninth Corps, in place of the Fifth and Sixth,
would have become the leading troops.

This was Grant's cardinal mistake on the 4th, and even
on the 5th he might have mitigated it, had he, on meeting
Ewell and *Hill*, ordered the Fifth and Sixth Corps to entrench.
From Meade's order,[1] issued at 6 p.m. on May 4, it would
appear that this was his intention, for the marches laid down
were short, and paragraph 8 of the order reads : " After
reaching the points designated, the army will be held ready
to move forward " ; in other words, it was to halt, and halting
meant entrenching.   Be this as it may, the points designated
were not reached, and in the attempt to reach them Grant
brought on a general engagement, in which premature attacks
were made ; for, as Swinton says : " The action on the 5th
May was not so much a battle as the fierce grapple of two
mighty wrestlers suddenly meeting."[2]   That is, though
Grant's army was not surprised, it was not ready to meet
the enemy in such a way as would prevent *Lee* influencing
his manœuvre.

On the evening of the 5th Grant determined[3] to attack
in force on the morrow.   He knew that *Longstreet*, at the
head of some 12,000 men, was on his way to join *Hill* ; consequently he was anxious to assume the offensive before he
could arrive, or make his influence felt.   Grant's plan was
as follows :

The Sixth and Fifth Corps were deployed across the
Orange Pike Road, and the Second Corps across the Orange
Plank Road ; the first two being faced by *Ewell*, and the
last by *Hill* ; between these two groups there was a gap
of about a mile in extent.   Grant's idea was to hold *Lee's*

[1] 68 *W.R.*, p. 371.　　[2] *Swinton*, p. 427.　　[3] 68 *W.R.*, p. 403.

left and annihilate his right.   To carry this idea out, he
ordered Hancock to assault *Hill's* front and left at 5 a.m.
on the 6th ; Warren and Sedgwick to attack *Ewell* and hold
him to his ground, and Burnside to advance through the
gap, and by wheeling to his left envelop *Lee's* right and
attack it in rear.

   Lee, who, until *Longstreet* arrived, was as desirous of delaying the battle as Grant was of reopening it, ordered *Hill*
to assault Hancock at dawn, and so delay his advance ;
but Grant was in no way disconcerted by this ruse, and
at 5 a.m. he moved Hancock forward.   An hour's desperate
fighting followed, when *Hill's* men broke back in confusion.
Of this fighting Grant writes :

   " I believed then, and see no reason to change that
opinion now, that if the country had been such that Hancock
and his command could have seen the confusion and panic
in the lines of the enemy, it would have been taken advantage
of so effectually that *Lee* would not have made another stand
outside of his Richmond defences." [1]

   But Hancock could see nothing, and hearing firing in the
direction of Todd's Tavern,[2] which he thought might be
Longstreet, he slackened his advance.

   At 6 a.m. the head of Burnside's corps, after a march
of forty miles, reached the Wilderness Tavern, but the
country was so dense that his further advance was long
delayed.   Meanwhile Hancock followed up *Hill*, who fell
back on *Longstreet* who was now arriving.   *Hill's* men,
regaining courage at the sight of reinforcements, turned
about and advanced with *Longstreet's*, driving Hancock
back to the position he held in the morning.   In this engagement *Longstreet* was accidentally wounded by his own men,
whereupon *Lee* took command of his right in person.   Withdrawing his men he reorganised them, and then, at 4.15 p.m.,
he assaulted Hancock's front, driving part of it in, but was
finally repulsed.

   Large stretches of the forest were now on fire, and many

---

[1] *Grant*, II, p. 197.   [2] This was between Sheridan and *Stuart*.

of the wounded were suffocated or burnt to death. What with the thickness of the undergrowth, the smoke, and the constant uncertainty of the whereabouts of the enemy, Burnside's, Sedgwick's, and Warren's attacks made little progress ; and Sedgwick, who had sent troops from his right to reinforce Hancock, was suddenly attacked on his right flank, and a panic resulted. Under cover of this and night *Lee* withdrew his army behind its entrenchments.

The losses during these two days' fighting were as follows :

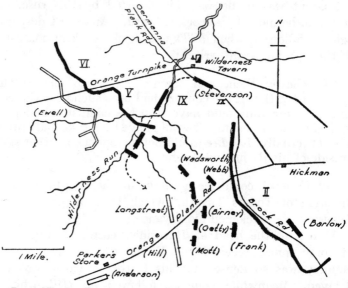

PLAN NO. 3. BATTLE OF THE WILDERNESS, 7 A.M. MAY 6, 1864.

Grant's army, 17,666 [1] ; *Lee's*, at least 11,400,[2] probably more.

On the 6th Grant's idea was a perfectly sound one ; he saw that *Longstreet* was the controlling factor, and that if he could round up *Hill* before *Longstreet* arrived, *Longstreet* single-handed would be left to meet him. His means were however, defective ; consequently his plan was a too ambitious one. Had Hancock and Burnside possessed a force of highly trained light infantry, there can be little doubt

[1] 67 *W.R.*, p. 133.   [2] *N. & L.*, p. 111.

that, in spite of the nature of the forest, *Hill's* corps would have been annihilated. Not only were the tactics of Grant's men far too rigid, but the size of his corps soon proved them to be cumbersome for forest warfare. To attain concentration of force, particularly on his left, Grant did not hesitate to break up his corps, and though this in the circumstances was good generalship, it resulted in confusion, loss of time, and loss in *moral*.

Tactically this battle was an indecisive one, strategically the greatest Federal victory yet won in the East ; for these two days' fighting satisfied *Lee* of his inability further to maintain the contest in the field. From the evening of May 6 until his attack on Fort Stedman the following year, never again did he dare to assume the offensive. It is true, as we shall see, that he sometimes attacked and often counter-attacked ; but from now onwards his strategy was purely defensive. In brief, his losses were so great, that though he could still move, tactically he was fixed. Thus had Grant's most important object been attained, and within forty-eight hours of crossing the Rapidan.

ADVANCE TO SPOTTSYLVANIA

By the evening of May 6 both sides were fought to a standstill. Thousands of men lay in the brushwood dead and dying, and the gloom of the forest was alone lit by the sudden flash of a rifle, or the flames of the burning undergrowth as they licked their way between the trees.

In this chaos of agony, it is of supreme interest to turn to the leaders. *Lee* was winded, never before had he met so formidable an antagonist ; he understood McClellan, Burnside, and Hooker—he was sorry to part from them ; but now he had met a man who refused to part from him, who was undisturbed by attack, and never unnerved by disaster—he paused. Not so Grant. He did not possess the imagination of *Lee* ; whilst the one put his trust in God, the other relied on his big battalions. It was a struggle between hope and faith, resistance against pressure, imagination against logic, and behind it all—a moribund cause battling with a virile one. The night of May 7 was indeed the curtain of a world drama—the struggle between the opposites in life.

Like Blücher—old " Marshal Vorwärts "—Grant's one idea was to advance. That night he determined to plant himself between *Lee* and Richmond, not to deprive Richmond of *Lee* but *Lee* of Richmond ; that is to say, he intended to place his army between *Lee* and his base of operations ; not to avoid *Lee*, but to compel him to come into the open and fight for the security of this base. Through his unerring common sense he divined that *Lee* had had enough of it, and on the night of the 6th, whilst sitting under a pine tree, he said to a staff officer—Colonel Theodore Lyman —" To-night *Lee* will be retreating south." [1] Most generals would have rested after such a battle, would have refitted their army in order to make certain of the next contest, and few would blame them for doing so ; but such disturbing influences, which govern the determination of lesser men, were impotent against Grant. If *Lee* was going to move, then he would move, and if possible before *Lee* could. The hour of this decision was in Sherman's judgment the supreme movement in Grant's life : " undismayed, with a full comprehension of the importance of the work in which he was engaged, feeling as keen a sympathy for his dead and wounded as anyone, and without stopping to count his numbers, he gave his orders calmly, specifically, and absolutely— ' Forward to Spottsylvania.' " [2]

Within twenty-four hours of the battle, the Army of the Potomac was once again on the line of march, not northwards in the footsteps of Hooker, Burnside, and Pope, but southwards towards Richmond. The effect on the men was electric, for as they moved off on the evening of the 7th they began to cheer and sing, one of them saying : " That night we were happy."

Grant issued his orders [3] at 6.30 a.m. on the 7th, upon

[1] *M.H.S.M.*, IV, p. 212.   [2] *B. & L.*, IV, p. 248.
[3] 68 *W.R.*, p. 481.

which Meade wrote his,[1] sending them out at 3 p.m. They were as follows :

The trains of the Sixth, Fifth, and Second Corps to move to Chancellorsville, and the Reserve Artillery by way of Chancellorsville to Block House (near Spottsylvania Court House).

The corps to move as follows : Fifth, at 8.30 p.m., by way of the Brock Road and Todd's Tavern to Spottsylvania Court House ; the Sixth at the same hour to Chancellorsville, then by way of Piney Branch Church to the Brock Road north of Block House ; the Second to follow the Fifth, moving to Todd's Tavern by way of the Brock Road.

The pickets of the Fifth and Sixth Corps to be withdrawn at 1 a.m., and those of the Second at 2 a.m. (the 8th) and follow the routes of their respective corps.

The Cavalry Corps to maintain a sufficient force on the right flank in order to prevent the enemy surprising the infantry columns.

The Ninth Corps to follow the Sixth.

A muddle occurred over the cavalry instructions ; for, before Sheridan's orders were received by his divisions, Meade, without consulting him, ordered the cavalry out to Corbyn's Bridge and the Brock Road, but failed to instruct them to hold Snell's Bridge and the Block House Road.

Meanwhile *Lee*, discovering the movement of Grant's trains, and supposing that his enemy was falling back on Fredericksburg, determined to move forward, not directly against his enemy's front, but against his retiring left flank ; consequently, on the morning of the 7th, he ordered *Anderson*,[2] now in command of *Longstreet's* corps, to move on Spottsylvania in the morning. As the woods were on fire, *Anderson* could find no suitable place to bivouac his men, and without informing *Lee*, he set out for his destination between 10 and 11 p.m. The next morning, *Early*, in temporary command of *Hill's* corps, was ordered " to move by Todd's Tavern, along the Brock Road, to Spottsylvania Court House, as soon as his front was clear of the

¹ 68 *W.R.*, p. 483.   ² 68 *W.R.*, p. 967.

enemy " [1]; and still later, *Lee* telegraphed to Richmond, that " the enemy has abandoned his position, and is moving towards Fredericksburg. This army is in motion on his right flank [i.e. the old left flank reversed], and our advance is now at Spottsylvania Court House," [2] namely, *Anderson's* corps.

The situation was now an extraordinary one, for both armies were operating under a misconception : Grant thought that *Lee* was falling back towards Richmond, and *Lee* thought that Grant was retiring on Fredericksburg ; *Lee* was attempting to move round Grant's original left, and Grant round *Lee's* right. Meanwhile *Anderson*, without orders, was advancing on Spottsylvania, and Warren was moving in the same direction. The crucial problem was : which of these two generals would arrive there first ?

Sheridan, whose command had been completely disorganised by Meade's over-hasty action, crossed the river Ny and pushed on to Spottsylvania ; then, hearing heavy firing in the direction of Todd's Tavern, he advanced towards that place to find himself in rear of two of *Anderson's* divisions. Meanwhile, on the Brock Road, part of the 1st Cavalry Division, which had been ordered by Meade to open the way to Spottsylvania, had become entangled in Warren's advance ; this delayed the Fifth Corps, and no sooner had it disentangled itself than it met *Stuart's* cavalry. A dismounted action followed, under cover of which *Anderson*, advancing along the Catharpin Road, crossed the Wooden Bridge over the Po, and drove Sheridan's 3rd Cavalry Division out of Spottsylvania.

At 11 a.m. Warren drove back the Confederate cavalry in front of him, and came up with *Anderson* who had already entrenched. *Lee* now became aware of the scope of Grant's movement ; and Grant, who had established his headquarters at Piney Branch Church, simultaneously learnt that his road was blocked, and as it happened, not so much through *Lee's* good luck as through Meade's blunder. It is true that had Grant moved from the battlefield of the Wilderness

---

[1] *Early's Memoirs*, p. 22.   [2] 68 *W.R.*, p. 974.

with his left (Hancock) leading, he would have forestalled *Anderson*; but not being certain what *Lee* would do, such a movement would have been extremely risky. Though disappointed by this unlooked-for opposition, he was in no way discouraged, and at once modified his plan to meet the change in circumstances.

At noon Grant received dispatches from Washington, and from these he learnt that Sherman's advance was progressing, and that Sigel was moving up the Shenandoah Valley. The news from Butler was, however, uncertain. On the 5th that general had occupied City Point, had reconnoitred towards Petersburg, and was entrenching " for fear of an accident to the Army of the Potomac [1] " ; further, he wanted " ten thousand of the reserves." Grant at once directed [2] Halleck to send the men, and as he was unable to unite with Butler until he had defeated *Lee*, he decided that Sheridan and the whole of the Cavalry Corps should " cut loose," and proceed on a raid against the north of Richmond, in order to relieve the pressure on Butler.[3]

On the morning of the 9th *Lee* established a strongly entrenched line along the ridge which separates the Po and the Ny, enclosing Spottsylvania in a blunt triangle of works. His position was a strong one, for in front of it lay a tangle of undergrowth and swamp-land : *Anderson* held the left, *Ewell* the centre, and *Early* the right. Facing the first two were Warren and Sedgwick ; Hancock was at Todd's Tavern, and Burnside was in reserve, moving towards Gate with one division at Piney Branch Church to protect the trains.

BATTLE OF SPOTTSYLVANIA

Lee's position between the rivers Po and Ny was one of great defensive strength. That he was fighting in his own country, that his men knew it intimately, and that

---

[1] 68 *W.R.*, p. 517.   [2] 68 *W.R.*, p. 561.

[3] 68 *W.R.*, p. 552. Further than this, a violent quarrel had taken place between Sheridan and Meade, presumably over Meade's change in Sheridan's orders, and I think Grant was not sorry to separate them.

the inhabitants informed him of Grant's every movement, were tremendous advantages; nevertheless, his losses had so depleted his army that he was compelled through this circumstance alone to distribute his troops in such a way that he would be able to exert the maximum resistance, and simultaneously, as occasion demanded, effect a concentration of force against any threatened point. To draw all his troops out in line would have deprived him of reserves; to have established strong reserves would have restricted his front; so, in place, he formed his army into a "hog's snout"; for not only would this formation be a difficult one to envelop should Grant attempt to encircle him, but should Grant mass against either of his flanks, the flank not attacked could act as a reserve to the one threatened.

Grant's object was a simple though difficult one. He realised that *Lee* was unable to maintain the contest in the open field, consequently that he himself had to maintain the offensive rôle. He could have manœuvred *Lee* out of his position, but this was the last thing he wanted to do; for Butler was now moving north, and until he could make his strength felt, to manœuvre *Lee* on to him might prove disastrous. Consequently, Grant decided to fix him by another attack; to hammer him as he had hammered him in the Wilderness, to drive him back in disorder, and then to unite with Butler and either knock *Lee* out, or pin him down within the entrenchments of Richmond, and so facilitate Sherman's manœuvre.

On May 9 a chance mistake, so apt to occur in an enclosed and badly mapped country, seriously influenced Grant's forthcoming operations. Part of Burnside's corps, as we have seen, was moving towards Gate; but the point so marked on the map was merely a roadside gate, and his 3rd Division, under Willcox, who was leading, very naturally passed it by, and, at about 7 a.m., when a mile south of Gate,[1] reached a farmhouse which was mistaken for Gayle. The correct name of this place was Beverly, but on Willcox's

[1] 68 *W.R.*, p. 581.

map it was marked Gayle, which in actuality was situated a mile and a half farther south. Thinking that Gayle was a misprint for " Gayte," which he supposed must be the Gate he had been ordered to march to, he reported his arrival at Gate to Burnside, who reporting it to Grant was ordered by him to close up his three forward divisions at that spot.

Lee, being informed that heavy columns were approaching his right, sent out a force to delay them. Grant learning of this, and simultaneously hearing that the Confederates on the Catharpin Road had been withdrawn, was of opinion that *Lee* was extending his right towards Fredericksburg,[1] with the object of either cutting the Federal line of communications, or of gaining the Telegraph Road—the direct road to Richmond and to Butler. He determined therefore on the following operation [2] : to hold *Lee's* right flank with Burnside's corps ; to engage and hold the right of *Lee's* left flank with Wright's [3] and Warren's corps, and to turn the left of *Lee's* left wing with Hancock's corps. His idea was, that as apparently *Lee* was weakening his left to reinforce his right, he would take advantage of this, and whilst the Fifth, Sixth, and Ninth Corps held *Lee* as in a vice, the Second would envelop his left, roll it up, attack his rear, and annihilate him. This plan was a bold one, and as we see it was based on a misconception.

Meade seems to have had no clear idea of what Grant intended ; for, in place of urging Hancock on, he instructed him to endeavour to ascertain the position and force of the enemy in his front and the location of his left flank. In fact, he asked him to carry out a reconnaissance and not an attack. Hancock, puzzled, acted cautiously. On the evening of the 9th his advance was slow, and *Lee*, grasping Grant's intention, moved two of *Early's* divisions from his right wing to his left. This bold move wrecked Grant's plan of rolling up *Lee's* left flank ; for, on the morning of

---

[1] 68 *W.R.*, pp. 561, 562.   [2] 68 *W.R.*, p. 582.

[3] On the morning of the 9th General Sedgwick was killed by a Confederate sharpshooter, and Wright succeeded to the command of the Sixth Corps. (68 *W.R.*, p. 577.)

the 10th, Hancock found the enemy so strongly entrenched that he was able to make little headway.

Grant, realising that he had been working under a misconception, and that *Lee* was not massing on his right, at once changed his plan. He decided on a general attack at 5 p.m.; Burnside was to advance against the enemy's

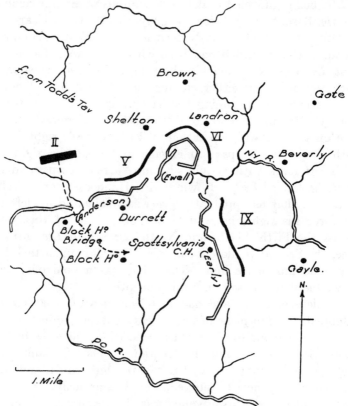

PLAN NO. 4. BATTLE OF SPOTTSYLVANIA, MAY 10, 1864.

right, and was ordered to make " all the show he could " as " the best co-operative effort " [1]; Hancock was to withdraw two of his divisions,[2] and uniting them with those

---

[1] 68 *W.R.*, p. 610.

[2] 68 *W.R.*, p. 600. Mott's division was already detached on Wright's left flank.

under Warren and Wright, to attack the enemy's centre at the same hour. This point of attack, the left face of the salient, was selected because the approaches to it were good, and artillery fire could support an assault made against it.

The original idea was that Hancock with six divisions (two of his own and Warren's four) and Wright and Mott with four divisions should attack simultaneously ; but as Hancock was delayed, and as Warren reported [1] that he could carry the works in front of him without Hancock's assistance, he received an order to do so at 4 p.m. ; [1] Wright and Mott being instructed to attack at the same time. This assault was a failure, and was unsupported by Wright and Mott, who were not ready to co-operate.

In no way discouraged, Grant decided to continue the attack, and Colonel Upton, one of Wright's brigadiers, and twelve selected regiments were ordered to storm the west face of the salient, the apex of which was simultaneously to be assaulted by Mott.

Upton's column was formed in four lines, and the advance was made through a wood, the far edge of which was but two hundred yards from the enemy's entrenchments. On his right flank he was supported by a battery of guns which kept up a constant fire until the moment to charge arrived. As the guns ceased fire, the column quickened its pace, then broke into the charge, and, in spite of a terrible front and flank fire, it swept over the enemy's parapets, then extending to the right and left it opened a large gap in his line, capturing some 1,200 prisoners. Unfortunately Mott's assault failed, with the result that Upton was attacked on all sides. In order to relieve him, Meade ordered Warren to carry out a second assault at 6.30 p.m. ; and though as an assault it failed, it succeeded in preventing *Anderson* reinforcing *Ewell* in the salient. Upton was eventually withdrawn under cover of night.

Meanwhile Burnside had moved forward, and, according to Grant, he " got up to within a few hundred yards of

[1] 68 *W.R.*, p. 600.

Spottsylvania Court House, completely turning *Lee's* right. He was not aware of the importance of the advantage he had gained," [1] and in these circumstances his attack became no more than a reconnaissance in force. That night he was ordered to close in on Wright's left. " This," says Grant, " brought him back about a mile, and lost to us an important advantage. I attach no blame to Burnside for this, but I do to myself for not having had a staff officer with him to report to me his position." [1]

The fighting on the 10th was but a gale heralding the storm. On the 11th came a lull, and the next day the hurricane ; for the ferocity of the fighting on this day has seldom been equalled.

The 11th was given up to preparation. In the morning Grant first wrote to Lincoln : " We have now ended the sixth day of very heavy fighting. The result to this time is much in our favour. But our losses have been heavy, as well as those of the enemy. . . . (I . . . propose to fight it out on this line if it takes all summer.) " [2]   The effect of this letter, as Captain Atkinson writes, " was instantaneous. It is hardly too much to say that from that moment dated Grant's real ascendancy over the people he represented." [3]   Next he prepared for a carefully mounted battle on the 12th, based on the experiences of Upton's successful assault.

His idea was to hold *Lee's* left flank, and assault his centre and right flank. He ordered [4] Meade to move Hancock's corps, less one division, under cover of darkness in rear of the Fifth and Sixth Corps to Brown's House north of the salient. Warren was to take over the front of the Second Corps in addition to his own, and the Sixth Corps was to hold its trenches with two divisions and to draw two out as a mobile reserve. At 4 a.m. Hancock and Burnside, seven divisions in all, were to attack ; Burnside from Beverly

---

[1] *Grant*, II, p. 225.

[2] 68 *W.R.*, p. 627.   The words in brackets are not mentioned in the Official Records.

[3] *Atkinson*, p. 275.   [4] 68 *W.R.*, p. 629.

House due westward against the right flank of the salient,
and Hancock against the apex of the salient.

Heavy rain was falling, when, at 10 p.m., Hancock's
corps moved out of its trenches to concentrate at Brown's
House. There it arrived at midnight, formed up, snatched

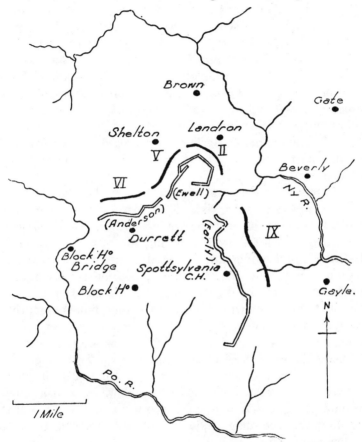

PLAN No. 5. BATTLE OF SPOTTSYLVANIA, MAY 12, 1864.

a little rest, and moved off towards the salient at about
4 a.m. ; for, the morning being very misty, Hancock had
postponed the attack until 4.35 a.m. Barlow's division
was on the left, Birney's on the right, and Mott's and
Gibbon's in rear.

The morning was excessively dark when Hancock's corps moved off through the mud and the mist, marching as it did on a compass bearing. As the enemy's position was neared there emerged from out the fog a line of chevaux-de-frise, a strong and continuous line of earthworks, manned by a double line of infantry, and " the black bellowing mouths of upwards of twenty pieces of artillery " . . . " I remember," says Barlow, " the thin picket line of the enemy, with their bewildered look, of which no one took any notice. There was a little pattering of bullets, and I saw a few of our men on the ground ; one discharge of artillery, that I remember, and we were up on the works with our hands full of guns, prisoners and colors." [1]

I will now condense Barlow's account, for as he was the leading participant in the assault, his is of exceptional interest.

The mass of men was irresistible, for the Confederates were completely surprised. The men surged over the parapet, and were at once thrown into inextricable confusion. The troops which followed them, in place of passing through the mob and forming an organised front, and in place of sweeping down the enemy's flanks, became confused with those of the successful first line. It was not the enemy's fire which interfered with troops re-forming, but the pouring in of supports and reserves. " You could see men of all commands intermingled and lying, in some places forty deep, on the outer side of the captured works, and on the slope which ran down from them." The truth is that, " so far as the assault was concerned, it was . . . the most brilliant thing of its kind of the war " ; but no one was prepared for the magnitude of the success. In General Barlow's opinion :

" It was an accident that we struck this angle, always a weak point in a line ; an accident that the morning was misty to an unusual degree ; an accident that we found a space for our rush so free from obstacles ; an accident that we so escaped the observation of the enemy's outposts and

[1] *M.H.S.M.*, IV, p. 250.

pickets that we were upon them before they could make
any substantial resistance." [1]

Accident though it may have been, success in war very
largely depends on accidents, and the ability of turning
them to account. This Hancock's corps did not do ; the
Confederates were stunned, and not until an hour after the
salient had been stormed did *Lee* launch his first counter-
attack. During these precious sixty minutes, organised
forces of Federals should have swept forward towards the
cross trench north of Harrison's House ; and had this work
been stormed successfully, *Lee's* army would have been cut
in two, and nothing but a miracle could have prevented its
annihilation.

The 'first Confederate counter-attack, launched about
5.45 a.m., struck not a formed but a confused mass of
men, and drove it out of the works. At 5.55 a.m. Hancock
asked [2] for support, and the two mobile divisions of the Sixth
Corps were sent to his aid. The battle now developed into
a hand-to-hand contest, in which one side or the other would
in a few minutes have been forced from the field had not
the trench line, parapet on one side and parados on the other,
proved an all but unstormable obstacle to Federals and
Confederates—in fact, this trench, like a coupling, not only
held the combatants together, but kept them apart. General
Grant of the Sixth Corps says :

" It was not only a desperate struggle, but it was literally
a hand-to-hand fight. Nothing but the piled-up logs or
breast-works separated the combatants. Our men would
reach over the logs and fire into the faces of the enemy,
would stab over with their bayonets ; many were shot and
stabbed through the crevices and holes between the logs.
Men mounted the works, and, with muskets rapidly handed
them, kept up a continuous fire until they were shot down,
when others would take their places and continue the deadly
work. . . . I was at the angle next day. The sight was
terrible." [3]

---

[1] *M.H.S.M.*, IV, pp. 252–6.   [2] 68 *W.R.*, p. 656.
[3] *Humphreys*, pp. 99, 100.

This contest, the ferocity of which was only equalled by its heroism, endured for twenty hours, and left the Second and Sixth Corps masters of the " Bloody Angle."

Meanwhile, the Ninth Corps attacked *Lee's* right flank, and though its assault was disappointing, it held nearly all of *Early's* command to its trenches; and the Fifth Corps, at 8 a.m., attacked *Lee's* left, but Warren was so slow in his movements that, outside keeping *Anderson* busy, no decisive advantage was gained.

Lee handled his men in a masterly manner, launching no less than five organised counter-attacks against the Second and Sixth Corps. It must be said, however, that to hold, as he did, the nose of the salient in strength was a tactical error. The rear trench across its base should have constituted his main line of resistance, and the " snout " should have been regarded as a mere outwork—a fortification which would break up an attack but not necessarily withstand it. This error could not be repaired during the battle; for, as no arrangements had been made to hold the rear line in strength, once Hancock broke through the " snout " it was imperative to force him out of it. To have attempted to withdraw would have meant that the retiring Confederates must have been swept in a confused mass over their reserves with Hancock's men on their heels.[1] *Lee* had to attack, the one thing he did not want to do. Not only did he lose the whole of *Edward Johnson's* division in the first rush, but also several thousands in killed and wounded in his attempts to hold the salient. He had indeed saved the day, but only at a price, and a price he could not afford.

According to General Humphreys, *Lee* lost between 9,000 and 10,000 officers and men on the 12th, of whom 4,000 were captured; and Grant, 6,820 killed, wounded, and missing.[2] Colonel Livermore calculates that, from the 8th to the 12th of May, Grant lost 14,322 men, and *Lee* about 12,000. The effective strength of Grant's army was, therefore, reduced by about 12·5 per cent., and *Lee's* by 19·7 per cent. " This result," writes Livermore, " would disprove the

---

[1] See *Humphreys*, p. 104.   [2] *Humphreys*, pp. 105, 106.

charge of a useless sacrifice of life by General Grant down to the 12th of May." [1]

Looking back on the operations of the 7th to the 12th of May, it cannot be questioned that *Lee's* luck was in, and Grant's was out. This fact does not, however, excuse any faults in generalship committed by Grant; for the test of true generalship is the presence not the absence of difficulties, and the proof—the means attempted in overcoming them. Grant's determination to move on the 7th was admirable, and to move forward from such a battlefield as that of the Wilderness, and after such a battle as the one fought there, shows a determination which is remarkable even in this remarkable man. His manœuvre to deprive *Lee* of Richmond is equally admirable, and curious to relate, his mistake, namely, that *Lee* intended to fall back on his base, was reciprocated by his antagonist, who thought that he himself was retiring on Fredericksburg. The truth is, that neither of these generals yet understood each other.

In this battle the dual system of command in the Army of the Potomac became conspicuous through its faultiness; yet, as I have already observed, it would have been extremely difficult in the circumstances for Grant to have devised a better one. Meade's interference with Sheridan is inexcusable; but his blunder over Hancock's orders is of a type which is inevitable when two men command.

In examining Grant's generalship in this battle, one pivotal factor must constantly be borne in mind, namely—Butler. If Butler's operation on the James is overlooked,

---

[1] *M.H.S.M.*, IV, p. 438. Captain Atkinson has an interesting remark to make on casualties. In spite of the desperate nature of the fighting, the losses on the 12th " show the startlingly low average of 1 per cent. per hour " (*Atkinson*, p. 300). The truth is, that hand-to-hand fighting is nothing like so costly as moving under fire in the open. The loss of 1 per cent. per hour in a charge lasting six minutes would, if the attackers were 10,000 strong, mean a loss of 10 men—a ridiculously low figure ! At St. Privat, in 1870, whilst advancing to the attack, the Prussian Guard lost 6,000 men in 10 minutes. In ancient fighting, very few men were killed until one side broke, when the slaughter which followed was annihilating—at Cannæ, 80,000 Romans were massacred.

no criticism is valid ; for Butler's advance formed the hinge of Grant's forward movement.

Anderson's premature advance was a stroke of luck for *Lee*. Willcox's blunder over Gayle and Gate was in no way an extraordinary one, such mistakes are not uncommon in war and must always be expected. Had Grant not sent all his cavalry away on a raid (this I will deal with in the next chapter) he would have been able to verify the situation of the Ninth Corps, and must have discovered *Lee's* true position. Failure to do so was an indirect cause of the hastily mounted assaults on the 10th, in which Upton's success convinced Grant that *Lee's* front could be broken. If this attack had proved successful, *Lee's* army would have been cut in half. Its initial success, largely due to the fact that the assault was adequately supported by artillery, was vitiated by failure to back it up with strong reserves.

On the 11th careful reconnaissances were made for another attack, which in its initial phase was still more successful than Upton's, for it came as a complete surprise ; and then, as we have seen, it failed in its main object, namely, the cutting of *Lee* in two, not because the reserves were too weak or too strong, but because they were allowed to follow so closely on the heels of the attackers that they became confused with them.   This faulty organisation cannot be charged against Grant or Meade, but must be debited to Hancock.

Was this assault, in the circumstances, the most effective operation which could have been undertaken ? To have outflanked *Lee* was out of the question : first, Grant did not wish to drive *Lee* back on Richmond before Butler had been given time to develop his operation ; secondly, the flanks of *Lee's* army were well protected by the river Po ; thirdly, *Lee's* defensive distribution was an admirable one, for, unless both flanks were simultaneously attacked, the one could support the other ; and fourthly, unless Grant could, by means of his cavalry, which on the 8th he had sent away, have isolated *Lee* from the civil inhabitants, no single move could have been kept secret.

Grant saw that the salient, in spite of tactical difficulties, was strategically the key to *Lee's* rear. Had he understood, as he never did, the true use of artillery, and had the assault been better organised, *Lee* must have been decisively defeated. We are told that on the 12th Hancock's artillery was able to fire over the heads of the assaulting troops, and sweep the interior of the salient.[1] This being so, Barlow's and Birney's divisions should have assaulted under cover of a bombardment ; or, if this were not possible, then a bombardment should have been opened on the Confederate supporting troops, directly the assault succeeded ; when after a twenty minutes' pause, Mott's and Gibbon's divisions should have been brought forward in small compact columns, and have passed through the assaulting troops, which should at once have been re-formed as a reserve.   It was no fault of Grant's that such a common-sense attack was not carried out, but, as we shall see in the next chapter, this simple lesson of the " Bloody Angle " was lost on him.

Finally, and in spite of its tactical errors, Spottsylvania was a crushing blow to *Lee*.   To be deprived of 9,000 to 10,000 effectives in five days' fighting, definitely meant that every available man would have to be sent to his aid, and that any idea of strongly reinforcing *Johnston* in Georgia was out of the question.   What Grant lost, Sherman gained.

[1] *Atkinson*, p. 285.

CHAPTER XII

FROM SPOTTSYLVANIA TO COLD HARBOR

MAY 13–20

THE battle of May 12 having failed in its ultimate object, Grant at once set about preparing for another. Works were thrown up, roads cleared, field telegraph lines laid, and extensive reconnaissances made of *Lee's* position. All these things were done, as Grant said, in order to get by " the right flank of the enemy " ; for in his next engagement he hoped that not only would an attack on *Lee's* right push the Army of Northern Virginia away from Butler, but that it would enable him to connect with the Army of the James, and so establish a new base of supply on the coast.

The battle was planned for the 14th, Warren's corps being moved over to Burnside's left ; but the rain coming down in torrents greatly delayed this change of front, which on the 15th assumed the following order—Hancock, Burnside, Warren, Wright in one line of entrenchments from the salient to Gayle (Plan No. 6). On the 16th, to lessen the length of the marching columns, Grant sent over a hundred pieces of artillery with their horses and caissons back to Washington, and on the 17th received his first reinforcements of 12,000 men. On the 18th an unsuccessful attack was made on the base of the salient, and that night Grant decided to abandon the offensive in the Spottsylvania area, and prepare another manœuvre round *Lee's* right. By the 20th the army was distributed between the rivers Ny and Po as follows : Warren's corps on the right ; Wright's in the centre, and Burnside's on the left, with Hancock's in reserve east of Gayle. Preparations were also set on foot to change the base of supplies from Fredericksburg to Port Royal on the Rappahannock.

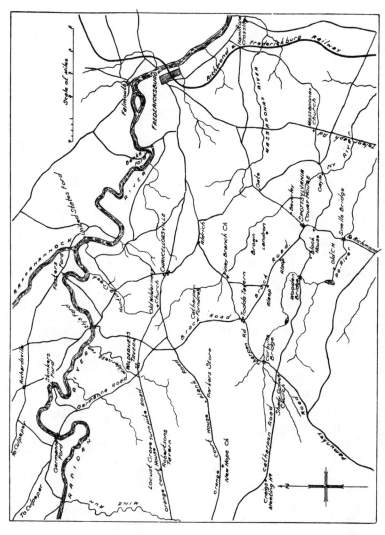

MAP No. 4.—OPERATIONS IN THE WILDERNESS AND AROUND SPOTTSYLVANIA COURT HOUSE, MAY, 1864.

General Butler's Operations

It will be remembered that the three subsidiary operations, simultaneously launched when Grant crossed the Rapidan, were those of Sherman, Butler, and Sigel. Sherman's advance was progressing satisfactorily, but on the 18th Grant heard that Sigel had been badly defeated at New Market and was retreating down the valley, and that Butler had been driven back from Drury's Bluff. This news might well have shaken a less determined general, for the co-operation of Butler and Sigel was essential to the maintenance of Grant's original plan. He was, however, in no way discouraged, and, as we have seen, had at once decided to continue the advance.

Butler's Army of the James consisted of two corps, the Tenth under Gillmore and the Eighteenth under Smith—of Chattanooga fame; its strength was about 38,000 officers and men. This army was assembled on the York river in order to mislead the enemy. On the night of May 4 it was embarked; steamed up the James, landing at City Point and Fort Powhatan. Its appearance completely surprised the Confederates, and as Butler was opposed by little more than the weak garrisons of Petersburg and Richmond, he should have pushed on at once. Instead, he delayed his advance, waiting to ascertain the success or failure of the battle of the Wilderness. At the time, *Beauregard's* forces were scattered; yet it should have been obvious to Butler that every hour's delay was a definite gain to the enemy.

On the 9th the army moved up towards Petersburg, driving the enemy back to Swift Creek, which was found to be uncrossable. Smith and Gillmore then suggested to Butler that he should bridge the Appomattox west of City Point, and " assault the works of Petersburg from the east." [1] Butler refused to listen to this advice; for he distrusted those whom he called " West Point men," and apparently was not on friendly terms with Smith.

Instead, hearing from Washington [2] that *Lee* was in retreat

[1] *B. & L.*, IV, p. 208.   [2] 68 *W.R.*, p. 555.

for Richmond, which was not the case, he decided to move
northwards in order to assist in the investment of the
capital. This decision was a fatuous one : first he painted

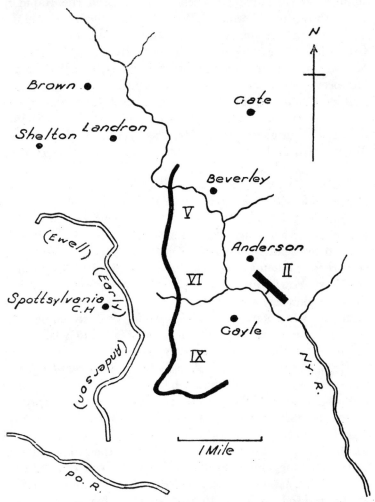

PLAN No. 6.   BATTLE OF SPOTTSYLVANIA, MAY 20, 1864.

a mental picture of what *Lee* intended to do, and secondly,
he ignored the existence of *Beauregard*. Having decided
on this advance, instead of crossing to the north side of

the James, and so placing this river on his left flank, on the 12th he set out northwards towards Drury's Bluff, some seven miles south of Richmond.

" The night of the 15th," writes Swinton, " everything was still. A thin film of cloud slightly obscured the sky, but it was not so heavy as to interfere seriously with the moonlight, and the heavens gave no token of what was presently to be seen. Before dawn a dense fog, arising from the margin of the James, overspread the whole face of the country with so opaque a pall that a horseman was not visible at a distance of ten yards. In the thick of this and before dawn, the sleeping camp was suddenly aroused by a savage outburst of musketry and artillery fire along the whole line. *Beauregard* had taken advantage of the fog. . . ." [1]

Butler's army was over-extended, nevertheless his front held, but his left being turned and threatened in rear by a division under General *Whiting*, he was compelled to fall back on Bermuda Hundred, where he entrenched himself between the James and the Appomattox; there, as Grant says, he was completely bottled up.

" Had the instructions of April 2 of General Grant been strictly carried out," writes General Smith, " and had Petersburg been promptly attacked on the 6th of May, it would doubtlessly have fallen, and the Southern lines of communication would have been at the mercy of General Butler." [2] Had this happened, the loss of the South Side and Weldon railways would have forced *Lee* to break up before Grant.

SHERIDAN'S RICHMOND RAID

Closely connected with Butler's movement from City Point, and largely dependent upon its success, was the raid carried out by Sheridan. That it accomplished nothing except the death of General *Stuart,* as some writers affirm, for instance Captain Battine,[3] is absurd; but that it did not form part of Grant's original plan is very true, for

---

[1] *Swinton,* p. 465. [2] *B. & L.,* IV, p. 212. [3] *Battine,* p. 375.

its origin may be traced to the quarrel between Sheridan and Meade on May 8. Grant, realising the danger of friction, saw that for the time being it was necessary to separate these two generals; and as was his invariable custom when faced by a difficulty, in place of seeking for some ideal solution, he accepted the lesser of two evils, in this case, separation, simultaneously turning this lesser evil to his advantage.

If Grant had realised the power of Sheridan's breech-loading carbines, by dismounting part of his cavalry he might have used this weapon with deadly effect in the woods of the Wilderness and around Spottsylvania. Like most generals, he does not seem to have paid much attention to weapon-power—the cutting edge of tactics. This being so, his cavalry were definitely an encumbrance in the forests; for no type of soldier is less suited to wood-fighting, and no other arm will block a road more completely than a large force of cavalry and its transport.[1] In the circumstances, I think that he was wise to part with his mounted troops; though whether he was wise to part with all three divisions is doubtful; yet, as he expected that the whole of *Stuart's* force would be encountered, not realising the power of the breech-loading carbine, it is difficult to say that he was wrong in maintaining Sheridan at full strength.

The objects of this raid were : to attack *Lee's* line of supply—his rear; to draw the Confederate cavalry away from the Army of the Potomac, and to reduce traffic from Fredericksburg forward. Critics of it frequently overlook the fact that Butler was at City Point, and under orders to move against Richmond. Had Butler occupied Petersburg, as he should have done, then damage to the railways [2] in rear of *Lee* would almost certainly have compelled *Lee* to fall back or risk starvation.

---

[1] In the World War, on several occasions, I have seen ten miles of road completely blocked by a force of cavalry less numerous than Sheridan's. The forage carts are the main difficulty.

[2] The damage done to the railways greatly delayed *Beauregard's* concentration.

Sheridan's orders were to move round *Lee's* left ; attack his cavalry wherever met ; cut the Virginia Central and Fredericksburg railroads, and then move south and join Butler. Starting out on the 8th, on the 11th, when a few miles from Richmond, he met the Confederate cavalry under *Stuart,* and defeated them, *Stuart* being mortally wounded. Next he entered the outer defences of Richmond, causing a panic in the capital ; joined up with Butler on the 14th, and on the 24th reported to the Army of the Potomac when on its march from the North Anna to Cold Harbor. During the sixteen days he was absent, a period of much administrative difficulty to Grant, who was in the process of changing his supply base to Port Royal, the Federal trains were never interfered with. On the other hand, there can be no question that *Lee* was seriously embarrassed by this raid ; for some ten miles of the Virginia Central railroad and several miles of the Fredericksburg were destroyed.[1] Colonel Livermore writes : " If Grant had succeeded in dislodging *Lee's* army from its intrenchments at Spottsylvania, the advantage from the interruption of their supplies might have been very great." [2] These points must be borne in mind when criticising Sheridan's operation.

MANŒUVRE TO THE NORTH ANNA

Grant had now for thirteen days been attacking *Lee* in the Spottsylvania area, and he realised quite clearly that whilst hastily entrenched positions could frequently be carried by assault, well-prepared ones could not, unless the assault came as a complete surprise. He now saw that if *Lee* would not come out of his entrenchments the battle must be shifted to new ground, and, in spite of bad news from the Valley, he determined on a risky manœuvre, namely, another flank march in face of his unbroken enemy ; so once again he decided to turn *Lee's* right.

---

[1] 67 *W.R.*, p. 776 ; 68 *W.R.*, p. 1025 ; 81 *W.R.*, pp. 686, 697.
[2] *M.H.S.M.*, VI, pp. 465, 466.

After the battle of the Wilderness his idea was that wherever *Lee* went Meade should follow ; this he now reversed, and in its place he substituted—wherever Meade went *Lee* should be compelled to follow.   So bold a change

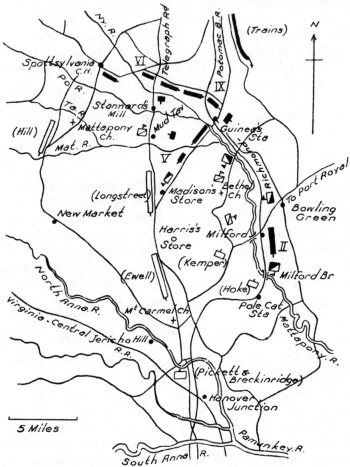

PLAN NO. 7.   ADVANCE TO THE NORTH ANNA, MAY 22, 1864.

in direction shows the elasticity of Grant's battle strategy ; further, it shows his courage, for the plan he intended to adopt, in order to persuade *Lee* to attack him, was a hazardous one.   Of this plan General Humphreys writes :

" It was supposed that, if one of the corps of the Army of the Potomac was sent some twenty miles distant on the road to Richmond, keeping the rest of the army ready to follow,[1] *Lee* might endeavour to attack the corps, thus separated before it could be reinforced, and upon the first indication of such intention (or even before it, after leaving full time for the intention to disclose itself, if it should exist) the rest of the army following the corps might be able to attack before *Lee* could intrench. If *Lee* did not make this attempt on the isolated corps, then the movement would become simply a turning or flank operation." [2]

In accordance with this idea, Hancock was ordered [3] to march by Guinea's (or Guiney's) Station and Bowling Green to Milford, cross the Mattapony river at this place, and fight the enemy wherever met. It was hoped when *Lee* found that the Second Corps had slipped by him, and was threatening his line of retreat on Richmond, that he would attempt to push it out of the way before the rest of Grant's army could come to its support. Should this happen, then Warren's, Wright's, and Burnside's corps would fall on *Lee's* left flank and rear.

In order that his march should not be observed, Hancock moved off at 11 p.m. on the 20th, arriving at Guinea's Station at dawn ; from where he pushed on towards Bowling Green. Humphreys suggests [4] that he should have moved by the Telegraph road, as he would then have immediately threatened *Lee's* line of retreat. This is correct, but Grant's difficulty was, that as Butler was bottled up in Bermuda Hundred, he was compelled to consider the security of his left flank with reference to his change of base to Port Royal, as well as entice *Lee* to attack the Second Corps. Again he was faced by a choice of two evils, and as usual he chose the lesser. That he did so shows his wisdom as events soon proved ; for, on the morning of the 22nd, in the neighbourhood of Milford, Hancock's cavalry were opposed by *Pickett's*

[1] 68 *W.R.*, p. 865.   [3] 68 *W.R.*, p. 910.
[2] *Humphreys*, p. 119.   [4] *Humphreys*, pp. 126, 127.

division from Petersburg. Here he learnt that *Hoke's* division, or part of it, had arrived from the James and was at Pole Cat Station, and that *Breckinridge*, from the Valley, was at Hanover Junction. Had Grant adopted Humphreys's idea of moving Hancock by Guinea's Station on to the Telegraph road, *Lee* might have turned on him ; whilst these newly arrived reinforcements, some 10,000 strong, fell on his flank and rear.

Meade had directed Hancock,[1] before he advanced, to keep him informed as to his situation ; this he failed to do, with the result that the movements of the remaining corps had to take place without any modification being made in the original plan ; these movements were as follows :

Early on the 21st Burnside, Warren, and Wright pushed their skirmishers forward to discover whether *Lee* was still in position. At 10 a.m. Warren began to withdraw, moving by Guinea's Station and Madison Store ; he was followed by Burnside, who arrived at Guinea's Station at 2 a.m. on the 22nd. Once Warren had withdrawn, Wright took over a shortened line of entrenchments at Gayle House, which he held until nightfall, when he set out to join Hancock. The trains were ordered to advance to Guinea's Station.

Early in the morning of the 21st, *Lee*, learning from his cavalry detachment at Guinea's Station that troops had passed through that place at daybreak, at once moved *Ewell's* corps over to his right ; but it was not until he discovered Wright's trenches evacuated that he set the whole of his army in motion, not to attack Hancock, but to place himself between his enemy and Richmond, and cover the Virginia Central railway. His retirement was directed on Hanover Junction ; *Ewell*, followed by *Anderson*, arriving there about midday the 22nd, and *Hill*, who had now returned to his corps, on the morning of the 23rd.

On the night of the 22nd the position of the Army of the Potomac was as follows : Wright's corps between Nancy Wright's and Madison's Store ; Warren at Harris's Store ; Hancock's at Milford, and Burnside's at Bethel Church.

---

[1] 68 *W.R.*, p. 910.

Grant's manœuvre had succeeded strategically, but tactically it had failed. *Lee* had been shifted from his strong
position, and was now in the open ; but he had not been
brought to battle, for the simple reason that though Hancock's movement threatened his right flank, it in no way
obstructed his rear. In the circumstances, *Lee* was wise
to leave Hancock alone.

Though disappointed, Grant lost no time in conforming
to *Lee's* move, and on the evening of the 22nd instructions
were sent to Meade [1] to advance at 5 a.m. on the following
day : Warren's and Wright's corps to Hawkins Creek
(Quarles's Mill) ; Hancock's to Chesterfield Ford (near where
the Richmond and Potomac railway crosses the North Anna) ;
and Burnside's corps to move at 3 p.m. to Jericho Bridge.
On the 24th Butler was instructed [2] to send north, under
General Smith, all forces not required to hold the lines at
Bermuda Hundred.

Though not ordered to do so, Warren, finding the North
Anna unoccupied, forded it, and by 4.30 p.m. the whole of
his infantry had crossed over. Here he was attacked, his
right flank being driven in by *Hill* ; but after a short engagement the enemy were ejected. Meade, hearing that Warren
was in difficulties, moved Wright's corps forward to support
him. Meanwhile, on the left, Hancock, crossing Long Creek,
moved towards Ox Ford, and by 7 p.m. drove the
Confederates back over the river, and secured Telegraph
Road Bridge. " Assuredly," writes Captain Atkinson,
" there was nothing on this day to show that Grant's army
was not capable of great deeds. The generalship of the
corps commanders, the bravery of their subordinate leaders,
and the steadiness of the men, were beyond praise." [3]

On the morning of the 24th Grant's distribution was as
follows : Warren's corps on the right entrenched beyond
the river, next on his left Wright's corps, and then Burnside's and Hancock's ; the last mentioned holding the road
bridge and the railway bridge except at its southern extremity.

---

[1] 69 *W.R.*, p. 81.   [2] 69 *W.R.*, pp. 145, 176, 177, 234, 235.
[3] *Atkinson*, p. 352.

About this time Grant was informed by some negroes [1] that *Lee* intended to fall back on Richmond. Accepting this information as reliable, he decided to push forward and attack his enemy before he could retire to the fortifications of the capital; consequently, Hancock and Burnside [2] were ordered, if possible, to cross the river and pursue *Lee* directly he began to retire. This information was soon found to be incorrect; for, in moving forward, Warren came up against a strongly entrenched line [3] running from Ox Ford towards Anderson's Station on the Virginia Central railway; and Gibbon's division of Hancock's corps reported similar works [4] running from Ox Ford to Hanover Junction. In fact, *Lee* was found to be in position with his whole army, occupying well-prepared works constructed during the previous winter.

Grant's situation was now an anxious one, for not only had he manœuvred *Lee* out of strong works at Spottsylvania into stronger ones on the North Anna, but his army was divided. His distribution was shaped like the letter " M," the central angle, or " V," of which was the North Anna, the left upright the Sixth and Fifth Corps, and the right upright the Second; whilst *Lee* again confronted him in a " hog snout " entrenchment, and was consequently well placed to concentrate against either flank at will.

Why did not Lee attack? Much mystery has been needlessly woven around this question, and frequently has the answer been suggested : that no attack was made because *Lee* was ill. On the 24th he had been confined to his tent, otherwise Warren would never have been allowed to cross the river. On the 24th he had said to General *Hill* : " Why did you let these people cross the river ? Why did you not drive them back as General *Jackson* would have done ? " and later on to his staff he exclaimed : " We must never let them pass us again ! We must strike them ! " If *Hill*

---

[1] 69 *W.R.*, pp. 148, 149.
[2] 69 *W.R.*, pp. 152, 154, 167. On this day Burnside's corps was permanently placed under the orders of Meade.
[3] 69 *W.R.*, p. 159.   [4] 69 *W.R.*, pp. 152, 153, 155.

had failed to strike on the 23rd, why did not *Lee* strike on
the 25th ? I do not think that it was sickness which prevented him from doing so, but the attrition he had suffered
in the Wilderness and at Spottsylvania.   To have attacked
Hancock, the most exposed of Grant's commanders, would
have entailed an assault on entrenchments, and with heavy
loss even if successful.   *Lee* could no longer afford such a
loss ; further still, as Grant had attacked him in every
position he had held since May 5, the probabilities were,

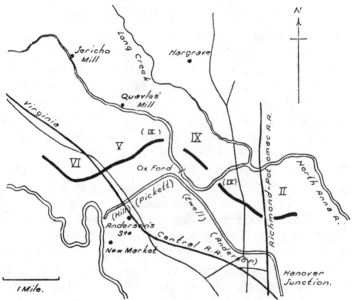

PLAN NO. 8.   OPERATIONS ON NORTH ANNA, MAY 23-6, 1864.

and the present Federal advance certainly supported this
contention, that Grant would attack again.   Should he do
so, then *Lee* was confident that he could hold him, inflict
the heaviest casualties on him, and should an opportunity
arise—counter-attack, and possibly cripple his enemy.
These, I think, are the true reasons why *Lee* did not attack.
He had been out-generalled not by manœuvre, but through
losses which he could not make good, and he realised this.
Grant has not only frequently but almost universally

been accused of seeing red whenever he saw a trench, of indulging in indiscriminate assaults, and of butchering his men; yet, at 10.45 a.m. on the 25th, what do we see him do? Directly he learns the exact position of *Lee*, and realises that his opponent is not retiring, and does not intend to retire, he decides on another manœuvre; this time of a still more hazardous nature than the one he carried out on the 21st, because he could not move until he had extricated his army.

Manœuvre to Totopotomoy Creek

On the afternoon of the 25th Grant directed [1] Meade to withdraw across the North Anna, and to move to Hanover Town. The greatest secrecy was to be observed, and a " heavy cavalry demonstration " against the enemy's left was ordered for the afternoon of the 26th. The next day a demand was made on Washington asking for all bridging material to be sent to Fort Monroe, so that it might be in readiness should the James have to be crossed.

The problem which faced Grant was as follows : to move the army to Hanover Town, and to deploy it south of the Pamunkey before *Lee* could advance and oppose the crossing. Its solution depended on time : at Hanover Junction *Lee* was about twenty miles from Hanover Town, and from Jericho, Grant's extreme right, the distance was thirty-four miles. It is true that several good crossings over the Pamunkey existed nearer than Hanover Town; but, apparently, Grant decided on this crossing as it was sufficiently far away to make it difficult for *Lee* to arrive there in time, should Grant gain a march on him. This would not have been the case had he chosen Littlepage's Bridge. Once across the Pamunkey, there was a chance of cutting in between *Lee* and Richmond, and so of compelling *Lee* to fight in order to regain his base.

Sheridan and his Cavalry Corps had now rejoined the Army of the Potomac; this was most fortunate for Grant, for without a large force of horse the manœuvre he con-

[1] 69 *W.R.*, p. 183.

templated would have been scarcely possible. The bulk of the cavalry, then assembled at Pole Cat Station, were ordered to watch, and seize if they were able to, Littlepage's Bridge and Taylor's Ford to the south of it, and to remain at these places until the infantry and artillery had passed. Russell's division of Wright's corps, supported by a strong force of artillery, was withdrawn from the line at dusk on the 26th, and without its trains was pushed forward by forced march to Hanover Town, where it was to seize the crossings over the Pamunkey, and establish a bridge-head for the army. Orders for the rest of the troops were issued by Meade at 10 a.m. on the 26th; in brief they were as follows : [1]

(1) The Sixth Corps to withdraw at dark by Jericho Bridge, and follow Russell's division to Hanover Town.

(2) The Fifth Corps to withdraw at dark by Quarles's Ford Bridge, and to move via Old Chesterfield to New Castle Ferry.

(3) The Ninth Corps to hold the fords and crossings from Ox Ford to Jericho Mills, and to follow the Fifth Corps to New Castle Ferry.

(4) The Second Corps, and Willcox's Division of the Ninth Corps, to hold the fords and crossings below Ox Ford, and follow the Sixth Corps to Hanover Town.

On Meade's suggestion, Smith and his corps from the James was ordered to disembark at White House on the Pamunkey.

This withdrawal, a most complex one in the time, was successfully carried out during the night of the 26th/27th, and on the following morning the Army of Northern Virginia found itself facing an empty trench line ; whilst, at 9 a.m., Sheridan's leading cavalry reported the occupation of Hanover Town, and the laying of two pontoon bridges across the Pamunkey. Two hours later, Russell and the advanced guard, after a magnificent march, joined up with Sheridan.

On the afternoon of the 27th a change in the routes of the

[1] 69 *W.R.*, p. 211.

army was made, the Sixth and Second Corps being ordered
to cross the river at Huntley's, four miles above Hanover
Town, and the Fifth and Ninth Corps to cross at Hanover
Town in place of at New Castle Ferry. About midday the
28th, the Sixth, Second, and Fifth Corps crossed to the
south side of the Pamunkey, the Ninth crossing at midnight, whilst the trains moved from Bowling Green to
Dunkirk. The general distribution from Crump's Creek on
the right to Totopotomoy [1] Creek on the left was—Sixth,
Second, Ninth, and Fifth Corps, with the Cavalry Corps in
the neighbourhood of Mechanicsville.

Grant's immediate problem was not to gain but to maintain the little remaining room left to manœuvre in. From
Sheridan [2] he learnt that *Ewell's* corps (now commanded
by *Early*) and *Anderson's* corps were four miles west of
Hawes' Shop, and that *Lee* had moved to Ashland on the
night of the 27th/28th. From this it was obvious that *Lee*
once again intended to oppose him. Grant, not wishing
to frighten *Lee* away, advanced a weak right towards
Shelton's, whilst he held back a strong left near Armstrong's
—Wright's and Hancock's corps holding three and a half
miles of front, and Burnside's and Warren's only a little
more than one. At the moment Grant's chief anxiety was
that *Lee* might fall back behind the Chickahominy.

On the 30th a definite drift southwards set in. On the
Federal side, Smith and the Eighteenth Corps [3] arrived at
White House, and at once began to disembark; and as
White House was about to become the new base of supply,
to protect this base and to shorten the distance between
Smith and Warren, Grant pushed Sheridan well out on his
left flank. Meanwhile, on the Confederate side, a similar
movement was taking place towards Old Cold Harbor,
which not only commanded Grant's line of communications

---

[1] Totapotamoy was the name of an Indian chief of the time of the settlement of Virginia. He is mentioned in *Hudibras* (Pt. II, Canto II) :
> " The mighty Tottipottymoy
> Sent to our elders an envoy."

[2] 69 *W.R.*, p. 274.

[3] A composite force containing much of the Tenth Corps.

with White House, but also his route to the James, should
he decide to cross to the north side of this river.

Realising that on the Totopotomoy every battle must be
one against entrenchments, and that if he attempted to
turn the Confederate right, *Lee* would extend his works to
the Chickahominy, which would again mean a frontal attack,
Grant decided to employ Smith's corps on June 1 as he had
employed Hancock's on May 21 ; that is, as a bait to draw
Lee eastwards. Should *Lee* fall on Smith, then he would
operate against *Lee's* left flank and rear ; in other words,
Grant's intention was to manœuvre against *Lee's* left and
cut him off from Richmond.

While Sheridan was reconnoitring towards Cold Harbor
and Mechanicsville, Grant warned Smith that " the movements of the enemy this evening on our left . . . indicate
the possibility of a design on his part to get between you and
the Army of the Potomac," then he added : " They will
be so closely watched that nothing could suit me better
than such a move." ¹ *Lee* did not, however, move east,
for, not aware that Smith had landed, he was contemplating
quite a different operation.

By the 31st the hostile lines stretched from east of Atlee's
Station to beyond Old Cold Harbor, a distance of about
nine miles, offering either side a chance to concentrate
against some weak spot. *Lee* intended to seize the opportunity, for not only was it necessary for political reasons to
throw Grant back, but never since May 4 was he more
favourably situated as regards numbers. Having been
strongly reinforced, he now had at his command some
70,000 men, and he reckoned that Grant had no more than
85,000 ² ; for he did not as yet know that Smith had joined
him.

Lee's plan was to hold Grant's front with the corps of *Hill*
and *Breckinridge* ; attack his centre with *Early's* ; and pivoting *Anderson's* on *Hoke* and *Fitzhugh Lee* at Cold Harbor,
to roll up Grant's left. *Lee* has been accused of not holding
Cold Harbor in sufficient strength, as it covered Smith's

¹ 69 *W.R.*, p. 371.   ² Grant had about 100,000.

advance from White House and commanded the approach to the James. But *Lee* did not know that Smith had arrived, nor could he know that Grant would cross the James. In any case, at the moment, he was not thinking of the future value of Cold Harbor, but of its immediate value ; and *Hoke's* Division supported by *Fitzhugh Lee* should have been able to hold this place against Sheridan ; but Torbert's magazine carbines proved so deadly that his dismounted troopers drove *Hoke's* infantry out of Cold Harbor. This done, Sheridan was about to withdraw, when he received an order to hold that place at all hazards.[1]

This order was sent to him, because Grant had gauged *Lee's* intention, and meant to turn it to his own advantage. Burnside and Warren were to hold their present positions ; Hancock was to defend the right wing of the army ; Wright to move from the right via Hawes' Shop to the left at Old Cold Harbor ; and Smith, with the Eighteenth Corps, was to march up from White House and come into line between Warren and Wright.

On the morning of June 1 *Anderson's* corps had two skirmishes with Sheridan's cavalry, and on both occasions was as sharply repulsed by the Spencer carbines as *Hoke* had been the day before. Their deadly fire, the arrival of the Sixth Corps at 9 a.m., and the absence of *Lee*, appear to have been the main causes which led to the abandonment of the Confederate offensive.

By noon Grant's forces were rapidly massing on his left, and as no Confederate attack had taken place, he decided to assume the offensive before *Lee's* men could strongly entrench themselves.

At 6 p.m. the attack was launched, an attack of especial interest, not because it proved fairly successful, but because it was made by exhausted troops and over open ground. Wright's corps had been on the move since 9.45 p.m. the day before, and Smith's corps, which foolishly had been hurried off from White House before the men could get

---

[1] 69 *W.R.*, p. 469, mentions the receipt of this order ; the order itself is lost.

their breakfasts, had marched twenty-five miles, leaving many stragglers on the road. On Wright's front the Confederate field of fire was 1,400 yards deep, and both corps were confronted by a strong line of rifle-pits covering a main line consisting of hastily dug trenches and log-works. The Eighteenth Corps carried the rifle-pits, but could get no farther. The Sixth was more fortunate, for it entered *Anderson's* main line, stormed a small salient on his right, and then moved towards New Cold Harbor, from where it was thrown back by a counter-attack. Some 750 Confederates were captured, at the cost of 2,200 Federals killed and wounded.

Three hours before this attack was launched, Hancock had been ordered to move from the right flank and take up a position on Warren's left; for it was Grant's intention, before *Lee* could withdraw over the Chickahominy, and whilst he had this river immediately in his rear, to launch a general attack against the New Cold Harbor position. For this formidable assault, Grant's corps were deployed from the right to the left as follows : Ninth, Fifth, Eighteenth, Sixth, and Second, and, at 10.15 p.m. on the 1st, Meade suggested the following operation to Grant : " What are your views about to-morrow ? I think the attack should be renewed as soon as Hancock is within supporting distance. . . . Warren " should " be ordered to attack in conjunction with the others. Burnside I would hold ready to reinforce Warren, if necessary." [1] To this Grant agreed.

To meet the concentration of force against his right, *Lee* ordered the following movements : *Early* and one division of *Hill's* corps to hold the left flank along the Totopotomoy ; *Breckinridge* and *Hill* to move from the left flank to beyond New Cold Harbor, the former coming into line on *Hoke's* right with *Hill* on his own right.

BATTLE OF COLD HARBOR, JUNE 3

In the history of the Civil War the battle of Cold Harbor has been given a tactical prominence which it certainly does

[1] 69 *W.R.*, pp. 432, 433.

not merit. It was not a great battle, or a decisive battle, or a very costly battle, for Lee's loss was slight [1] and Grant's only amounted to 5,617, of whom 1,100 were killed and 4,517 wounded.[2] Why, then, has it been so greatly magnified ?

The reasons are not far to seek—they are political. The North looked for a speedy termination of the war, and was disappointed. Intrigue was rife ; the Presidential election was approaching ; the cost of the war was growing apace, and every day saw heart-rending lists of casualties. To the politicians and to the masses generally, Cold Harbor was the checkmate of Grant, and as is ever the case with the people, from an unfounded optimism they sank into an unfounded pessimism. They had in their ignorance expected victory, and now in their ignorance they accepted defeat, a defeat of their own making ; for the true strategical value of Cold Harbor was not that Grant had failed to overthrow *Lee*, nor was it that he was now compelled to seek a new solution ; but that his check, not a checkmate, disappointed the *canaille*, who being denied *Lee's* blood in place demanded his own. The newspapers, ever eager to feed the masses on the carrion of events, turned on Grant—he had failed, he was no more than a butcher, and " had provided either a cripple or a corpse for half the homes of the North." [3] To vilify him, casualties were exaggerated, not by publishing fictitious returns, but by lumping together whole periods and debiting the totals to June 3. Thus, from the 1st to the 12th of June the losses were 12,737, and from the 27th of May to the 12th of June, including sick—17,129. Figures like these, juggled to suggest the losses of the assault, did Grant and the Northern cause more harm than the actual check he sustained. Even to-day they have not lost their sting ; for in the opinion of many, Grant still represents the butcher type of general.

To turn to the cause of all this falsification : was Grant

---

[1] *Swinton*, p. 487, doubts whether the Confederate losses on June 3 reached 1,300. See also Grant's report—67 *W.R.*, pp. 21, 22.

[2] *Humphreys*, p. 191 ; Livermore says—6,000 to 7,000.

[3] *New York Daily News.*

justified in launching this attack? My own answer is: No, he was not; but I do consider that there were extenuating circumstances.

Few generals better understood the influence of politics on war than Grant. He realised quite clearly the vital necessity of an early success; for, ever since the opening of the war, the North had suffered from a political enteric fever. For thirty days he had wrestled with the most noted general of the Confederacy, in a theatre of war as unsuited to offensive action as it was well suited to defensive. He had driven *Lee* from the Rapidan to the Chickahominy, and was left with no further room to manœuvre in. *Lee's* flanks could not be turned, consequently outside abandoning the campaign he had no choice but to attack frontally. To abandon the campaign would at once have been proclaimed a disaster; a disaster which would have depressed the North and have elated the South; a disaster which in its ill effects would have exceeded those of the check Grant actually experienced. At Missionary Ridge the assault had succeeded beyond all expectation; Upton's assault was successful and so was Barlow's. On June 2 there was as good a chance of success as in these engagements, and the need for it was greater.

The attack was, however, postponed. At first it was to take place on the morning of the 2nd, then at 5 o'clock in the afternoon, then the next day. Meanwhile, Burnside's corps was to move out of the line and come into reserve in rear of Warren, and these two corps, in place of supporting the three south of them, were to become an offensive mass of attack. There would then be two assaults, launched simultaneously; that of the Eighteenth, Sixth, and Second Corps near New Cold Harbor, and that of the Ninth and Fifth Corps north of this spot.

As this concentration was about to take place, *Early*, on the afternoon of the 2nd, attacked Grant's right; and Grant, realising that *Lee* could not be strong everywhere, and that as he had shown strength on his left, in all probability his right, about New Cold Harbor, was not as

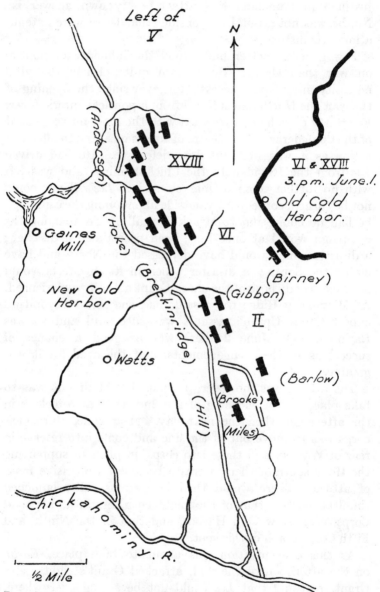

Left of
V

N

(Anderson)

XVIII

VI & XVIII
3.p.m. June.1.
○ Old Cold
Harbor.

(Hoke)

○ Gaines
Mill

(Breckinridge)

VI

○ New Cold
Harbor

(Birney)

(Gibbon)

II

○ Watts

(Barlow)

(Hill)

(Brooke)

(Miles)

Chickahominy. R.

½ Mile

PLAN NO. 9. ASSAULT OF II, VI, AND XVIII CORPS AT COLD HARBOR,
JUNE 3, 1864.

strong as he had expected, postponed the assault until
4.30 a.m.[1] the next day.

Grant's error was a two-fold one : first he postponed the
attack for twenty-four hours, and so gave *Lee* ample time
to strengthen his position (in all probability this delay was
unavoidable) ; secondly, he ordered an attack all along
the line, and in the assault on the New Cold Harbor position
he massed on a frontage of 4,000 yards no less than 60,000
rifles, that is fifteen rifles to each yard of front. Here he
fell, and by no means for the first or last time, into a common
error, an error which has caused more needless loss in war
than any other, namely : that battles can be won by masses
of men ; or, in other words, that human tonnage is the
coefficient of victory. Obviously this assumption is not
only illogical but absurd ; for on a modern battlefield it is
not men who count, but weapon-power—bullets and shells.
If Grant had as clearly understood that tactics are based
on weapon-power as he did that strategy is based on movement, and that as movement depends on supply, so does
offensive power depend on protection, he would never have
assaulted at Cold Harbor as he did, nor would he have
sent over a third of his guns back to Washington because
he could not employ them to the full in the Wilderness and
at Spottsylvania.

I will now, remembering the conditions of war which faced
Grant, attempt to show what he might have done on the
morning of the 3rd with the forces and weapons at his disposal.

Lee's line was some six miles long, extending vaguely
from the Shady Grove Church road on his left to the Chickahominy on his right ; behind his right this river was a serious
obstacle to retire over. This frontage may be divided
roughly into two tactical zones : the northern—north of the
eastern extremity of Gaines's Mill lake ; and the southern—
south of this point. I will now suggest a definite operation.

Grant should have held the northern zone defensively
with the Ninth and Fifth Corps ; and he should have selected
the left of the southern zone as the objective of his decisive

[1] 69 *W.R.*, p. 479.

attack. He should, after dark on June 2, have drawn the Sixth Corps out of the line, and have ordered the Second Corps to take over its front, and have massed his artillery in two groups, one on the right of the Second Corps and the other on the right of the Eighteenth. The Eighteenth Corps should have been allotted a strong force of dismounted cavalry armed with Spencer carbines, and General Smith should have been ordered to penetrate the enemy's front between the two streams running from the east into Gaines's Mill lake. Hidden away behind the Eighteenth Corps front, the Sixth Corps should have been kept in mobile reserve.

As regards the attack, I consider that it might then have been carried out as follows :

The front to be penetrated to be bombarded by the two groups of guns for about one hour, and under cover of this bombardment small parties of dismounted cavalry to have been pushed forward to within about 100 yards of the Confederate works. The sudden cessation of the bombardment to be the signal for the assault, to be carried out by a line of battalion columns at deploying intervals, advancing under cover of the magazine carbine fire of the dismounted cavalry. These columns to be followed by supporting columns in similar formation, which, directly the enemy's trench line was carried, would move outwards, forming two defensive flanks along the two streams. The guns then to switch north and south, throwing their shells over these defensive flanks, whilst others immediately would support them. This would terminate the first phase of the attack.

The second to consist in passing the Sixth Corps through the gap made by the Eighteenth, and then swinging it southwards towards New Cold Harbor, its rear being protected by the Eighteenth Corps holding the southern margin of the Gaines's Mill lake. By such a manœuvre, the Sixth Corps would have taken the whole of the left of *Lee*'s right wing in reverse, and, directly this wing broke, the Second Corps would have advanced, and have driven it into the Chickahominy.

I do not say that such an attack would have succeeded ;

but one thing is certain—it would not have led to such a complete failure as did Grant's general attack, each division of which was taken in enfilade [1] as well as being decimated by a strong frontal fire.   The fate of his assault was decided in less than an hour [2] ; General McMahon says [3] that the time

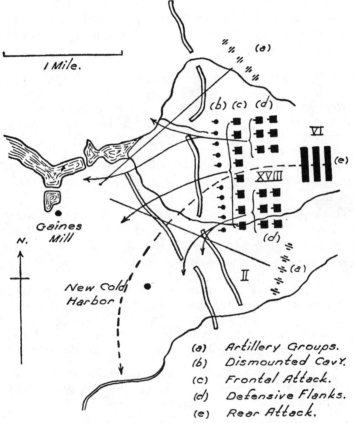

PLAN No. 10.   SUGGESTED TACTICS, JUNE 3, 1864.

taken in the actual advance was not more than eight minutes ; Swinton [4] says—ten.   Barlow's division gained the enemy's advance works but was unable to hold them ; the other assaults broke down, and fortunately Meade decided to

[1] *B. & L.*, IV, pp. 217, 218.   [3] *B. & L.*, IV, p. 217.
[2] *Humphreys*, p. 182.   [4] *Swinton*, p. 485.

suspend the attack before Burnside's and Warren's corps were heavily engaged. Swinton's statement[1] that Grant ordered a second assault has been proved to be incorrect.[2]

Grant's own excuse for this assault was, that as *Lee*, ever since the battle of the Wilderness, had refused to take the offensive, he considered him " whipped." [3] He believed that the *moral* of *Lee's* army was spent, and that one tremendous blow would overthrow it. Badeau says of Grant's offensive tactics generally :

" I have often heard him declare, that there comes a time in every hard-fought battle, when both armies are nearly or quite exhausted, and it seems impossible for either to do more ; this he believed the turning-point ; whichever after first renews the fight, is sure to win." [4]

Unfortunately for Grant, though he expected, and rightly, the highest heroism from his own men, he failed to realise that his enemy was of the same stock.

This repulse had a most disheartening effect on the North. The Army of the Potomac now stood where it had in June, 1862, and it strangely seemed that McClellan's experiences were about to repeat themselves. Yet, writes Ropes :

" General Grant was in no way disheartened nor was he in the least affected by the tremendous experiences of his campaign. He at once went to work, with as cool a head as he ever applied to any military problem in his life, to effect the crossing of the James and to capture Petersburg." [5]

" To Grant, the optimist of supreme moral strength, and supreme ' faith in success,' Cold Harbor was not a death-blow but a mistake to be repaired." [6]

Indeed, it was more than this, for within ten days its failure was to put his generalship to the highest test.

[1] *Swinton*, p. 487.   [4] *Badeau*, I, p. 85.
[2] *M.H.S.M.*, IV, p. 446.   [5] *M.H.S.M.*, IV, p. 399.
[3] 69 *W.R.*, p. 206.   [6] *Atkinson*, p. 463.

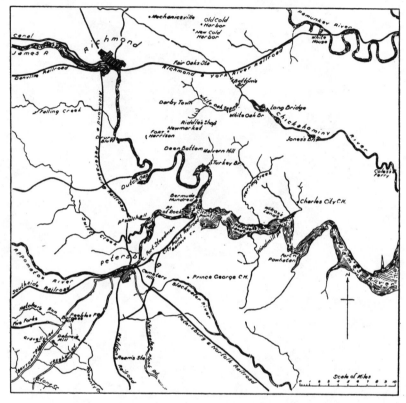

MAP No. 5.—OPERATIONS AROUND RICHMOND AND PETERSBURG, 1864–5.

CHAPTER XIII

PETERSBURG CAMPAIGN

CROSSING THE JAMES

A CHECK is not necessarily a checkmate, and though Grant has been credited with little imagination, from the moment he first considered his overland campaign, his common sense, as we have seen, pointed out to him the possibility of the situation which now confronted him. That this was so, marks his generalship as being of a high order, for a reasoned clairvoyance is exceedingly rare in war.

Without this foresight, the situation which now faced him would indeed have been a depressing one. Before him stood *Lee* strongly entrenched; his right protected by the Chickahominy and White Oak Swamp, his left secured by circumstances, for a Federal movement in this direction would uncover Grant's base at White House. Further still, behind *Lee* lay Richmond and Petersburg—the Piræus of this Athens, connected to it by a " long wall " consisting of formidable fortifications stretching from Fair Oak Station to Drury's Bluff, and thence southwards across Butler's front to Fort Stedman. These fortifications included— trenches and redoubts protected by abattis, chevaux-de-frise and inundations, and were provided with listening galleries and bomb-proof shelters, very similar to those constructed in 1914–18. On the other hand, behind his adversary trembled Washington, ever nervous that any move south of the James would uncover the capital; for not understanding Grant's strategy, the politicians of the Union were unable to realise that *Lee's* recent losses prohibited a successful invasion of the North. This fear is clearly proved by the fact that no sooner was the battle of Cold Harbor at an end than Halleck proposed to Grant that he should invest Richmond from the north bank of the James.

Grant saw the fatuity of this suggestion : if he could not break *Lee's* front by a direct assault, how was he to break through the fortifications of Richmond defended by *Lee* ? and how was he to invest the city, seeing that its main lines of supply ran through Petersburg ? If *Lee's* front could no longer be attacked, then, paradox though it may seem, he would attack *Lee's* rear, hinging this operation on his ever-shifting base. Grant's army had suffered heavy casualties, but he had received in all some 40,000 reinforcements, and was now at the head of 115,000 men.[1] *Lee* faced him with 80,000, but the source of his reinforcements was drying up ; his main strength lay, however, in his tactics, which were defensive ; further still, the country was friendly to him, and in the neighbourhood of Richmond he had no immediate line of supply to protect.

Realising that north of the James nothing could be accomplished " without a greater sacrifice of life " than he " was willing to make," [2] Grant determined, under cover of a cavalry operation directed against the Virginia Central railroad about Beaver Dam, " to move the army to the south side of the James River by the enemy's right flank," so that he " could cut off all his sources of supply except by the canal." [3] From a campaign against *Lee's* army he would turn to a campaign against *Lee's* supplies ; the idea was the same, namely, to fix *Lee*, but the method was entirely different —one of rapid surprise movements in place of massed attacks. It was in no ways a continuation of his overland campaign, but rather a reversion to his original idea that an operation south of the James might be necessary,[4] an operation which was only practicable because the overland campaign had grievously exhausted *Lee*.

On June 7 Sheridan, at the head of two divisions of cavalry, was ordered to move to Charlottesville, whilst

[1] *Grant*, II, p. 289.   [2] *Grant*, II, p. 280.
[3] 67 *W.R.*, p. 22 ; 69 *W.R.*, pp. 598, 599. The James River Canal.
[4] 67 *W.R.*, p. 17.

Hunter advanced up the Valley against Lynchburg. On the 8th, hearing that the Federal cavalry had crossed the Pamunkey, *Lee* ordered *Hampton* to follow them with two cavalry divisions ; *Fitzhugh Lee's* division being instructed to support this force as speedily as possible. Further than this, he sent *Breckinridge* back to the Valley, and, on the 11th, directed *Early* and his division to move by way of Charlottesville against Hunter's rear with the object of destroying this force, and then march down the Valley and threaten Washington ; which threat, *Lee* rightly considered would prove the surest protection of Lynchburg and the upper stretches of the Valley—regions so vital to him. Thus Sheridan's manœuvre, for it was much more than a raid, proved of advantage to Grant, and was far from being " useless," as Ropes considers it.[1]

Lee's attention having been diverted northwards, Grant, as Badeau rightly says, set out on an operation which " transcended in difficulty and danger any that he had attempted during the campaign." [2] It was—to withdraw " an army within forty yards of the enemy's line " ; to cross the swamps of the Chickahominy ; to bridge the James, a tidal river 700 yards wide ; to shift his base of supplies from White House to City Point, 150 miles apart, and to advance on Petersburg.

" The whole plan of the national commander at this juncture," writes Badeau, " assumed magnificent proportions. Sherman was advancing towards Atlanta and the sea, and Canby had been ordered to begin the attack against Mobile to meet him, so that the rebel forces west of the mountains were all engaged : Hunter was moving up the Valley of Virginia ; Crook and Averill (*sic*) were converging from the west and south-west, to cut off entirely the supplies reaching Richmond from these directions ; Sheridan was advancing to complete the destruction and isolation on the north, while Grant himself moved with the bulk of his forces against Petersburg and the southern railroads. . . ." [3]

Grant's first action was strongly to entrench his front at Cold Harbor in order to establish a secure base from

[1] *M.H.S.M.*, V, p. 164. [2] *Badeau*, II, p. 346. [3] *Badeau*, II, pp. 346, 347.

which to manœuvre. His next, to move Warren's corps
secretly to near Bottom Bridge on the Chickahominy.[1]
Meanwhile, on the 9th, Butler, foolishly, so I think, was
allowed to move Gillmore's division, supported by Kautz's
cavalry,[2] against Petersburg; for this small force effected
nothing, except awakening *Beauregard* to the danger of
his position.

The place selected to cross the James was at Wilcox's
Landing, well protected on its western flank by Herring
Creek. Here the river is 2,100 feet wide, and in mid-channel
some twelve to fifteen fathoms deep. The bridge constructed
at this place was supported on ninety-two boats, and was
thirteen feet wide. " It was braced by three schooners
anchored in eighty-five feet of water, near the centre. The
whole was laid in ten hours, and was finished at midnight " [3]
—a truly remarkable performance.

The order of march decided on was as follows : [4]

Warren and Hancock were to cross the Chickahominy at
Long Bridge ; Wright and Burnside at James's Bridge, and
the trains were to move from White House to Windsor
Shades and Coles's Ferry ; these movements being protected
by Wilson's cavalry, one brigade on the right and one on the
left ; the former to withdraw at the same time as Warren
and Hancock did, in order to protect the rear of the army
as it moved south. Smith and the Eighteenth Corps were
to move to White House, thence by transport to Bermuda
Hundred.

The withdrawal began at nightfall on the 12th, under cover
of Hancock's and Wright's corps. Upon crossing the
Chickahominy, Warren covered the passage of the army
towards the James, and then followed Hancock, who moved
to Charles's City Court House ; Wright's and Burnside's
corps marching to the same place by separate roads.

Warren's move in rear of White Oak Bridge was intended
to deceive *Lee* into supposing that either the Army of the
Potomac was about to move against Richmond from Riddle's

---

[1] 69 *W.R.*, p. 730.　　　[3] *M.H.S.M.*, V, p. 22.
[2] 67 *W.R.*, p. 22.　　　[4] 69 *W.R.*, pp. 747–9.

Shop, or attempt to cross the James at Turkey Bridge, the direct road to Bermuda Hundred.

Hancock's corps reached Wilcox's Landing on the afternoon of the 13th ; Wright's and Burnside's arriving at Charles City Court House that same day. By midnight the 16th, over half the infantry of the army, 4,000 cavalry, a train of wagons and artillery thirty-five miles long, and 3,500 beef cattle [1] were assembled on the south side of the James : as far as staff duties are concerned, this is surely one of the finest operations of war ever carried out.

This astonishing manœuvre was effected within a few miles of *Lee's* army, and, be it remembered, in a hostile country swarming with spies. Why did not *Lee* strike ? Here was presented to him an opportunity of attacking his enemy in detail and in flank, and, in spite of his numerical inferiority, of concentrating superiority of force against a most favourable target. There can be but one answer to this question, namely, that *Lee* had been completely out-generalled. An adept in audacious flanking movements, he failed to credit Grant, by reputation a stolid, unimaginative fighter, with an equal daring. He was completely deceived, first by Sheridan's movement, and secondly by Warren's. He was petrified by Richmond, and imagining that the capital was threatened, on the 13th he moved *Anderson's* corps over White Oak Swamp, halting it between Malvern Hill and Riddle's Shop, and then *Hill* was moved to support him. Nót until the 18th, as we shall see, did *Lee* believe that Grant had crossed the James ; on the 15th, 16th, and 17th he lay idle.

" Thus the last, and perhaps the best, chances of Confederate success," writes General Alexander, " were not lost in the repulse of Gettysburg, nor in any combat of arms. They were lost during three days of lying in camp, believing that Grant was hemmed in by the broad part of the James below City Point, and had nowhere to go but to come and attack us. The entire credit for the strategy belongs, I believe, to Grant." [2]

[1] *M.H.S.M.*, V, p. 23.   [2] *Alexander*, p. 547.

General Smith's Advance on Petersburg

The Eighteenth Corps was withdrawn from its trenches at
Cold Harbor after dark on the 12th, and on the evening of
the 14th Smith reported to General Butler at Bermuda
Hundred.   What instructions did he receive ?

Grant had failed to destroy *Lee* by force of arms ; this was
obvious to General Smith, who was not only a highly trained
officer, but a critic of Grant's action at Cold Harbor, which
he considered " was fought in contravention of military
principles." [1]   He himself says that on the 12th no intimation was given him of the object of his move.[2]   This was
true enough, for his mission was so important that the utmost
secrecy was essential.   On the 11th Grant had written to
Butler that he might expect the Eighteenth Corps on the
14th, and that if practical he was to seize and hold Petersburg.[3]   On the 14th he visited Butler and discussed the
whole operation with him.[4]   Grant saw quite clearly what
Beauregard saw, namely, that Petersburg was now " the
citadel of the Confederacy."   If he could not destroy *Lee's*
army by force of arms, then he would destroy it by grasping
" the arteries of the Confederacy at the throat " ; consequently, the object of the expedition against Petersburg
was obvious, it was to seize its railways and so strangle *Lee*.

On arriving at Bermuda Hundred Smith was informed that
he was to move his troops for an attack on Petersburg at
daybreak, and that Kautz's cavalry, 2,400 strong, as well
as some 3,700 other troops were to join him, bringing his
force up to between 16,000 and 18,000 men.   Smith says :

" On receiving my verbal orders from Butler at about
sunset, no plan was formulated for me to follow. . . .   The
information given me by General Butler was that the works
protecting Petersburg were not at all formidable, and that
General Kautz a few days before had ridden over them with
his cavalry, an assertion endorsed by General Kautz himself
in a personal interview." [5]

[1] *B. & L.*, IV, p. 229.   [3] *Grant*, II, p. 285 ; 69 *W.R.*, p. 755.
[2] *M.H.S.M.*, V, p. 79.   [4] *Grant*, II, p. 293 ; 67 *W.R.*, p. 25.
                    [5] *M.H.S.M.*, V, p. 80.

Butler, though an indifferent general, was an informatively minded man, and there can be little doubt that he supplied Smith with detailed information regarding the enemy. Smith complains that no plan was formulated for him, yet he would have been the last man in Grant's army to have accepted a plan from Butler, and this Butler knew from recent experiences. That he should have been given a plan was out of the question ; for, being ordered to direçt the operation, obviously he was the proper authority to formulate it. The truth would appear to be, that although Smith was a highly educated soldier he was not a commander. At Chattanooga he was astonished when he learnt that Grant had allowed Thomas to work out his own plan ; [1] now he was astonished that he was not given a ready-made one, which, had he been, he would have simply criticised and suggested another.

Smith's troops were disembarked two miles below Port Walthall. On the morning of the 15th, Kautz was sent forward [2] and struck a line of rifle-pits which was carried by the supporting infantry, who, pushing on, at about 10 a.m. came under range of the guns of Petersburg. From this hour until 5 p.m. Smith reconnoitred the position, for he was " determined to take no step in the dark." He then decided not to attack in column, but to advance " a heavy line of skirmishers with my artillery massed upon the salient near General Brookes's centre." [3] Ordering up his artillery, he learnt that the horses had been sent to water ; this delayed the attack until 7 p.m. By 9 p.m. the position was carried ; but hearing that *Beauregard* was being reinforced, and that Hancock's corps was approaching, he deemed " it wiser to hold what we had than . . . to lose what we had gained . . . " [4] ; these are his own words.

[1] *M.H.S.M.*, VIII, p. 193.   [2] 80 *W.R.*, p. 705.

[3] *M.H.S.M.*, V, pp. 82, 83. The wit of the rank and file is more often than not a reliable measure of a general's worth. Of Smith his men used to say that he made his movements at the " double-slow step," and the conundrum was early started round the camp-fires : " How long is it going to take us to get to Richmond if we go out three miles a day and come back at night ? " (*M.H.S.M.*, XIV, p. 103.)

[4] *M.H.S.M.*, V, p. 84. From the following correspondence it is obvious that Butler must have fully explained to Smith the importance of taking

Smith must have known that *Beauregard's* force was a
weak one ; in any case he knew that the Petersburg lines
were about seven and a half miles long on the south side of
the Appomattox, and to defend these with any certainty
would require at least 20,000 men ; further, he must have
known that *Beauregard* had nothing like this number. In
actuality there were 2,200 artillery and infantry in Petersburg, and about 4,500 guarding the Bermuda Hundred lines.
Opposed to Smith were only 1,200 men, and though he did
not know this, as General Wilcox says : he " feared to run
any risk " and " preferred to sleep on his arms that night." [1]

For a moment I will turn to Hancock. By the early
morning of the 15th he had crossed the whole of his corps to
Windmill Point. The day before, he had been instructed
by Grant, through Butler, to wait there until rations [2]
were sent him, and then to move by the most direct route
to Petersburg. Hancock reported that he had already three
days' rations with him,[3] which fact Meade did not pass on
to Grant, and quite inexcusably kept Hancock waiting for
these rations which he did not want, until, at 10.30 a.m.
on the 15th, Grant, having heard that he was still at Windmill
Point, ordered him to advance.

Meade, who on the 14th had been informed of Smith's
movement,[4] should (rations or no rations) have ordered

Petersburg. At 7.20 p.m. on June 15 he telegraphed Smith : "I grieve for
the delays. Time is the essence of this movement. I doubt not the delays
were necessary, but now push and get the Appomattox between you and
Lee. Nothing has passed down the railroad to harm you yet." At 9 p.m.
Smith replied : "I must have the Army of the Potomac reinforcements
immediately." At 9.30 Butler telegraphed back : "Hancock has been
ordered up by General Grant and my orders. Another army corps will
reach you by 10 a.m. to-morrow. It is crossing. They have not got 10,000
men down yet. Push on to the Appomattox." Then, ten minutes later :
"Did you make the attack contemplated ? What was the result ? Please
answer by telegram." The answer was sent off at midnight, and was as
follows : "It is impossible for me to go further to-night, but unless I mis-
apprehend the topography I hold the key to Petersburg. General Hancock
not yet up. . . ." (81 *W.R.*, p. 83.)

[1] *M.H.S.M.*, V, p. 120.   [2] 81 *W.R.*, p. 36.   [3] 81 *W.R.*, p. 25.

[4] Grant says, that he " communicated to General Meade, in writing, the
directions I had given to General Butler and directed him [Meade] to cross

Hancock forward at about 5 a.m.; had he done so the
Eighteenth Corps would have been in position to support
Smith early in the afternoon ; instead it arrived in the even-
ing.   Had Hancock arrived but two hours earlier, Colonel
Livermore is of opinion that " Petersburg would have fallen
that night," [1] and so was *Beauregard.*

Whether Grant or Meade was to blame for this muddle is
really immaterial, for Smith had been given no promise of assistance, and it was not until 4 p.m. on the 15th that he was informed that Hancock was advancing on Petersburg. The blame
is General Smith's ; for not only should he have attacked much
earlier in the day, but, failing to do so, when Hancock arrived
he should have made a night attack.   Grant says :

" The night was clear, the moon shining brightly, and
favourable to further operations.   General Hancock, with
two divisions of the Second Corps, reached General Smith
just after dark, and offered the services of these troops
as he (Smith) might wish, waiving rank to the named commander, who he naturally supposed knew best the position
of affairs and what to do with the troops.   But instead of
taking these troops and pushing at once into Petersburg,
he requested General Hancock to relieve a part of his line
in the captured works, which was done before midnight." [2]

Fortunately for *Lee, Beauregard* played his part with
consummate skill.   He was a man of enterprise and daring,
highly imaginative, for he could often foresee the movements
and actions of his enemy.   In his present situation, he
measured up Smith with extreme accuracy ; he bluffed him
into believing that Petersburg was strongly held, by making
a great noise with his artillery, and by boldly throwing
forward his skirmishers as if they were supported by strong
columns in rear.

On the 14th he telegraphed [3] to *Bragg* that Grant was

Hancock's corps over under cover of night, and push them forward in the
morning to Petersburg ; halting them, however, at a designated point until
they could hear from Smith " (*Grant*, II, p. 294).   Meade asserts that he
never received this information (80 *W.R.*, p. 315).

[1] *M.H.S.M.*, IV, p. 454.   [2] 95 *W.R.*, p. 24.   [3] 81 *W.R.*, pp. 648, 652.

reinforcing Butler, and that his position might at any moment be rushed : to this he received no reply. Then he telegraphed [1] *Lee* that Butler had been reinforced by the Eighteenth Corps—again no answer. Next he sent [2] an aide to *Lee* to explain to him the exact situation ; but *Lee* only said that he must be in error in believing that Smith was south of the James—and this at the very moment when Smith was attacking Petersburg. On the 15th he was reinforced by *Hoke* [3] and some 4,000 men, who were returned to his command by *Lee* ; but as he learnt that Hancock was approaching, not waiting for authority he ordered [4] General *B. J. Johnson* to evacuate the lines in front of Bermuda Hundred at dawn on the 16th, and to march to Petersburg. At 9.45 a.m. on the 16th he telegraphed [5] *Lee* that Hancock's corps had crossed the James on the 14th, and that reinforcements were urgently needed. To which *Lee* replied : [6] " Has Grant been seen crossing James river ? " And then, at noon on the 17th, [7] " Until I can get more definite information of Grant's movements, I do not think it prudent to draw more troops to this side of the river," and " Have no information of Grant's crossing James river, but upon your report have ordered troops to Chaffin's Bluff." [8] At 3.30 p.m. this day he ordered [9] *W. H. F. Lee*, then at Malvern Hill, to " push after the enemy, and endeavour to ascertain what has become of Grant's army." On the 18th, at 12.40 a.m., *Beauregard* telegraphed [10] *Lee* that he was confronted by the whole of Grant's army ; to which *Lee* answered, " Am not yet satisfied as to General Grant's movements ; but upon your representations will move at once to Petersburg." [11]

I have entered into this detail with a purpose, not to

[1] 81 *W.R.*, p. 653. [4] 81 *W.R.*, p. 657. [7] 81 *W.R.*, p. 664.

[2] *B. & L.*, IV, p. 540. [5] 81 *W.R.*, p. 660. [8] 81 *W.R.*, p. 665.

[3] 81 *W.R.*, p. 658. [6] 81 *W.R.*, p. 659. [9] 81 *W.R.*, pp. 663, 665.

[10] 81 *W.R.*, p. 666.

[11] *B. & L.*, IV, pp. 540–3. Yet, according to 81 *W.R.*, p. 667, *Lee* telegraphed *Early* on the 18th : " Grant is in front of Petersburg. . . . Strike quick as you can." And as early as 3.30 a.m. he had telegraphed to the Superintendent of the Richmond and Petersburg railroad : " Can trains run through to Petersburg ? . . . It is important to get troops to Petersburg without delay." (81 *W.R.*, p. 668.)

belittle *Lee,* who was a really great general, but to show the peculiar psychological effect of war on a general's mind. *Lee* was so certain that he understood Grant, that his certainty became an obsession which obliterated the clearest proof of what was actually happening. Here, at Malvern Hill, he was as certain that Grant would attack him, as Sherman at Pittsburg Landing was certain that he would not be attacked. Grant's surprise at Shiloh was great, yet no greater than *Lee's* on the James. At Shiloh Grant risked the loss of an army, on the James *Lee* risked the loss of the war, and had it not been for a brilliant subordinate, a soldier who has never received full justice, he would have lost the war on June 15.

It will be remembered that, on the 15th, *Beauregard* ordered *B. J. Johnson* to withdraw from Bermuda Hundred, and march with all speed to Petersburg. Though circumstances demanded this bold move, it drew the cork from the bottle in which Butler had been confined for just a month. *Beauregard* undoubtedly hoped that, as *Hill's* and *Anderson's* corps were only a few miles away at Malvern Hill, the pickets he had ordered *Johnson* to leave in the trenches would be rapidly reinforced.

On the evening of the 15th Lieutenant-Colonel Greeley, of the 10th Connecticut Volunteers, crept out on his hands and knees towards the Confederate trenches, and discovered that a withdrawal was in progress. At once reporting this fact to General Terry, at about 4 a.m. on the 16th Terry moved [1] forward his command, and was soon in possession of the enemy's main line of trenches, which extended from the James to the Appomattox. This done, Terry advanced his whole force as far as the Richmond and Petersburg railway, and a little later was met by part of *Anderson's* corps and driven back on to the old Confederate main line. Grant hearing [2] of Terry's advance, and realising the importance of occupying the Richmond and Petersburg road and railway, at once ordered [3] Wright's corps to report to Butler at Bermuda Hundred. Unfortunately, however, Butler so

----

[1] 81 *W.R.,* p. 105.   [2] 81 *W.R.,* p. 97.
[3] 81 *W.R.,* p. 99.

little realised the situation that he withdrew Terry,[1] and
made no use of Wright.

Whilst Terry was moving towards the Richmond railway,
Burnside's corps was brought forward to Hancock's left,
and Warren's was ordered to advance directly Burnside had
cleared the river. At 6 p.m. Hancock, supported by two
brigades of the Eighteenth Corps on his right and two brigades
of the Second on his left, assaulted and carried some redoubts
on his front. *Beauregard*, nothing daunted—though his
14,000 men were facing nearly 80,000—counter-attacked [2]
again and again, leading Meade to believe that he was far
stronger than he actually was.

On the 17th *Beauregard*, receiving no further reinforcements, and in order to maintain his fighting front, was compelled to evacuate the whole of his works from half a mile
east of the Jerusalem Plank road westwards to the Appomattox. Had Meade, in place of hammering at his enemy's
front, moved one corps by the Jerusalem Plank road, or
west of it, as *Beauregard* says, " I would have been compelled
to evacuate Petersburg without much resistance. But
they persisted in attacking on my front, where I was
strongest." [3] In the morning Potter's division of Burnside's corps carried the Shand House Ridge, but was not
supported ; in the afternoon an identical mistake was made
when Ledlie's division of the same corps was launched in
another assault. In both these cases Ropes is of opinion
that had support been forthcoming Petersburg might have
been taken,[4] and in spite of *Beauregard's* counter-attacks.
Of Ledlie's attack Burnside says : " The line was carried
and held till ten o'clock at night, when his advance was
driven in by an overpowering force of the enemy." [5] This
is indeed a compliment to *Beauregard's* leadership, seeing
that he was outnumbered by at least five to one.

Late on the 17th Meade ordered [6] the Fifth, Ninth, and
Second Corps to assault the enemy's works at 4 a.m. on the
following day. When the advance was made, it was found

---

[1] 81 *W.R.*, pp. 99, 106.   [3] *M.H.S.M.*, V, p. 121.   [5] 80 *W.R.*, pp. 522, 523.
[2] 80 *W.R.*, p. 168.   [4] *M.H.S.M.*, V, p. 182.   [6] 81 *W.R.*, p. 118.

that *Beauregard* had slipped back ; this withdrawal and the
nature of the ground seem to have completely unhinged
the co-operation between the divisions of Meade's corps, for
the rest of the day was spent in a series of unconnected
and misdirected assaults, which in my opinion were far more
culpable than the grand assault at Cold Harbor, and more
costly, for the total losses between the 15th and 18th
numbered over 10,000.[1]

It is instructive to look back on the operations of these
three days, for they show how faulty tactics and indifferent
leadership can wreck the most brilliant strategy and command.   By the morning of the 15th Grant had completely
out-generalled *Lee*. *Lee's* obsession left Petersburg all but
undefended, and had it not been for one man—*Beauregard*,
who at the time was worth 10,000 reinforcements—Petersburg, as Grant says, must have fallen.   On the other side,
an erudite soldier, blinded by book learning, wrecked the
profoundest strategy.   Grant has time and again been
blamed for needless assaults, yet had he been in Smith's
place, Petersburg would have been carried by assault on
the 15th, and the war would have been shortened by six
months ; for it is ludicrous to suppose, as Swinton does,[2] that
it could have for long continued once Petersburg was taken.
Six months less war would have probably meant 100,000
less casualties.   Smith had witnessed the assault on
Missionary Ridge, but with all his erudition it taught him
nothing.   He had taken part in the assault at Cold Harbor,
and its failure obsessed him.   He was a good thinker but
a bad doer, for neither on the evening of the 15th, nor the
night of the 15th, nor on the morning of the 16th, would
he accept the responsibility to assault and chance failure.
A general who fears to fail should never take the field, for
fear in itself is the foundation of failure.

Had Hancock arrived before dark on the 15th, as he says,
he would have assaulted, but unfortunately he was sick
and in an ambulance at the rear of his column when he
received the order to press on—on such small things do

[1] *Humphreys*, p. 224.   [2] *Swinton*, p. 506.

battles depend. If Hancock could have taken supreme command, it is probable that he would have carried Petersburg on the 16th or 17th ; but Meade, an indifferent tactician, many of whose blunders I feel have been off-loaded on to Grant, appeared on the scene. Once before Petersburg he showed no tactical skill whatever, and failing standing still did the next best thing *Beauregard* could have hoped for, namely—attack him on a narrow front. Meanwhile Butler, finding himself uncorked, like the jinn in the Arabian Nights, was persuaded, even with less trouble than the time before, to creep back into his bottle.

Some think that the Army of the Potomac was a blunt tool when it reached Petersburg ; that it had been demoralised by losses, and had no heart left to press an attack. I agree with Ropes [1] that there is little evidence that this was the case. That after six weeks' continuous fighting it had not suffered some deterioration is of course absurd ; but its physical losses had been made good, and its loss in *moral*, due to casualties, and the influx of raw recruits, was largely counter-balanced by the spirit of victory which animated it. Grant had never turned back, and come what might, the men felt that he never would. At Petersburg the courage of the soldiers leaves nothing to be desired ; but as Ropes says, this courage was squandered. He writes :

" The Army of the Potomac at Petersburg possessed, in spite of its disappointments, failures, and severe losses, a temper and daring quite sufficient for its task. The blame of the failure to take Petersburg must rest with our generals, not with our army." [2]

Lastly, turning to Grant, what do we see ? Recrimination ?—no ; excuses ?—no ; blame ?—no. His plan has been wrecked ; victory has been bungled out of his hands ; clouds are gathering in the Valley of Virginia : that he has failed is obvious, and he accepts failure not as a defeated man, but as one who sees in every failure a fresh incentive to further action. His reticence at this moment is truly

---

[1] *M.H.S.M.*, V, p. 183.   [2] *M.H.S.M.*, V, p. 184.

heroic; it is work and not failure which absorbs him.
Nothing unhinges him, or weakens his faith in himself and
in final victory. He soars above his subordinates, forgetting
their mistakes so that he may waste not a moment in
shouldering aside their blunders and getting on with his
task. If he cannot destroy *Lee*, then he will destroy his
communications ; if he cannot destroy his communications,
then he will invest Petersburg. Though means vary, his
idea remains constant ; he holds fast to *Lee*, so that Sherman's
manœuvres may continue.

War on the Railways

The assaults on Petersburg having failed, and because
Lee on June 18 moved the bulk of his army across the
James, Grant had once again to modify his plans. As he
could not take Petersburg by storm, he determined to invest
it, and, by strongly entrenching his front, reduce the number
of men required for the defensive, and so concentrate as
large an offensive force as possible to work westwards south
of the city against its railways.

The railways vital to the supply of *Lee's* army may be
divided into two groups, namely, those entering Richmond
and those entering Petersburg ; with the Richmond and
Petersburg railroad in between.

The first group comprised the Richmond and York River
and the Fredericksburg railroads—now of little use, and
the Virginia Central and Danville railroads which were
vital ; the second—the City Point and the Petersburg
and Norfolk railroads, already in Grant's hand, and the
Weldon and Southside (or Lynchburg) railroads, the
first of which was of high value, for it linked Petersburg
to Wilmington. Once the Petersburg lines were captured,
the bulk of the Confederate traffic would be thrown on to
the Danville railway, which was incapable of carrying
all of it. Grant's plan was, therefore, to occupy the Weldon
and Southside railways in order to compel the evacuation
of Petersburg ; and then, by turning the Confederate works

west of Bermuda Hundred, operate against the Danville
railway, the occupation of which would not only force the
surrender of Richmond, but sever *Lee* from Wilmington
and the Atlantic, and consequently cut him off from
European supplies. It is true he could still retire into the
interior, or unite with *Johnston*, but without an administrative base—and his vital supply base was Europe—he would
soon have been reduced to bow-and-arrow warfare.

Having stabilised his position, on June 21 Grant launched
the first of a series of combined movements against the
railways ;[1] Hancock's and Wright's corps advancing on
the Weldon line, which Grant hoped would be occupied on
the 22nd, and from where an advance could then be made
on the Southside line. At the same time Wilson and 5,500
cavalry were directed to move on Burksville,[2] and destroy
the Southside and Danville railways at this place.

The attempt on the Weldon line failed, mainly through
lack of co-operation between the two corps engaged. Wilson's
raid met, however, with considerable success—but at heavy
cost ; for on the 12th Sheridan, in contact with *Hampton*
at Trevylian's Station, learning that *Early's* corps was
on its way to Lynchburg, and that *Breckinridge* was at
Gordonsville or Charlottesville, considered that it was
not possible to join Hunter, and so decided to return, whereupon *Hampton* was set free. Sheridan reached the White
House on the 21st, from where he escorted 900 wagons to
the pontoon bridge at Bermuda Hundred ; after which the
base at White House was closed.

At Burksville, Wilson destroyed the entire junction and
sixty miles of the Southside and Danville lines. On his
way back he was all but surrounded, and by July 2, when
he returned, had lost 1,500 men, 12 guns abandoned, and
nearly all his wagons burnt or captured.

This raid, like all of Grant's, has been condemned by
most critics. It is true that it was a risky operation, seeing
that when Sheridan retired *Hampton's* cavalry were free
to turn on Wilson ; nevertheless, though Wilson himself

[1] 81 *W.R.*, pp. 258, 267.   [2] 81 *W.R.*, pp. 256, 258.

condemns his raid, as well as Sheridan's,[1] he relates that after the war General *J. M. St. John*, who, at the time of the raid, was in charge of the military railways of the Confederacy, said to him :

" I want to tell you what I never told any Federal officer. That raid of yours against the Danville and Southside railroads was the heaviest blow the Confederacy ever received, until it was destroyed at the battle of Five Forks." [2]

The day Sheridan turned back from before Gordonsville, Hunter was at Lexington, and on June 17 but five miles from Lynchburg, the third largest city in the Confederacy. The next day, meeting with *Early's* corps, he retired westwards into the Kanawha Valley, leaving the Shenandoah Valley open to *Early*,[3] who at once determined to head for the Potomac. On the 27th, with some 17,000 men,[4] he reached Staunton, and on July 11, moving through Rockville, appeared within range of the guns of Washington, to the utter consternation of the Union Government.

Washington at this time was garrisoned by 9,600 troops, supported by an equal number of details of little value, consequently it was precariously situated. Fortunately, however, on the 5th Grant had ordered [5] the Sixth Corps to Washington, this corps arriving at the very moment *Early* approached the city. *Early*, learning of its presence, recrossed the Potomac on the 14th, and moved to Leesburg and then towards Strasburg.

On the 23rd Grant ordered [6] the Sixth Corps back to the James, but *Early* hearing of this turned about and drove Crook's force through Winchester to Bunker Hill. The news of Crook's defeat caused Grant to cancel [7] his order recalling the Sixth Corps, and to send 4,600 [8] men of the Nineteenth Corps to Washington. He now made up his mind once and for all to close the Valley by systematically

---

[1] *M.H.S.M.*, XIII, p. 73.   [2] *M.H.S.M.*, XIII, p. 74.   [3] *Pond*, p. 38.
[4] *Pond*, p. 47. *Early* says—12,000 (see *B. & L.*, IV, p. 493).
[5] 82 *W.R.*, pp. 44, 45.   [7] 82 *W.R.*, p. 422.
[6] 82 *W.R.*, p. 408.   [8] *Pond*, p. 99.

devastating it, so that no army could support itself in that region. To attain this end he suggested [1] to the Government to merge the Departments of West Virginia, of the Susquehanna, of Washington, and the Middle Department (Delaware and part of Maryland) into one, the Middle Military Division, and to place Sheridan in command of it. This was agreed to, and on July 7 the Sixth, Nineteenth, and Eighth Corps were placed under this gallant young officer.[2]

Though *Early's* raid on Washington did not interrupt Grant's war on the railways, it did lead to a considerable weakening of his main army, and it is interesting to remember this when examining his operations from now onwards until the end of the year. This weakening is clearly set forth in the following table worked out by Colonel Livermore,[3] showing the numbers " present for duty " in the two armies from June to December :

Date.					Grant.	Lee.
June 30	.	.	.	.	137,454	65,562
July 31	.	.	.	.	93,542	61,623
Aug. 31	.	.	.	.	69,206	55,622
Sept. 30	.	.	.	.	88,308	51,200
Oct. 31	.	.	.	.	99,728	56,911
Nov. 30	.	.	.	.	103,442	66,717
Dec. 31	.	.	.	.	124,278	65,692

Whilst *Early* was moving down the Valley, the second combined operation against the railways was planned. It was to consist in a mine attack on a redan not far from Cemetery Hill, and a feint against the Virginia Central and Fredericksburg railways from the vicinity of Richmond to the North and South Anna rivers. This was to be carried out by Hancock's corps, and three cavalry divisions under Sheridan. Its object was to induce *Lee* to weaken his front at Petersburg, and in this it was entirely successful, for no sooner had Hancock crossed the river at Deep Bottom, than *Lee* moved two divisions from the south bank to the north ; this left only three infantry and one cavalry divisions

---

[1] 82 *W.R.*, p. 436. [2] Sheridan was born in 1831.
[3] *M.H.S.M.*, VI, p. 461.

in Petersburg. On the night of the 29th July Hancock withdrew to the south bank, as the mine was to be exploded at 3.30 a.m. the next day.

Tunnelling for the mine was begun on June 25, and was finished on July 23. The main gallery was 511 feet long with two lateral galleries in which 8,000 lb. of powder were packed.[1] Meade, from the start, was against the experiment. He said " that it was all clap-trap and nonsense ; that such a length of mine had never been excavated in military operations, and could not be . . . etc., etc. ; "[2] and Grant at first approved of it only because it would keep his men occupied. It was here that the cause of the eventual disaster originated. As so often happens in war, whilst a few enthusiasts saw the possibilities of the novelty proposed, the high command took little interest in it.[3] First Ferrero's coloured division was selected to lead the assault, then the remaining divisional commanders drew lots for the post of honour—a most unmilitary procedure—the lot falling on Ledlie, an incompetent coward. The mine was fired at 4.40 a.m. on the 30th, a crater about 150 feet long, 60 wide, and 25 deep being formed. At once it was occupied by a confused mob of men packed so close together that General Stephen M. Weld says, " I literally could not raise my hands from my side."[4] Meanwhile, Ledlie was sitting in a bombroof in the rear " soliciting and obtaining whiskey to stimulate his courage."[5]

No one had foreseen the panic the Confederates were thrown into, consequently no one was prepared to exploit it. Had this been done, Captain Charles H. Porter is of opinion that : " The city certainly would have been captured, and *Lee's* army, hopelessly divided, would have been disastrously beaten. It is almost impossible to conceive of the results which would have happened from a successful advance to that crest [Cemetery Hill], if the enemy had

---

[1] *B. & L.*, IV, pp. 546–8 ; 80 *W.R.*, pp. 136, 137. [2] *B. & L.*, IV, p. 545.
[3] In the World War examples of this are—the tactical use of tanks by the British Army in 1916, and the German gas attack in April, 1915.
[4] *M.H.S.M.*, V, p. 210. [5] *M.H.S.M.*, V, p. 218.

been pushed as he might have been. Their cause would have received a blow that would have been well-nigh disastrous." [1] The panic over, the Confederates advanced and literally slaughtered their enemy in the crater, the Federal losses numbering nearly 4,000.[2]

The Petersburg mine operation was, in my opinion, one of the most disgraceful episodes of the war, and Grant cannot be exonerated from blame ; for when a novel means of attack is decided upon, it is the duty of a general-in-chief to take a personal interest in it. It is true that after the event Grant blamed himself for having allowed Ledlie to lead the assaulting column ; [3] nevertheless, this honesty does not excuse him for not having done so.

The next combined attack was made against the Richmond fortifications in the vicinity of Bailey's Creek, and against the Weldon railway.

Grant, having heard that *Lee* intended to reinforce *Early* in the Valley, determined to frustrate this move. Hancock's corps [4] was secretly conveyed by steamer from City Point to Deep Bottom, and disembarked on the morning of August 14. Meanwhile, on the 18th, Warren's corps [5] marched to the Weldon railway, brushed aside a cavalry brigade, and occupied Globe Tavern, about four miles south of the outskirts of Petersburg. This operation was entirely successful ; *Lee*, believing that another checkmate move was intended, hastened over to his left and assumed command in person ; this led to a weakening of his right, and to Warren's success. Though the Weldon railway was now severed, it could still be used by the Confederates as far as within a day's haulage by wagon to Petersburg.

To follow up Warren's success, on the 22nd, Hancock was recalled [6] and sent to destroy the Weldon line near

---

[1] *M.H.S.M.*, V, pp. 230, 231. This is corroborated by Grant, who says : " Such an opportunity of carrying fortifications I have never seen, and do not expect again to have." (*Badeau*, II, p. 483 ; see also 80 *W.R.*, p. 134.)

[2] *B. & L.*, IV, p. 560. 　　　[4] 88 *W.R.*, pp. 148–50.

[3] *Badeau*, II, p. 486. 　　　[5] 88 *W.R.*, p. 176.

[6] 88 *W.R.*, p. 332.

Rowanty Creek, south of Ream's Station ; this expedition proved unsuccessful.

A month later another combined operation somewhat similar to the last was attempted. On September 28 Ord and Birney crossed the James at Dutch Gap,[1] and at 7.30 a.m. the next day assaulted Fort Harrison and Fort Gilmer ; the former being carried and held by Ord [2] against a determined counter-attack. On the south side of the river Warren advanced towards the Boydton (or Boydtown) Plank road, and captured the enemy's entrenchments at Peebles Farm [3] ; these were rapidly linked up to the Federal works on the Weldon railway.

The capture of Fort Harrison deserves more than a passing mention, for it clearly shows that as late as the autumn of 1864, when the art of field fortification was of a high order, well-led troops could still carry out successful though costly frontal attacks. The lesson the capture of this fort teaches us is that had Ord been in command of the Eighteenth Corps on June 15, Petersburg would most certainly have fallen.

Fort Harrison, a six-sided redoubt, each face measuring 1,463 feet, stood on a bluff flanked by breastworks and smaller redoubts. On crossing the James at 5 a.m. on the 28th, Ord formed Stannard's division into two columns, each about a thousand strong, deploying in front of them the 96th New York regiment commanded by Colonel Edgar M. Cullen—a youth twenty years of age ; he supported Stannard by Heckman's division in similar formation. The advance was made in the dark, and no halt was allowed until the open field land a mile from the fort was reached ; here Ord carried out a ten to fifteen minutes' reconnaissance of the ground. After the columns had been re-formed, caps removed and bayonets fixed, the advance was continued in perfect order in spite of the enemy's artillery fire. Stannard, considering the advance too slow, sent an order for the columns to break into double-quick time. " When this

---

[1] 88 *W.R.*, pp. 1046, 1082–9.   [2] 87 *W.R.*, p. 20.
[3] 87 *W.R.*, p. 21.

was given in a loud voice, the men shouted in reply, ' No,
no—the distance is too great.' " [1] Many men now began to
fall, and Ord fearing a failure sent forward the whole of
his staff to encourage them. A pause under cover was
made in order to regain breath, then Colonel Roberts,
commanding the Third Brigade, rose and in a quiet voice
said : " Come, boys, we must capture this fort—now get
up and start." [2] All sprang forward, rushed the ditch,
scrambled up the parapet, and entered the fort. Ord then
re-formed his men and held it.

Before winter put an end to operations, one further combined attack was carried out. A force of 32,000 men, drawn
from the Second, Fifth, and Ninth Corps, was moved against
the South Side railway. [3] At daylight on October 27 Hancock crossed Hatcher's Run, but met with no success and
was withdrawn. Simultaneously Butler was ordered [4] to
push through White Oak Swamp and carry the works which
protected the Williamsburg road and the Richmond and
York River railway. *Longstreet*, who had returned to duty
on October 19, divining Butler's intention drove him back
with the loss of 1,100 men. [5]

The tactical results of these various attacks were small,
and their value will be misunderstood should they be considered solely as attempts to reduce Petersburg. This
fortress, which became the main tactical objective after
Cold Harbor, had since Smith's failure become in this respect
a secondary one. Attacks were made on it, rather to terrify
the Government at Richmond than to take it, for Grant
realised that if Richmond were perpetually threatened,
the Government would insist on *Lee* maintaining a powerful
force in its neighbourhood. This Grant saw would simultaneously protect Washington, Sheridan, and Sherman.
Though his tactics failed, his strategy succeeded. That
it did succeed, the following incident will show. When
Fort Harrison was captured, J. B. Jones wrote in his diary :

[1] *M.H.S.M.*, XIV, p. 93.
[2] *History of the Thirteenth New Hampshire Volunteers*, p. 479.
[3] 89 *W.R.*, p. 340.   [4] 88 *W.R.*, pp. 331, 332.   [5] *Humphreys*, p. 306.

" The offices and government shops were closed and the tocsin was sounded for hours. All the local troops were hurried out to defend the city, and guards on foot and horse-back scoured the streets with orders to arrest every male person between the ages of seventeen and fifty and send them to Cary Street for service. Two members of Mr. Davis's Cabinet were caught in this sweeping out, the Postmaster-General and the Attorney-General. Such was the need of fighting men that the type-setters of all the newspapers, who had a general exemption, were taken into the ranks, and the *Richmond Whig* was the only paper published the next morning." [1]

[1] *Jones*, II, p. 295.

CHAPTER XIV

CAMPAIGNS OF SHERMAN, SHERIDAN, AND THOMAS

Military and Political Situation

It will be remembered that Grant's overland campaign was the pivot of a series of campaigns the security and success of which depended on the Army of the Potomac holding *Lee*. The most important of these subsidiary operations was Sherman's advance from Chattanooga, which was strategically so closely related to the campaign in Virginia that it is quite impossible to appreciate the one without reference to the others.

Immediately after the battle of Chattanooga, *Bragg* fell back to Dalton, and on December 18 was replaced by *Joseph Johnston*, a high-minded, patient, and indefatigable general who by most historians has been ranked only second to *Lee*. Meanwhile Grant, at the head of a formidable army, about 120,000 strong, decided to prepare for a move on Atlanta, and from there fight his way to Mobile. It will be remembered that this intention was communicated to Sherman and Thomas, the first of these generals succeeding Grant in command of the Military Division of the Mississippi on March 17. On April 4, as we have already seen, Grant sent him his plan for the forthcoming campaign, and at 11 a.m. on April 28 ordered him to move on May 5.

Sherman entered the campaign with an effective force of nearly 100,000 men and 254 guns,[1] and was faced by *Johnston* at Dalton at the head of an army 43,000 strong.[2] His object was definite, for as he writes in his *Memoirs*:

---

[1] *Atlanta*, p. 25.

[2] *Atlanta*, p. 28. Ropes says, probably 60,000 strong. (*M.H.S.M.*, X, p. 135.)

" Neither Atlanta, nor Augusta, nor Savannah, was the objective, but the ' army of *Jos. Johnston,* go where it might.' " [1]   Thus in the West and in the East the objectives were similar, in both cases they are the opposing armies ; but whilst *Lee* was operating in what may be called a topographical corridor at the far end of which was Richmond, *Johnston,* with his right flank resting on the southernmost spurs of the Alleghanies, had at his disposal a vast area of good defensive country to manœuvre in ; consequently Sherman's tactical problem was very different from Grant's.

Whilst Grant's plan was taking form, politics in the North were causing him grave anxiety.   He saw quite clearly that as Lincoln's accession to power resulted in the declaration of the war, his defeat in the forthcoming Presidential election would almost certainly be followed by a disastrous peace. He was well aware that Southern hopes were fixed on this possibility ;   Senator Hill from Georgia on March 14, 1864, had expressed himself as follows :   " I think, therefore, that policy, as well as necessity, indicates that we should now make a direct appeal to the people of the United States against Lincoln and his policy and his party, and make them join issue at the polls in November—we shaping that issue." [2] It was this shaping of the issue by the South that Grant feared ;   he knew that the South could not win the war by force of arms, but if through prolonged resistance, or political machinations, it could tire the North out, or prevent Lincoln's nomination or re-election, the Union cause was faced by disaster.   It must have been clear to Grant, that unless *Lee* could be decisively defeated in the East before the summer closed, a somewhat problematical event, the next most effective operation was the forward movement of Sherman ;   for by carrying the war into the heart of the Confederacy the *moral* of the North would be stimulated in proportion as that of the South was lowered.   To magnetise the North into supporting Lincoln was àt this moment Grant's political object, his tactical one, as we have seen,

---

[1] *Sherman,* II, p. 26.

[2] *Annual Report of the American Historical Association* (1911), II, p. 635.

being to hold *Lee*, so that Sherman's strategy might attain full liberty of movement.

ATLANTA CAMPAIGN

The theatre of war in which Sherman was now called upon to operate was an exceedingly difficult one ; maps worthy the name did not exist, and he did not possess an intimate knowledge of the country. Not only was this theatre most unsuited for offensive action, but *Johnston* had every intention of using it defensively, for being out-numbered by about two to one, he was not in a position to attack. Dalton he strongly fortified, as he judged rightly from the nature of the country that Sherman would be com-pelled to advance along the line of the railway. Realising that Sherman must assume the offensive, and considering him of an impulsive nature, he trusted that he would exhaust his strength in useless assaults, until such time as he him-self was reinforced, when he would be in a position to meet him on more equal terms. In this he was to be disappointed ; for though Sherman was pre-eminently a fighting general, he was by no means a reckless one. Imaginative, and fertile in resources, he saw clearly that in spite of his numerical superiority every mile he advanced would lengthen his communications and so reduce his strength. He determined, therefore, not to do what *Johnston* wished him to do ; but instead, by constant manœuvre, to keep a grip on him whilst Grant was hammering *Lee* in the East. Consequently, the operations which were now to take place are of great interest, not merely as a psychological struggle between the wills of two able generals, but as a contrast to Grant's campaign in Virginia.

On May 4 the campaign opened [1] : the Army of the Cumberland under Thomas, 60,000 strong, in the centre ; the Army of the Tennessee under McPherson, 25,000 strong, on the right, and the Army of the Ohio under Schofield, 14,000 strong, on the left : Sherman's idea being that

[1] *Atlanta*, p. 25.

whilst Thomas and Schofield pinned *Johnston* down to his entrenchments, McPherson should turn his left through Snake Creek Gap, and cut in behind him at Resaca. If this operation were successful, the chances were that the campaign would be ended by a single battle.

The idea of this manœuvre must be credited to Thomas, for it was he who suggested it to Sherman some time before the campaign opened. He proposed to march his army [1] through the Gap, and so concentrate an overwhelmingly strong force against *Johnston's* rear. Sherman seems, however, to have considered so large a force unnecessary ; why, it is difficult to say, for at Snake Creek Gap opposition might well be expected. Deciding that McPherson and his two corps would be sufficient, on May 5th he sent the following order :

" I want you to move . . . to Snake [Creek] Gap, secure it and from it make a bold attack on the enemy's flank or his railroad, at any point between Tilton and Resaca. . . . I hope the enemy will fight at Dalton, in which case he can have no force there [? at Resaca] that can interfere with you. But, should his policy be to fall back along the railroad, you will hit him in flank. Do not fail in that event to make the most of the opportunity by the most vigorous attack possible." [2]

On the 8th McPherson advanced through Snake Creek Gap unopposed. " How this gap," writes *Cleburne* in his report, " which opened upon our rear and line of communications, from which it was distant at Resaca only five miles, was neglected, I cannot imagine " [3] ; but unoccupied it was. Hearing of this move, on the 9th *Johnston* sent three divisions to Resaca, and McPherson, finding the position too strong to be attacked, fell back to the entrance of the gorge. In his *Memoirs* Sherman blames McPherson for doing so ; he says :

" He had in hand 23,000 of the best men in the army, and could have walked into Resaca (then held by a small

---

[1] *Atlanta*, p. 31.   [2] 75 *W.R.*, pp. 39, 40.   [3] 74 *W.R.*, p. 721.

brigade), or could have placed his whole force astride the railroad above Resaca, and there have easily withstood the attack of all *Johnston's* army, with the knowledge that Thomas and Schofield were on his heels. Had he done so, I am certain that *Johnston* would not have ventured to attack him in position, but would have retreated eastward, by Spring Place, and we would have captured half his army. . . . Such an opportunity does not occur twice in a single life, but at the critical moment McPherson seems to have been a little timid. Still, he was perfectly justified by his orders." [1]

What were they ? The answer is given by Sherman himself in a dispatch sent to Halleck at 8 p.m. on the 9th, namely : " After breaking the road good his orders are to retire to the mouth of Snake Creek Gap, and be ready to work on *Johnston's* flank, in case he retreats south." [2]

Should McPherson have disobeyed this order ? The answer is given by *Cleburne* in his report; he says :

" But McPherson . . . after penetrating within a mile of Resaca, actually returned, because, as I understood, he was not supported, and feared if we turned back suddenly upon him from Dalton, he would be cut off, as doubtless would have been the result. . . . If McPherson had hotly pressed his advantage, Sherman supporting him strongly with the bulk of his army, it is impossible to say what the enemy might not have achieved—more than probably a complete victory." [3]

I have gone into this detail with a purpose, namely, to show the difference between Sherman's and Grant's generalship. Grant, whenever he determined to carry out a decisive movement, never failed to concentrate the maximum force in order to effect it. Should this force be commanded by a subordinate, giving its commander a general idea, he left all detail to the commander himself. In this operation Sherman accepted Thomas's idea ; but, failing to appreciate the difference between a rear and a flank attack, he only allotted sufficient force for an outflank-

[1] *Sherman*, II, p. 34.   [2] 75 *W.R.*, p. 88; see also 75 *W.R.*, pp. 40, 41.
[3] 74 *W.R.*, p. 721.

ing operation, and ordered McPherson to carry it out, and then complains of over-caution when McPherson does not throw himself across *Johnston's* rear. It would appear, however, that it was not McPherson who was over-cautious, but Sherman himself. He kept Thomas in the centre, presumably to cover his base—Chattanooga; had he realised that Thomas at Resaca, severing *Johnston* from his base, would equally well have been able to carry out this protective rôle, he would undoubtedly have moved him there. The truth is that Sherman did not so fully understand the nature of the rear attack as Grant did.

McPherson having failed, Sherman advanced the bulk of his army through Snake Creek Gap, with the result that *Johnston*, on the night of the 12th, fell back to Resaca, and on the 15th retired across the Oostanaula river. From now onwards until July 17, when he was relieved of his command by *Hood*, he was ably flanked out of every position he held by Sherman, and as ably extricated himself from each successive envelopment. From the Oostanaula, he fell back on the Etowah, then to Allatoona, then to New Hope Church, then to Marietta, and lastly to Kenesaw Mountain, where he was able, on June 18, with 71,000 men,[1] to confront Sherman. Here Sherman changed his tactics, determining on an assault; his reasons being as follows :

(1) The weather was so bad, that to continue outflanking *Johnston* was impossible until he could accumulate a sufficiency of supplies; and should he sit down and wait for good weather and good roads, he feared that *Johnston* might seize the opportunity to detach troops to *Lee*.

(2) As he himself writes :

" The enemy and our own officers had settled down into a conviction that I would not assault fortified lines. All looked to me to outflank. An army to be efficient must not settle down to a single mode of offense, but must be prepared to execute any plan which promises success. I

---

[1] *B. & L.*, IV, p. 282; *B. & L.*, IV, p. 252, says 62,000. Some time before *Johnston* had been reinforced by *Polk's* corps. On May 31 Sherman's total effective strength was 112,819 (72 *W.R.*, p. 115).

wanted, therefore, for the moral effect to make a successful assault against the enemy behind his breastworks." [1]

The first of these reasons is a sound one, and the one which Grant had so frequently to follow in Virginia; the second, in my opinion, is fallacious; for I do not believe that successful troops ever require to be stimulated by slaughter. I have on several occasions seen this argument applied practically, and have still to discover its value. Attacks delivered for the sole purpose of raising the *moral* of the soldier are never justifiable, unless *moral* is so low that a sudden shock is required to reawaken courage. In this case Sherman's assault was useless, and it was beaten back at a loss of 2,500 men. [2]

From the Kenesaw entrenchments, on July 2, *Johnston* fell back to the Chattahoochee, and then on the 17th the Richmond Government, tired of his continual retreats, and not understanding his difficulties, replaced him by *Hood*.

Hood was far from being an indifferent general, and his courage is above question. His position was about as unenviable a one as a general could be faced with: his back was against Atlanta; his army, though far from being demoralised, had for over two months been in almost unceasing retreat; above all, he was expected to assume the offensive and do something dramatic, and he certainly succeeded in doing both, but unfortunately to the detriment of his side.

On the 20th he attacked Sherman at Peach-Tree Creek and lost some 5,000 men. [3] Then he fell back on Atlanta, attacked again, and lost about double this number. [4] At Atlanta his position depended on his being able to preserve the Macon railway; here once again he attacked, losing probably 5,000 men. By now Richmond had its bellyful of the offensive, for, on August 5, Jefferson Davis wrote to him saying: "The loss consequent of attacking him [Sherman] in his intrenchments requires you to avoid

---

[1] 72 *W.R.*, p. 68.
[2] *Atlanta*, p. 127.
[3] *B. & L.*, IV, p. 253.
[4] *Atlanta*, pp. 175, 176.

that, if practicable." [1] This censure left him with some dramatic move as his only alternative.

On August 25th Sherman began his final manœuvre ; on the 28th the Montgomery railway was reached, whereupon *Hood's* position became untenable. On September 1 he evacuated Atlanta, and the next day " the gate city of the South " was entered by Sherman's army.

From May 4 to September 2 the total losses were approximately—Federals 32,000, and Confederates 35,000 [2] ; a heavy toll in spite of the fact that the tactics of this campaign were mainly manœuvre and the defensive. Deducting the 20,000 men lost under the command of Hood, the remaining 15,000, to be debited to *Johnston*, shows that his tactics were correct.

" For my own part," says Grant, " I think that *Johnston's* tactics were right. Anything that could have prolonged the war a year beyond the time that it did finally close, would probably have exhausted the North to such an extent that they might then have abandoned the contest and agreed to a separation." [3]

Sherman's tactics could scarcely have been improved upon ; yet, in spite of the fact that he generally avoided assaults, his losses were almost as great as his enemy's. The reason for this was, that in order to manœuvre with his wings—McPherson and Schofield—he was compelled to keep his centre—Thomas—in constant contact with the enemy. With the exception of his first move, his idea of holding with his centre, and, as occasion demanded, of outflanking with his wings, was altogether an admirable one. Because of the theatre of war, which was roomy, the superiority of his force, and the defensive tactics of his enemy, he was able to replace assaults by manœuvres. *Johnston*, discussing this question with *Swinton*, once said to him : " I know I should have beaten him [Sherman] had he made assaults on me as General Grant did on *Lee*." [4] Though

---

[1] 76 *W.R.*, p. 946. [2] *Wood and Edmonds*, p. 393 ; possibly 40,000 each.
[3] *Grant*, II, p. 167. [4] *Swinton*, p. 495.

such an assertion is beyond proof, it is not altogether value-less, for it shows that if so able a general as *Johnston* failed to appreciate the difference between Grant's and Sherman's campaigns, and the influence of topography on the operations in Virginia and Georgia, there is some excuse for Grant's strategy being so generally misunderstood.

SHERIDAN'S CAMPAIGN, AUGUST 7 TO DECEMBER 19

To turn from Sherman to Sheridan is of great interest, if only as a personal study. Whilst both were generally bold in their actions, the former was more experienced and cautious, whilst the latter was more intuitive and dashing. The one was daring, the other sometimes reckless ; both possessed imagination, but whilst Sherman's was kept in restraint, Sheridan's was frequently given full leash. A good tactician, Sheridan was no strategist ; but in spite of this defect, his selection to command the troops in the Valley was probably the best which could have been made. The situation required a young and really active general to close this " race-course of armies," so that the incessant Confederate advances on Harpers Ferry, which by some wag had been rechristened *Harper's Monthly*, might definitely be ended. Further than this, Grant had determined to devastate this region so that no Confederate army would be able to operate in it and simultaneously live on the country.

Having secured Washington against a sudden raid, Grant's intention was for Sheridan to move against Lynch-burg—the Atlanta of Virginia. This was the strategic part of his mission which, as we shall see, he failed to appreciate. He never seems fully to have understood that his campaign was not a unique one, but part of a combined operation, in which the destruction of *Early's* army was but a stepping-stone to the encirclement of *Lee*.

Sheridan's command—the Army of the Shenandoah—consisted of three corps : the Sixth under Wright, the Nineteenth under Emory, and the Eighth under Crook, supported by three cavalry divisions—Torbert's, Wilson's, and Averell's. On August 10 Sheridan moved from Halltown towards Winchester, *Early* falling back to Fisher's Hill ; Sheridan, hearing that *Early* had been reinforced, fell back, devastating the country between Strasburg and Winchester. This retreat was quite unnecessary, for though *Early* had been reinforced by *Anderson*, Sheridan must have known that he was still far stronger than his enemy. On the 25th, when *Early*, finding Sheridan's position too strong to be attacked, left a small force under *Anderson* to contain him, whilst he moved towards Williamsport,[1] an opportunity, as seldom occurs in war, was presented to Sheridan to place his army across his enemy's communications and without endangering his own. He did nothing, however, and so strong grew the feeling in Washington, that Grant left City Point [2] and hurried to Sheridan to discover his difficulties. Simultaneously with this visit, *Lee* was compelled, through shortage of men, to call upon *Early* to return to him the force under *Anderson*.

Sheridan's plan was to operate against *Early's* line of retreat, a plan which accorded fully with Grant's views ; but when, on September 19, he attacked *Early* at Opequon Creek, 40,000 men being launched against 17,000,[3] he failed to do this, and though he decisively defeated the Confederate general, this battle cost him nearly 5,000 casualties.[4] It may be true, as Sheridan says, that he sent the enemy " whirling through Winchester," [5] but, in my opinion, *Early* is not altogether wrong in criticising his generalship, for his own dispositions were so faulty that he should have been annihilated.

On the 20th *Early* withdrew to Fisher's Hill, to be followed by Sheridan, who, on the 22nd, attacked him in rear, and

---

[1] *Pond*, p. 137.   [2] *Grant*, II, p. 327.

[3] Strengths as usual are difficult to arrive at. Keifer (*Slavery and Four Years of War*, II, p. 109) gives Sheridan's strength as 25,000, and *Early* (*Swinton*, p. 558) estimates his own strength at 11,500. In either case Sheridan outnumbered him by over two to one ; further still, neither side made use of entrenchments in this battle.   [4] *Phisterer*, p. 217.

[5] In 91 *W.R.*, p. 110, the words are " driving him through Winchester."

once again severely defeated him. The Valley was now at the Federal mercy, consequently Sheridan once again set to work to devastate it.

Early defeated, Grant, with the persistence so characteristic of him, at once returned to the strategic problem in Sheridan's campaign, namely, the destruction or isolation of Lynchburg. He considered that as Lynchburg could not at present be directly attacked, a move should be made against the Virginia Central railroad between Gordonsville and Charlottesville, and also against the James River canal. Sheridan objected [1] to this, believing that the sole object of his campaign was to devastate the Valley, and that to move against Lynchburg, or Gordonsville and Charlottesville, were not feasible operations even if the railway in rear of him were repaired. Instead, he proposed [2] to maintain Crook's corps in the lower Valley, and to return the Sixth and Nineteenth to Grant.

Grant was right and Sheridan was wrong ; for, as will shortly be seen, any depletion of the forces in the Valley was altogether premature. Nevertheless, Grant, as was his custom once he had placed a subordinate in a responsible position, instead of sending a definite order merely suggested a leading idea ; should the subordinate not like it, then, failing his removal, Grant, with one exception, never pressed the idea upon him ; for he always held that the man on the spot should be allowed a free hand in deciding what in the circumstances he considered best. In the present instance, on October 3, he authorised [3] Sheridan to carry out his plan.

No sooner was this decision made, than Sheridan withdrew to Strasburg ; simultaneously, *Lee* reinforced *Early*, who started in pursuit of the retiring Federals, and occupied Newmarket on the 7th. On the 10th Sheridan crossed Cedar Creek, and, on the 13th, the uncrushable *Early*, hearing that Sheridan was about to dispatch part of his force to the assistance of Grant, moved forward to Fisher's Hill. On the 15th Sheridan was called [4] to Washington to discuss the

---

[1] 91 *W.R.*, p. 249 ; see also, 91 *W.R.*, pp. 177, 202, 210.
[2] 91 *W.R.*, p. 250. [3] 91 *W.R.*, p. 266. [4] 91 *W.R.*, p. 355, dated October 13.

feasibility of sending Merrit's cavalry division, reinforced by Powell's from the Luray Valley, through Chester Gap, against the Virginia Central railroad.[1]

No sooner had he left, when Wright, who was now in command at Cedar Creek, heard that *Longstreet* was marching to *Early's* assistance. In spite of this, it does not appear that he considered it worth while to send out a strong force of cavalry to picket and watch his enemy ; the result was, that before sunrise on the 19th he was even more completely surprised than Grant had been at Shiloh.

I cannot here in detail describe the battle which now took place, though it is one of the most interesting and instructive of the war. *Early's* astonishing boldness is a fine example of audacity succeeding. Under cover of fog he rolled up Wright's left, taking his centre in rear, and had it not been for the magnificent behaviour of the Federal cavalry, Wright would in all probability have been totally defeated.[2]

Meanwhile, at 8.30 a.m. on the 19th, Sheridan, on his return from Washington, set out from Winchester, and was soon met by a stream of fugitives. Galloping on, he reached the battlefield at 11.30 a.m. to find that Wright had the situation well in hand ; nevertheless his arrival and his gallant behaviour inspired his troops with the utmost confidence in themselves, and when, at 4 p.m., they advanced to the attack the result was the rout of *Early's* army.

I will only quote one incident which took place in this battle, as it bears on a point I have already examined, namely, the value of the magazine carbine. Early in the day Sheridan's army lost twenty-four guns. At about 4.30 p.m. Colonel A. C. Hamlin pointed out to General Custer a large force of broken enemy retreating south, and obtained his permission to charge them. His men were armed with sabres, revolvers, and magazine carbines. He moved forward at the head of his regiment and a detachment of the 5th New York cavalry. Then in his own words :

" The 5th New York swung out and struck the enemy at my left, while I led my regiment straight to the front, thus

1 *Pond*, p. 212.   2 *M.H.S.M.*, VI, p. 145.

keeping in advance. The enemy when we struck them were a dense body, covering several acres, and the broken and disorganised rushed upon those in better order, so that all were thrown into confusion. My men with carbines, lying along the side of their horses' necks, fired point blank upon this mass. When the seven shots were gone carbines were slung and revolvers drawn. At one point some of the enemy fell and others fell over them, until the ground for the distance of nearly half an acre was covered with a struggling mass of fallen men. We swung just to the left of this fallen body, and smashed our way right through the main force of the enemy, who slowly gave way, and then rushed to the right and left. Here we overtook the first gun." [1]

The Federal victory was a costly one, for Sheridan's losses numbered 5,764,[2] exceeding *Early's* by about 1,500.[3]

After this defeat *Early* fell back on Newmarket, whereupon Grant once again pressed Sheridan to move on to the Virginia Central railroad; but Sheridan still considered[4] that such an operation was impracticable. Again being urged to do so, on December 19 [5] he sent some 8,000 cavalry under Torbert against this railway; but the expedition met with no success, as it was now too late in the year for such an operation.[6]

In my opinion Sheridan's generalship throughout this campaign was, in spite of his many successes, indifferent. It is true that his victories had a most important influence on the political situation, and that his devastations still further restricted *Lee's* ever-decreasing resources and protected Washington by making it most difficult for a Confederate army to subsist in the Valley. It is also true that his campaign did succeed in holding a force of the enemy which President Davis would otherwise have sent to *Johnston*; but his persistent resistance to Grant's wishes shows that he had no grasp of the higher meaning of generalship. When, after Cedar Creek, he was urged by Grant to move against the railway, his answer that it " would demoralise the troops,

---

[1] *M.H.S.M.*, VI, pp. 202, 203.
[2] *Pond*, p. 239.
[3] *Phisterer*, p. 218.

[4] 91 *W.R.*, pp. 464, 465.
[5] 91 *W.R.*, p. 804.
[6] See *M.H.S.M.*, VI, pp. 55, 56.

now in magnificent trim," [1] shows this clearly enough, and I entirely agree with Lieutenant L. W. V. Kennon when he says :

" Grant's judgment was sound, while Sheridan's action practically nullified his victories won in the field. It seems not unlikely that if he had complied with Grant's instructions immediately after the battle of Fisher's Hill, Richmond would have fallen in September or October, 1864, instead of April, 1865." [2]

SHERMAN'S MARCH THROUGH GEORGIA

Once Atlanta was in Sherman's hands the next problem was : in what direction should he move ? It had always been Grant's idea to push him through to the Atlantic coast (see Appendix V), but *Hood's* army had not yet been annihilated, and though Mobile Bay [3] was now in Federal hands, Mobile itself was not taken until March 11, 1865. Wilmington, Charleston, and Savannah were still held by the Confederates, and unless a seaport connected to Atlanta by rail could be occupied and converted into a base of supply, it was a hazardous operation for Sherman to cut loose from his communications and move south or east. On September 10 Grant wrote to Sherman as follows :

" As soon as your men are sufficiently rested and preparations can be made, it is desirable that another campaign should be commenced. We want to keep the enemy continually pressed to the end of the war. If we give him no peace while the war lasts, the end cannot be far distant. Now that we have all of Mobile Bay that is valuable, I do not know but it will be the best move to transfer Canby's troops to act upon Savannah, while you move on Augusta. . . ." [4]

The failure to take Mobile was the factor which was unbalancing the Federal strategy. Sherman's base of

---

[1] *M.H.S.M.*, VI, p. 55.   [2] *M.H.S.M.*, VI, p. 57.   [3] Occupied August 5, 1864.
[4] 78 *W.R.*, p. 355. Canby's movement against Mobile had miscarried. He had been compelled strongly to reinforce Rosecrans on account of General *Price's* activities in Missouri.

supplies was still at Louisville, 474 miles away, and in all
he had to protect 950 miles of railway, establish large intermediate supply depots and garrison them, as well as patrol
the Tennessee river by cavalry and gunboats. As it was
intended that Sherman should move forward, it was imperative for him to cut loose from his communications—this
Grant had foreseen before the opening of the campaign.
Sherman saw this clearly enough, and had already, on August
13, written to Halleck as follows :

" In making the circuit of Atlanta as proposed . . . I
would like to know the chances of our getting the use of the
Alabama river this campaign. I could easily break up the
railroads back to Chattanooga, and shift my whole army
down to West Point and Columbus, a country rich in corn,
and make my fall campaign from there." [1]

But it was of little use moving in this direction as long as
Mobile was in enemy hands.

On September 20, in reply to Grant's letters of the 10th
and 12th he put forward a host of proposals : " But, the
more I study the game," he writes, " the more I am convinced that it would be wrong for me to penetrate much
further into Georgia without an object beyond " ; then he
suggests that if Grant will secure Wilmington and the City of
Savannah, he will meanwhile keep *Hood* employed, and put
his own army " in fine order for a march on Augusta,
Columbia, and Charleston. . . ." [2]

Whilst Sherman's active mind was pouring forth suggestions to Grant, *Hood* was also considering his future movements. It was clear to him that he must abandon his
present line of retreat, as he was now on the edge of the
highlands, and once in the open country he would be at the
mercy of Sherman's superior force. To cover Selma,
Montgomery, Columbus, and Macon, and to threaten a
Federal advance from Atlanta on Augusta, on September 20
he withdrew to Palmetto Station, twenty-five miles south-
west of Atlanta on the railway to Montgomery, and there

[1] 76 *W.R.*, p. 482.   [2] 78 *W.R.*, p. 412.

he entrenched. Sherman reported this move and said :
" He is eccentric, and I cannot guess his movements as I
could those of *Johnston*, who was a sensible man and only
did sensible things." [1] He was not, however, left long in
doubt, for Jefferson Davis, journeying from Richmond
to visit *Hood*, publicly announced at a number of places
that Atlanta was to be recovered, that Sherman would
meet the fate of Napoleon in his retreat from Moscow, etc.
To the Tennessee troops he said : " Be of good cheer, for
in a short while your faces will be turned homeward, and
your feet pressing Tennessee soil." [2]

The result of this proclamation was that Sherman ordered [3]
Thomas back to Chattanooga, a wise precaution : for on
the 29th *Hood* crossed the Chattahoochee, and by October 2
it was obvious that his intention was to strike the railway
in the vicinity of Marietta. Leaving one corps to hold
Atlanta, Sherman set off in pursuit. Soon he found that
there was but little chance of bringing *Hood* to battle, thereupon his thoughts returned to his proposed march on
Savannah. On the 9th he wrote to Grant as follows :

" It will be a physical impossibility to protect the roads,
now that *Hood, Forrest, Wheeler*, and the whole batch of
devils are turned loose without home or habitation. . . .
By attempting to hold the roads we will lose 1,000 men
monthly, and will gain no result. I can make the march
and make Georgia howl." [4]

And again on the 11th :

" Instead of guessing at what he means to do, he would
have to guess at my plans. . . . I can make Savannah,
Charleston, or the mouth of the Chattahoochee." [5]

Sherman's pursuit was nevertheless continued until he
was a hundred miles from Atlanta ; when, on the 19th, he
saw that his chances of bringing his extremely mobile

---

[1] *M.H.S.M.*, VIII, p. 506. In 78 *W.R.*, p. 431, he says : " I do not see
what he designs by this movement."
[2] *Badeau*, III, p. 51.   [3] 78 *W.R.*, pp. 464, 465.   [4] 79 *W.R.*, p. 162.
[5] 79 *W.R.*, p. 202.

adversary to book were hopeless. This day he informed Thomas that he intended to abandon it, and " make a hole in Georgia and Alabama " ; then he added : " If you can defend the line of the Tennessee in my absence of three months, it is all I ask." [1] Again on the 20th he wrote : " To pursue *Hood* is folly, for he can twist and turn like a fox, and wear out any army in pursuit." [2]

As it will be remembered, the primary object of Sherman's campaign was to destroy *Johnston's*, now *Hood's* army ; and Grant, who never liked changing the idea of a campaign, on November 1 wrote to Sherman as follows :

" Do you not think it advisable now that *Hood* has gone so far north to entirely settle him before starting on your proposed campaign ? With *Hood's* army destroyed you can go where you please with impunity. I believed, and still believe, if you had started south while *Hood* was in the neighbourhood of you he would have been forced to go after you. Now that he is so far away, he might look upon the chase as useless, and will go in one direction whilst you are pushing in the other. If you can see the chance for destroying *Hood's* army, attend to that first, and make your other move secondary." [3]

Here we are faced by one of the most interesting strategical problems of the Civil War, namely : should Sherman follow *Hood*, or should he march to the Atlantic ?

Hood's action had surprised Sherman ; as to this there can be no doubt ; further still, there can be no doubt that for several days he was bewildered. *Hood* had moved south, obviously to avoid fighting in open country, and so that he could threaten the flank of any Federal move against Augusta. Sherman should have advanced on him like lightning ; instead he remained at Atlanta. Grant, a far abler strategist than Sherman, at once recognised this missed opportunity ; and seeing that he seldom censured a subordinate as long as he intended to employ him, his words, " I believed, and still believe, if you had started south," are nothing short of a reproval.

[1] 79 *W.R.*, p. 365.   [2] 79 *W.R.*, p. 378.   [3] 79 *W.R.*, p. 576.

Next, Jefferson Davis visited *Hood*, and broadcasted the fact that *Hood* was going to march into Tennessee. Every historian I have consulted has ridiculed Davis for making his plan public; but surely it was the publicity of *Hood's* move into Tennessee which Davis wanted in order to compel Grant and Sherman to consider the defence of Tennessee instead of the offence in Georgia—and why? In my opinion the reason is obvious, namely, that Davis was terrified at the idea of the war being carried into Georgia and the Carolinas. The action of these States had largely caused the rebellion; they were truculent and independent; they had already given Davis much trouble; in short, he was afraid that if they were invaded they might carry the doctrine of State-rights to its logical conclusion—that is, they might object to support the Confederacy. *Hood's* plan was political.

Lastly came *Hood's* move, and he gained so good a start over Sherman that Sherman was unable to catch him; and be it remembered, the country was hostile to Sherman.

Hood's advance was strategically a sound one, and had it been possible for *Kirby Smith* in Arkansas to have reinforced him—and in spite of the Federal command of the Mississippi this was not altogether impossible—he would have been right in moving as he eventually did on Nashville. Not being reinforced, he should have terrorised Tennessee, and then turning south have followed up Sherman, waging a guerrilla war on his foraging parties.

Grant, at a distance, as usual avoided giving a direct order, and in place asked the question—" Do you not think it advisable " to follow up *Hood* ? Strategically on the map it appeared more than advisable, it was essential. But Grant knew that war is not made solely on maps, and he wanted Sherman to consider the question with the minutest care; this he did most ably. On November 2 he pointed out that no single army could catch *Hood*, and that Thomas would have a force strong enough to hold him. Then he writes: " I am convinced the best results will result from defeating Jeff. Davis's cherished plan of making me leave

Georgia by manœuvring. . . . If I turn back the whole effect of my campaign will be lost." [1] He saw that *Hood's* army was only his primary objective as long as it covered Georgia, the Carolinas, and *Lee's* rear, and because it covered them. Now that they were no longer covered, these vital localities became in themselves his primary objective ; and as long as he could guarantee the security of the country in rear of him, he would have violated the principle of direction had he continued in pursuit of *Hood*. On the 6th he again wrote to Grant, saying :

" On the supposition always that Thomas can hold the line of the Tennessee . . . I propose to act in such a manner against the material resources of the South, as utterly to negative Davis's boasted threats and promises of protection. If we can march a well-appointed army right through his territory, it is a demonstration to the world, foreign and domestic, that we have a power which Davis cannot resist. This may not be war, but rather statesmanship ; nevertheless, it is overwhelming to my mind that there are thousands of people abroad and in the South who will reason thus : If the North can march an army right through the South, it is proof positive that the North can prevail in this contest, leaving only open the question of its willingness to use that power.

" Now Mr. Lincoln's election, which is assured, coupled with the conclusion thus reached, makes a complete, logical whole. Even without a battle the results, operating upon the minds of sensible men, would produce fruits more than compensating for the expense, trouble, and risk." [2]

But Grant was already convinced by his lieutenant, for on the 2nd he had written to him : " With the force, however, you have left with General Thomas, he must be able to take care of *Hood* and destroy him. I really do not see that you can withdraw from where you are, to follow *Hood*, without giving up all we have gained in territory. I say, then, go on as you propose." [3]

On the 14th Sherman concentrated 60,000 men at Atlanta, and on the following morning the great march began. It

---

[1] 79 *W.R.*, pp. 594, 595.   [2] 79 *W.R.*, p. 660.   [3] 79 *W.R.*, p. 594.

terminated with the occupation of Savannah on December 21, three hundred miles having been covered in twenty-four days, and untold damage done to the country. That it did not directly weaken *Lee* is true, for he was so firmly gripped by Grant that he could not spare a man to be sent against Sherman. That indirectly it did so is proved by the ever-increasing stream of deserters who flocked south to succour their devastated homes. That economically it weakened him is certain, for Georgia had become the granary of the Confederacy; but it must be remembered that to cut off this supply, all that was necessary was to destroy the railways, and that it was not necessary utterly to devastate the land. That his march had a decisive strategical and political influence on the war is beyond question, but because of Sherman's ruthlessness and wasteful destruction it had a bad influence on the peace which followed the war. For instance, he says : " I shall then feel justified in resorting to the harshest measures, and shall make little effort to restrain my army." [1] " I do sincerely believe that the whole United States, North and South, would rejoice to have this army turned loose on South Carolina to devastate that State, in the manner we have done in Georgia " [2] ; and " The truth is the whole army is burning with an insatiable desire to wreak vengeance upon South Carolina. I almost tremble at her fate." [3] In Georgia Sherman estimated the entire damage done at $100,000,000, of which only $20,000,000 " inured to our advantage," the remainder being " simple waste and destruction." [4] Ideas and actions such as these are reminiscent of the Thirty Years' War, and discredit the noble words on the plinth of this great soldier's statue at Washington—" The legitimate object of war is a more perfect peace." [5]

[1] 92 *W.R.*, p. 737.
[2] 92 *W.R.*, p. 743.
[3] 92 *W.R.*, p. 799.
[4] 92 *W.R.*, p. 13.
[5] Sherman once said : " War is cruelty, and you cannot refine it " ; even if this were true, which it is not, it is no good reason why war should be barbarised.

THOMAS AND THE BATTLE OF NASHVILLE

Qui ne risque rien n'attrape rien was a favourite saying of Napoleon, a saying which fully justified Sherman's advance eastwards when *Hood* turned westwards. If *Hood* beat Thomas, now holding the line of the Tennessee, both Grant and Sherman would be handed down to history as reckless and amateur generals. If *Hood* were beaten, the same and by no means logical judgment would be passed on him. The chances were, however, in Sherman's favour, because it was unlikely that *Hood* could be reinforced ; the farther he moved north the weaker he would become, and the more difficult would he find it to replenish his ammunition, and the more likely was it that he would meet Thomas with his forces concentrated. As is always the case in war, the whole problem revolved round the question—what would the man on the spot do ? *Hood,* a bold general, had failed to read correctly the mind of Sherman ; Sherman, had he rightly interpreted the personality of Thomas, one of the ablest tacticians of the war ? We shall see.

When, on November 15, Sherman moved off from Atlanta, *Hood,* at the head of 41,185 infantry and artillery and 12,753 cavalry,[1] was at Florence ; on the 20th he moved forward to frustrate the invasion of Georgia by an invasion of Tennessee. As early as September 29 Thomas had been sent to Nashville, and on October 10 Sherman had ordered him to concentrate all troops within reach " at some converging place, say Stevenson." [2] Three days later similar orders were sent to him by Grant through Halleck,[3] and on the 19th Schofield's corps was sent back to reinforce him. Thomas, however, in place of falling back and concentrating, which was obviously the correct thing to do, preferred to hold the Tennessee from Decatur to Eastport, when, on the 25th, *Hood* appeared in force before the former of these towns, and then on the 29th marched to Florence.

---

[1] *Cox*, p. 12.   In *B. & L.*, IV, p. 435, *Hood* gives his strength as 30,600.
[2] 79 *W.R.*, p. 191.   [3] 79 *W.R.*, p. 252.

Again Thomas was ordered to concentrate,[1] and again he refused to abandon his advanced posts ; this order was repeated, but as Badeau says : " Thomas's way of making war was different from Sherman's." [2]

From this initial failure to concentrate arose all Thomas's troubles ; for, on November 2, *Forrest* with his cavalry appeared before Johnsonville, and the Federal forces in Tennessee were still scattered. Schofield, at the head of some 22,000 men, was rushed from Nashville to meet him, and then moved to Pulaski. On the 20th Thomas's army numbered 59,500 men, but of these 25,000 were still scattered, and the remainder was now confronted by *Hood* at the head of a concentrated force of 30,600 infantry and 7,000 cavalry.[3]

As *Hood* advanced, Schofield, in accordance with Thomas's orders, fell back towards Nashville, where a general concentration was to be effected. Instead, had Thomas been in any way ready to advance, he should have moved forward and supported Schofield, but, as Grant says, he made no effort to do so.[4] Schofield's position was now a critical one, for on the 30th, at Franklin, he was compelled to accept battle ; but, most fortunately for Thomas, he beat off every assault, and at a loss of 2,326 men inflicted no less than 6,300 casualties on *Hood's* army.[5]

Now was Thomas's chance, and had he been a great general he would have seized it. *Hood's* intention to crush Schofield before he could reach Nashville had been frustrated, his losses had been severe, his position was now a desperate one. Thomas should have advanced at once and have overwhelmed him ; instead, what did he do ? On December 1 he wrote to Halleck that he intended to retire to the fortifications round Nashville until his cavalry were equipped.[6]

It is necessary, so I think, in a study of Grant's generalship, to examine in some detail the situation which now faced him, especially as we are confronted by the only occasions upon which he personally directed the operations of a sub-

---

[1] 79 *W.R.*, p. 497.
[2] *Badeau*, III, p. 186.
[3] *Badeau*, III, p. 188.
[4] *Grant*, II, p. 379.
[5] *Cox*, pp. 96, 97.
[6] 94 *W.R.*, p. 3.

ordinate. *Hood's* army was reduced to 44,000 men,[1] Thomas, on November 20, had under his command "present for duty" 71,463[2] ; deducting recent casualties and non-effectives, Thomas must have considerably outnumbered *Hood*, why then did he not assume the offensive ? The reason is that he was not certain of winning ; he would not accept any risks, and he could not see that the situation demanded them, otherwise the whole of Grant's campaign in Virginia might be jeopardised, for at any moment political panic might dissolve his grand operation by diverting forces to Tennessee.

Thomas was one of the great historical figures of this war, and he has been handed down to history as one of its leading generals, because of his gallant behaviour at Chickamauga,[3] and because of his eventual overwhelming success at Nashville ; yet, in my opinion, his generalship was, except in battle itself, beneath contempt. I will now justify this statement, and prove that Grant's decisions in this campaign were sound.

Thomas was old as generals went in this war, having been born in 1816. At West Point his fellow cadets had nicknamed him "Slow Trot," and as so often is the case, youth, with unfailing accuracy, appreciated his predominant characteristic. He was a man of firm and fervent loyalty, deliberate, cautious, and sure. He once said to a battery commander who had carelessly allowed his harness to break, that "the fate of a battle may depend on a buckle," and he undoubtedly believed that such small things were of supreme importance in war. "He made it a rule . . . to finish up all his work to the minutest detail before any important movement was begun. . . . Wherever his signature was required, even if it were only in a copy-book, he invariably signed his name himself."[4] He had the mind of a quarter-

---

[1] *Cox*, p. 101 ; according to *B. & L.*, IV, p. 474—39,000 ; and according to *Hood*—23,000 (*B. & L.*, IV, p. 435).   [2] 93 *W.R.*, p. 52.

[3] He was, however, largely responsible for the crucial mistake in this battle. See *M.H.S.M.*, X, pp. 229, 230.

[4] *M.H.S.M.*, X, p. 199. He was called "Old Safety." "Maj.-Gen. George H. Thomas, if it can be so put with due respect, may be called the

master, and would have made a most valuable one, for he did not like the responsibility of command.[1] Of his present delay, Colonel Stone, his assistant adjutant-general at the battle of Nashville, says : " He realised too keenly the importance of victory to allow anything that might help secure it to be neglected. Compared with the destruction of *Hood's* army nothing else was of any account."[2] This is not meant only to be a statement of facts, but a proof of his generalship ; in my opinion it is proof positive that he was totally lacking in strategical sense.

On December 2 Stanton informed Grant that " the President feels solicitous about the disposition of Thomas to lay in fortifications for an indefinite period, ' until Wilson [his cavalry general] gets equipped ' " ; whereupon Grant telegraphed Thomas : " Should he [*Hood*] attack you it is well, but if he does not you should attack him before he fortifies " ; and again : " After the repulse of *Hood* at Franklin it looks to me that instead of falling back to Nashville we should have taken the offensive against the enemy." To which Thomas replied: "I earnestly hope, however, that in a few more days I shall be able to give him a fight."

On the 5th Grant telegraphed Thomas : " It seems to me, whilst you should be getting up your cavalry . . . *Hood* should be attacked where he is. Time strengthens him, in all probability, as much as it does you." To which Thomas answered on the 6th : " As soon as I get up a respectable force of cavalry I will march against *Hood*." Grant losing patience wired : " Attack *Hood* at once, and wait no longer for a remount of your cavalry. There is great danger in delay resulting in a campaign back to the Ohio river." Thomas's reply was : " I will make the necessary dis- position and attack *Hood* at once . . . " ; but no move was made.

---

elephant of our army animals—slow, ponderous, sagacious, not easily roused to wrath, but when aroused terrible and invincible " (*Iowa and the Rebellion*, Ingersoll, p. 644).

[1] 23 *W.R.*, pp. 539, 555. [2] *M.H.S.M.*, VII, p. 496.

On the 7th Stanton telegraphed Grant : " Thomas seems unwilling to attack because it is hazardous, as if all war was anything else but hazardous. If he waits for Wilson to get ready, Gabriel will be blowing his last horn." Thereupon Grant telegraphed Halleck : " If Thomas has not struck yet he ought to be ordered to hand over his command to Schofield." To which Halleck replied : " If you wish General Thomas relieved from [command] give the order." Realising that Lincoln did not support Thomas's removal, Grant telegraphed Thomas : " Now is one of the fairest opportunities ever presented of destroying one of the three armies of the enemy." To which Thomas answered that his cavalry were not in a condition to move.

On the 9th Halleck telegraphed Thomas : " If you wait till General Wilson mounts all his cavalry, you will wait till doomsday, for the waste equals the supply." Thereupon Thomas replied that the weather had broken, and that the roads were impassable. Before this telegram was received, Grant had asked Halleck to replace him by Schofield. This order was made out but not sent, and Grant learning from Thomas that the roads were now covered with sheets of ice, suspended the relieving order, and again urged Thomas on.

On the 11th Grant telegraphed Thomas : " If you delay attacking longer the mortifying spectacle will be witnessed of a rebel army moving for the Ohio river, and you will be forced to act, accepting such weather as you find. Let there be no further delay." To which Thomas answered : " I will obey the order as promptly as possible, however much I may regret it " ; and the next day to Halleck he telegraphed : " Under the circumstances, I believe that an attack at this time would only result in a useless sacrifice of life."

At length Grant could tolerate Thomas's inaction no longer, and on the 13th he ordered General Logan to proceed to Nashville and take over the command of the Army of the Cumberland. On the following day he set out from City Point to assume command in person. Meanwhile, Halleck had telegraphed Thomas : " Every day's delay on your part, therefore, seriously interferes with General Grant's plans." On his arrival at Washington on the 15th Grant learnt that Thomas had attacked.[1]

Having massed at least 55,000 men [2] against *Hood*, Thomas won by able tactics, as well as through force of numbers, a decisive victory. He captured fifty-three guns and 4,500 prisoners ; *Hood's* killed and wounded are unknown, but they probably numbered rather less than the 3,000 lost by the army of the Cumberland. That he was able to gain so complete a victory is proof positive that his prolonged delay was unnecessary. His chief concern was the mounting of his cavalry, but by postponing the battle until the middle of December, he found that the roads were so broken up that an effective pursuit was impossible.

Though victory is the aim of a general, it is not necessarily a measure of his worth ; for whilst popular opinion sees only greatness in results, the student of war should seek for greatness in the steps which lead up to results. To make certain of winning a battle, and thereby risk losing a campaign, is no qualification towards earning the laurels bestowed on a great commander.

POLITICAL AND STRATEGICAL VICTORY

On May 5, 1864, Grant opened the throttle of his great combined campaign. He hoped that before the summer had run its course the war would be ended, but he in no way founded his strategy on this hope. His grand tactical idea of holding and encircling has already been explained ; but because it demanded not an exorbitant but a continuous loss of life in Virginia and a crowding of these losses into a brief period—May and June—its costliness appeared exaggerated, and undoubtedly had an adverse influence on the political mind. Realising this, Grant was faced by a

---

[1] This correspondence will be found in 94 *W.R.*, pp. 15–18, 55, 70, 84, 96, 97, 114, 116, 143, 155, and 180.　　[2] *B. & L.*, IV, p. 473.

dual problem, namely, how to maintain the strategy of his combined campaigns, and simultaneously gain such tactical successes as would raise the *moral* of the North and consequently assure Lincoln's re-election.

Because of his able strategical distribution, as long as *Lee* could be held within the Richmond fortifications, which meant that a sufficiently powerful army must constantly threaten the city, it was possible for Grant to divert a large force to the Valley, which simultaneously prevented the Confederate Government diverting reinforcements to *Johnston*. By a shifting of force towards the circumference, Grant was able, without destroying his centre of gravity, to solve the intricate grand strategical problem which grew more and more intense as the autumn approached.

Within his Government, the opposition to Lincoln was that " he was felt to be too easy-going . . . to be unbusinesslike in his methods . . . and . . . in capacity and temperament . . . inadequate to the responsibility of the head of the Nation at such a momentous period." [1] When early in July Lincoln was nominated for re-election at Baltimore, within the ranks of his own party there existed a group of influential men who wished him to withdraw his candidature. In August General McClellan was nominated to oppose him, when the *Charleston Courier* amongst other things said : " Our success in battle insures the success of McClellan. Our failure will inevitably lead to his defeat." [2] Then came the battle of Mobile Bay (August 5) ; the occupation of Atlanta (September 2) ; the battle of Opequon Creek (September 19) ; the battle of Fisher's Hill (September 22), and the battle of Cedar Creek (October 19). These battles were not only of great value to Grant in furthering the war, but of immense importance to Lincoln in gaining his election, without which the war would in all probability have collapsed. So strong had these victories made Lincoln's position, that when, on October 17, E. B. Washburne, of Illinois, wrote to him : " It is no use to deceive ourselves. . . . There is

---

[1] *Memoirs and Letters of Charles Sumner*, IV, p. 195.
[2] *Nicolay and Hay*, IX, p. 353.

imminent danger of our losing the State," Lincoln scribbled on the envelope " Stampeded." [1]

Then came November 8, a dull rainy day in Washington, and Lincoln was re-elected, receiving 212 electoral votes, whilst 22 went to McClellan. Though this event " was a greater triumph over the principles of the rebellion than any military victory could be," [2] it must not be over-looked that it was mainly the effect of military causes, the most important of which were the occupation of Atlanta and Sheridan's success in the Valley ; a success so close to the physical Washington that the moral Washington was revitalised as if by magic.

The influence of Lincoln's second election was felt not only in every corner of the immense theatre of war, but through-out the civilised world. It halved Grant's difficulties by enabling him to concentrate solely on the strategy of the war. It daily increased his strength by daily weakening *Lee's*. Ten days after this election, *Lee* wrote to President Davis : " Desertion is increasing in the army notwithstanding all my efforts to stop it." [3] Then came the battle of Franklin (November 30) ; the battle of Nashville (December 15–16), and Sherman's entry into Savannah (December 21) ; and on this last-mentioned day we find a Lieutenant-Colonel *J. H. Duncan* in *Hill's* corps writing : " Desertions are becoming amazingly numerous." [4] At the time desertion was attributed to an " inefficiency of rations and the failure of the paymaster to pay the men off." [5] Shortage of rations may have been *a* cause, but it was not *the* cause. " To what end is the struggle prolonged ? " This thought, above all others, was the dry rot of the Confederacy.

The end of the war was now in sight ; the political founda-tions of the North were sound and deep-rooted ; Grant's attrition had paralysed *Lee*, and his grip held him fast in Richmond ; Sheridan had given *moral* to the North, and beyond the silence of winter in Virginia " there came,"

---

[1] *Nicolay and Hay*, IX, p. 372.
[2] *Letters of Charles Eliot Norton*, I, p. 282.
[3] 89 *W.R.*, p. 1213.
[4] 96 *W.R.*, pp. 1144, 1145.
[5] 96 *W.R.*, p. 1148.

as Swinton says, " rolling across the plains of the Carolinas, beating nearer and nearer, the drums of Champion's Hill and Shiloh." [1] Unless Sherman were stopped, come what might, the Confederacy was doomed. This was the tactical problem of 1865 : could the South win, even only as their forefathers had won at Guildford Court House ? [2] If so, then they might yet aspire to a second Yorktown.[3]

[1] *Decisive Battles*, p. 480.   [2] March 16, 1781.
[3] October 19, 1781.

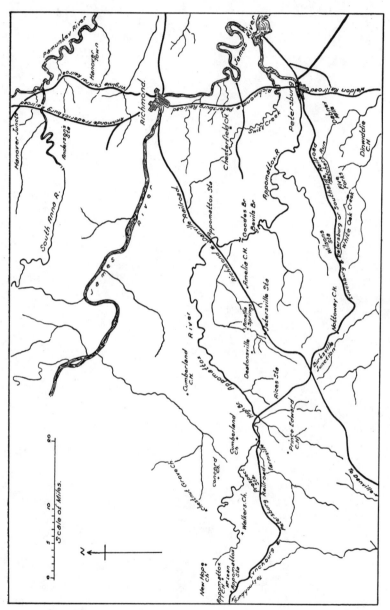

Map No. 6.—Campaign on the Appomattox, 1865.

CHAPTER XV

APPOMATTOX CAMPAIGN

The Grand Manœuvre

As the year 1864 closed, Grant's problem of how to continue to hold *Lee* became an anxious one. He realised what *Lee* himself realised, namely, that the only hope of stopping Sherman advancing northwards from Savannah was to oppose him in force, and that this could not be done unless the Richmond defences were evacuated. To effect such a movement during the winter months would in any case be difficult, but what was far more uncertain than the weather was Grant's intention : what did he intend.to do with Sherman ? Would he move him by sea to the James ; or march him inland ; or for the time being keep him at Savannah ? Besides, to evacuate Richmond not only meant a moral loss which was altogether incalculable, but the loss of Wilmington, and consequently of nine-tenths of the blockade-runner traffic, which daily was becoming more and more necessary to the maintenance of the war. The fact is, that though physically still unconquered, Grant's campaigns had through moral and economic pressure, as well as through physical attrition, fixed *Lee* to Richmond. It was not because *Lee* did not see the danger of his position that he determined for a while to hold on to the capital, but because he saw the extreme moral and economic danger of evacuating it.

Though Grant may not have appreciated *Lee's* situation as clearly as *Lee* himself did, he realised the importance of bringing the war to an end. The finances of the North were steadily growing worse, and what he feared was that *Lee* might break away into the interior and set the whole centre of the United States ablaze with a guerrilla war. He determined, therefore, whilst winter rendered it difficult for *Lee* to move, to encompass him in a circle of advancing columns, and by continuing his economic attack, more and more demoralise the civil will of the Confederacy.

His first problem was to occupy the seaports. Charleston, Mobile, and Wilmington still held out ; but the first two were now of little importance, Charleston having been closed as a port of entry in September, 1863, and Mobile in August the following year. Why, in the spring of 1864, Grant had not insisted upon the closing, if not capture, of Wilmington, it is hard to guess ; unless his attention was so fixed on the land operations that he overlooked the enormous value of this port. It is no exaggeration to say that towards the end of 1864 it had become the jugular vein of the South, for from July, 1862, until the fall of Fort Fisher on January 15, 1865, at least one hundred vessels were engaged in running in and out of Wilmington. The capture of Fort Fisher, which protected the entrance to the harbour, was, says Vice-President Stephens, a blow equal to the loss of Vicksburg.[1]

Grant never realised that Wilmington was of greater importance to the Confederacy than either Atlanta or Lynchburg, and it was not until Sherman was marching through Georgia that he decided [2] an effort must be made to occupy this town, and that if it fell a force must be sent from there to co-operate with Sherman. In this suggestion we see the beginning of a general plan to tighten the circle— that is, completely to envelop *Lee*.

Once *Hood* had been disposed of by Thomas, Grant decided on the general idea of his spring campaign. With the Army of the Potomac he intended to watch *Lee* rather than attack him, and to hold this army in readiness to spring on *Lee* should he attempt to break away. Next he considered moving Sherman north by sea, and then decided, as we shall see, to move him inland on to a point south of Richmond to be decided on by Sherman himself. In co-operation with Sherman, a force was to take Wilmington [3] and

---

[1] *M.H.S.M.*, XIII, p. 406 (see also 78 *W.R.*, p. 412): [2] 92 *W.R.*, pp. 611, 612.
[3] The entrance to Wilmington was protected by Fort Fisher. Towards the end of December General Butler made an attempt to carry the fort, and

move towards Raleigh, and Sheridan was to move on Lynchburg, whilst Thomas moved a force of cavalry east-wards on Columbia. These four columns were to close in on *Lee* whilst Grant held him ; or should *Lee* break away, they were to hem him in whilst Grant pursued. Sub-sidiary to this grand operation, Grant intended to take Mobile, and in co-operation with this attack Thomas was to move south from Nashville towards Selma. Mobile—Montgomery once occupied, should *Lee* break away and slip past Sherman he would be confronted by this second net.

On December 16 [1] Grant suggested to Sherman that when he had taken Savannah he should make it a base for an operation against Charleston or Augusta. In answer, on the 24th, Sherman said that from Savannah his idea was to advance on Branchville, thence on Columbia, and after Wilmington was occupied, to move on Raleigh. " The game," he writes, " is then up with *Lee*, unless he comes out of Richmond, avoids you, and fights me, in which case I should reckon on your being on his heels." [2] Grant was pleased with this idea, as it would demoralise the South, " and prevent the organisation of new armies from their broken fragments," and so on the 27th [3] he ordered Sherman to prepare to start the northern march as soon as he was able to do so.

The march began on February 1 ; Sherman's army was 60,000 strong, and the distance to be travelled to Goldsboro was 425 miles. Of this operation Sherman says : " Were I to express my measure of the relative importance of the march to the sea, and of that from Savannah northwards, I would place the former at one, and the latter at ten, or the maximum." [4]

When Sherman was ordered to move into the Carolinas, Thomas was instructed to send Schofield from Clifton on the Tennessee to the Potomac ; this move taking place on

failed. In consequence he was relieved of his command of the Army of the James, and was replaced by General Ord. In January a second attempt was made, and Fort Fisher fell on the 15th.

[1] 92 *W.R.*, p. 636 ; this letter is signed by Halleck.
[2] 92 *W.R.*, p. 797.   [3] 92 *W.R.*, p. 820.   [4] *Sherman*, II, p. 221.

January 15. Three days later, hearing that *Beauregard* had gone west " to gather up what he can save from *Hood's* army to bring against Sherman," Grant informed Halleck that Selma and Montgomery could now be reached. " I do not believe, though," he writes, " that General Thomas will ever get there from the North. He is too ponderous in his preparations and equipments to move through a country rapidly enough to live off it." He then suggests that Canby should make a winter campaign from Mobile Bay, and that Thomas should move on Selma.[1]

Schofield, on arriving from the West, was at once placed in command of all forces in North Carolina. On the 31st Grant gave him the following instructions : first to secure Wilmington, and secondly to occupy Goldsboro, repairing the railway as he advanced. " The enterprise under you," he writes, " has two objects. The first is to give General Sherman material aid, if needed, in his march north ; the second, to open a base of supplies for him on his line of march." [2] On February 22 Wilmington was abandoned, and Schofield entered the town.

On the day upon which Schofield received the above instructions Thomas was ordered to send a strong force of cavalry under General Stoneman towards Columbia in South Carolina to visit such portions of this State as could not be reached by Sherman. Knowing Thomas's habitual slowness, Grant ended by saying, " Let there be no delay in the preparation for the expedition, and keep me advised of its progress." [3] On February 14 he again wrote to Thomas pointing out that, as Canby's movement against Mobile and the interior of Alabama would " attract all the attention of the enemy and leave an advance from your standpoint easy," he should move south " to attract as much of the enemy's force as possible, to ensure success to Canby . . . to destroy the enemy's line of communications and military resources," and " to destroy or capture their forces brought into the field. . . ." [4]

[1] 94 *W.R.*, pp. 609, 610.
[2] 99 *W.R.*, p. 190.
[3] 103 *W.R.*, p. 617.
[4] 103 *W.R.*, p. 708.

These movements should have taken place about February 20, yet on March 16 Stoneman was still at Louisville, Kentucky. This quite inexcusable delay on the part of Thomas is even more flagrant than his dawdling before Nashville. As an independent commander he was an impossible subordinate.

The snows in the mountains having sufficiently melted, on February 28 Sheridan set out for Staunton. Already on February 8 Grant had ordered [1] him, as soon as the weather permitted, to move a force of 10,000 cavalry on Lynchburg. Between Staunton and Charlottesville *Early* was met, and his army annihilated. Sheridan then occupied Charlottesville, and broke up the railway towards Gordonsville and Lynchburg ; the condition of the roads, however, prevented him reaching Lynchburg itself, so he turned south to join up with Grant, arriving at White House on March 19.

Whilst these various operations were in progress, Grant maintained a waiting attitude. On February 4 he wrote to Stanton :

" I do not want to do anything to force the enemy from Richmond until Schofield carries out his programme. . . . I shall necessarily have to take the odium of apparent inaction, but if it results, as I expect it will, in the discomfiture of *Lee's* army, I shall be entirely satisfied." [2]

On March 3 he said to Meade : " For the present, it is better for us to hold the enemy where he is than to force him south. . . . To drive the enemy from Richmond now would endanger the success of these two columns [Sherman and Schofield]." [3] On the 14th, however, his encircling manœuvre had so far succeeded that he sent Meade the following instructions : " From this time forward keep your command in condition to be moved on the very shortest possible notice, in case the enemy should evacuate, or partially evacuate Petersburg, taking with you the maximum of supplies your trains are capable of carrying." [4] He did so

---

[1] 96 *W.R.*, pp. 495, 553, 605, 606.   [3] 96 *W.R.*, p. 806.
[2] 96 *W.R.*, p. 365.   [4] 96 *W.R.*, p. 962.

because he had heard that everything possible was being moved from Richmond to Lynchburg, and that Richmond would have been evacuated had not Sheridan's destruction of the railway delayed this move.

The grand manœuvre was now about to give way to the grand attack. On March 23 Sherman and Schofield joined hands at Goldsboro, and on the 24th Sheridan set out from White House to rejoin the Army of the Potomac. That day Grant issued his orders [1] to Meade and Sheridan for a movement against *Lee's* right.

LEE'S PROBLEM AND DIFFICULTIES

If Grant's difficulties were many, *Lee's* were legion. He knew that the Confederacy was sinking, and that nothing short of a miracle could save it. All he could hope for was to wait until the situation had grown so critical that the public mind would be dumbfounded, and under cover of this coma, to slip away, move south and deal Sherman a staggering blow. Such an attack, he thought, might revive the *moral* of the South, and, reinforced by this sudden elation, he might be able to carry the war eastwards, not to win it, but to gain a surrender on terms. On January 19, by an act of Congress, he was appointed commander-in-chief of all the Confederate forces, whereupon he recalled *Joseph Johnston* from unemployment, placing him in command of all the troops which could be concentrated against Sherman. Some writers think that he now lost his nerve; but though a man advanced in years and faced by a situation which would have paralysed many a younger general, it seems to me that seldom before was he more alert, active, and resolute.

The people had lost heart in the war, discontent was rife, many of the newspapers were openly hostile. A Raleigh editor voiced this feeling when he wrote :

" Peace and equality might be had now by conciliation and compromise ; but if we go on and lose, we lose all and

---

[1] 95 *W.R.*, pp. 50, 51 ; for Meade's order issued on the 27th, see 97 *W.R.*, pp. 198, 199.

become the slaves of the conquerors. . . . This is the people's war, and we are satisfied from our intercourse with them that an immense majority are for stopping it." [1]

Conscription had become odious, desertions were increasing daily—" This morning forty-five came in a single squad, from a single regiment—a South Carolina regiment at that." [2] North Carolina regiments were equally affected,[3] which points to the demoralising influence of Sherman's advance. Soon it became apparent to *Lee* that the army could only be kept together by military executions ; [4] thus the cement of *moral* had to be replaced by tamping down fear, and when discipline is maintained only by terror an army may at any moment expect an explosion.   A hundred thousand deserters were now scattered over the Confederacy, and so common had this crime become, that in popular estimation its stigma disappeared.   Nor was this all : " The States of North Carolina, South Carolina, Georgia . . . passed laws to withdraw from service men liable to it under existing laws," and these laws had the support of local authorities.[5]   Thus writes General *Preston*, head of the Confederate Bureau of Conscription.   On March 16 a call for negro recruits was published in the Richmond papers,[6] and eight days later *Lee* wrote to Davis saying : " The services of these men are now necessary to enable us to oppose the enemy." [7]

What remained of the railways of the South was rapidly falling to pieces, and means of repairing them did not exist. The commissariat was in a state of chaos, and the army was standing on the brink of starvation.[8]   The whole situation pointed to one possible solution only, namely, the move south ; not solely to halt Sherman, but in order to live, for in North Carolina supplies were still plentiful.   On February 19 *Lee* wrote to the Secretary of War as follows : " I fear it may be necessary to abandon all our cities, and

---

[1] *History of the United States*, Rhodes, V, p. 75.
[2] 99 *W.R.*, p. 558.
[3] *M.H.S.M.*, XIV, p. 223.
[7] 97 *W.R.*, p. 1339.
[4] 96 *W.R.*, p. 1258.
[5] 108 *W.R.*, p. 1065.
[6] *Jones*, II, pp. 444, 450.
[8] 96 *W.R.*, pp. 1034, 1035, 1211, 1216–18, 1220, 1223–5, 1240, and 1285.

preparation should be made for this contingency." [1]   Then
he proposed [2] that should he have to abandon his present
position he would march to Burksville; and on the 22nd
he wrote [3] to *Johnston*, "Until I abandon James river
nothing can be sent from this army.   Grant, I think, is now
preparing to draw out by the left with the intent of envelop-
ing me. . . ."   Three days later he issued orders to begin
removing stores from Richmond to Lynchburg. [4]

The question now arises, why did not *Lee* abandon Richmond early in March and unite with *Johnston*?   Some
Southern writers say that President Davis refused to leave
the city. [5]   This is contradicted by Davis himself, who
writes [6] that *Lee* had informed him that his horses were
not in condition for such a move, and *Fitzhugh Lee* says
much the same thing. [7]   This probably was a reason, but
I am of opinion that it was not the whole reason.   In spite
of the roads, *Lee* could have moved earlier than he did, and
it appears to me that why he did not move was that he
saw the war was already lost; that his personal pride was
against such a move; and, more important still, that he
could not trust his army away from immediate danger.
As long as his men faced their enemy they would fight;
but it seems to me what he feared was: should they break
their clinch, would not they break away altogether?   On
March 23 he heard from *Johnston* [8] that Sherman had
joined hands with Schofield, and in reply he sent back a
cheerful answer. [9]   In a way it almost seems that he was
relieved by this event; for now that the chance of falling
upon Sherman before Schofield could reinforce him had
vanished, he could pause yet a little longer.   Then of a
sudden he decided to assume the offensive, [10] the first since
Spottsylvania.

[1] 98 *W.R.*, p. 1044.   [3] 96 *W.R.*, p. 1247.
[2] 96 *W.R.*, p. 1244.   [4] 96 *W.R.*, p. 1257.
  [5] *Four Years with General Lee*, Taylor, p. 146; and *Reminiscences of the
Civil War*, Gordon, p. 393.
  [6] *Davis*, II, p. 648.   [8] 99 *W.R.*, pp. 1453, 1454; 100 *W.R.*, p. 682.
  [7] *Fitzhugh Lee*, p. 371.   [9] 99 *W.R.*, p. 1454.
[10] 97 *W.R.*, p. 1338.

On March 24 he ordered Fort Stedman to be assaulted early the next day, for from one of his many spies he had learnt of Grant's projected advance. Grant, as we shall see, had planned to hold his entrenchments lightly, and under cover of this screen to move 80,000 men round *Lee's* right flank. Colonel Livermore is of opinion [1] that as *Lee* recognised he could not hold his entrenchments, and simultaneously meet such a force, his object was to throw Grant's right back in confusion, and under cover of this attack withdraw and reinforce his own right. Personally, I doubt this explanation, and consider that General *Gordon* is more correct when he says that *Lee* told him " there seemed but one thing that we could do—fight. To stand still was death. It could only be death if we fought and failed." President Davis bears out this statement in part, for he informs us that *Lee's* idea was to strike at City Point to compel Grant to weaken his left in order to reinforce his right.[2] Finally, General *Walker*, who commanded the assault on Fort Stedman, states that the object of this attack was to penetrate the Federal army, pass a force of cavalry through to City Point and capture Grant himself.[3] If such were really *Lee's* idea, then this attack on the brain of his enemy's army (a counter-thrust to disorganise the Federal army) is one of the most remarkable tactical conceptions of this war. The attack, however, failed, *Lee* losing 4,000 men to Grant's 2,080.[4] The initiative was now Grant's absolutely.

BATTLE OF FIVE FORKS

Grant's determination to move was, so I think, based on the fact that Sherman would not be able to advance to the Roanoke river until April 10, and that, as *Lee's* army was rapidly crumbling, a chance was offered to him to end the war without Sherman's immediate assistance. The suggestion that it was made for political reasons [5] is, I con-

---

[1] *M.H.S.M.*, VI, p. 478.   [3] *S.H.S.*, XXXI, p. 29.
[2] *Davis*, II, p. 649.   [4] 95 *W.R.*, p. 156, and *Humphreys*, p. 321.
[5] *Badeau*, III, p. 441 and *B. & L.*, IV, p. 718.

sider, secondary, because to wait for Sherman might mean that *Lee*, in place of uniting with *Johnston*, would retire into the mountains, and a prolonged guerrilla war might result. Grant determined, therefore, to advance, and as usual his plan was a flexible one, based on the idea of turning *Lee's* right, not only to interpose his forces between him and *Johnston*, but to cut him off from the still fertile districts of the South.

First, he considered advancing his left in order to attenuate *Lee's* already over-extended front, moving Sheridan and his cavalry against the Danville Railroad; and if then it were found impossible to break *Lee's* centre, secondly, he planned " to swing the Army of the Potomac entirely to the left, cutting loose from his base, and leaving only sufficient troops at City Point and in front of Petersburg to take care of themselves." [1] Finally, on March 24, he issued his orders,[2] modifying this plan as follows :

The whole of the Army of the Potomac, except the Ninth Corps (Parke),[3] and for the time being the Sixth Corps (Wright), and three divisions of the Army of the James (Ord) were to constitute the turning force; whilst the Ninth and Sixth Corps were to hold the trenches in front of Petersburg, and the Twenty-Fifth Corps (Weitzel) those north of the James and at Bermuda Hundred. The turning force would then comprise 66,000 men, and the holding force 34,000. Sheridan with 14,000 cavalry[4] was to advance ahead of the Army of the Potomac under special instructions.

On the night of the 27th Ord was to proceed to the left of the Army of the Potomac and relieve the Second Corps, now under Humphreys. On the morning of the 29th the Fifth Corps (Warren) and the Second Corps were to move off in a south-westerly direction crossing Hatcher's Run, and Sheridan was to pass through Dinwiddie and then turn north and west against the Danville railway. The

---

[1] *Badeau*, III, p. 134.   [2] 95 *W.R.*, pp. 50–2.

[3] Burnside was replaced by Parke after the Petersburg Mine fiasco.

[4] For calculations as to numerical strengths, see *Livermore's* table (*M.H.S.M.*, VI, pp. 502–6.)   For Grant's Order of Battle, see Appendix VI.

Sixth Corps was to remain in the trenches between the Twenty-Fifth and the Ninth Corps and await the turn of events. The Ninth and Sixth Corps were to be massed ready to break the enemy's front should *Lee* strip it. " A success north of the James," says Grant, " should be followed up with great promptness," but only if " the enemy had detached largely." Foreseeing that *Lee* would most certainly be compelled to weaken his front in order to strengthen his right, Grant says :

" It cannot be impressed too strongly upon commanders left in the trenches, not to allow this to occur without taking advantage of it . . . in case of an attack from the enemy [*Lee's* normal action before withdrawing], those not attacked are not to wait for orders . . . they will move promptly, and notify the commander of their action. . . . In like manner, I would urge the importance of following up a repulse of the enemy."

On the 28th Sheridan's instructions [1] were, after passing through Dinwiddie, " to cut loose and push for the Danville road," then he was to destroy the South Side railroad between Petersburg and Burksville, after which he was to return or join Sherman. On the night of the 29th Grant modified this order, saying: " I now feel like ending the matter. . . . I do not want you, therefore, to cut loose at once and go after the enemy's roads at present. In the morning push around the enemy if you can and get onto his right rear." [2]

On the night of the 29th Grant's army south of the James was distributed in the following order : from left to right—Warren, Humphreys, Ord, Wright, and Parke ; the head of the column, Warren's left, being at Mrs. Butler's at the intersection of the Boydton and Quaker roads. Meanwhile, *Lee*, learning of Grant's advance, immediately reduced his forces east of Hatcher's Run and reinforced

---

[1] 97 *W.R.*, p. 234. According to *Grant* (II, p. 437), Sheridan was disappointed with these instructions, consequently Grant said to him : " ' General, this portion of your instructions I have put in merely as a blind. . . .' I told him that . . . I intended to close the war right here, with this movement, and that he should go no farther."   [2] 97 *W.R.*, p. 266.

those west of this stream in order to attack Grant's advancing
columns. By this means, on the 31st, he was able to oppose
23,000 to Grant's 48,000 west of the Run, holding to the
east of it only 11,000 to face Grant's 54,000.[1] Hearing that
a concentration towards *Lee's* right was in progress, Grant,
on the 30th, at once planned to take advantage of it, and
withdrawing Ord from the turning force, he prepared to
deliver a general assault [2] east of Hatcher's Run directly
the weather became favourable, for during the night of the
29th/30th the rain had rendered the ground impassable
for wheeled traffic.[3]

On the night of the 29th Grant, seeing that should he
be able to occupy Five Forks *Lee* could no longer remain in
Petersburg, ordered [4] Sheridan to seize this road centre
early the next morning; but when Sheridan moved out
he found it already occupied in force.; whereupon Grant
determined to send Warren's corps to Sheridan's assistance,
and also to penetrate the weakened lines in front of his
right front.

Lee, recognising the danger he was exposing himself to
by stripping his front, heavily attacked Warren on the
morning of the 31st, driving him back from White Oak
road, which was, however, reoccupied by the Fifth Corps
that evening.

This same morning *Pickett*, who had arrived at Five
Forks on the 30th, advanced against Sheridan, who was
forced back on Dinwiddie. " Here," Grant says, " Sheridan
displayed great generalship." [5] He dismounted his cavalry
and compelled his enemy to deploy in a wooded and broken
country, and though for a time he was able to hold back
Pickett's infantry, at length he reported his position as critical.
Lee's audacity had once again told, but his front was now

---

[1] For strengths see *Livermore* (*M.H.S.M.*, VI, p. 485).

[2] 97 *W.R.*, pp. 267, 268, 286, 289, 305.

[3] " The roads had become sheets of water ; and it looked as if the saving
of that army (Sheridan's) would require the services, not of a Grant, but
of a Noah. Soldiers would call out to officers as they rode along : ' I say,
when are the gunboats coming up ? ' " (*B. & L.*, IV, p. 709).

[4] 97 *W.R.*, pp. 266, 323.   [5] 95 *W.R.*, p. 54.

a mere skeleton, and as *Pickett* was separated from his left wing, he also was critically situated.

In place of being discouraged, Grant was elated. At last, after many weary months of trench fighting, he had drawn a large enemy force out of its works. At 8.45 p.m. he instructed [1] Meade to order Warren to draw back to the Boydton road and to send an infantry division to Sheridan's support.

Warren had already a brigade on the Crump road, and by moving by this road his division would be brought directly on to the rear of *Pickett's* force fronting Dinwiddie. At 9.45 p.m. Meade asked [2] Grant for authority to send the whole of Warren's corps by this road to attack *Pickett* in rear; to which Grant at once answered [3] : " Let Warren move in the way you propose, and urge him not to stop for anything." At 10.15 p.m. Meade ordered [4] Warren to make this advance : to " strike the enemy in rear," and to be " very prompt in this movement."

Warren, a brave and able soldier, was over given to detailed preparations ; further—the roads were bad, the country was unfamiliar to him, the night was dark, and his men were tired. He was expected to gain touch with Sheridan at midnight, but some of his units did not leave their position until 5 a.m. on April 1, and others were hours late.[5]

At 3 a.m. on the 1st, supposing Warren to be in position, Sheridan sent him the following order : " Attack at daylight anyway, and I will make an effort to get the road this side of Adam's house ; and if I do, you can capture the whole of them." [6] Warren did not, however, appear, but knowing that he could not be far off, Sheridan moved out against *Pickett*, who, learning of Warren's advance, crossed Chamberlain's bed, and thus escaped the impending rear attack.

Whether Warren was really to blame for this lost opportunity is doubtful, for the situation which confronted him on the night of March 31 was an exceptionally difficult one. Sheridan considered, however, that he was to blame ;

---

[1] 97 *W.R.*, p. 340.   [3] 97 *W.R.*, p. 342.   [5] 95 *W.R.*, pp. 838, 869.
[2] 97 *W.R.*, p. 341.   [4] 97 *W.R.*, p. 367.   [6] 97 *W.R.*, p. 420.

nevertheless, not waiting to discover the reasons of the delay, he determined to drive *Pickett* into his works at Five Forks, engage his right with his cavalry and roll up his left with the Fifth Corps.

Warren reported to Sheridan at 11 a.m. and was ordered to advance towards Five Forks, then to move off the road towards Gravelly Run Church and take up position obliquely to *Pickett's* left flank on the White Oak road. He was instructed to place two divisions in front and hold one in reserve, so that as soon as he struck the enemy's left he could

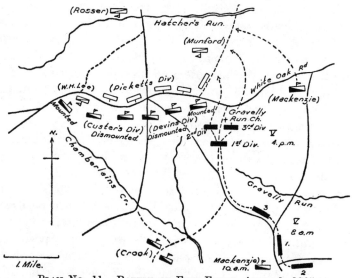

PLAN No. 11. BATTLE OF FIVE FORKS, APRIL 1, 1865.

wheel the reserve division to his right and carry out a complete envelopment. Directly Warren was engaged, the cavalry were to assault the enemy's front.[1]

Warren, in place of advancing at the best speed his tired troops were capable of, approached with great deliberation,

---

[1] When they did, Horace Porter says: " The natty cavalrymen with tight-fitting uniforms, short jackets, and small carbines, swarmed through the pine thickets and dense undergrowth, looking as if they had been especially equipped for crawling through knot-holes. Those who had magazine guns created a racket in those pine woods that sounded as if a couple of army corps had opened fire." (*B. & L.*, IV, p. 714.)

taking three hours to move two miles.[1] At about 4 p.m.
the Fifth Corps advanced, Ayres's division on the right,
Crawford's on the left, and Griffin's in reserve. Ayres's
met with a repulse, his right flank being uncovered by
Crawford failing to wheel to his left. Warren could not be
found in the densely wooded country ; but Sheridan, who
was on Ayres's right flank, seeing his men falling back, at
once placed himself at their head, and led them forward,
breaking through *Pickett's* left, and carrying his works at
the bayonet point. Shortly after this gallant charge he
relieved Warren, ordering him to hand over the command
of the Fifth Corps to Griffin.[2]

Sheridan's success was complete, for not only was *Pickett*
routed with a loss of 4,500 prisoners,[3] but the South Side
railroad was now at Grant's mercy, consequently the fate
of Petersburg was sealed.

Fall of Petersburg and Richmond

On the night of the battle of Five Forks Grant was at
Dabney's saw-mill ; the rain had ceased falling, and he was
seated outside his tent wrapped in the blue overcoat of a
private soldier, when the silence was broken by a cheer.
An aide-de-camp galloped up with the first news of Sheridan's
victory ; soon he was followed by another, Colonel Horace
Porter, who leaping off his horse, in his excitement clapped
the general-in-chief on the back. Grant was unperturbed ;
already during the afternoon he had issued a warning
order to Humphreys, Wright, and Parke to assault at 4 a.m.
the next day. Having heard what Porter had to say,
he went into his tent, and by the light of a candle wrote the
following dispatch to Meade : " Generals Wright and Parke
should both be directed to feel for a chance to get through
to the enemy's line at once, and if they can get through

---

[1] 95 *W.R.*, pp. 825–7, 838–40.

[2] Sheridan, in his *Memoirs* (II, p. 161), is very unfair to Warren. For the
Court of Inquiry on Warren, see *B. & L.*, IV, pp. 723, 724 ; and *Humphreys*,
pp. 357–61. For praise of Warren, see *Swinton*, pp. 598–600.

[3] *Humphreys*, pp. 353, 354.

should push on to-night. All our batteries might be opened at once, without waiting for preparing assaulting columns. Let the corps commanders know the result on the left, and that it is still being pushed." [1] He then came out of his tent, and said to those standing by the camp fire : " It is a windy night, I have ordered an immediate assault along the lines." [2]

Grant's one idea now was to engage the enemy along the whole entrenched front, so as to prevent a concentration against Sheridan. Having sent the above dispatch to Meade, he instructed [3] Ord to " feel the enemy and push him if he shows signs of giving way," and Weitzel he ordered [4] to " be ready also to push any wavering that may be shown in your front." A little later on he ordered [5] Meade not to assault without a bombardment, and to Ord he wrote [6] : " If it is impracticable for you to get through in your front, I do not want you to try it. . . . I want you to see, though, if the enemy is leaving, and if so follow him up." He sent out these instructions because he realised that *Lee* must fall back, and that the time to attack him was as he retreated. The assault was fixed for 4 a.m.[7] on the 2nd, and Sheridan was instructed to advance on the South Side railway, moving towards *Lee's* right flank, Miles's division being sent down the White Oak road to protect his right. At midnight an intense bombardment was opened.

Lee, in spite of his defeat at Five Forks, seems to have believed that Grant would not assault the Petersburg front. He could have retired on the night of the 1st/2nd to Amelia Court House, but in place he ordered *Field's* division, about 4,000 strong, from the Richmond front to Petersburg,[8] and awaited Grant's next move. It came swiftly, for at 4 a.m. the men of the Armies of the Potomac and James swept through the Confederate works west of Petersburg,[9] and penetrating to the Appomattox cut *Lee's* army in two.

[1] 97 *W.R.*, p. 397.	[4] 97 *W.R.*, p. 438.	[7] 97 *W.R.*, p. 423.
[2] *Badeau*, III, p. 502.	[5] 97 *W.R.*, p. 399.	[8] 97 *W.R.*, p. 1373.
[3] 97 *W.R.*, p. 431.	[6] 97 *W.R.*, p. 431.	[9] 95 *W.R.*, pp. 603, 1017.

Lee now recognised that Richmond was untenable, so he notified [1] the Confederate Secretary of War that he intended to withdraw north of the Appomattox, concentrating his divided forces on the Danville railway; simultaneously he advised that Richmond should be evacuated that night.

All west of *Lee's* centre was now being driven by Sheridan beyond the Appomattox, and all east of it was forced into Petersburg by Grant wheeling his left flank inwards. The question then arose : should the inner works be assaulted ? Meade and others strongly urged that they should be carried by the bayonet, but Grant wished to avoid unnecessary slaughter, consequently no assault was ordered for that evening; in place, at 7.40 p.m., he wrote [2] Meade : " I believe it will pay to commence a furious bombardment at five a.m. to be followed by an assault at 6, only if there is good reason for believing the enemy is leaving."

At 4 a.m. on the 3rd Parke succeeded in penetrating the enemy's works, and an hour and ten minutes later Meade reported [3] to Grant that Petersburg was in his hands.

Meanwhile, in Richmond all was in confusion. Jefferson Davis had fled; the people had not been warned of the disaster; no steps to police the city were attempted, so the mob ruled that night. Casks of liquor were rolled into the streets and their heads knocked in. White and black men, women, and children fought around them ; then they pillaged the commissariat stores, the shops, and the houses. The jails were broken open and the city was set on fire, smoke and flame struggling to obscure and to reveal the drunken orgy. An orgy of riot and lust, a pandemonium now and again shaken into the terror of panic as the shock of the explosion of a ram or a gunboat on the James, fired by the flying Government, brought the flaming houses crashing into the streets, and threw high into the blackness of the night—amidst sparks, dust, and smoke—the doom of the Confederacy.

[1] 97 *W.R.*, p. 1378 ; see also 97 *W.R.*, pp. 1370, 1379.
[2] 97 *W.R.*, p. 458.   [3] 97 *W.R.*, p. 511.

An hour after dawn, whilst the rioters were still trampling each other in their search for plunder, a cry arose in the streets of " Yankees ! Yankees ! " It was the advanced guard of General Weitzel's corps, and a few minutes later the Stars and Stripes once again floated over Richmond.

Thus Richmond fell : and symbolic of the strange oneness of peace and war, of the conflict of man with nature and of man with man, as Colonel George A. Bruce approached the burning city, " on the verge of this maelstrom of smoke and fire " he saw a " farmer ploughing in a field while cinders from the burning capital were falling at his feet." [1]

PURSUIT AND SURRENDER

Directly Grant heard from Meade that Petersburg had fallen, he ordered [2] him to leave one division to hold the city, and with the rest of his army to take the river road and advance to the Appomattox. Correctly surmising that *Lee* would have to follow the Danville railway in order to gain the Roanoke and to supply himself, Grant at once decided not to follow him and become involved with his rear-guards, but instead to get ahead of him and so intercept his line of retreat.[3] Sheridan, anticipating the fall of Petersburg, had not waited for orders, and was already in hot pursuit of *Lee's* right wing which was marching northwards for Bevil's Bridge. The advanced guard of *Lee's* left wing reached Amelia Court House on the 4th, and what remained of the Army of Northern Virginia was reunited there the next day.[4]

On the 3rd, before leaving Petersburg, Grant had written to Sheridan saying : " The first object of present movement will be to intercept *Lee's* army and the second to secure

---

[1] *M.H.S.M.*, XIV, p. 130. This remainds me of an incident during the World War. A French peasant woman came to me one day in a great state of excitement and said a soldier had stolen her pickaxe. I attempted to pacify her by informing her that her countrymen had just gained a great victory. To which she replied : " Ça m'est égal—mais où est ma pioche ? "

[2] 97 *W.R.*, p. 512.   [3] *Grant*, II, p. 456.

[4] 95 *W.R.*, pp. 1285, 1283, 1289, 1301.

Burksville," [1] consequently Sheridan continued his movement westwards, and on the evening of the 4th occupied
Jetersville Station, there learning that Lee was at Amelia
Court House. Thereupon he ordered the Fifth Corps to
entrench across the railway, and urged Meade to push up
the Second Corps and attack.[2] Meade decided, however,
not to do so until the arrival of the Sixth Corps, and by the
time it came up night was beginning to close in.[3] Irritated
by Meade's lack of audacity, the impetuous Sheridan wrote
to Grant : " I wish you were here yourself. I feel confident
of capturing the Army of Northern Virginia if we exert
ourselves. I see no escape for *Lee*." [4] On receiving this,
Grant, who was at Nottoway Court House, at once set
out for Jetersville, sixteen miles away. A scout

" rode at the head of the little column [four or five staff
officers and fourteen men]," writes Badeau, " with one of
the aides-de-camp by his side, who silently cocked a pistol,
and all through that march was ready to fire at the slightest
symptom of treachery. They peered into the woods on
either hand lest the forest should conceal a foe, and sometimes
caught sight of rebel camp fires twinkling in the distance.
But the scout was loyal, and at ten o'clock, after a four
hours' ride, the party came upon Sheridan's outposts." [5]

Lee's road was blocked ; his retreat on Danville had been
intercepted. He himself says that his delay at Amelia
Court House " was fatal and could not be retrieved " ; he
attributes it to the cutting of the Danville railway which
" rendered it impracticable to procure from Danville the
supplies ordered to meet us at points of our march " ; [6]
but the true reason was that he had started his retirement
too late. The road to the Roanoke being cut, he decided
to march upon Farmville, to which place supplies had been
ordered by rail.

[1] 97 *W.R.*, p. 528.   [3] 97 *W.R.*, p. 576.
[2] 97 *W.R.*, pp. 557, 558.   [4] 97 *W.R.*, p. 582.
[5] *Badeau*, III, p. 562 ; 97 *W.R.*, p. 577, and *Grant*, II, p. 469.
[6] 95 *W.R.*, p. 1255. The story that a supply train had been sent on to
Richmond past Amelia Court House without unloading is a myth. See
M.H.S.M., VI, pp. 493, 494.

On the afternoon of the 5th *Longstreet's* corps set out for Farmville, but unaware of this move, Meade at 7 p.m. ordered [1] the three corps at Jetersville, namely, the Second, Fifth, and Sixth, to advance on Amelia Court House at 6 a.m. on the 6th and attack the enemy. Grant was, however, of opinion [2] that *Lee* would retire during the night; he explained to Meade that he did not want to follow the enemy but to get ahead of him,[3] to intercept his line of retreat and not to push him along it. According to Sheridan, Meade was instructed to modify his orders; but this was not done, and it was not until 9.30 a.m. the following morning, when a Confederate column was seen moving west, that he changed his direction and moved on Deatonsville.[4] This movement brought Sheridan and the Sixth Corps parallel to and abreast of the enemy's left; the Fifth Corps on his right, and the Second Corps in his rear, which corps before nightfall captured many wagons, six guns, and 1,700 prisoners.

Meanwhile, Ord's corps was pressing on to Rice's Station; and hearing of its approach, *Lee* urged on *Longstreet* to that place,[5] with the result that he became separated from the troops following him, and Sheridan and the Sixth Corps, interposing between him and these troops, overwhelmed the latter and captured 6,000 men.[6] *Longstreet*, pushing on, annihilated a small force sent forward by Ord to destroy the bridge at Farmville. Thus ended the operations on the 6th.

Grant, thinking that *Lee* would attempt to reach Danville by Prince Edward Court House, ordered the Fifth Corps and three divisions of cavalry to march to that place on the 7th, Ord's corps proceeding to Farmville.[7] *Lee* was, however, unable to gain time for such a move, for at Farmville he had to halt to ration his men from a supply train. Instead he decided to cross to the left bank of the Appomattox at Farmville and High Bridge, gaining Danville by the road leading through Appomattox Court House.

[1] 97 *W.R.*, pp. 577, 578. [4] 95 *W.R.*, pp. 681, 682.
[2] 97 *W.R.*, p. 577. [5] *Longstreet*, p. 611.
[3] *Grant*, II, p. 469; *Sheridan*, II, pp. 177, 178. [6] *Humphreys*, pp. 383, 384.
[7] 95 *W.R.*, pp. 1109, 906, 841; 97 *W.R.*, pp. 620, 634, 635.

On the 7th the Second Corps, crossing High Bridge before the Confederate rear-guard could destroy it, came up with *Lee's* main body at Cumberland Church, and so hotly engaged it that he was compelled to form line and halt there for the rest of the day.[1] At nightfall *Lee* disengaged his weary troops and, marching thirty-five miles westwards to Appomattox Court House, the battle-worn Army of Northern Virginia reached its last bivouac on the evening of the 8th.[2] Whilst this retirement was taking place, Grant ordered[3] the Second and Sixth Corps to move north of the Appomattox and press the enemy's rear; whilst south of the river, Sheridan, followed by the Fifth and Ord's corps, was directed on Appomattox Station, information having been received that *Lee* intended to resupply his army at that place.

On the evening of the 8th Sheridan reached Appomattox Station, from where he pushed *Lee's* advanced troops back towards the Court House. On the morning of the 9th *Lee* advanced to attack him, when Sheridan's cavalry, " parting to the right and left," disclosed the Fifth and Ord's corps in line behind them. Simultaneously the Second and Sixth Corps arrived in rear of *Lee's* men. The white flag was then raised.[4]

On the 7th Grant realised that the Confederate cause was lost, consequently, to prevent further bloodshed, he wrote to *Lee* asking him to surrender " that portion of the C. S. Army known as the Army of Northern Virginia." [5] *Lee* also knew that the end had come ; his army was rapidly disintegrating, in fact he no longer had any idea of the number of men he commanded, and in answer he asked what terms of surrender would be offered ? [5] On the 8th Grant replied that the only condition was, " that the men and officers surrendered shall be disqualified for taking up arms against the Government of the United States until properly exchanged." [6] *Lee* answered that he did not think that the emergency had arisen to call for the surrender of

[1] *Longstreet*, p. 167.
[2] 95 *W.R.*, p. 1266.
[3] 97 *W.R.*, pp. 621, 633.
[4] 95 *W.R.*, pp. 1109, 1110.
[5] 97 *W.R.*, p. 619.
[6] 97 *W.R.*, p. 641.

his army, but as his sole object was the restoration of peace he was willing to meet Grant.[1] To which Grant rightly replied, on the morning of the 9th, that he had no authority to treat on the subject of peace, and that " the terms upon which peace can be had are well understood." [2] *Lee* then asked for an interview.[3]

The meeting took place at McLean's house,[3] in a "naked little parlor, containing a table and two or three chairs." After a brief general conversation *Lee* said :

" I asked to see you, General Grant, to ascertain upon what terms you would receive the surrender of my army ? "

Grant explained that the officers and men must become prisoners of war, all munitions, weapons, and supplies being surrendered. Then he said : " Do I understand, General *Lee*, that you accept these terms ? "

" Yes," replied *Lee*, " and if you will put them into writing, I will sign them."

Grant then wrote out the terms,[4] and whilst he did so he glanced at *Lee*, and noticing the sunlight glinting on his sword, he added a paragraph that the officers should be allowed to retain their swords, horses, and personal property. He then handed the paper to *Lee*.

Lee put on his spectacles and after reading the draft was much touched by this unexpected indulgence, which he said would have a very good effect upon his army. He then asked whether the horses of the cavalry and artillery, which were the property of the soldiers, might not also be exempted.

Grant answered that he could not alter the terms of surrender, but that he would instruct his officers who received the paroles " to allow the cavalry and artillery men to retain their horses and take them home to work their little farms."

Lee then wrote out his letter of surrender,[5] after which he made one further request ; he asked that his starving men might be fed. Grant inquired of him the number of

---

[1] 97 *W.R.*, p. 641.   [2] 97 *W.R.*, p. 664.
[3] The following facts are mainly taken from *Badeau*, III, pp. 602–12.
[4] 97 *W.R.*, p. 665.   [5] 97 *W.R.*, p. 666.

rations he wanted, but *Lee* did not know, so 25,000 rations were decided upon.[1]

Lee then left the house, and said to his soldiers as they crowded round him : " Men, we have fought through the war together. I have done the best I could for you."

Grant rode over to his lines, and, hearing the firing of salutes, he at once ordered them to cease, saying : " The war is over, the rebels are our countrymen again, and the best sign of rejoicing after the victory will be to abstain from all demonstrations in the field."

The 10th was a lovely day, the sky was blue and cloudless, and spring was in the air ; Grant rode out to the Confederate picket line. There he met *Lee*, also *Longstreet* who had been at his wedding, *Cadmus Wilcox* who was his groomsman, *Heth*, a subaltern with him in Mexico, and many others whom he had known and who had known him in days long before the war. They thanked him for being allowed to retain their swords, and one said to him : " General, we have come to congratulate you on having wound us up." To which Grant replied : " I hope it will be for the good of us all."

---

[1] When *Lee's* army surrendered, there were in it only 7,892 " organised infantry with arms " (97 *W.R.*, p. 1266). The numbers paroled were— 22,349 infantry, 2,576 artillery, 1,559 cavalry, and 1,446 miscellaneous troops. (*M.H.S.M.*, VI, p. 501.)

CHAPTER XVI

GRANT'S GENERALSHIP, 1864-5

THE CREATIVE PERIOD

IN my opinion, few periods in military history have been so misunderstood as the one under review ; and consequently few generals-in-chief have suffered greater injustice than Grant. The reason for this misunderstanding is obvious, directly it is appreciated that the Civil War was the first of its kind ; by which I do not mean that it was the first of all such wars, but the first of all modern wars ; and though strategically it can be compared to wars which preceded it, tactically it can only be judged correctly by those which followed it. In fact, a writer who possessed no knowledge of the tactics of previous wars, and some knowledge of tactics since 1865, could not possibly have displayed so intense an ignorance of the nature of the tactics of this war as has been done by so many of the learned yet purblind historians who have obscured the very nature of the war through excess of strategical knowledge and paucity of tactical understanding.

For instance—Ropes, and no man can doubt his knowledge or interest in the war—has but a faint idea of its tactical nature. To him there is no trace of Marlborough, Wellington, or Napoleon in Grant's last campaign—" its terribly bloody battles, its encounters of every day . . . the noble trees cut down by musket bullets . . . the thousands upon thousands of brave men slain and maimed, and, above all, the indecisive results, amaze, terrify, repel, dishearten us." And again :

" The experience of the Army of the Potomac in the campaign was in fact a new experience for soldiers. Sacrifices were demanded every day of the rank and file of the army which had hitherto been required only occasionally, and then only from those selected for some special post of honour or danger."

These things he cannot understand :

" To lie in a new-dug rifle-pit a hundred yards from the enemy for several days under constant fire is much like the experience of the engineer troops in a siege. To rush from this rifle-pit upon the enemy's works is the act of a forlorn hope, whose gallant performance is the admiration of a storming column, itself selected for a special and dangerous service. But it is not every day that the sap is pushed forward or the breach assaulted." [1]

Why cannot he understand them ; why does he talk of Marlborough and Wellington, of new experiences, of rifle-pits, prolonged battles, siege-works, and indecisive results ? Because he does not understand that the rifle bullet has completely revolutionised tactics. His knowledge enables him to place his finger on the pulse of war, yet he cannot count its heart throbs, nor can he diagnose its fever. He is blind to the reality of rifle warfare ; yet, though he wrote the above extracts in 1884, he was no blinder than the majority of generals of thirty years later. The rifle bullet utterly changed tactics, and unless this is understood all knowledge is a blank, worse—a danger.

The 1864–5 campaign in Virginia was the first of the modern campaigns ; it initiated a tactical epoch, and did not even resemble the wars of ten years before its date. It was not a campaign of bayonets, but of bullets ; bayonets were rarely crossed, and there were few bayonet wounds " except accidental ones," writes Surgeon-Major Albert G. Hart ; then he says : " I think half a dozen would include all the wounds of this nature that I ever dressed." [2] It was a campaign of bullets. On the battlefields of the Wilderness and of Spottsylvania the Confederate ordnance officers collected for recasting more than 120,000 pounds of lead, [3]

---

[1] *M.H.S.M.*, IV, pp. 365, 405. [2] *M.H.S.M.*, XIII, p. 265.
[3] *B. & L.*, IV, p. 244.

and even if this amount represents a twentieth part of the bullets fired, then, at two ounces apiece, the number expended was 19,000,000. When did Marlborough, or Wellington, or Napoleon face such a hail of projectiles ?

It was the bullet which created the trench and the rifle-pit ; which killed the bayonet ; which rendered useless the sword ; which chased away guns and horsemen ; which, from May 5, 1864, to April 9, 1865, held the contending forces in " constant close contact, with rare intervals of brief comparative repose," [1] and which prevented the rapid decisions of the battles of preceding centuries. In 1861-5 the rifle bullet was the lord of the battlefield as was the machine-gun bullet in 1914-18.

Yet in spite of this deadly instrument of war, and in spite of the fact that Grant never fully appreciated its powers, his achievements are remarkable. From his camps north of the Rapidan, in a little over a month, he fought his way through a hundred miles of most difficult country ; he crossed three rivers in face of the enemy ; he made nine flanking movements ; he changed his base of supplies four times, fed his army, sheltered it, and transported his sick and wounded to the rear.[2] He moved forward 4,000 wagons and an immense train of reserve artillery without the loss of a gun, a wagon, or an animal captured by the enemy, and he was never once surprised or compelled to halt for more than a few days at a time. How were these things possible ? They were possible because Grant realised that weapon-power is the secret of tactics. He was not afraid to use the rifle, and he was not afraid to meet the rifle. Had he only carried this supreme understanding of what fighting demands to its logical conclusion, namely, that high

---

[1] *Humphreys*, p. 118.

[2] The daily percentage of sick in May was less than, and in June almost the same as, it was in camp in April (*Medical and Surgical History of the Rebellion*, Pt. I, p. 329). Typhoid fever and dysentery were the scourges of the war. According to *Phisterer* (p. 70), the total deaths in the Union forces were 304,369, out of which 186,216 were accountable to disease, and ?4,184 died of unknown causes. Roughly, two men died from sickness in hospital to each man killed or mortally wounded in battle.

superiority in weapon-power is ninety-nine per cent. of
victory, he would have more fully realised the value of
artillery, and have never ceased to call for more and more
magazine rifles and carbines. What he did not understand,
and what no general of his day understood, and few since
have understood, was that the art of war had been revolutionised by the rifle, and to apply old tactics to new weapons,
was tantamount to applying a whip to a locomotive.

GRANT'S STRATEGY

In reviewing Grant's generalship during the last year of
the war, it is all-important to keep his object clearly in
mind, and especially so because those who criticise his
strategy and tactics frequently overlook it. It was to
establish unity of strategical direction and to end the war
in the shortest possible time, because, as we have seen, the
political condition of the North brooked no delay. Had
Grant felt certain of Lincoln's re-election, his problem would
have been a less difficult one ; but not knowing this, his
aim in May, 1864, was to end the war before the presidential
elections took place. Throughout this period, the spring
and summer of 1864, politics dominated strategy as strongly
as topography dominated tactics, and though Grant never
failed to realise this, many of his critics have, and by forgetting the political foundations of his campaign, they have
suggested strategical edifices which, in the circumstances,
either could not have been built, or would have toppled
over at the first shock.

To bring the war rapidly to an end demanded concentration of force against the decisive point, which does not mean
concentrating against the front of the enemy's main army,
but against its rear. To effect this concentration, the
Army of Northern Virginia had to be held as in a vice, and
we have seen how Grant held it, and this holding did not
depend only on hitting, but also on an elaborate combination of manœuvres carried out on the James and in the
Shenandoah Valley, as well as a frequent shifting of the
main base of supply under protection of the fleet.

The primary strategical localities were Washington, Chattanooga, and Fort Monroe; the secondary strategical localities, Lynchburg, Atlanta, Mobile, and Wilmington—the economic outposts of Richmond and of *Lee's* army. Grant's grand strategy included all these points, and with the exception of Wilmington, the value of which Grant never seems to have fully appreciated, the others he kept constantly in mind. Whilst no other of the Federal generals, such as Sherman, Sheridan, and Butler, had at any time to consider more than one or two of these centres, Grant had constantly to keep all in view, and, as conditions fluctuated, to readjust his plan of operations without changing his strategical direction. This point is also commonly overlooked by those who criticise Grant, and especially by those who compare his campaign to Sherman's.

If the point I have so often mentioned is kept in mind, namely, failing the annihilation of *Lee's* army early in the campaign, the whole of Grant's strategy depended upon his ability to hold this force, the various movements he carried out and ordered become clear. He opened his campaign by a manœuvre round *Lee's* right flank, and he ended the war by a similar movement, a movement so ably and speedily carried out that the pursuit of his enemy to Appomattox Court House remains a model of its kind. As the summer advanced, his strategical problem became more and more intense. By holding *Lee*, which meant hitting *Lee*, he was able to detach large forces to the Valley when *Early* threatened it. It may be said that this shows that his holding operation had failed, for Sheridan was only sent there because *Lee* had detached *Early*. Strategically this is correct, but tactically *Early's* force was never strong enough to compel Grant to abandon his campaign; and had it not been for *Lee's* losses in the Wilderness and at Spottsylvania, this might not have been the case. Further, it must not be overlooked that throughout this campaign Grant's subordinates missed opportunity after opportunity. Butler, Smith, Meade, and Sheridan, each in turn failed to take advantage of circumstances which seldom

occur in war, until at length Grant's strategy was almost
overwhelmed by impatient popular opinion. In the late
summer and autumn these failures compelled him to carry
out a number of operations, not only to maintain the direction
of his strategy, but to stimulate the *moral* of the North. His
attempts to strike the Richmond railways may be compared
to his Bayou campaign before he moved south of Vicksburg ;
for they had a dual aim—to hold *Lee* and to maintain political
enthusiasm. Had he simply laid siege to Petersburg, he
would have been accused of doing nothing.

Whilst these operations were in progress, Sherman's lever,
supported on Grant's fulcrum, was steadily moving eastwards. " Sherman's repose at Savannah," so announced
the *Richmond Dispatch* in January, 1865, " is the repose of
a tiger," and only because *Lee*, the hunter, was penned up
in Richmond, and could not get out and stalk his prey.
As Swinton says :

" The splendidly appointed legions which Sherman led
out of Atlanta were able to journey unmolested to the sea.
They marched whithersoever they listed ; the few squads
of gray beards and boys whom they met got briskly out of
their way or were trampled under foot. It was indeed less
a campaign than a tour of triumph." [1]

Though somewhat of an exaggeration, this is a picturesque
paraphrase of what took place, and what was only possible
because of *Lee's* losses in May and June.

Sherman was without question one of the great generals
of the war, in spite of the fact that he never fought a great,
let alone a decisive battle. His superb march captivated
popular imagination ; but this is no reason why the student
of war should be thrown off his balance.

To compare Sherman's strategy with Grant's is really
fatuous, and though I have already touched on this subject,
for a moment I will return to it, as it will help to explain
Grant's tactics which I intend to examine later on.

[1] *Decisive Battles of the War*, Swinton, p. 471.

Sherman never manœuvred his enemy into a position where he was brought to bay, for the very good reason that *Johnston* never gave him an opportunity of fighting him until he reached Atlanta, and as *Johnston* was there relieved by the impetuous *Hood*, in his turn Sherman was relieved from a pitched battle at that place. It is true that both Sherman's and Grant's armies were in constant and close contact with their enemies, nevertheless whilst Sherman forced *Johnston* back from Dalton to Atlanta, a distance of about a hundred miles in a little over two months, Grant pushed *Lee* back a similar distance, that is from the Rapidan to Petersburg, in forty days. He assaulted field works on eight days and Sherman on seven, and whilst Sherman carried out eight outflanking movements Grant undertook nine; the last of which, his move to the James, was the most brilliant manœuvre of its kind during the war. Here the comparison ends, and is, in truth, utterly superficial; because the ideas behind these two campaigns are utterly different. Grant's, I will again repeat, was either to annihilate or hold through hitting, whilst Sherman's was to advance through holding based on threatening to hit. Whilst Grant through losses paralysed his opponent, and under cover of this paralysis outflanked him, Sherman, and to his credit, adopted a system of strategical entrenchments, works constructed to cover his outflanking movements. By entrenching his centre, he was able to secure these movements; in other words, he threatened his enemy's front in order to turn his flank. Though Grant, after his failure to take Petersburg, adopted similar tactics, it would have been suicidal for him to have done so before; because *Lee* would simply have fallen back on Richmond, and had he refrained from attacking Grant on May 5, which was an act of doubtful wisdom, he would have reached Richmond with his army almost intact. Had he done so, he could then have detached a formidable force to strike at Washington or to reinforce *Johnston*. What most historians quite inexcusably overlook is, that throughout his campaign Grant had Washington behind him whilst Sherman had Chattanooga. The one was a political centre and the seat of government, the other was a strategical centre and a base of supply.

GRANT'S TACTICS

As a strategist Grant has been understood, but as a tactician he has been misunderstood, because critics will separate these two branches of the art of war, examining each as if it were enclosed in a water-tight compartment. It is possible to develop an offensive tactics from a defensive strategy, as Hannibal did ; equally is it possible to develop an offensive strategy from a defensive tactics, as was done by Quintus Fabius ; but normally a general who is called upon to conquer a foreign land, or a hostile people, is compelled by circumstances to act offensively in both these branches of his art. This is the point which so many critics of the Civil War have overlooked. It was not an ordinary war, a war in which victory depended on the vanquishing of the enemy's armed forces, but a war against a nation in which the will of the people had to be broken. The one highly trained army corps, suggested by Lord Wolseley, had it existed, and had it defeated the Confederate forces in 1861, and had it occupied Richmond, would have been no nearer winning the war than *Beauregard* was, or would have been, had he occupied Washington after the battle of Bull Run. What soldier critics, even more so than civilian, so frequently fail to understand is, that in most modern wars, and certainly so in such wars as the Civil War, there is a vast difference between gaining a victory and winning a war, because a war in its full sense can only be won when the defeated nation, or people, agree to accept the will of their conqueror, and not merely acknowledge that his army is more powerful than their own. This was the reason why wars originating from religious causes were so long and so terrible.

In a former chapter I have shown that to the North the war could only be won by the destruction of a civilisation which was antagonistic to its own, and that consequently no satisfactory conclusion could be arrived at through mere adjustments between its civilisation and that of the South. I pointed out that conquest was forced upon the North, therefore I am of opinion that Grant was right in deciding that both his tactics and strategy must be offensive ; for it was obvious to him that the longer the war lasted the less likely would the North hold out ; for the North was fighting for a wounded principle, and the South for the life of its ideal.

When examining his tactics, it is generally overlooked that to him the physical attack was but one of the three forms of attack, the other two being the moral and economic (or material) attacks ; attacks which were waged against the will and resources of the Confederacy, and not merely against the strength of her armies. The attacks of Sheridan in the Valley and of Sherman in Georgia and the Carolinas were in nature moral and economic, whilst his own in Virginia was a physical onslaught so unrelenting and fierce that it shielded these attacks from physical interference. To turn a fertile valley into a wilderness has little effect on the civil will, should the invader be driven away and the wilderness be occupied by a friendly army. This Grant understood, but what he did not realise was that as the Confederacy possessed few industries, and was consequently dependent on Europe for most of the luxuries and many of the necessities of life and of war, in place of destroying vast quantities of cotton—the " gold " of the South—it would have proved far more economical had he tightened up the blockade and left the cotton bales intact, to help towards paying for the war once peace was re-established.[1]

To turn to the physical attack—the conquest of armed forces—Grant's difficulties have already been examined, and all that is necessary for me to repeat here is, that his outstanding tactical difficulties were the power of the rifle

[1] On November 6, 1864, Sherman suggested (79 *W.R.*, p. 660) to Grant a variety of possible moves forward from Atlanta, one being to the Appalachicola river, because near Albany and Fort Gaines he could destroy 400,000 bales of cotton. "This, at the price of the day, would have meant a loss to the country greater than the burning of Chicago." (*M.H.S.M.*, VIII, p. 523.)   The Chicago fire in 1871 destroyed $196,000,000 worth of property.

and forest warfare. The Minié rifle had trebled the range of the old musket, and not only did this result in the zone of fire separating the combatants being considerably increased, but, in consequence, by prolonging the time taken to assault, it enabled the defender to utilise this time in throwing up breastworks, and so rendered defensive action stronger than the attack. Behind an earthwork the infantry soldier was supreme,[1] and though at the beginning of the war trenches were seldom dug, the instinct of self-preservation rather than the faculty of reason soon sought their alliance. Grant, so I am of opinion, never really understood the relationship between rifle and trench. At Shiloh he overlooked trenches altogether, at Missionary Ridge he treated them with caution, and in the Wilderness, and at Spottsylvania, because trees and undergrowth partially reduced the depth of the zone of aimed fire, he rushed them with masses of men. It is curious that he never learnt the secret of this relationship, seeing that he had a wonderful grasp of the value of the rear attack. He saw the end, but he failed to see the means —the tactics of the rear attack. He did not understand that given artillery, infantry, and cavalry, a *combination* of these three arms was required. First, a strong skirmishing line to gain contact ; secondly, a mass of artillery to bombard ; thirdly, a powerful line of infantry to assault, *should the enemy attempt to overwhelm the guns or to withdraw from their fire* ; and fourthly, a force of cavalry to manœuvre round one of the enemy's flanks, and by attacking or threatening to attack his rear *distract his front*. What Grant did not understand was that a battle, like a campaign, is a combination of physical, moral, and economic pressure : the artillery bombardment, the fear of infantry assault, and the cavalry manœuvre against the communications

---

[1] This should have been as obvious as $2 \times 2 = 4$, because the infantryman in a trench can fire steadily, can load rapidly, and only presents one-fifth of the target, frequently less, when compared to his counterpart in the open. Nevertheless, in 1914, when the range of the rifle had been trebled, and the average rate of fire quintupled, attempt after attempt was made by German, French, British, and Russian generals to carry entrenched fronts by assault.

sufficiently close to the rear of the hostile army so as to compel it, or part of it, to face about. In this respect he was on a footing with all other generals of his day, and, what is still more extraordinary, with most generals of to-day ; further still, the enclosed country he was compelled to fight in was the very worst possible for artillery and cavalry action. Failing to realise the power of the Spencer carbine,[1] and frequently not being able to haul his guns through the forests, he relied on infantry assaults, made not only with the idea of disrupting the enemy's front, but of so disorganising it, that under cover of its reorganisation he could gain time to carry out a flank march. In the circumstances it is difficult to say that Grant was wrong, seeing that the attack was forced upon him.

In open country these out-flanking manœuvres would certainly have been carried out by cavalry, but in thickly wooded country cavalry operations are normally excessively slow, not because the troopers cannot move rapidly, but because their trains are confined to a few and usually indifferent roads. The main trouble is of course the forage carts, which for only a moderate force of cavalry run into hundreds. Grant has been criticised for detaching Sheridan's cavalry before the battle of Spottsylvania and before his advance on Petersburg. In the first case, as I have already stated, I consider that he should have left a division or part of a division with Meade, but in the second case Meade had with him quite sufficient cavalry to carry out all necessary reconnaissance. He has also been criticised for having at first ordered Sheridan to cut loose from the army on March 29, 1865 ; but apparently he did so because at the time he was afraid that unless *Lee's* communications were cut he might slip away altogether. Directly he found that *Lee* had not moved, whether on his own initiative or on Sheridan's recommendation, he cancelled this order.

---

[1] " I never knew a well-directed assault by troops armed with Spencers to fail, nor have I ever seen any line that could stand before seven successive discharges of Spencer carbines." (Major-General James H. Wilson in *M.H.S.M.*, XIII, p. 85.)

The true use of cavalry—for cavalry could still operate in this war—is well set forth by General Wilson, who says :

" To make a proper use of cavalry, you must get it into such a position that it can assail the flank or rear of an enemy, or operate upon his communications with effect. If I were called upon to command a force of 60,000 men, with authority to organise it as I pleased, I would have at least 20,000 on horseback. By using the mounted force to assail the flank and rear of the enemy, I should expect to conduct a more successful campaign than could be done by any other possible means in these days. The scattering of cavalry promiscuously along the front of an army is no longer necessary. Of course you must use cavalry to find out where the enemy is, and to gain early information of his movements, but a few squadrons can do it as well as a whole division."

Grant understood this better than *Lee*, for he never wasted his cavalry as did his great opponent when he detached *Stuart* to operate against McClellan's rear in the Peninsula campaign, or when he sent this same general into the blue before the battle of Gettysburg, which operation did not perturb Meade.[1] But it was not until the battle of Five Forks that he fully understood that—" With good cavalry acting in conjunction with good infantry, you can accomplish almost anything in modern warfare. It is simply marvellous what can be done with men who are properly mounted. You can get them onto the flank and rear of the enemy every time." [2] Such is General Wilson's conclusion.

ASSAULTS AND LOSSES

To turn from combined tactics to Grant's use of infantry, as I have explained in a former chapter, in his day, as to-day, the theory of the attack was based on the assault, that slowly dying rudiment of old pike warfare. This is clearly expressed by McClellan when, early in the war, he wrote to Buell saying : " I believe in attacks by concentrated masses." [3]

[1] 43 *W.R.*, p. 67.   [2] *M.H.S.M.*, XIII, pp. 87, 88.   [3] 7 *W.R.*, p. 457.

Lee also believed in such attacks, and frequently ordered them, notably at the battle of Gettysburg where the Confederates advanced in a solid wedge and were repulsed with fearful slaughter.   But like Grant after his second assault at Vicksburg, and after his assault at Cold Harbor, *Lee* possessed the moral courage to acknowledge his mistake, for after this battle he wrote to *Longstreet ;* " If I had only taken your counsel, even on the 3rd [July, 1863], and moved around the Federal left, how different all might have been." [1] Again, at this battle, had Meade only delivered a counterattack when *Lee* was repulsed, his victory might well have been a decisive one.[2]

Throughout the war we are faced by this difficult problem : assault after assault failed ; three were carried out on May 5, four on May 6, two on May 8, five on May 10, an unknown number on May 12, one on May 18, and one on May 19, and none of them led to decisive results ; yet at Missionary Ridge and Fort Harrison, to quote only two examples, results were decisive ; in the first case, because *Bragg's* front was distracted by Hooker's outflanking attack, and in the second, because the most careful preparations were made.   Again, had McClernand assaulted at Champion's Hill, or had Smith assaulted at Petersburg, in the first case the siege of Vicksburg would have been unnecessary, and in the second the war would undoubtedly have been shortened. Here we are confronted by a choice between two evils—to assault and risk heavy casualties, or to refrain from assaulting and so prolong the war, a war in which two men died from sickness to every man killed on the battlefield.   Rightly or wrongly, Grant chose what he believed to be the lesser evil of these two, and in spite of the fact that the tactical theatre favoured the defence.   There can be little doubt that his assaults did shorten the war, and, in the long run, in all probability, they led to an economy in life; yet there can

---

[1] *B. & L.*, III, p. 349.

[2] Lincoln always felt that this assault should have been made, and regretted that he did not go to Gettysburg himself " and push matters on the field." (*Nicolay & Hay*, VII, p. 278.)

be no doubt that they were costly, though not more costly, as I will show, than those carried out by *Lee* and other generals.

The criticism on these assaults has been both general and severe : a good example, and not altogether an unfair one, is the following taken from General Francis A. Walker's book, *History of the Second Army Corps* [1] :

" The terrible experiences of May and June in assaults on intrenched positions ; assaults made, often, not at a carefully selected point, but ' all along the line ' ; assaults made as if it were a good thing to assault, and not a dire necessity ; assaults made without adequate concentration of troops, often without time for careful preparation, sometimes even without examination of the ground—these bitter experiences had naturally brought about a reaction, by which efforts to outflank the enemy were to become the order of the day, so that the months of July and August were largely to be occupied in rapid movements, now to the right and now to the left of a line thirty to forty miles in length, in the hope of somewhere, at some time, getting upon the flank of the unprepared enemy—the sentiment of headquarters, and perhaps the orders, being adverse to assaults."

What General Walker does not, however, appreciate is the difference between the overland campaign and the Petersburg campaign ; nor does he make due allowance for the topographical difficulties which faced Grant. It is easy enough to talk of " carefully selected points " and " examination of the ground," but when a battle is fought in a jungle selection and examination are impossible. Napoleon once wrote of Turenne, that he

" constantly observed the two maxims : first, never attack a position in front, when you can obtain it by turning it ; secondly, avoid doing what the enemy wishes, and that simply because he does wish it. Shun the field of battle which he has reconnoitred and studied, and the more particularly that in which he has fortified and entrenched himself." [2]

[1] Quoted by *Church*, p. 276.
[2] *Memoirs of Napoleon*, Montholon, III, p. 95.

Grant did not always follow these excellent maxims, not because he did not appreciate their value, but because circumstances did not allow of his following them. Whenever he could he aimed at a rear attack, and when he could not a frontal attack did not terrify him. He did not, however, purposely seek frontal attacks as has been so often implied. Even at Cold Harbor when he definitely decided to attack frontally, he did so because had he moved south of the Totopotomoy entrenchments, *Lee* would have extended his works to the Chickahominy, and an equally dangerous frontal attack would have had to be made, some distance south of his actual one, and obviously such an attack would have strategically been more unfavourable to Grant. Further still, it must be remembered that all tactical details were left to Meade. Colonel Lyman, one of Meade's aides-de-camp, says: " I recall but one instance in which the details of attack were arranged at headquarters [Grant's], and that was for the explosion of the Petersburg mine; and had those orders been obeyed, the town would have fallen." [1] Both he and Meade have been blamed again and again for failing to reconnoitre, and the best answer to this criticism is given by Meade himself, who, two days after the battle of Cold Harbor, said: " In this country I must fight a battle to reconnoitre a position." [2]

To turn now to the vexed question of the casualties resulting from these assaults. From the common criticism levelled against Grant's last campaigns, the only conclusion is that he was a callous butcher. Yet, as is well known, Grant had a horror of bloodshed. His usual question after a fight, writes Horace Porter, was " How many prisoners have been taken ? " Further—" No man ever had such a fondness for taking prisoners. I think the gratification arose from the kindness of his heart, a feeling that it was better to win in this way than by the destruction of human life." And again—When a number of his officers urged him to assault the inner lines at Petersburg on the afternoon of April 2—

[1] *M.H.S.M.*, V, p. 6.   [2] *M.H.S.M.*, V, p. 9.

" he was firm in his resolve not to sacrifice the lives necessary to accomplish such a result. He said the city would undoubtedly be evacuated during the night, and he would dispose the troops for a parallel march westward, and try to head off the escaping army." [1]

Losses in themselves convey much to the imagination but little to the reason, and as the popular mind is always governed by emotions and spectacles, there is some excuse why popular imagination was stampeded by Grant's casualties ; but there is absolutely no excuse why students of war should accept popular opinion as historical truth, for popular opinion is nearly always wrong. To judge losses correctly, circumstances, results, and the initial and final strengths of the contending forces must be examined and compared.

On May 4 Grant's army numbered about 115,000 officers and men of all arms, and *Lee's*—62,000 ; between this date and June 14 he received in all 46,934 reinforcements,[2] and *Lee* received about 12,000 [3] ; Grant's losses in killed, wounded, and missing were—54,926,[4] *Lee's*, as far as can be estimated—31,800 ; but this figure leaves out of account cavalry casualties, and the operations on May 8–9 on the North Anna. Accepting *Lee's* losses at 33,000 and Grant's at 55,000, then the percentages of losses to totals were as follows : Grant 34 per cent., and *Lee* 43 per cent. Considering the nature of the country, there was nothing exceptional in this, for in the Peninsula campaign McClellan lost about 43,000, or 31 per cent. of his total force, and *Lee* about 28,500, or 40 per cent. of his. Nor was there a marked disproportion in the battles themselves ; thus, in the Wilderness Grant lost 15·5 per cent. of the effective force of his army, and about 17·3 per cent. of those actually engaged ; whilst *Lee* lost 17·1 per cent. of his total force, and 18·1 per cent.[5] of his effective force. At Spottsylvania it was much the same, as mentioned in Chapter XI.

[1] *B. & L.*, IV, pp. 715, 718.   [3] *Humphreys*, pp. 124, 125.
[2] *M.H.S.M.*, IV, p. 450.   [4] 67 *W.R.*, p. 188.
[5] *N. & L.*, p. 111.

It is true that in actual bulk numbers Grant's losses exceeded *Lee's* by about 20,000 ; but as after the battle of the Wilderness *Lee* remained on the defensive there is nothing remarkable in this. Nor in single battles were Grant's losses excessive when compared to the battles fought by many of the other generals : thus, at Gettysburg, Meade's losses were—23,049, and *Lee's*—28,063 ; at Chickamauga Rosecrans lost 16,336, and *Bragg* 20,950 ; and at Malvern Hill McClellan lost 15,849, and *Lee* 20,634. If anything, *Lee* rather than Grant deserves to be accused of sacrificing his men. According to Lieutenant-Colonel George A. Bruce, an able writer :

" *Lee* in five months of 1862 . . . lost nearly 60,000 men in four battles, and still found *Jackson's* part of his army one hundred miles south and the remainder only sixty miles north of their starting-points, whilst in 1864 Grant moved forward a hundred miles in a little over a month, and moved toward final victory." [1]

Further still, it will be remembered that Sherman in his Atlanta campaign, so frequently held up as the model Grant should have followed, lost some 32,000 men, or approximately 33 per cent. of his original force. Though these figures do not convey much, they do show, so I think, that Grant's losses have been greatly exaggerated by historians, and that much of their criticism has consequently been unjust.

GRANT AND LEE

It was the drift of circumstances rather than premeditation which compelled Grant to play on the stage of this war the part of a destroyer. Not only a destroyer of men, but a destroyer of everything and anything which could be utilised in war, and above all the destruction of the will

---

[1] *M.H.S.M.*, XIII, pp. 452, 453. According to Colonel Livermore, the losses of the Armies of the Potomac and James, from May 4, 1864, to April 9, 1865, were 124,166 ; and in the same period *Lee's* losses were 112,563, possibly 20,000 more " if full reports of the Confederate commanders were at hand." (*M.H.S.M.*, IV, pp. 455, 456.)

of the Confederacy to continue the conflict. On June 7, 1864, Major *John Tyler*, an officer on *Lee's* staff, expressed this feeling clearly in a letter to General *Price* when he wrote :

" From first to last Grant has shown great skill and prudence combined with remorseless persistency and brutality. He is a scientific Goth resembling Alaric, destroying the country as he goes and delivering the people over to starvation. . . . The game going on upon a military chessboard between *Lee* and Grant has been striking and grand, surpassing anything I have heretofore witnessed, and conducted on both sides with consummate mastery of the art of war. It is admitted that *Lee* has at last met with a foe who watches [matches] his steel, although he may not be worthy of it. Each guards himself perfectly and gives his blow with a precise eye and cool sanguinary nerve." [1]

In this conflict a close examination will show that whilst *Lee* fought like a paladin, as a general-in-chief he was inferior to Grant. Grant maintained his direction by a most careful adjustment, and constant readjustment, between concentration and distribution of force ; he never changed his controlling idea, though he frequently modified his means of action. *Lee*, I maintain, was an indifferent general-in-chief, not because he failed to win battles, but because his strategy, though it often led to brilliant tactical successes, was not of the type which could win the war. This, then, is their difference : Grant understood the meaning of grand strategy, *Lee* did not. He never seems to have realised the uselessness of squandering strength in offensive actions as long as the policy of the Richmond Government remained a defensive one. He never seems to have been able to focus the war as a whole, as one picture. He could see bits of it clearly enough, but the whole was beyond his vision ; consequently, outside the Army of Northern Virginia, his influence on the grand strategy of the war

[1] 108 *W.R.*, p. 994.

was negligible. His strategy, so I think, is very justly apprised by Colonel Bruce when he says :

" If a manufacturer or merchant worth a million dollars should enter into a trade warfare with a competitor worth two millions, and so aggressively carry it on as to entail a loss to each of $250,000 a year, the result would be that at the end of four years one would be bankrupt and the other still rich. This was the kind of war inaugurated by General Lee." [1]

In truth, *Lee's* one and only chance was to imitate the great Fabius, and plot to win the war, even if in the winning of it he lost every battle fought. His instincts were, however, against such a course. Aristocratic, imperious, proud, and above all temperamental, against Burnsides, Popes, and Hookers he cultivated such a god-like disdain for his enemy —the tradesmen of the North—that his " embattled " cotton growers swept all before them, throwing the enemy back as the sea hurls the shingle up the beach,—only to drag it down again as the waves recede. Unlike Grant, he never seems to have analysed his victories, to discover how and why it was he had won Malvern Hill, Manassas, Fredericksburg, and Chancellorsville, and this lack of self-searching led him to the folly of Gettysburg.

" The disastrous movement of *Lee* into Pennsylvania," writes Mr. Dargan, a member of Congress from Mobile, to the Confederate Secretary of War, " and the fall of Vicksburg, the latter especially, will end in the ruin of the South without foreign aid in some shape. . . . The failure of the Government to reinforce Vicksburg, but allowing the strength and flower of our army to go North, when there could be but one fate attending them, has so broken down the hopes of our people that even the little strength yet remaining can only be exerted in despair." [2]

Here at Vicksburg and Gettysburg we have presented to us in practical values the measure of the generalship of Grant and *Lee*. The one had a clear object in view, though

[1] *M.H.S.M.*, XIII, p. 468.   [2] 128 *W.R.*, p. 664.

still far distant, for Vicksburg was but a stepping-stone towards it ; the other rushed forth to find a battlefield, to challenge a contest between himself and the North.

The truth is, the more we inquire into the generalship of *Lee*, the more we discover that *Lee*, or rather the popular conception of him, is a myth ; by which I do not mean that he was not a great soldier, but that he was not a great general-in-chief. Unlike Grant, he did not create a strategy in spite of his Government ; instead, by his restless audacity, he ruined such strategy as his Government created. His outflanking movement against Pope was audacious in the extreme, and it succeeded. His battle strategy was hazardous, but he ably improved upon the mistakes of his antagonists. His movements before the battle of Antietam, or Sharpsburg, are nothing short of reckless. In this battle, as I have already mentioned, he neglected to entrench, though entrenchments would have been as serviceable to him as to Grant at Shiloh, and as one writer says : " in a struggle in which he was forced to play the part of a Wellington without a Blücher, but in which, fortunately for him, he was not opposed by a Napoleon." [1] Again at Fredericksburg his audacity is superb ; estimating the inertia of Burnside, he accepts risks which are so patent to the occasion as to be valueless as a general lesson. At Chancellorsville he emulates Kutusoff at Austerlitz—but successfully, his outflanking movement being secured by Hooker's inertia. Then, suddenly at Gettysburg, there is a blank ; his magic fails him.

At 5 p.m. on July 1 *Longstreet* turned to *Lee* : " We could not " (he said) " call the enemy to a position better suited to our plans. All that we have to do is to file around his left and secure good ground between him and his capital." " If he is there to-morrow " (said *Lee*) " I will attack him." (*Longstreet* was astonished.) " If he is there to-morrow it will be because he wants you to attack. . . ." [2]

[1] *Journal of the Military Service Institution*, March, 1898, p. 230.

[2] *Fitzhugh Lee*, p. 276 ; *Military Memoirs of a Confederate*, Alexander, p. 386 ; *Longstreet*, p. 358.

Then on July 3 he carried out his famous and costly frontal attack of which *Fitzhugh Lee* writes :

" A consummate master of war such as *Lee* was would not drive *en masse* a column of fourteen thousand across an open terrene thirteen or fourteen hundred yards, nearly every foot of it under a concentrated and converging fire of artillery, to attack an army on fortified heights, of one hundred thousand, less its two days' losses, and give his entering wedge no support ! Why, if every man in that assault had been bullet proof, and if the whole of those fourteen thousand splendid troops had arrived unharmed on Cemetery Ridge, what could have been accomplished ? Not being able to kill them, there would have been time for the Federals to have seized, tied, and taken them off in wagons, before their supports could have reached them. Amid the fire and smoke of this false move these troops did not know ' someone had blundered.' " [1]

Though this is written to exonerate *Lee*, it really condemns him, for there can be little doubt that it was he who blundered. He had never analysed Fredericksburg and Chancellorsville, and, failing to do so, these successes led him to believe that he could take any risks he liked with his enemy. He was a wonderful judge of character, but over-apt to rely entirely upon such judgments. He could sum up McClellan, weigh Pope and Burnside, and measure up Hooker ; but Meade he failed to appraise, though Meade was quite an ordinary general, and Grant he never understood.

The ability to judge character is certainly as valuable a gift as a general can possess, but unless it is weighed against the circumstances of each situation it is apt at times to prove a dangerous one. Here we find a marked difference between the personalities of Grant and *Lee*. Of Grant, Badeau tells us that " he often said of those opposed to him : ' I know exactly what that general will do '; ' I

----

[1] *Fitzhugh Lee*, p. 289.

am glad such an one is in my front ' ; ' I would rather fight
this one, than another ' " [1] ; but he never relied entirely
upon this knowledge. He would use it as a plummet line,
but not as a trowel : he did not build with it, but instead
rectified his plan by it. Only with his own subordinates,
when once he had gauged their value and sounded their
worth, would he leave all detail to them, handing over to
them his idea. What his trusted subordinates were to him,
in many ways the Federal generals were to *Lee*, but in
place of giving them an idea *Lee* extracted *his* idea from them,
and once he had done so, the normal detail of the art of war
he frequently abandoned to chance. Whilst *Lee's* intellect
was almost feminine in nature, Grant's was entirely masculine;
the one sensed a situation, the other reasoned it out, not
possessing that quick and subtle imagination which electrified
Lee.

Lee realised, however, the weakness of his strength, when
he said that he was sorry to part with McClellan, because
the Federal Government might eventually find a general
whom he would not understand. Unfortunately for him,
this premonition came true, for he never understood Grant ;
had he done so he would never have attacked him as he
did on May 5, and he would never have allowed Grant to
cross the James. Even at the very end he failed to understand him ; he went to McLean's house to meet Grant,
and he went there with a mental reservation as to the
surrender of his army. Before sending his last letter to
Grant he ordered his men to be prepared to cut their way
through the enemy, should Grant demand the surrender
of his army as prisoners of war.[2] Instead, the " crude "
democrat of the North, the son of a tanner, offered terms
more liberal than *Lee* ever hoped for, and behaved with a
delicacy and consideration as if he were dealing with a
sensitive woman. *Lee's* intuition never fathomed Grant's
personality, and why ? I think the answer to this question
is best given in the words of Colonel Bruce :

[1] *Badeau*, III, p. 141.
[2] *Army of Northern Virginia*, Memorial Volume, p. 47.

" It has been said more than once that General Grant had not the gift of imagination. It is true that he had not that kind of imagination that sees an enemy where none exists ; that multiplies by five the number of those who happened to be in his front ; that discovers obstacles impossible to overcome whenever there is a necessity to act ; that sees the road open and the way clear to victory when the foe is far away and not threatening ; that conjures up, on his near approach, a multitude of impossible movements being made on the flanks and on the rear ; that sets the brain of a commander into a whirl of doubt and uncertainty which generally ends in a hasty retreat or ignominious defeat. . . ."

This type of imagination *Lee* could grasp as if it were a material thing ; but Grant was not of this type.

" It was not through knowledge gained from books, but through the gift of an historic imagination in part that he was enabled to see the true character of the great conflict in which he was engaged, its relation to the past and its bearing on the future ; that enabled him to take in at a glance the whole field of the war, to form a correct opinion of every suggested and possible strategic campaign, their logical order and sequence, their relative value and the interdependence of one upon another ; and finally at Appomattox, the moment *Lee* let drop his flag, to see that the end had come and the whole Southland was once more a part of a common country and her conquered soldiers were again his countrymen." [1]

This type of imagination *Lee* could not understand, because in *Lee*, with all his greatness, there was something parochial ; whilst in Grant there was something cosmic. At the outbreak of the war *Lee* joined the South because he was a Virginian ; Grant threw in his lot with the North because he believed in the United States. *Lee* could penetrate the provincially minded man, the man who thinks in units, Hookers, Burnsides, and such-like ; but he could not grasp

[1] *M.H.S.M.*, VII, pp. 7, 8.

the nature of a man who, however uncultured he might be, possessed the soul of Browning's Grammarian—

> " That low man seeks a little thing to do,
>   Sees it and does it :
> This high man, with a great thing to pursue,
>   Dies ere he knows it.
> That low man goes on adding one to one,
>   His hundred's soon hit ;
> This high man, aiming at a million,
>   Misses an unit."

Lee's misfortune as a soldier was that, ever since the opening of the war, he had been fighting in the political theatre, and Grant had been fighting in the strategical theatre, a theatre of war in which he, more than any other man, incubated the strategy of 1864–5. Then he came East, bringing with him his strategy, and *Lee* was confronted not only by a man he could not understand, but by a problem and a war which were utterly novel to him. He had been fighting generals who lacked direction, and who had no conception of how to win peace ; who, possessing little or no strategy, floundered through a tactical gloom, only to be derided by the politicians who should have supported them. Then came Grant ; Lincoln stood like a rock behind him, when, on May 5, he opened the first of the modern battles in the history of war. Not a day's, or a two, or even a three days' engagement, but a relentless tussle of weeks and months.

Grant's difficulties were many, but they were minor and incidental when compared to *Lee's*. *Lee* had no political foundation to work from ; he had no clear-cut plan of campaign, and he served a waning cause. The fight he put up exceeded in courage and grandeur anything he had as yet accomplished ; for at last he was confronted by an antagonist worthy of his steel. Hitherto his strategy and tactics had been offensive, now they were defensive ; and by combining rapidity of movement with earthworks he blocked Grant's advance at every turn, holding Richmond and Petersburg for nine months against every attack. What is so supremely heroic is, that after his failure to crush

Grant in the Wilderness, it must have been apparent to
him that ultimate victory had eluded his grasp ; yet, in
spite of every discouragement—the fall of Atlanta, the
triple defeat of *Early*, the destruction of *Hood's* army,
the loss of Savannah and Wilmington and the capture of
Fort Harrison—with his back against the wall he parried
every thrust, until Sherman's advancing columns and Grant's
unceasing pressure brought the Confederacy to collapse.
As a general, *Lee* must stand or fall by his last campaign ;
for, though he won no battle, it was the most skilful, masterful,
and heroic he was ever engaged in.

Grant's difficulties are of another kind. The government and the people of the North are behind him, and
though they quibble and question, on the whole they are
loyal. Sea-power is at his elbow, consequently the base of
his strategy is secure. Unlimited resources are at his call,
and his army knows that it is approaching victory. Yet
the theatre of war is hostile to him ; the forests frown on
him ; the swamps sneer at him—he is beset by many difficulties. Every movement is, however, well secured, and
his forward movement is unceasing. But Grant is not a
subtle tactician ; he realises the value of each arm, yet
time has been insufficient for him to weld this knowledge
into an amalgam. His losses compel him to adopt the
simplest possible methods, because the man-power of his
army is always changing. His tactics are simplicity itself
—the forward thrust, under cover of which each successive
flanking movement is made ; but failure to understand the
true use of artillery, and the great difficulty of using this
arm in wooded country, threw the onus of his numerous
holding attacks on to his infantry, who, consequently,
suffered heavy casualties. Battling with earthworks, rivers,
swamps, and men, here again we find another heroic soul ;
accepting all consequences, never being obsessed by misfortune, fearing no danger, bearing up against disappointments, Grant strode onwards from battlefield to battlefield,
fashioning each loss into a stepping-stone towards the next
hoped-for success.

Then came the end, peace was once again established, though not the peace Grant had prayed and fought for; but a peace as cruel as war, for it was—

"Dawn not Day!
While scandal is mouthing a bloodless name at *her* cannibal feast,
And rake-ruin'd bodies and souls go down in a common wreck,
And the press of a thousand cities is prized for it smells of the beast,
Or easily violates virgin Truth for a coin or a cheque.

"Dawn not Day!
Is it Shame, so few should have climb'd from the dens in the level below,
Men, with a heart and a soul, no slaves of a four-footed will?
But if twenty million of summers are stored in the sunlight still
We are far from the noon of man, there is time for the race to grow."

Perhaps Grant saw it so, I think he must have, and that the dawn was turning "a fainter red," for both in war and peace he was a man possessed of the "larger hope."

PART IV

THE GENERALSHIP OF PEACE

CHAPTER XVII

THE FOUNDATIONS OF WAR

THE SPIRIT OF THE PEACE

THE surrender of *Lee* to all intents and purposes brought the Civil War to an end ; yet, within five days of this event, the assassination of President Lincoln flamed through the smoke of departing war heralding in a new conflict : the struggle of reconstruction and of peace ; a struggle which for a time was to prove as bitter as the war itself and far less honourable. The loyalty of *Lee* and the fortitude of Grant—those spells " by which to reassume an empire o'er the disentangled doom," were forgotten, and all that might have been learnt from the war was left unlearnt in a scramble for place, power, and plunder.

For a moment let us pause and consider this problem, for the problem of war is worth understanding, and, so it seems to me, is no better understood to-day than it was in 1865. William James, one of the most lucid of philosophers, once wrote :

" Every up-to-date dictionary should say that ' peace ' and ' war ' mean the same thing, now *in posse*, now *in actu*. It may even reasonably be said that the intensely sharp competitive *preparation* for war by the nation *is the real war*, permanent, unceasing ; and that battles are only a sort of public verification of mastery gained during the ' peace ' intervals." [1]

Much wisdom lurks in these words, and sufficient to unbar this mystery ; for if war is so closely related to peace as to be its obverse, surely then, by examining war and peace as phases of one activity, we shall be able to discover

[1] " The Moral Equivalent of War," in *Memories and Studies*, p. 273.

why nations prepare for war, and why wars are waged, and perhaps how they can be restricted.

To-day the Civil War appears to have been but little short of an act of madness, for it would now be difficult to find a single individual of intelligence prepared to say that it would have been advantageous to the United States and the world had the South won. This has long been recognised ; already many years ago General *E. P. Alexander*, the commander of the Confederate artillery at Gettysburg, said :

" The world has not stood still in the years since we took up arms for what we deemed our most invaluable right—that of self-government. We now enjoy the rare privilege of seeing what we fought for in the retrospect. It no longer seems desirable. It would now prove only a curse. We have good cause to thank God for our escape from it, not only for our sake, but for that of the whole country, and even of the world." [1]

Yet in 1861 there were over five millions of men and women who fervently believed the contrary ; who were willing to face the turmoil of war ; to assist in the slaughter of their fellow countrymen, and carry fire and sword over half a continent for an idea which we now know to have been a veritable illusion. Nevertheless it is impossible to conceive, as conditions then were, of any other test except that of war of the hollowness of this myth. So also, accepting the conditions which prevailed when the conflict was over, it is equally impossible to suggest how the turmoil of the first twenty years of the peace which followed the war could have been avoided.

The military chaos of 1861–2 was rapidly replaced by a military cosmos : mobs of men were organised into armies, were ably officered, trained, well led and well equipped. On April 6, 1865, two divisions of the Federal Second Corps formed a line of battle over a mile long, and, preceded by skirmishers and supported by a third division, marched

---

[1] *Military Memoirs of a Confederate*, E. P. Alexander, p. viii.

fourteen miles across country through forests, undergrowth, and swamps " with a precision which would have
been creditable on parade," [1] and " with a rapidity and
nearness of connection " which astonished General Humphreys.[2] Yet, less than three years before, what do we see ?
Mobs of men dressed as soldiers, followed by congressmen
in carriages, women in barouches, sightseers, psalm singers,
tricksters, vendors, and newspaper men climbing trees—
and what do they see ? A regiment and a battery turn
about and march off the field of Bull Run, because their
term of enlistment has expired. Then pell-mell one regiment
after another breaks, and barouches, carriages, journalists,
women, and soldiers stampede towards Washington. So
also after the war, the emotionalism of untasted battle
is replaced by the gross materialism of plundering peace,
a materialism which sucked all classes into its vortex, and
belched into the Southern States political adventurers,
speculators, and " carpet baggers " who spared no trouble
in purloining the public funds, and in seizing all cotton
they could lay their hands on. Scandal followed scandal ;
the " Whisky Ring " shocked the Government, and the
" Crédit Mobilier " shocked the nation ; yet out of this
turmoil of graft and swindling crept a Gargantuan power—
the United States as we know her to-day.

The drama of this age of reconstruction, like a brach-
hound following close on the trail of the wolf, is profound.

Behind the ploughshares over the newly turned earth
came a multitude of frenzied sowers casting the seeds of
future greatness to the winds of speculation, some to fall
on fertile ground and some on rock. Waste is seen at every
turn, but out of it there sprouted forth an ever-increasing
prosperity ; for the overthrow of the patriarchal system
of the South opened the whole land to the conquest of
steam-power—the real, the creative conflict. Even during
the war itself, the industries and population of the North
refused to shrivel before the blaze of the guns. Between 1860
and 1865, the inhabitants of the North increased by over

[1] *M.H.S.M.*, VI, p. 498.   [2] 95 *W.R.*, p. 682.

3,000,000 and 4,500,000 acres of public land were taken up by settlers. Then, from 1865 to 1890, what do we see? The population of the entire land is doubled and the capital invested in manufactures rises from one thousand million dollars to six thousand million, whilst the cotton crop of the South, which in 1860 was about two thousand million pounds, in 1890 rises to four thousand million.

In spite of the devastation wrought by the war, what other human activity could have wielded over this land so magical a wand; could, through changing an idea, have whispered an " Open Sesame " throughout a continent ?

By breaking a political shackle the war bound North and South into a unity by means of an economic link; for the economic independence of the Southern workers led directly to the economic interdependence of the whole of the United States, now truly united, being freed from economic barriers and internal moral frontiers. And in this dramatic change, this magical growth, the factor which governed the strategy of the war, governed the strategy of the peace, namely, communications.

In 1860 the Alleghany mountains severed the West from the East, and the great river system of the Mississippi drew the West from the North and led her towards the South. Then, when the war was ended, 'the greatest creation of the Industrial Revolution—the railway—challenged the rivers. In 1865 the railroad mileage of the country was 35,000 miles, in 1890—166,000 miles; this reverberating band of steel, like an immense tuning fork, brought harmony to the land, not only through freedom of movement but through freedom of intercourse, creating new ideals.

" . . . When I think how the railroad has been pushed through this unwatered wilderness and haunt of savage tribes; how at each stage of the construction, roaring impromptu cities, full of gold and lust and death, sprang up and then died away again, and are now but wayside stations in the desert; how in these uncouth places Chinese pirates worked side by side with border ruffians and broken men

from Europe, gambling, drinking, quarrelling and murdering
like wolves ; and then when I go on to remember that all
this epical turmoil was conducted by gentlemen in frock
coats, with a view to nothing more extraordinary than
a fortune and a subsequent visit to Paris—it seems to me as
if this railway were the one typical achievement of the age
in which we live, as if it brought together into one plot all
the ends of the world and all the degrees of social rank,
and offered to some great writer the busiest, the most extended, and the most varied subject for an enduring literary
work. If it be romance, if it be contrast, if it be heroism
that we require, what was Troy to this ? "

Thus writes Robert Louis Stevenson in *Across the Plains* ;
and to me it seems that this glowing picture of might and
vice and progress triumphant depicts more truly than
volumes of dry statistics the spirit of the peace which was
begotten of this war.

THE CREATIVE POWER OF WAR

Turning now to the period in which we live, the spirit
which emanated from out the World War was very similar
to that which emerged from the American Civil War, not
only because the main causes of both these wars were
in nature economic, but because the World War was in fact
an European Civil War, a duel between two political doctrines :
on the one side the right of nations to control their destinies,
and the thinly veiled attempt of Germany to establish
a hegemony, Cæsarism, or European federation, on the
other. There is little doubt in my mind that had Germany
succeeded in re-establishing the Roman Empire (and I
do not say that she would have or could have), that is a
union of European nations, the results might in time have
been as beneficial to Europe as those in America which accrued
from the conquest of the South by the North. Accepting
conditions as they were during the generation which preceded
the World War, then it would appear that the only instrument which could have accomplished this federation was

war, for to attempt it diplomatically was obviously out of the question.

During the World War, science and industry played the leading parts, and as in 1861–5 the power of the bullet rapidly began to replace the power of the bayonet—that is, the scientific weapon replaced the barbaric weapon—so do we find during 1914–18 that the supreme tactical problem is the elimination of the bullet, which problem is solved by the reintroduction of armour and its carriage by petrol-driven machines—that is, by weapons which are the military expression of the economic age which gave birth to the war.

After the war the same process continued ; for, as in 1865, out of its emotionalism emerged a vindictive spirit. Whilst in America the plundering of the South was carried out by " carpet baggers " and such-like people, in Europe the plundering of the defeated powers was legislated for by the treaty of Versailles. Between 1865 and 1875 it was not realised that to plunder the South was to plunder the United States, and even to-day, more than ten years after the conclusion of the World War, it is not yet realised by millions of Europeans that to plunder Germany is to plunder Europe ; for though politically European nations are not federated, economically they are interdependent, and are becoming more and more so every year.

To-day the fashion is to blacken war, carefully avoiding any examination of its causes. The will of the proletariat, which in every democratic country still remains the final arbiter in politics, has decided that the easiest way to destroy the weeds of war is to cut off their heads, leaving their roots firmly embedded in the peaceful soil. Their intellectual method—it seems almost an insult to call it such—is identical to their spiritual method during the Middle Ages. Then it was to blacken the Devil in order to save souls ; now it is to blacken war in order to save bodies. The apotheosis of the value of human life is quite a fictitious one. There are few things cheaper in this world than the lives of men and women ; their value is an illusion begotten of the instinct of self-preservation which controls each separate person. The 500,000 men killed and died in 1861–5 were not long missed, nor did their death detrimentally influence the prosperity of their country. In the World War the same applies to the 10,000,000 who perished during it, and could they be raised from the dead they would seriously encumber our social difficulties ; their return being far more disastrous to the present peace than their departure was to the past war.

Because 10,000,000 men died in the war, war is anathematised, but when 10,000,000 men, women, and children died during the winter of 1918–19 of so common a complaint as influenza, what did rational people do ? They said : " Isn't it terrible ? " and a few sniffed oil of eucalyptus.

Cannot we introduce into this subject of war a little common sense ? Cannot we bring ourselves to look at war as we look at influenza or diphtheria ? Because we have an ulcerated throat, do we attempt to anathematise the infection away ? Instead, do we not examine the drains of our peaceful and frequently ill-built houses ? Yet when it comes to a question of war, we go off our heads, and behave like mediæval magicians.

The destructiveness of war is always apparent, but its creative influences are generally hidden away from even the more highly educated of the multitude. If the drains in a house are defective the alternative to sore throats is to repair them. Repair means destruction in one form or another, and if the drains are in a terrible condition it may become necessary to replace them altogether—that is, to destroy them utterly so that a new condition of life may be established. Destruction is not necessarily evil, and, in my opinion, had the Civil War in America been better understood, the causes of the Civil War in Europe quite possibly might have been eliminated.

THE CIVIL AND THE WORLD WARS

Grant's cold reasoning and common sense perceived an angle of this question when he stated that " the Southern

rebellion was largely the out-growth of the Mexican war."
His philosophy was that nations, like individuals, are
punished for their transgressions; in other words—wars,
like fevers, may be traced to certain poisons which sicken
nations as they do individuals. Had he lived to-day he
would have been amazed at the idea that disarmament could
prevent wars; he, so I think, would have argued: armaments are the outward and visible sign of some inward
discontent, and to disarm a nation in order to prevent war
is about as sensible as depriving a surgeon of his instruments
in order to do away with tumours. From this he might
well have concluded that the World War was nothing more
than the military apotheosis of the Industrial Revolution,
and that its materialistic orgy of destruction was but the
counterpart of the materialistic orgy of construction which
preceded it. That this war, like the Civil War, was but
an effect following a cause, rendering tangible and visible
to all the virtues and vices of the state of peacefulness which
preceded its outbreak. Further still, when once the war
was at an end, should popular opinion condemn it as brutal,
then the masses must realise that its brutality was no more
and no less than a reflection of the brutality of the age which
gave it birth.

Had he been of a studious nature and an acute observer
of events, his common sense might have led him to see that
though it was a coincidence that the year which witnessed
the birth of Napoleon also saw the patenting of Watt's
pumping engine, it was no coincidence that the theory
of absolute war and the general utilisation of steam-power
evolved from out the same period, for in idea they are blood
relations. The spirit of both is coercion through physical
force, and their aim—the conquest of human and physical
spaces. Though Napoleon may never have contemplated
the establishment of a world empire, that is, a fusing of
national spaces into one complete federation, his destiny
was to manifest this idea. Though the dream of James
Watt, a somewhat petty-minded man, seems seldom to
have soared above that of an average mechanic's, his destiny

was to liberate the idea of the unity of geographical spaces, and the possibility of converting the world into one intricate self-supporting city.   Finally, it might have struck Grant how extraordinarily alike were these two wars, and what a crime it was to Western Civilisation that the natural history of the Civil War was not studied by European statesmen ; for had it been, the events which were about to take place in Europe would have been better understood.

In 1870 there occurred a sudden change in the economic structure of the Old World.   From 1830 onwards Great Britain, now highly industrialised, flooded her neighbours with her manufactures, and was confronted by no serious competitor.   Then came the Franco-Prussian War ;   the defeat of France, and an influx into Germany of £200,000,000 of French gold.   Though the first effect of this bullion was to unhinge the stability of German finances, within a few years it enabled Germany to follow the course trodden by England, and, passing from an agricultural to an industrial footing, she soon became the competitor of Great Britain.

Once Germany was industrialised the result was a dislocation of world markets.   Not only did competition take place between her and Great Britain, but between all manufacturing countries.   These, to defend themselves against what was called " peaceful penetration," resorted to protective tariffs and customs.   Thus did protection, that is, economic pressure and resistance, become a diplomatic weapon.   Strictly speaking it is no weapon at all, because trade is mainly international, and for its health depends upon interdependence and not independence.   When in the pre-industrial period a nation decided to go to war with another, the war was normally a duel between the two nations, and all or most other nations were onlookers. But when a diplomatist exerts economic pressure, by resisting or imposing a tariff, he influences all countries, some more and some less, and not merely the country he intends to coerce.   The result is immediate, it is a hostile international feeling, and it is this feeling which sometimes begets armaments, as between the years 1871–1914, and which sometimes

does not, as was the case during 1815–61 ; but which if not
checked, armaments or no armaments, inevitably leads to
war.

The result was that shortly after the Franco-Prussian
War down to the outbreak of the World War, the law of
economic interdependence was constantly infringed. Trade,
which for the prosperity of all nations should be free, was
dammed and restricted by political action. To circumvent
protection the eighties witnessed a frenzied search after new
markets and new sources of supply. The uncivilised world
was rapidly divided up among the competing powers.
Germany, then controlled by the nationally minded Bismarck, was a bad last in the land-grabbing race, and by the
time her growing industries had satisfied her home needs
there was little left for her to grab.

Governments acted as they did because the political part
attempted to swallow the international whole, by which
I mean—that when each country was self-supporting, each
politically and economically was autonomous, but once every
industrial country began to depend on the world as a whole,
each became economically so intricately interwoven with the
other that all except political autonomy was shared in common. As this was not realised, a solution to economic
difficulties was sought through political pressure, just as
in years gone by the Papacy, a religious organisation,
attempted to solve temporal problems by spiritual power.
The result of this earlier intermixture of two incompatibles
was a series of devastating religious wars, and so also, from
about 1890, the attempt to solve an international problem
by political means resulted in a series of economic wars
which eventually embroiled the entire civilised world in
the war of 1914–18. Thus it happened that this war was
the culminating act of a war period which in itself was
symptomatic of the economic friction and chaos produced
throughout the world during the preceding generation by
statesmen attempting to solve international problems by
national means. An economic war was declared, which
was the true war, and its sole object was national profit

at any price. Wages were kept low, and the result was
social unrest; protective tariffs were imposed, and the
result was international irritation. As' things were, the
civilised world was riding for a fall—a World Revolution
or a World War; and as politicians and statesmen naturally
dread the former more than the latter, because it means
their overthrow, when economic pressure could be carried
no farther they appealed to the guns, and from 1894 to
1918 artillery seldom ceased its thunder.

When war was declared in 1914, each nation blamed the
other for its outbreak. This was natural enough, but what
none could see was that a war between any two great industrial nations must rapidly evolve into a world war, and
directly influence every civilised man and woman. For
years past the citizens of each separate country had been
proud to consider themselves as nationals; the war very
soon established conditions which showed them that in
spite of their patriotism, the world was an economic whole,
and that economically they were far more international
than national. Stocks fell, and people became bankrupt;
food grew scarce, and rationing had to be resorted to.
The Englishman, glorying in the fact that he was English
to the backbone, for year after year had sat down at his
dinner table entirely oblivious that on it was daily placed
before him the spoil of five continents, and that nearly
everything he ate and drank came from any other land
except his own. The very foundations of his life were
international, yet he was delighted when he heard that
Germany was nearing industrial ruin.

How different in detail and yet how closely related in
essential causes were the origins of these two wars! Both
were expressions of the Industrial Revolution, both were
preceded by an economic turmoil, the one originating largely
out of the 1870 war, the other out of the invention of the
cotton gin, for both this war and this invention resulted
in an enormous influx of gold into Germany and the Southern
States respectively. Once the South became a cotton-
growing region, and once Germany became industrialised,

an economic war began, in the one case with the Northern States and in the other with Great Britain. Then, in both cases followed a series of tariff skirmishes and battles, and extensive land-grabbing operations on the one hand in Africa and Oceania, and on the other in Mexico. The Mexican War added vast territories to the United States; then occurred the clash between North and South—who should control them? The clash in Europe was very similar; for Germany, finding no more unoccupied land to grab, cast an envious eye on the colonies of other nations. Ultimately came war, and it showed, as nothing else could have, that South and North were interdependent; so also did the World War show that Europe was interdependent; but it resulted in no union of the nations. Within a generation of the reunion of the North and South on an economic foundation which was free from friction, not only were the entire ravages of the war made good, but a prosperity was experienced totally undreamt-of by the wildest visionary in 1861.

We see, therefore, that the Americans solved their problem, and by establishing a more perfect peace proved their war to have been a legitimate one. As regards the World War, this proof still rests a heavy load on the shoulders of European statesmen, and it is not likely to be off-loaded until they learn that peace can only be rendered certain through unity, and that unity can only be established through harmonising differences in place of building ramparts around them. To set up economic barriers between nations, reinforced by trade bastions and commercial sally-ports, in. order to restrict the flow of wealth and to raid the wealth of foreign countries, is, in conception, purely mediæval, and but little removed from the brigandage of the old barons who built castles on hill-tops from which they could swoop down and plunder the neighbouring valleys.

Grant, who by most of his countrymen has been denied the faculty of imagination, was nevertheless a man of quite extraordinary vision; a vision which was prophetic. He saw that the Civil War was the first and the last war of its kind in the United States, and that it had eliminated the economic cause of war in the Republic. He said : " I think that if there ever is another war in this country it will be one of ignorance and superstition combined against education and intelligence " [1]; consequently the somewhat comic skirmishes which have recently taken place between Fundamentalists and Modernists are interesting to watch. In 1877, when in Glasgow, he said :

" Though I may not live to see the general settlement of National difficulties by arbitration, it will not be many years before that system of settlement will be adopted, and the immense standing armies that are depressing Europe by their great expense will be disbanded, and the arts of war almost forgotten in the general devotion of the people to the development of peaceful industries. I want to see, and I believe I shall see, Great Britain, the United States, and Canada joined with common purpose in the advance of civilisation ; an invincible community of English-speaking nations that all the world beside could not conquer." [2]

And finally—" I believe that our Great Maker is preparing this world in His good time to become one nation, speaking one language, and when armies and navies will no longer be required." [3] It is remarkable, and in a way mysterious, that this man who more than any other assisted towards maintaining the Union, should towards the end of his life glance longingly towards a still greater federation.

[1] *Church*, p. 435.   [2] *Church*, p. 429.   [3] *Woodward*, p. 370.

CHAPTER XVIII

THE FOUNDATIONS OF PEACE

Causes of Discord

THE peace which followed the Civil War and the peace which followed the World War were equally chaotic, because, during each of these conflicts, statesmen lost sight of the legitimate object of war, which is to establish a better peace; and, in place of aiming at this ideal, mistook the means for the end, substituting for it the destruction of the enemy. Then, when the enemy's fighting power was destroyed, not realising that the object of peace is contented prosperity, they set about to punish the defeated side, which, disarmed, was unable to resist their " legalised " forays.

In both cases the immediate peace is indeed a sorry picture, for the heroism of war is replaced by a bullying spirit, and its self-sacrifice by greed. As long as these things are possible, and as long as statesmen behave as they did in 1865 and in 1919, and are applauded by their nation for doing so, just so long will war remain the lesser evil to purge the world of this greater one.

It might be thought, even by the most ignorant and irrational, that sufficient blood had been shed in both these wars, yet no sooner were they ended than the demagogues of the North demanded the blood of *Lee,* and the demagogues of Great Britain the life of the German Emperor. Grant, recognising the criminal folly of indicting *Lee* of treason, went to President Johnson, and told him that if the paroles which he had granted were violated he would resign his commission; this brought Johnson to book. In the second disgraceful blood-lust, Lloyd George, having been returned to power on the plank of " à la lanterne ! " was astute enough to turn the light out.

As the object of peace is to establish a state of contented prosperity, and as wars find their origin in discontent, until discontent ceases to inflame peacefulness it logically follows that this object must remain unattainable. The two main sources of war are fear and greed in their many forms ; yet it must not be assumed that fear and greed are absolute evils, for they spring from the instincts of self-preservation and acquisitiveness, which are as essential to life and progress as are those of self-sacrifice and charity. Without fear men would plunge into every danger, and the human race would soon be annihilated ; and without the desire to acquire things society would be bankrupted by prodigality and sloth. It is not in themselves that these qualities are undesirable, but only in so far as circumstances convert them into evils. Thus, in peace and war, fear is the sentinel of armies and peoples, and possession the reserves which stand behind both, ever ready to repulse or make good unexpected dangers and disasters.

When, with an impartial mind, we examine the whole question of peace, we see how closely it is related to the organisation of war : the bands of workers, guilds, companies, trades, professions, and associations, the tools, machines, and implements they use, and the various forms of management which direct their course and administer to their needs, all have their counterparts in war. Secondly, we are faced by the conditions of labour, which may be divided into two groups—those which are national and which can be controlled by the people themselves, and those which are international and which can only be controlled by the various peoples in co-operation. As stability of peace is an essential of growth, because no crop can be harvested if the fields are constantly being ploughed up, out of their instruments of peace nations have evolved specialised instruments of war—militias, armies, navies, and air forces—the object of which is to canalise fear along two main lines of action : to establish and maintain internal order and tranquillity, without which a nation must be in ceaseless anarchy ; and by a readiness to meet in battle any foreign invader, to maintain the integrity of a nation's frontiers—the walls and roof of a people's grand residence.

For thousands of years such have been the national and international means of security, which on the whole have proved themselves to be of profound service and utility to the progress of civilisation. To-day they are anathematised, because they are not understood, and because peace itself is not understood. Often is it asserted that another war would wreck Western Civilisation ; but, if I am correct in my theory that wars are the purgatives of peaceful rottenness, unless by some other means peace is cleansed of its diseases, the elimination of the power to wage war, that is to evacuate social excrement, must certainly end in the destruction not only of our present civilisation but of civilisation itself.

Sloth and internal corruption, when they can find no outlet in foreign wars or in creative rebellions, simmering on in the intestines of nations, constitute the dry rot of kingdoms, empires, and republics. War has had its use, for hitherto progress has demanded that from time to time things be thrown into its melting-pot ; for progress is fed on the mixed cultures evolved in conflict, yet in itself there can be no doubt that the military spirit is antagonistic to civilisation, because it is the child of its imperfections.

This is forgotten by the prohibitionists of war. They overlook, in the excess of their zeal, its enormous creative influences. Their fervour and fear blind them to the facts of history, for few if any of the greater wars this world has witnessed, such as the Crusades, the Seven Years' War, the Napoleonic Wars, and the American Civil War, have been followed by periods of decadence or of prolonged poverty. Obsessed by faith in an ideal, they cannot realise the moral necessity of war in the past. It was, as Maudsley writes in *The Pathology of Mind*, " the divinely appointed instrument of human progress," and " carnage the immoral-seeming means by which the slow incarnation of morality in mankind has been effected." [1]   It has hardened races to

---

[1] *The Pathology of Mind*, Henry Maudsley, p. 26.

withstand changes in social structure; it has constituted a school for heroism and a playground for valour. "That which invests war, in spite of all the evils that attend it, with a certain moral grandeur, is the heroic self-sacrifice it elicits," thus writes Lecky in his *History of European Morals*.[1] The era of great wars is the era of great empires, and as Ruskin noted: great nations are born in war and decay in peace. Nor must it be supposed that virtue is patent to modern warfare, for as ancient as the code of Manu is the chivalry of war; in this code poisoned arrows and other cunning devices are prohibited. Even in the turbulent days of the Religious Wars in Europe, Rabelais pointed out that "according to right military discipline, you must never drive your enemy to despair."[2]

Is this an apologia for war? "Yes," as long as peace remains corrupt; but "No" should mankind, in place of anathematising war, diagnose the diseases of peace and eliminate them. As long as they fail to do so, we are faced on the one side by slaughter, destruction, pestilence, and famine, and on the other by decadence; a decadence well depicted by Botticelli in his famous painting[3] in which satyrs may be seen stripping Mars of his armour as he lies sleeping by the side of Venus.

Hitherto, in order to maintain peace, mankind has relied on a cure—armaments; and to replace cure by total prevention, that is by the eradication of fear and greed, the causes of war, is in conception as absurd as an attempt to prevent gluttony and immorality by interdicting eating and union between the sexes. Does this mean that we must leave things as they are? No, it means that we are faced by an extremely difficult and consequently interesting problem. It means that in place of attempting to eliminate fear and greed we should change those conditions in which fear and greed must lead either to war or decadence.

Where, then, is our starting-point? It is the Industrial

---

[1] *History of European Morals*, 1902, W. E. H. Lecky, Vol. I, p. 95.
[2] *The Works of Rabelais*, Chap. XLIII.
[3] In the National Gallery, London.

Revolution, which a hundred and seventy years ago began to convert a " muscular " world into a " mechanical " one. This revolution founded our present-day civilisation ; it was the direct cause of the Civil War, it was the direct cause of the World War, and if we are guided by its current in place of eddying about in its backwash we shall find in it the direction of world peace.

Peace means work, work leads to trade, and during the modern period of history trade has expanded until it has become international. In Europe no country is self-contained or self-supporting, and daily is America becoming less so. To work and to barter, these are the abutments of the arch of our civilisation ; consequently prosperity depends on output, and contentedness on wages.

In 1866 the peace which was established was an economic peace, its nature was radically different from the peace of 1860, because slavery was abolished ; and as trade within the United States was free and unrestricted, the placing of all men, black and white, on a wage-earning footing resulted in establishing a higher degree of contentedness than existed before the war. In 1919 the change in the organisation of peace was negligible ; for though during the war trade became so completely internationalised that belligerents pooled their economic resources (and even their commands), directly the war ended governments re-established their old tariff barriers which had played so large a part in causing its outbreak.

The old systems of work and of fighting were by hand and hand-to-hand, they were based on rule-of-thumb derived from years of blind experimental work, of trial and error ; they were a dodge rather than an art, for there was no true science behind them. The new systems of work and of fighting are more complex, because the tools and weapons are the product of science, and to attain simplicity these systems, which depend for production on scientific instruments, must themselves be organised scientifically.

We thus obtain two major series of peace problems : the first is to establish contentedness in work through scientific management; and the second—to free trade of all restrictions, so that it may become completely internationalised and the common property of mankind, in place of the individual property of separate nations. To attain this freedom demands scientific statesmanship. Grant was supremely right when he said that in the United States there could never be another war except between ignorance and superstition and education and intelligence. To attain to a clean and contented world peace, which will lead to a federation even greater than that of the United States, we must bend all our might towards eliminating, not war, but the causes of war—the ignorance and superstititions which still grip the mind and heart of the civilised world. As these are modified, so will that spirit of conflict which begets revolutions and foreign wars subside, and this is what I believe Grant had in mind, perhaps in an inarticulate form, whem he said he believed " that our Great Maker is preparing this world . . . to become one nation." It was a vision of the future, the stepping-stones towards which were unseen.

NATIONAL HARMONY

During the first half of the Civil War its predominant feature was its lack of discipline, and I have called these two and a half years the experimental period out of which, through trial and error, were evolved soldiership and generalship; which, with reference to civil work, I will examine in turn.

The establishment of order and of discipline, of management and the replacement of rule-of-thumb by common sense, that is action and thought adapted to circumstance, in no way destroyed the virtues of war—heroism, valour, self-sacrifice, obedience, duty, and comradeship—rather it enhanced them. As the output of victory grew greater suffering grew less, not because men did not frequently suffer as greatly, but suffering had now a purpose, it was accomplishing a common aim; each dead or maimed soldier pointing gloriously towards the birth of a better peace.

Thus, to the few who could see, the war became a visible symbol of the spirit of the peace which should follow it ; a spirit which of its own accord could not embue peace with the heroism of self-sacrifice of soldiership, but which halting by the road-side of the commercial world silently waited for the workers to adopt it.

Grant, a dismal failure in the peace which preceded this war, like this spirit, halted by the way-side, because this spirit was of himself. Then it lurked out, for like no common worker we find him ever looking ahead. He meditates on the present and projects it into the future ; thus he renders visible a goal, and having rendered it visible he maintains his direction towards it, believing that every success is only the fulcrum upon which to rest the lever of yet another effort. Surely we have presented to us here one of the greatest secrets of civil progress : always to be looking ahead, to maintain the right and righteous course in spite of all obstacles, and never to be satisfied with our poor little accomplishments, and never to be obsessed by our greater ones.

To-day the world is beginning to realise what this spirit means, and in the form of scientific management, the cradle of which rightly belongs to America.

Henry Ford in one of his books says : " The farmer follows luck and his forefathers," [1] and is not this exactly what the soldiers of the North did in the years 1861–3 ? Further : " We fortunately did not inherit any traditions and we are not founding any," [2] and was not this one of the great military advantages of the Southern soldier, for whilst the Northern soldier was attempting to copy the systems of European generals, he was adapting his tactics to the circumstances of each field ?

Frederick Winslow Taylor is just as informative. He writes : That employers and employees are organised for war rather than for peace ; " that every single act of every workman can be reduced to a science " ; that rule-of-thumb methods are inefficient ; that the aim of scientific manage-

---

[1] *Ford*, p. 16.　　　　　　[2] *Ford*, p. 98.

ment is to accomplish work " with the smallest combined expenditure of human effort," and that management consists
in responsibility, in co-operation, and in developing a science
of work and a science of training.[1] Surely these were the
military lessons of this war—discipline, applying principles
to conditions, avoiding shibboleths, maintaining and aiming
at economy of force, and the responsibility and co-operation
of generalship. Surely these lessons could have been learnt
from this war, had writers—I dare not call them students
—ceased to hallucinate themselves by looking upon war
in the following terms :

" A great mind and a fine soul are unnecessary baggage
among the qualities that go into the making of a successful
general. War is an anachronism in the modern world, a
survival from primitive society. It has no more place in
the complex modern social structure than a dinosaur has in
a drawing-room. The most successful generals are primitive
men, whose opinions on everything outside of war and
soldiers are often—and indeed generally—extremely naive
and childish." [2]

Though this sweeping condemnation must include such
men as Philip of Macedon, Alexander, Cæsar, Edward III,
William the Silent, Gustavus, Cromwell, Marlborough,
Frederick, Clive, Washington, and Napoleon, and many
another of the great statesmen of the world, and though
the dinosaur disappeared because the world got too clean
for it, it is curious and perplexing to find this particular
writer saying :

" It ought to be an axiom of history that economic issues
are the inspiring motives behind all moral attitudes. The
story of mankind, in its broadest sense, is nothing but a
record of the successive adjustments of social status to
economic facts. Sometimes these adjustments are leisurely
and slow in movement, and society adapts itself by almost
imperceptible degrees to new forms of existence. At other
times they are projected with a high initial velocity because
their explosive elements are too powerful to be controlled.

---

[1] *Taylor, F. W.*, pp. 10, 11, 16, 36, 64.   [2] *Woodward*, p. 182.

In that case history records a war or a revolution. The fundamental difference between social evolution and war is simply a matter of their respective rates of speed." [1]

A most wise and penetrating conclusion, but one which, so it seems to me, has too much brain in it to fit even a literary brontosaur.[2]

To return to the drawing-rooms of civilised society, where incidentally most wars are hatched, what we want here is less gossip and dawdling and more thought and work. On the one hand we find generals who know nothing of the process of peace, and on the other captains of industry who know even less of the procedure of war ; and yet peace and war are but one conflict at different rates of speed, as Mr. Woodward so admirably puts it. Napoleon's ideal general is as much a captain of industry as a captain of war, and a great employer of labour, if he would succeed, must possess the penetration of Henderson's great general as well as the judgment and industry of Faraday's philosopher. When he does, then shall we find not so much a division between management and work as a harmony between these two. On the one side must there be knowledge, and on the other discipline, and between these must come harmony created by the staff. Not only must the master know what the men can do, but the men must understand what the master wants them to do, and this is only possible when the staff is in closest touch with the conditions which surround the workers and the direction of the management.

Work, like fighting, demands the expenditure of intelligence, of goodwill, and of muscular energy ; consequently we are faced by three spheres of work—the mental, moral, and physical, and one law governing these three spheres, the law of economy of force. Henry Ford writes : " Save ten steps a day for each of twelve thousand employees and you will have saved fifty miles of wasted motion and misspent

---

[1] *Woodward*, p. 109.

[2] The " Thunder-Lizard." Its body is supposed to have weighed about two hundred tons, and its brain a little less than two ounces.

energy." [1] Clausewitz says : " Every unnecessary expenditure of time, every unnecessary *détour*, is a waste of power, and therefore contrary to the principles of strategy." [2] This is a case of great minds thinking alike, not coincidentally, but because the main problem in peace and in war is identical ; it is to effect economy, that is to avoid waste. The science of work and the science of war are based on this law, and, as I will show, the principles of war are just as applicable to working as to fighting, forming the foundations of the art of both these activities. In this art the strategical side is management and the productive side tactics ; and in both, this art is nothing more than action, mental and physical, correctly adapted to circumstances.

Just as the object of a campaign is to gain victory at the least possible loss and cost, so the object of all productive work is to secure the maximum prosperity of employer and employed at the least cost to the public : the instruments are the workers and their tools ; the theatre of work—the markets ; the conditions of work—time, space, material, law, finance, and service, and the enemy not only trade competition but lack of efficiency. In war, a grand strategist, general or statesman, does not fix his final object at the destruction of the enemy, which is but a means of attaining it, but at establishing a condition from out of which a better peace can be evolved. In civil trade it is the same. To destroy by under-selling, and then to aim at high profits through over-charging, does not establish a better condition of trade but a worse one, because it is not to the advantage of the public.

To turn now to the principles, all of which are expressions of economy of force : direction, which aims at attaining the object, is obviously as necessary in industry as in fighting, and as obviously does it depend for its stability on the proper distribution of work and concentration on essentials. Glass-topped tables and morocco-covered chairs are as unessential in an office as aides-de-camp and French chefs in the field ; they are luxuries and not necessities.

---

[1] *Ford*, p. 76.   [2] *On War*, Clausewitz, III, p. 153.

In the moral sphere, determination and endurance are as essential in peace as in war. A business in which the management is lacking in fortitude, in perseverance, and in sympathy, and the workers in courage, discipline, loyalty, and comradeship, is in either an actual or a latent state of mutiny. And again, surprise, which in civil work is better named originality, is one of the most potent factors or principles of all. Without foresight and research, the best-founded business may suddenly find itself attacked in rear by some new invention or by some change in taste or demand, and if it has not an ample reserve of capital in hand it may rapidly be reduced to bankruptcy. Originality in all its many forms is the soul of progress.

Turning to the physical sphere of work : offensive action is the energy expended in work ; security is the avoidance of useless loss of energy, and mobility and rapidity in accomplishing the task set. When some new tool or means of work is invented, every task becomes an experiment ; and those businesses which apply old methods to new means, and adhere to this application, are generally doomed because mobility is violated and security is overlooked. Activity is a great asset in work, but it must carry with it flexibility, that is power to change as circumstances change, and power to adapt itself rapidly to new conditions.

I think I have now written sufficient to show that a study of war need be no less barren to the civilian than a study of business to the soldier. As in war human nature is put to the highest test, the study of the psychology of war forms an admirable foundation to the psychology of work. When once the psychological problems of industry are solved— and all our present industrial difficulties are in one form or another expressions of human nature—social discontent will disappear, and the cause of rebellions, revolutions, and civil wars will be eliminated. This condition established, our remaining problem is to remove economic friction between foreign powers.

INTERNATIONAL HARMONY

When we turn to the foreign policies of nations, the natural
history of the Civil War is most instructive, and had statesmen closely studied it during the years following the Franco-
Prussian War they must have become aware of the fact that
international relationships were tending towards a catastrophe. They would have seen that as out of the myth of
slavery emerged the Civil War, so out of the myth of the
economic autonomy of nations must emerge a still greater
conflict. Before the coming of the Industrial Revolution,
slavery though morally wrong was an economic reality,
and it did not seriously influence the relationship between
North and South ; but once industry crept into the North,
and steam-power began to weave the separate States into
an economic whole, it lost its value and this was definitely
proved after the war.

To-day, European statesmen are obsessed by a similar
myth, the myth of National Rights in place of State Rights,
which include not only the political right of a nation to
control its internal affairs, but the economic right of controlling its external trade which is only partly its own. It
is not realised that, whilst before the Industrial Revolution,
the bulk of trade being national, such a right did exist,
since its coming, steam-power having woven the civilised
world into an economic unit, this right no longer exists.
To maintain the politics of an agricultural age in an industrial
age, is, as I have stated in the last chapter, equivalent to
the attempt made by the Papacy after the Crusades to solve
temporal problems by spiritual power. This attempt led
to several hundred years of conflict terminating only in
1648 ; and the present attempt to solve international
problems by national politics must inevitably follow a
similar course. As in 1861, old tactical ideas were applied
to new tactical conditions, so to-day are statesmen, in spite
of the lessons of the Civil and World Wars, attempting to
apply the machinery of old political myths to create, destroy,
or modify new international realities.

The world of fifteen years ago, a world which is fast crystallising into a myth, for it is losing its reality, was pre-eminently a world of forces kept stable until it exploded through the fear of war. This fear was the undercurrent of all foreign policies, and it swamped the growing reality that the world was becoming yearly more and more an economic whole. Since the war, this fear has largely disappeared; consequently European equilibrium has vanished. Politically this is most notice-able, for we now find two definite classes of politicians —the new autocrats and the old opportunists. The first, whether they hail from Italy or Spain, are Russian in essence, for they rule by force whether anti-democratic or anti-aristocratic.

The second class is mainly composed of the old pro-fessionals, men of the hoplite mind, and men of the force-world of before-war days; men who then may have been big men, but who, having been brought up in a war atmosphere, and who, having lost their nerve in the present peace atmosphere, know of no other implements than the old ones, and are unable to use them because present con-ditions are unsuited to their use. They are men of peace, in that they desire to get back to a state which is dead, but in no way are they creators of peace—that is, they know not how to render the present state of peacefulness creative; consequently in place of working they fall back on talking away difficulties. These men are as dangerous in winning the peace as they were dangerous in attempting to win the war; because, obsessed by a myth, the reality in which they live is obscured to their minds. Unity of command is lacking, government is mainly by conferences and com-mittees—councils of war—and the onus of responsibility is passed round the table much as it was by the Confederate generals at Fort Donelson. No man stands out a grand and solitary figure; mental pictures are constantly painted of what the people think and as to what the people will or may do: when the bulk of the people do not think at all; for as Henry Ford long ago discovered, to most minds thought is " absolutely appalling," [1] and what very naturally the masses want to do is to enjoy themselves thoroughly and cheaply. When a crisis takes place, these men are paralysed as Rosecrans was at Chattanooga, and feverishly they stoop to the ground, scoop up dust which they throw into the air, not to blind only the credulous, but to cut out from their own sight the hideous glimpses of reality which each crisis evokes.

The real difficulty is that politicians as well as captains of industry " must be trained right as well as born right " [2] ; the old idea that men are born to a job, if ever true, is to-day fallacious. Grant was not born to win the Civil War—he trained himself to win it, and in his training myths played a small part. By close observation and reflection, he brought himself to realise the interdependence of politics and strategy ; and not until present-day statesmen create a grand strategy of peace as Grant created a grand strategy of war, that is a relationship between national politics and international affairs, will a solution to world difficulties be discovered, and a line of direction established between the pressure and resistance of these two.

A study of history, and especially a study of the history of the Civil War, the period which immediately preceded it, and the period which followed it, a *post-mortem* examination in fact—for this is the object of historical study—will show where the statesmen of Europe are right and where they are wrong ; because this study will teach them the anatomy of federation, and without economic federation there can be no certainty of peace. It will also show them that the world of to-day is a world in which the forces of the past are in conflict with the ideals of the future, as liberty was once in conflict with slavery. To-day slavery consists in binding ourselves to the myth that nations are economically independent and that prosperity can be cultivated by trade barriers and protective tariffs. Were it possible to-morrow to establish universal free trade throughout the world, then within a generation would nations be so completely de-

---

[1] *Ford*, p. 103.   [2] *Taylor, F. W.*, p. 6.

capitalised, for wealth would become so distributed, that international war would be deprived of its reason and would become inane.

The problem of peace is therefore one of realising which ideas will do the least harm and the greatest good to humanity, and what existing forces must be dissolved so that ideas are not crippled or killed. It is of necessity a choice between two evils, a new conflict for an old conflict—creation in place of destruction. The creative spirit, and not the offensive, or protective, or competitive, or subversive, is the soul of contented and prosperous peace. " Let us have peace," said Grant ; then, it seems to me, that free trade following free labour is its royal road, for as service to a people is the ultimate object of national work, service to all peoples is the ultimate object of international trade.

CHAPTER XIX

GRANT AS CITIZEN AND MAN

THE CITIZEN

IN this final chapter I come to the keystone in the arch of human conflict—man. Man establishes peace and creates war; he works and he fights, ever building up things and systems as mortal and moral as he is himself. Yesterday one thing was good, to-day it is evil, and to-morrow it is gone. Thus progress marches onwards, over dead things, lifeless ideas and phantom forces, moribund empires and decayed civilisations. No end is permanent; there is no final goal: but the means are ever the same, expression of the will of man and the powers of his body; for tools and weapons are but servants accomplishing his desires and economising these forces.

Whatever type of war we examine man is the predominant factor; he fights as he thinks, and he thinks as he sees and feels, and these in their turn shape and form themselves according to the surroundings in which he lives. If barbarous, then his warfare is barbarous; if cultured, then according to the degree of culture is his warfare less barbarous.

Grant, though born but a little over a hundred years ago, and still remembered by many living men, for he died on July 23, 1885, lived in a rough-and-tumble age, an age of conflicting ideas and struggling energies, in which the Civil War was but its climax. Of all types of men he seems to have been the least suited by nature to find his place in this turmoil; for he was a peace-loving man, one who frankly hated war, who was sickened by the sight of bloodshed, and one who, had he only realised that there is no essential difference between peace and war, and that brutality is sometimes as necessary as kindliness, and shrewdness more

413

productive than simplicity, might well have done better for himself and better for others before the war and after it.

Like many men of a retired nature he required the pressure of necessity to bring out his strength. He never seems consciously to have realised this; he was so matter-of-fact, not only as regards others but as concerned himself, that when circumstances drew his greatness out into visible manifestation, he appears never to have noticed it. In activity or in rest, when selling faggots or when retrieving a disaster on the battlefield, his balance is unaltered; he is neither carried away by success nor is he depressed by failure. Outwardly he is a very ordinary man, inwardly a philosopher, a fatalist, a man who refuses to pass under the yoke of events as long as an opening has been left unexplored; and then, if none can be found, a man who accepts fate, not as an ultimate end but as a stepping-stone towards another beginning.

It was because the conditions of peace seemed so unreal when compared to those of war, that as a civil worker and a politician he was a failure. He had a true political sense, for he could see big things and big ideas; but he possessed no political cunning, he could not see the littleness of the little men who surrounded him. Honesty to him was always the best policy, and not being a man of the world, he failed to see that though honesty is necessary to social evolution, at times cunning is vital, and that the more animal human society is the more vital does cunning become. In war he could always differentiate between the lesser or greater of two evils; but in peace time he could not, because he so often failed to understand that conditions were evil, or that there was a choice. The simplicity and honesty of war unconsciously appealed to him, whilst the complexity and dishonesty of peace, being so alien to his nature, he left to be entangled rather than disentangled by others.

The age was against him; it was a formative age, the age of a nation's adolescence. Creative impulses were many; the commingling of steam-power and man-power was churning up human affairs and throwing the scum to the top.

The war had detonated an enormous energy, an energy which could not at once be canalised towards productive ends; which has not even as yet been fully absorbed, for it can still be seen boiling over in the great cities of the United States in the form of virile criminality: a throw-back to the commercial spirit of the Dark Ages, and therefore but an out-of-date, or unfashionable, counterpart of present-day trading, banking, and money-making generally. Such criminals are not decadents, their vices are virile not senile. Monsters dreaming of lecheries they are too indolent to perform disgust us; but a scalp hunt or a hold-up will fascinate even the most cultured of men, because in every healthy man there still lurks the barbarian.

Grant was plunged into this turmoil. The idol of the people, for eight years he was enthroned in the temple of their rascality. For eight years he stood there a symbol of a past and future greatness, a solitary figure without a present, remaining himself, not changing or being able to change, witnessing corruption, injustice, and dishonesty, and hardly realising that they were such because of his unshakable incorruptibility, sense of justice, and faith in men. Had he been less obedient to his ideals, had he been more of the soldier who destroys to create and less of the man, the farmer he once was, who sows and waits on God's goodwill to ripen his crops, he might have influenced his generation more fully than he did.

That he had a political sense is proved by his visions of future greatness. I have mentioned his ideas of an Anglo-Saxon bond and of universal peace; but besides these he had more practical visions, such as the construction of a canal across Nicaragua, and the absorption of the smaller nations by the greater in order to reduce the causes of war. But the immediate problems, which in war he had always seen, in peace either he could not see or seeing could not understand.

Grant at Galena and Grant at Donelson are two totally different personalities; but Grant with his carpet bag setting out to visit McClellan at Cincinnati, and Grant as general-in-chief carrying a portmanteau and accompanied by his son entering Willard's Hotel on March 8, 1864, are in every respect the same persons.

He had signed the hotel register as " U. S. Grant and son, Galena, Ill.," and not knowing who he was, the clerk allotted to him a room on the fifth floor. Then looking at the book he could not have been more astonished " had he been struck by a cyclone." He said : " I expected General Grant to appear with a retinue of staff officers and servants, and could not suppose that the plainly attired and unassuming officer, who looked as if he might be a captain or major, was about to take command of all the Union armies." [1]

This incident goes a long way towards explaining Grant's failure as a politician—he could not change the man within him. He could fight men but he could not fight systems—

" But these are the days of advance, the works of the men of mind,
    When who but a fool would have faith in a tradesman's ware or his
        word ?
Is it peace or war ?   Civil war, as I think, and that of a kind
    The viler, as underhand, not openly bearing the sword."

Generalship in this type of war was beyond him.

The Man

Turning to Grant as man, we find a simple, unostentatious and lovable character. Very human, sincere, and generous. Very American, for he revered success, and wealth as a symbol of success. When he voyaged round the world he met, so he said, only four great men—Beaconsfield, Bismarck, Gambetta, and Li Hung Chang ; a curious quartette, and especially so when compared to Grant himself ; for no one of these four bore the slightest resemblance to him, they all had succeeded in things at which he had failed, yet he and they had been in their own way successful.

His common sense I have already examined. Johnston, one of his biographers, says : " His success was the success of sheer common sense—which is almost the same thing as generalship—and of American democracy." [2] This is

---

[1] *General Grant*, James Grant Wilson, p. 212.
[2] *Leading American Soldiers*, R. M. Johnston, p. 137.

largely true, for precedents, conventionalities, and normal behaviour had no influence over him. When, in March, 1863, Halleck wrote a letter to Grant and Rosecrans offering a major-generalship to whoever of the two first gained a decisive victory, Rosecrans adopted the conventional attitude : he felt " degraded at such an auctioneering of honors." Otherwise Grant : he folded his copy up, put it in his pocket, and went on with his plan of campaign. Halleck was born a tactless ass, consequently no anger or offended dignity would alter this fact—Grant's action saved time, Rosecrans's only increased friction.

His common sense was due to his reasoning nature; he always had a reason for what he did, good, bad, or indifferent ; chance and luck he did not believe in. " He was accustomed," writes Greene, " to take things as they were and to devote his whole energies to making the best of them." [1] He had little of the poet in his composition and much of the mechanic, in that he was extremely practical, accepting situations rather than creating them, and working without complaint with the means he had at hand. " Venice would be a fine place if it were drained," he said, and many have thought the same, especially in summer time, but have not had the moral courage to belittle their eyes in order to support their noses.

General James B. Fry, who met Grant when a cadet at West Point and then again in the last year of his life, says of him :

" He had no readiness in showing off his acquirements ; on the contrary, his acquirements did not appear until forced to the front, and then they showed him off without his knowing it. . . . He did not hesitate in choosing the best course, no matter who proposed it ; and in military affairs he would execute a plan prescribed by higher authority with as much vigor and fidelity as if it had been his own. . . . Neither responsibility, nor turmoil, nor danger, nor pleasure, nor pain, impaired the force of his resolution, or interrupted the steady flow of his intellect. . . . He could not dwell upon theories, or appear to advantage in hypothetical cases,

[1] *Greene*, p. 108.

and even in practical matters his mental processes were carried on beneath the surface. Until he was ready to act he gave no sign by word or expression of his own train of thought or the impression made upon him by others, though they might make him change his mind and induce action different from what he had intended. He generally adhered to his first convictions, but never halted long between two opinions. When he changed he went over without qualification or regard of consequences, and was not disturbed by lingering doubts or regrets." [1]

Matter-of-fact in his views on life, he was equally so as regards religion. His faith, as W. E. Woodward writes, appears to have been " a kind of ethical paganism." [2] He believed that " all evil must be punished in some form at some time," whether the evil be personal or national. In brief, his beliefs do not appear to have been far removed from those of Thomas Paine ; for reason, honesty, truth, justice, and humanity were the chief articles of his faith. In his last letter to his wife he says :

" Look after our dear children and direct them in the paths of rectitude. It would distress me far more to hear that one of them could depart from an honourable, upright, and virtuous life than it would to know that they were prostrated on a bed of sickness from which they were never to arise alive." [3]

Loyal citizenship and duty in this world were his creed, and if religion consists in living up to an accepted standard of faith, and daily reflecting this faith in thought and deed, then Grant was a truly religious man.

To turn now to his relationship with his fellows, General Burnside once said of him : " If there is any quality for which General Grant is particularly characterised, it is that of magnanimity. He is one of the most magnanimous men I ever knew. He is entirely unambitious and unselfish." [4] In his many reports and dispatches there is never a boastful word, or an exaggeration as to his actions, and those of others he always considered first, and was unstinting in

[1] *Fry*, pp. 295, 296, 301.   [3] *Woodward*, p. 500.

[2] *Woodward*, p. 369.   [4] *Church*, p. 3.

his praise where praise was due. Jealousy was entirely foreign to his nature, and when he placed his trust in others it was implicit, for in those whom he once took to his heart he had unlimited faith. " It was a principle with him never to abandon a comrade ' under fire ' ; and a friend in disgrace, as well as a friend in trouble, could depend upon him until Grant himself found him guilty." [1] Probably the bitterest moment in his life was the day he discovered that Ferdinand Ward had speculated away his fortune and violated his trust ; then he said sorrowfully : " I have made it the rule of my life to trust a man long after people gave him up ; but I don't see how I can trust any human being again."

Grant felt this wrong more than most men would have, not because his financial loss was overwhelming, but because to him his moral loss was crushing. Outwardly imperturbable and self-composed, like most Americans he was of an emotional nature, but living in an unemotional age he was slow to show it. When McPherson was killed he was overcome with grief, as Alexander was when he lost Hephæstion. Retiring to his tent he wept for his departed friend. His feelings for others, friend or foe, were deep and sincere. I have already mentioned his delicacy towards *Lee* when he surrendered, and how the glint on his sword set him thinking, as he himself says, " that it would be unnecessary humiliation to require the officers to surrender their swords " [2] ; and how he stopped the salute of a hundred guns in order not to triumph over his fallen enemy.

Many other cases of this gentleness of nature might be quoted, and of these, I think, three will suffice. When on April 8, 1863, Sherman wrote to Rawlins objecting to Grant's proposed move south of Vicksburg, and recommending the calling of a council of war to settle on " the best general plan of campaign," [3] Grant read this letter carefully, made no comment, carried on with his plans, and never after mentioned its existence, in spite of the fact that, after the investment of the city, several prominent politicians attributed the conception of the campaign to Sherman.

[1] *Fry*, p. 297.   [2] *B. & L.*, IV, p. 738.   [3] *Badeau*, I, p. 616.

Similarly, when Grant hurried from City Point to Charleston in September, 1864, in order to visit Sheridan, he had a plan of campaign in his pocket.

" But I found him so thoroughly ready to move," he said to Badeau, in 1878, " so confident of success when he did move, and his plan so thoroughly matured, that I did not let him know this, and gave him no order whatever except the authority to move. . . . I was so pleased that I left, and got as far as possible from the field before the attack, lest the papers might attribute to me what was due to him." [1]

Again on May 12, 1864, when General *Edward Johnson,* who had been captured in the attack on the salient, was sent to his headquarters, " Grant, out of consideration for his feelings, passed round the dispatches from Hancock instead of reading them aloud." [2]

Of his friendships, the one which has always appealed to me most was *Buckner's,* an old classmate of his, and whose surrender to him at Donelson was the beginning of his fame. When in 1854 Grant resigned his commission, soon afterwards he found himself in New York with but a dollar or two in his pocket, and it was *Buckner,* then a captain, who supplied him with sufficient funds to pay his way home. Grant never forgot this kindness, and when *Buckner* surrendered Fort Donelson to him he said : " Look here, *Buckner,* I fear you may be short of money before you can communicate with your friends ; if so, let me be your banker, and repay me at your convenience." [3] And then right towards the end, in the summer of 1885, when Grant had been moved to a cottage at Mount McGregor, near Saratoga, *Buckner* would, from time to time, come and see him, and talk over with him the days which had gone, when they were at West Point and when they met at Donelson.

Though reticent and normally a silent man, Grant was by no means devoid of humour and wit. He disliked doubtful stories and spiteful jokes, gossip he could not tolerate, nevertheless at times he could be sarcastic, and was not

[1] *Badeau,* III, p. 28.   [2] *Atkinson,* p. 287.   [3] *Formby,* p. 444.

slow with a pointed reply. He disliked Charles Sumner heartily, one of the few men he really did dislike, because he thought he had secured his support on the question of the annexation of San Domingo, and then found that he opposed it. One day, when informed that Sumner did not believe in the Bible, he promptly exclaimed, " Oh, no ; he wouldn't—he didn't write it." When Meade opened the Wilderness campaign by unfurling a headquarters flag of magenta, gold, and silver, he looked at it for a moment, and then said : " Is Imperial Cæsar about here ? " And one day seated outside his tent at Vicksburg, when asked by some politicians from Illinois to state his views, the answer they got was as follows : " There is one subject with which I am perfectly acquainted, and if you like to talk about that, I am your man." " What is that, General ? " " Tanning leather," replied Grant.[1]

DISCIPLINE

Such was the man, the man in himself, who won the Civil War for the North and for the world ; who ruled his country to the best of his ability during eight tumultuous years of reconstruction ; who witnessed one great era in American life founder, and another emerge from out of chaos. A massive and solitary figure in peace and war, simple in his life, possessed of no false pride of self, faithful to his friends, generous to his enemies, enduring and resolute in battle, patient in toil, in sickness, and in misfortune ; to me it seems that the greatest lesson he can still teach his fellow countrymen is : that the heroism which fashions great men and great nations is above all to be sought in self-control, in discipline of body and mind : for " Wisdom is glorious, and never fadeth away," and " the very true beginning of her is the desire of discipline ; and the care of discipline is love," [2]—the enthusiasm of youth.

[1] *New York Herald*, January 5, 1864.
[2] *Wisdom of Solomon*, VI, 12, 17.

THE BOOK ENDS

APPENDICES

APPENDIX I

THE SURPRISE AT SHILOH

BEFORE publication, the MS. of this book was submitted by me to an eminent military writer, and as his opinion was emphatically that the Federal Forces at Shiloh were not surprised, and as he said, " to picture Sherman as dominating and leading Grant astray like a child is simply laughable," I consider it only right to enter into greater detail than I originally intended, and this, I think, can be better done in an appendix than in the text of this book.

The root cause of the surprise is to be discovered in the question of command. Six general officers are concerned : namely, Halleck in supreme command, but at a distance ; Smith at Pittsburg Landing ; then Grant at Savannah with Smith still in control at the Landing, and a very sick man ; Sherman, the moving spirit at the Landing ; McClernand an unknown quantity as regards seniority, and finally Buell under Halleck, but not under Grant until April 5.[1]

On March 16 [2] Buell was ordered by Halleck to advance on Savannah and join Grant, presumably with the idea of carrying out an offensive against Corinth under Halleck. On the 17th Grant arrived at Savannah and, again presumably, because Smith was too ill at the time, he wrote [3] to Sherman, then " *Commanding U.S. Forces, Pittsburg, Tenn.*," " I have ordered all troops here to report to you immediately, except McClernand's division." On the 20th this fact was corroborated by Sherman himself, when, from headquarters, Pittsburg Landing, he wrote [4] to Colonel Lauman, Commanding Second Division : " Sir, General Smith is on board the *Hiawatha*, unwell, and requests that I should give the necessary directions for encamping the troops as they arrive." Some muddle over this dual and nominal command must have occurred, for on March 26 the following order was published [5] by Grant : " Major-General C. F. Smith,

---

[1] 11 *W.R.*, p. 94. [3] 11 *W.R.*, p. 43. [5] 11 *W.R.*, p. 67.
[2] 11 *W.R.*, p. 42. [4] 11 *W.R.*, p. 53.

425

the senior officer at Pittsburg, is hereby appointed to command
that post during the continuance of headquarters of the district
at this place or until properly relieved. He will be obeyed and
respected accordingly." The next day Grant learnt of McClernand's promotion to the rank of Major-General " without the
date of promotion of either him or General Smith being known,"
and referred [1] this question to Halleck, who referred it to the
Secretary of War, answering [2] Grant on March 31, " I know
nothing about it, except that General McClellan directed me to
place General Smith in command of the expedition until you
were ordered to join it." On receipt of this information, Grant,
who was receiving " feeble support " from many of his officers,[3]
decided to remain at Savannah until Buell arrived, but in order
to overcome the difficulty as to whether Sherman or McClernand
should control affairs at Pittsburg Landing, he opened an advanced
headquarters at this place.[4]

On April 4 the situation was as follows : Sherman, according
to his own statement in the *United States Service Magazine,*
1865, was " forming as it were the outlying picket," and as
Prentiss's division was in the middle of his command, for three
of Sherman's brigades were on Prentiss's right and one on his
left, it may be concluded that Prentiss was under his orders,
or at least affiliated to him. This day Grant, hearing [5] from
Lewis Wallace that enemy reinforcements had arrived at Purdy,
ordered [6] W. H. L. Wallace to be prepared to reinforce him at
once. Informing [6] Sherman of this order, Grant went on to say :
" I would direct, therefore, that you advise your advance guards
to keep a sharp lookout for any movement in that direction
[towards Purdy], and should such a thing be attempted, give all
the support of your division and General Hurlbut's, if necessary."

In spite of certain gaps in the evidence, there is no doubt in
my own mind that from the day he arrived at Savannah
Grant looked upon Sherman as the controlling spirit at the Landing, and that shortly before the battle took place Sherman
was in command (nominal, if the critic wishes to stress this
point) of three divisions—his own, Prentiss's, and Hurlbut's ;
that McClernand, for obvious reasons, was not placed under him,
and that Lewis Wallace and W. H. L. Wallace were under Grant,
who feared an attack on Crump's Landing, but not on Pittsburg

[1] 11 *W.R.,* p. 70.   [3] 11 *W.R.,* p. 73.   [5] 11 *W.R.,* p. 90.
[2] 11 *W.R.,* p. 82.   [4] 11 *W.R.,* p. 84.   [6] 11 *W.R.,* p. 91.

Landing. This is borne out by Sherman in his report [1] in which he says :

" On Sunday morning early, the 6th instant, the enemy drove our advance guard back on the main body, when I ordered under arms my division, and sent word to General McClernand asking him to support my left ; to General Prentiss, giving him notice that the enemy was in our front in force, and to General Hurlbut, asking him to support General Prentiss."

That Grant did rely on Sherman's judgment seems to me self-evident. Sherman selected the sites of the forward encampments with two ideas in his head—that an advance was shortly to be made, and that room should be left for Buell's army. No continuous line of battle, offensive or defensive, was contemplated, and this can be seen from the gaps left between the forward groups. There were no entrenchments, and though Grant was to blame for this, Sherman stated at the trial of Colonel T. Worthington : " To have erected fortifications would have been an evidence of weakness, and would have invited an attack." [2] In fact he did not believe that the Confederates would attack. On April 4 Colonel Buckland and Major Ricker carried out [3] a reconnaissance, and were fired on by " three or four pieces of artillery, at least two regiments of infantry, and a large cavalry force." According to Buckland,[4] Sherman was displeased with what he had done, as he " might have drawn the whole army into a fight before they were ready " ; yet as to the events of this day (in the Worthington trial report), Sherman said : " On Friday, the 4th, nor officer, nor soldier, not even Colonel Worthington looked for an attack, as I can prove." Major Ricker says :

" When we got back to the picket lines we found General Sherman there with infantry and artillery in line of battle, caused by the heavy firing of the enemy on us. General Sherman asked me what was up. I told him I had met and fought the advance of *Beauregard's* army, that he was advancing on us. General Sherman said it could not be possible. *Beauregard* was not such a fool as to leave his base of operations and attack us in ours—mere reconnaissance in force." [4]

The critic may say that Buckland and Ricker are unreliable witnesses, since they are quoted by Boynton who did not like

---

[1] 10 *W.R.*, p. 248. [3] 10 *W.R.*, pp. 91, 92.
[2] *Boynton*, p. 28. [4] See *Boynton*, p. 32.

Sherman. If so, I will turn to Sherman himself. In his report on the battle he wrote : " On Saturday [April 5] the enemy's cavalry was again very bold, coming well down to our front, yet I did not believe that he designed anything but a strong demonstration." [1] To Grant he telegraphed : " The enemy has cavalry in our front, and I think there are two regiments of infantry and one battery of artillery about 2 miles out." [2] This dispatch was followed up by a report to which was attached Colonel Buckland's. In this report Sherman said [3] : " I infer that the enemy is in some considerable force at Pea Ridge, that yesterday morning they crossed a brigade of two regiments of infantry, one regiment of cavalry, and one battery of field artillery to the ridge on which the Corinth road lays." The idea of " some considerable force " did not alarm Sherman, for the reasons given in his report on the battle, already quoted. Otherwise surely he would have elaborated his sketchy defence order issued on the 4th—" In case of alarm, night or day, regiments and brigades should form promptly on their parade grounds and await orders. Of course, if attacked the immediate commanders present must give the necessary orders for defense." [4] Had Sherman on the 5th considered that " some considerable force " meant the bulk, or whole, of *Johnston's* army, then his action was criminal in not making this fact clear to Grant, and in leaving his defence orders as they were. This day Grant telegraphed Halleck : " The main force of the enemy is at Corinth." [5] That Sherman never intended to convey the idea. of the presence of the whole of *Johnston's* army is obvious from his report dated April 10.[6] In it he says that shortly after 7 a.m. on the 6th he rode forward to an open field before Appler's regiment, was fired on and had his orderly killed. " About 8 a.m. I saw the glistening bayonets of heavy masses of infantry to our left front in the woods . . . and became satisfied for the first time that the enemy designed a determined attack on our whole camp." This evidence is conclusive—the attack was unexpected, but was this unexpected attack a surprise ?

It is true that the firing of the Federal pickets gave just sufficient warning of the enemy's approach, and that as Grant wrote : " The five divisions stationed at this place were drawn

[1] 10 *W.R.*, p. 248.   [3] 10 *W.R.*, p. 90.   [5] 11 *W.R.*, p. 94.
[2] 11 *W.R.*, p. 93.   [4] 11 *W.R.*, p. 92.   [6] 10 *W.R.*, p. 249.

up in line of battle." [1]   But where ?   Not on a carefully selected
position, but in most cases in their camps or immediately outside
of them ; a broken line offering to the enemy a number of flanks,
the turning of which resulted in a number of local surprises,
and a considerable amount of panic.   Here are a few extracts
from regimental and other reports.

SHERMAN'S DIVISION

Colonel Hildebrand, Commanding Third Brigade: " The
Seventy-seventh and Fifty-seventh Regiments were thrown
forward to occupy a certain position, but encountered the
enemy in force within 300 yards of our camp." [2]

Lieut.-Colonel Parker, Forty-eighth Ohio : " Our regiment met
the enemy about 200 yards in front of our color line.   They came
up so suddenly that for a short time our men wavered." [3]

Colonel Cockerill, Seventieth Ohio : " Formed up 200 paces
from the color line and opened fire." [3]

Major Taylor, Chief of Artillery, Fifth Division : " The enemy
appeared in large masses, and opening a battery to the front
and right of the two guns, advanced across Owl Creek." [4]

Captain Barrett, First Illinois Light Artillery : " We were
stationed near the outposts, and on the alarm being given, at
about 7.30 o'clock on Sunday morning, the battery was promptly
got in readiness, and in ten minutes thereafter commenced firing
on the right of the log church, some hundred yards in front of
General Sherman's headquarters, where the attack was made
by the enemy in great force." [5]

PRENTISS'S DIVISION

Colonel Quinn, Acting Commander Sixth Division : " At
3 o'clock a.m. of that day several companies were ordered out
from the First Brigade of this division to watch, and endeavour,
if possible, to capture a force of the enemy who were prowling
near our camp. . . . The firing grew closer and closer. . . .
The division was ordered into line of battle by General Prentiss,
and immediately advanced in line about one quarter of a mile
from the tents, where the enemy were met in short firing distance." [6]

---

[1] 10 *W.R.*, p. 109.   [3] 10 *W.R.*, p. 270.   [5] 10 *W.R.*, p. 276.
[2] 10 *W.R.*, p. 262.   [4] 10 *W.R.*, p. 273.   [6] 10 *W.R.*, p. 280.

Colonel Moore, Twenty-first Division : " A terrific fire was opened upon us from the whole front of the four or five regiments forming the advance of the enemy, which my gallant soldiers withstood during thirty minutes." [1]

McCLERNAND'S DIVISION

General McClernand, Commanding First Division : " Early on the morning of Sunday, the 6th of April, hearing sharp firing at short intervals on my left and front, in the direction of Sherman's and Prentiss's divisions, I sent a messenger to General Sherman's headquarters to inquire into the cause of it. Soon after my messenger returned with General Sherman's request that I should send a battalion of my cavalry to join one of his, for the purpose of discovering the strength and design of the enemy." [2]

Colonel Marsh, Twentieth Illinois : " Moving rapidly to the left I was assigned a position by General McClernand, which I had scarcely assumed when the enemy were seen approaching in large force and fine style, column after column moving on us with a steadiness and precision which I had scarcely anticipated." [3]

Lieut.-Colonel Engelmann, Forty-third Illinois : " My orders to turn out were met by the inquiry, ' For what purpose ? ' And to my response, ' That it was to meet the enemy which was engaged with our troops but a short distance in front,' they said that the firing then heard was none other than our own men firing off their pieces [to uncharge them]. The infatuation that no enemy was about was so general, that I was also to a great extent affected by it, and rode forward in the direction from which the firing proceeded to obtain certainty." [4]

Lieutenant Nispel, Second Illinois Light Artillery : " On the morning of the 6th instant, the company being on the drill ground, I received an order from Major Schwartz to ' prepare for immediate action.' " [5]

HURLBUT'S DIVISION

Colonel McHenry, Seventeenth Kentucky : " My regiment was ordered into line early on Sunday, 6th instant, upon a sudden and unexpected attack which had been made upon our front lines by the enemy." [6]

---

[1] 10 *W.R.*, p. 282.
[2] 10 *W.R.*, pp. 114, 115.
[3] 10 *W.R.*, p. 133.
[4] 10 *W.R.*, p. 143.
[5] 10 *W.R.*, p. 146.
[6] 10 *W.R.*, pp. 240, 241.

Confederate Reports

Colonel Preston, Aide-de-Camp to General Johnston : " Through this field General *Cleburne's* Brigade moved in fine order, with loud and. inspiring cheers, to attack the camp. The surprise was complete. It [the camp] was carried between 7 and 8 o'clock, and its colors, arms, stores, and ammunition were abandoned. The breakfasts of the men were on the table, the officers' baggage and apparel left in the tents, and every evidence remained of unexpected conflict and sudden attack." [1]

Captain Dubroca, Thirteenth Louisiana : " We first encountered the enemy in one of their camps, which I suppose was the first of their camps still occupied. There we were formed in line of battle." [2]

Colonel Hodge, Nineteenth Louisiana : " I continued to move forward rapidly until we came in sight of the enemy's camp, when . . . I halted the regiment, having previously deployed them into line." [3]

That when the attack came the bulk of the Federal troops fought gallantly is borne out by many of the Confederate reports ; [4] that Sherman's leadership was heroic is also certain ; [5] but that the whole of the Federal army was not surprised is to my mind contrary to facts. It is true that the Federal pickets may not have been surprised, for they were already in contact with their enemy ; they appear to have been for the most part only three-quarters of a mile in advance of the camps, with no cavalry vedettes in front of them. Behind them was no defensive line, the troops falling in inside and outside their encampments, which is a proof that no attack was expected. Once their flanks were turned, as in the circumstances was inevitable, they broke or were driven back, the greater part in confusion, the surprise detonating like a delay-action bomb. For this, in my opinion, Grant and Sherman must share the responsibility.

[1] 10 *W.R.*, p. 403.
[2] 10 *W.R.*, p. 491.
[3] 10 *W.R.*, p. 492.
[4] 10 *W.R.*, pp. 408, 566, 574, 581.
[5] 10 *W.R.*, pp. 98, 110.

APPENDIX II

THE ATTACK OF GENERAL THOMAS AT CHATTANOOGA

THE following account of the attack by the Army of the Cumberland on November 24 is summarised from *The Army of the Cumberland at Chattanooga*, by Joseph E. Fullerton, Brevet Brig.-Gen., U.S.V., Assistant Adju.-Gen., Fourth Army Corps, an eye-witness of the event. (See *B. & L.*, III, pp. 724–6.)

General Grant ordered the attack at 3.30 p.m. In Sheridan's division the order was : " As soon as the signal is given, the whole line will advance, and you will take what is before you." No mention of rifle-pits is made.

At 4.20 p.m. the signal guns were fired. On the first line of rifle-pits being captured :

" There was a halt of but a few minutes, to take breath and to re-form lines ; then, with a sudden impulse, and without orders, all started up the ridge. . . . As soon as this movement was seen from Orchard Knob, Grant quickly turned to Thomas, who stood by his side, and I heard him say angrily : ' Thomas, who ordered those men up the ridge ? ' Thomas replied, in his usual slow, quiet manner : ' I don't know ; I did not.' Then addressing General Gordon Granger, he said, ' Did you order them up, Granger ? ' ' No,' said Granger ; ' they started up without orders. When those fellows get started all hell can't stop them.' General Grant said something to the effect that somebody would suffer if it did not turn out well, and then, turning, stoically watched the ridge. . . .

" As soon as Granger had replied to Thomas, he turned to me, his chief-of-staff, and said : ' Ride at once to Wood, and then to Sheridan, and ask them if they ordered their men up the ridge, and tell them, if they can take it, to push ahead.' As I was mounting Granger added : ' It is hot over there, and you may not get through. I shall send Captain Avery to Sheridan, and other officers after both of you.' As fast as my horse could carry me, I rode first to General Wood, and delivered the message. ' I didn't order them up,' said Wood, " they started up on their own account, and they are going up, too ! Tell Granger, if we are supported, we will take and hold the ridge ! ' As soon as I reached General Wood, Captain Avery got to General Sheridan, and delivered his message. ' I didn't order them up,' said Sheridan ; ' but we are going to take the ridge ! ' " Before Sheridan received the message taken by Captain Avery, he had sent a staff-officer to Granger, to inquire whether " the order to take the rifle-pits meant the rifle-pits at the base, or those on the top of the ridge."

Governor John A. Martin, of Kansas, Colonel of the 8th Kansas Volunteers, of Willich's brigade, Wood's division, in a letter to General Fullerton, dated November 16, 1886, says :

On reaching the first line of rifle-pits " General Willich came up, and I said to him, ' We can't live here, and ought to go forward.' He gave me directions to move ahead, and I at once ordered my regiment forward. By that time, or about that time, it seemed to me that there was a simultaneous advance of many of the regiments in different parts of the line, and I got the impression that possibly orders had been communicated for an advance on the ridge, which I had not received ; hence I hurried my regiment forward as rapidly as possible. . . . I was impressed with the idea, I know, that a sharp rivalry had sprung up between several regiments, including my own, as to which should reach the summit first.' "

APPENDIX III

LEE'S ORDER OF BATTLE, MAY, 1864

General Headquarters.—General R. E. Lee, Commanding; Brig.-General W. N. Pendleton, Chief of Artillery.

Cavalry Corps.—Maj.-General J. E. B. Stuart, Commanding (succeeded by Maj.-General W. Hampton); Hampton's Division, Maj.-General W. Hampton (succeeded by Maj.-General M. C. Butler); Fitzhugh Lee's Division, Maj.-General F. Lee; W. H. F. Lee's Division, Maj.-General W. H. F. Lee.

First Corps.—Lieut.-General J. Longstreet, Commanding (Maj.-General R. H. Anderson from May 7); Pickett's Division, Maj.-General G. E. Pickett; Field's Division, Maj.-General J. B. Field; Kershaw's Division, Maj.-General J. B. Kershaw.

Second Corps.—Lieut.-General R. S. Ewell, Commanding (May 25, Maj.-General J. A. Early); Early's Division, Maj.-General J. A. Early (May 8–21, Brig.-General J. B. Gordon; May 21–5, Maj.-General J. A. Early; from May 25, Maj.-General S. D. Ramseur); Rodes's Division, Maj.-General R. E. Rodes; Johnson's Division, Maj.-General E. Johnson (after May 12 re-formed as Gordon's Division, Maj.-General J. B. Gordon).

Third Corps.—Lieut.-General A. P. Hill, Commanding (May 7–20, Maj.-General J. A. Early); Anderson's Division, Maj.-General R. H. Anderson (May 7, Brig.-General W. Mahone); Heth's Division, Maj.-General H. Heth; Wilcox's Division, Maj.-General C. M. Wilcox.

APPENDIX IV

GRANT'S ORDER OF BATTLE, MAY, 1864

General Headquarters.—Maj.-General G. G. Meade, Commanding; Maj.-General A. A. Humphreys, Chief of Staff; Brig.-General H. J. Hunt, Chief of Artillery; Brig.-General R. Ingalls, Chief Quartermaster; Brig.-General S. Williams, Assistant Adjutant-General.

Cavalry Corps.—Maj.-General P. H. Sheridan, Commanding; 1st Division, Brig.-General A. T. A. Torbert; 2nd Division, Brig.-General D. McM. Gregg; 3rd Division, Brig.-General J. H. Wilson.

Second Corps.—Maj.-General W. S. Hancock, Commanding; 1st Division, Brig.-General F. C. Barlow; 2nd Division, Brig.-General J. Gibbon; 3rd Division, Maj.-General D. B. Birney; 4th Division, Brig.-General G. Mott (discontinued May 14); 4th Division (Heavy Artillery), Brig.-General Tyler (from May 16, discontinued May 26).

Fifth Corps.—Maj.-General G. K. Warren, Commanding; 1st Division, Brig.-General C. Griffin; 2nd Division, Brig.-General J. C. Robinson (broken up May 9); 3rd Division, Brig.-General S. W. Crawford; 4th Division, Brig.-General J. S. Wadsworth (May 6, Brig.-General L. Cutler).

Sixth Corps.—Maj.-General J. Sedgwick, Commanding (May 9, Maj.-General H. G. Wright); 1st Division, Brig.-General H. G. Wright (May 9, Brig.-General D. A. Russell); 2nd Division, Brig.-General G. W. Getty (May 6, Brig.-General F. Wheaton; May 11, Brig.-General T. H. Neill); 3rd Division, Brig.-General J. B. Ricketts.

Ninth Corps.—Maj.-General A. E. Burnside, Commanding; 1st Division, Brig.-General T. G. Stevenson (May 11, Col. D. Leasure; May 12, Maj.-General T. L. Crittenden); 2nd Division, Brig.-General R. B. Potter; 3rd Division, Brig.-General O. B. Willcox; 4th (Coloured) Division, Brig.-General E. Ferrero.

APPENDIX V

SHERMAN'S MARCH TO SAVANNAH

WHO originated the idea of the march to Savannah ? From the War Records there can be little doubt that it was Grant.

In his *Memoirs* Sherman writes :

" I have often been asked by well-meaning friends, when the thought of that march first entered my mind. I knew that an army which had penetrated Georgia as far as Atlanta could not turn back. It must go ahead, but when, how, and where, depended on many considerations. As soon as *Hood* had shifted across from Lovejoy's to Palmetto I saw the move in my ' mind's eye ' ; and, after Jeff. Davis's speech at Palmetto, of September 26th, I was more positive in my conviction, but was in doubt as to the time and manner. When General *Hood* first struck our railroad above Marietta we were not ready, and I was forced to watch his movements further till he had ' carromed ' off to the west of Decatur. Then I was perfectly convinced, and had no longer a shadow of doubt. The only possible question was as to Thomas's strength and ability to meet *Hood* in the open field." [1]

This places Sherman's claim from September 20, 1864, onwards.

In my opinion the idea arose out of Grant's Mobile project, for directly after he assumed supreme command he sent Sherman a map marked with red and blue lines, the former showing the territory occupied by the Federal forces at the opening of the campaign of 1864, and the latter the proposed lines of operations for the campaign. The blue lines were as follows :

(1) From Saluda, Va., via Richmond and the James river to Lynchburg ; thence via Liberty to the Blue Ridge.

(2) From New Berne to Raleigh, N.C.

(3) From Tunnel Hill to Atlanta, Ga.

(4) From Atlanta via Milledgeville to Savannah.

(5) From Atlanta via Montgomery and Selma to Mobile.

(6) From Sabine Pass to Shreveport, La., then up the Red river.

[1] *Sherman*, II, pp. 166, 167.

The letter accompanying this map has been lost,[1] but the map itself shows quite clearly Grant's idea of the rear approach, or manœuvre, and the general encirclement of the Confederate armies in an ever-contracting area. From it can be seen at a glance that the forces at Chattanooga were to move on Atlanta, there divide, one half moving on Mobile, and the other via Milledgeville on Savannah.

On April 2nd Sherman received the above letter, and on the 5th wrote in reply :

" From that map I see all, and glad am I that there are minds now at Washington able to devise ; and for my part, if we can keep our counsels I believe I have the men and ability to march square up to the position assigned me and to hold it. . . . No time shall be lost in putting my forces in mobile condition, so that all I ask is notice of time, that all over the grand theater of war there shall be simultaneous action." [2]

Again on April 10 he wrote :

" Your two letters of April 4th [in which Grant outlined his plan of campaign] are now before me, and afford me infinite satisfaction. That we are now all to act in a common plan on a common center, looks like enlightened war." [3]

The occupation of Mobile Bay on August 5 caused Grant to modify his plan, and on September 10 he wrote to Sherman the letter quoted on p. 817 of the text. On the same day Sherman replied as follows :

" I do not think we can afford to operate farther, dependent on the railroad. . . . If I could be sure of finding provisions and ammunition at Augusta or Columbus, Ga., I can march to Milledgeville and compel *Hood* to give up Augusta or Macon. . . . If you can manage to take the Savannah River as high as Augusta, or the Chattahoochee as far up as Columbus, I can sweep the whole State of Georgia. Otherwise I would risk our whole army by going too far from Atlanta." [4]

From this telegram it would appear that on September 10, only in certain contingencies which depended on Grant, did Sherman consider an advance east of Atlanta a feasible operation.

---

[1] 59 *W.R.*, p. 261. For the map, see *Church*, p. 230.
[2] 59 *W.R.*, p. 262.   [3] 59 *W.R.*, p. 312.   [4] 78 *W.R.*, pp. 355, 356.

On the 12th, in reply, Grant sent Colonel Porter to Sherman with a letter in which he explained his forthcoming campaign, and that he intended to operate against Wilmington. Then, evidently perturbed by Sherman's difficulties, he continued :

" What you are to do with the forces at your command I do not see. The difficulty of supplying your army except when you are constantly moving beyond where you are, I plainly see. If it had not been for Price's movements Canby could have sent 12,000 more men to Mobile. From your command on the Mississippi an equal number could have been taken. With these forces my idea would have been to divide them, sending one half to Mobile and the other half to Savannah. You could then move, as proposed in your telegram, so as to threaten Macon and Augusta equally. . . . My object now in sending a staff officer is not so much to suggest operations for you as to get your views." [1]

Sherman sent these in his letter of the 20th, quoted on p. 318 of the text.

From the above there can be little doubt as to who originated the march to Savannah. The idea was Grant's, the elaboration and eventual execution Sherman's.

[1] 78 *W.R.*, p. 364.

APPENDIX VI

GRANT'S ORDER OF BATTLE, MARCH 31, 1865

ARMY OF THE POTOMAC

General Headquarters.—Maj.-General G. G. Meade, Commanding ; Brig.-General H. J. Hunt, Chief of Artillery.

Cavalry Corps.—Maj.-General P. H. Sheridan, Commanding ; 1st Division, Brig.-General T. C. Devin ; 2nd Division, Maj.-General G. Crook ; 3rd Division, Brig.-General G. A. Custer.

Second Corps.—Maj.-General A. A. Humphreys, Commanding ; 1st Division, Brig.-General N. A. Miles ; 2nd Division, Brig.-General W. Hays ; 3rd Division, Brig.-General G. Mott.

Fifth Corps.—Maj.-General G. K. Warren, Commanding ; 1st Division, Brig.-General C. Griffin ; 2nd Division, Brig.-General R. B. Ayres ; 3rd Division, Brig.-General S. W. Crawford.

Sixth Corps.—Maj.-General H. G. Wright, Commanding ; 1st Division, Brig.-General F. Wheaton ; 2nd Division, Brig.-General G. W. Getty ; 3rd Division, Brig.-General T. Seymour.

Ninth Corps.—Maj.-General J. G. Parke, Commanding ; 1st Division, Brig.-General O. B. Willcox ; 2nd Division, Brig.-General R. B. Potter ; 3rd Division, Brig.-General J. F. Hartranft.

ARMY OF THE JAMES

General Headquarters.—Maj.-General O. C. Ord, Commanding.

Cavalry Division.—Brig.-General R. S. MacKenzie, Commanding.

Defences of Bermuda Hundred.—Maj.-General G. L. Hartsuff, Commanding.

Twenty-Fourth Corps.—Maj.-General J. Gibbon, Commanding ; 1st Division, Brig.-General R. S. Foster ; 3rd Division, Brig.-General C. Devens ; Independent Division, Brig.-General J. W. Turner.

Twenty-Fifth Corps.—Maj.-General G. Weitzel, Commanding ; 1st Division, Brig.-General A. V. Kautz ; 2nd Division, Brig.-General W. Birney.

INDEX

440

Other DACAPO titles of interest